ALL-COLOUR QUESTION AND ANSWER

ENCYCLOPEDIA

800 questions and answers and 600 colour pictures all about the Earth, man, natural history, transport, communication, science, history and art

Hamlyn
LONDON · NEW YORK · SYDNEY · TORONTO

Contents

Original title: *Encyclopedie in vraag en antwoord*

ISBN 0 600 37427 0
Filmset in England by Photocomp Ltd, Birmingham
Printed in Italy

Translators: Anthea Ridett, Anthony Lloyd and Nicholas Fry
Chief editor, original edition: E. De Vocht

Introduction

An encyclopedia for children should be enjoyable as well as informative and every effort has been made to ensure that readers of this one will be delighted in every way.

The general presentation and the question-and-answer format ensure that it can be read from cover to cover, simply dipped into in spare moments, or used for specific reference.

The contents have a very wide range, including such a variety of topics as prehistoric man, modern man's most recent technological developments, the vast world of nature and the extraordinary world of communication satellites.

The illustrations are outstanding and the helpful captions play a major part in making this a memorable book, which will be a valuable addition to any child's, or indeed the family's, bookshelves.

The Earth

Earth and Cosmos

The Earth is much, much more than just a home for men, animals and plants. It's a planet which travels through space, rotating about its own axis and around the sun. All around it is the cosmos *– the Universe, with its countless planets and stars.*

What did people think about the cosmos in ancient times?

Below: **The Milky Way, the heart of the stellar system, is made visible by the white trail it leaves in the sky. It consists of an innumberable quantity of stars so close to each other that they seem to form a faintly luminous cloud. Their number is estimated at about 100 to 200 thousand million. This stellar system has a diameter of about 100,000 light years. (Light travels at a speed of 300,000 km per second and therefore covers roughly 9.5 trillion km in one year). This photograph shows what the Milky Way would look like if we could see it from outside.**

The Egyptians, Babylonians, Chinese and Indians had already begun to study the sky about four to five thousand years ago, and the most notable advances were made by the Egyptians and Babylonians. The Greeks were hesitant in their approach. In about 600 B.C. they succeeded for the first time in explaining the laws of nature on the basis of their own experience and research, and not merely in accordance with tradition. It was the Greeks who gave birth to astronomy, the science of heavenly bodies, and their schools of astronomy on the coast of Asia Minor became famous. The Greek philosopher Thales of Miletus was able, even at this early stage, to predict the eclipse which occurred in 585 B.C. From the fact that the sun rose in the east each morning and set in the west each evening, and because he saw that the moon and stars moved across the sky on clear nights, Anaximander, a fellow-countryman of Thales, concluded that everything in the sky revolved. It was also thought that the Earth was stationary and that the heavens revolved around it. Towards the end of the fifth century B.C. an eclipse of the Moon seemed to indicate that the Earth threw a circular shadow. From that time Greek scholars, such as Aristotle (384-322 B.C.), began to be convinced that the Earth was a sphere.

Roughly a hundred years later, Eratosthenes of Alexandria (*c.* 276-194 B.C.) succeeded in calculating the Earth's circumference with a high degree of precision. The distance from the Earth to the Moon was also known fairly exactly at this early period.

The achievements of the famous astronomer Ptolemy of Alexandria in the second century A.D. finally put an end to the ancient conception of the Universe. He wrote a work known as the *Almagest* which summed up the astronomical knowledge of the age.

After Ptolemy's time the story of astonomy continued with the Arabians. Many of the star names we use today are Arabian. For example, the bright red star in the constellation of Taurus (the Bull) is called Aldebaran – the Arabic name for 'eye of the bull'.

However, other Greeks had, surprisingly, come even nearer to the truth several centuries before Ptolemy. Towards the end of his life the philosopher Plato (427-347 B.C.) discovered that it was incorrect to regard the Earth as the centre of the Universe. The astronomer Aristarchus (310-230 B.C.) taught that if the stars appeared to revolve around the Earth this was only an illusion, and that in fact it was the Earth which turned about its own axis. He also asserted that the Earth revolved around the Sun. The Greeks did not believe him: having as yet no idea of the force of gravity, they found it difficult to imagine that they themselves were revolving around the Sun upon the Earth.

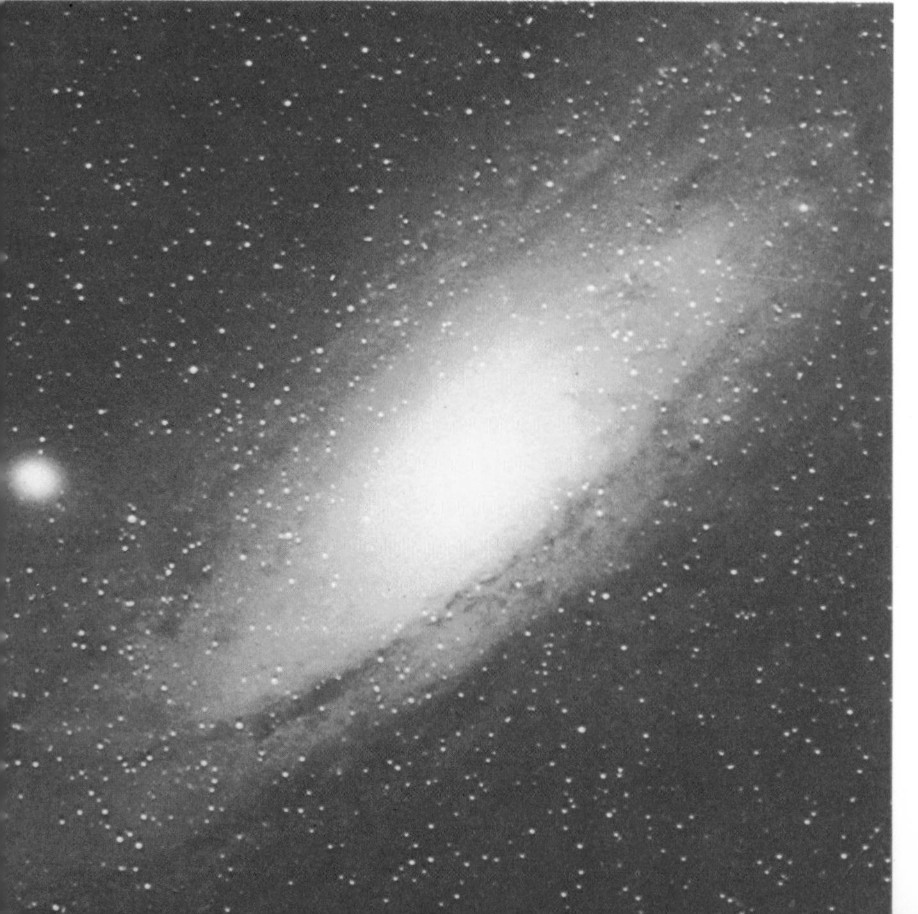

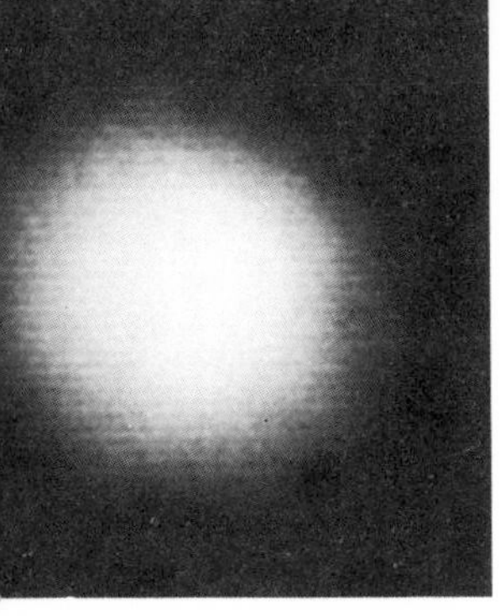

Above: The first photograph of a star other than our own sun. This is *Betelgeuse*, the reddish-orange star of Orion.
Below: The nebula of Orion is a great luminous and lustreless patch discovered in 1610. It consists of a gas which burns gently under the intense, hot radiation of the stars. This makes it luminous.

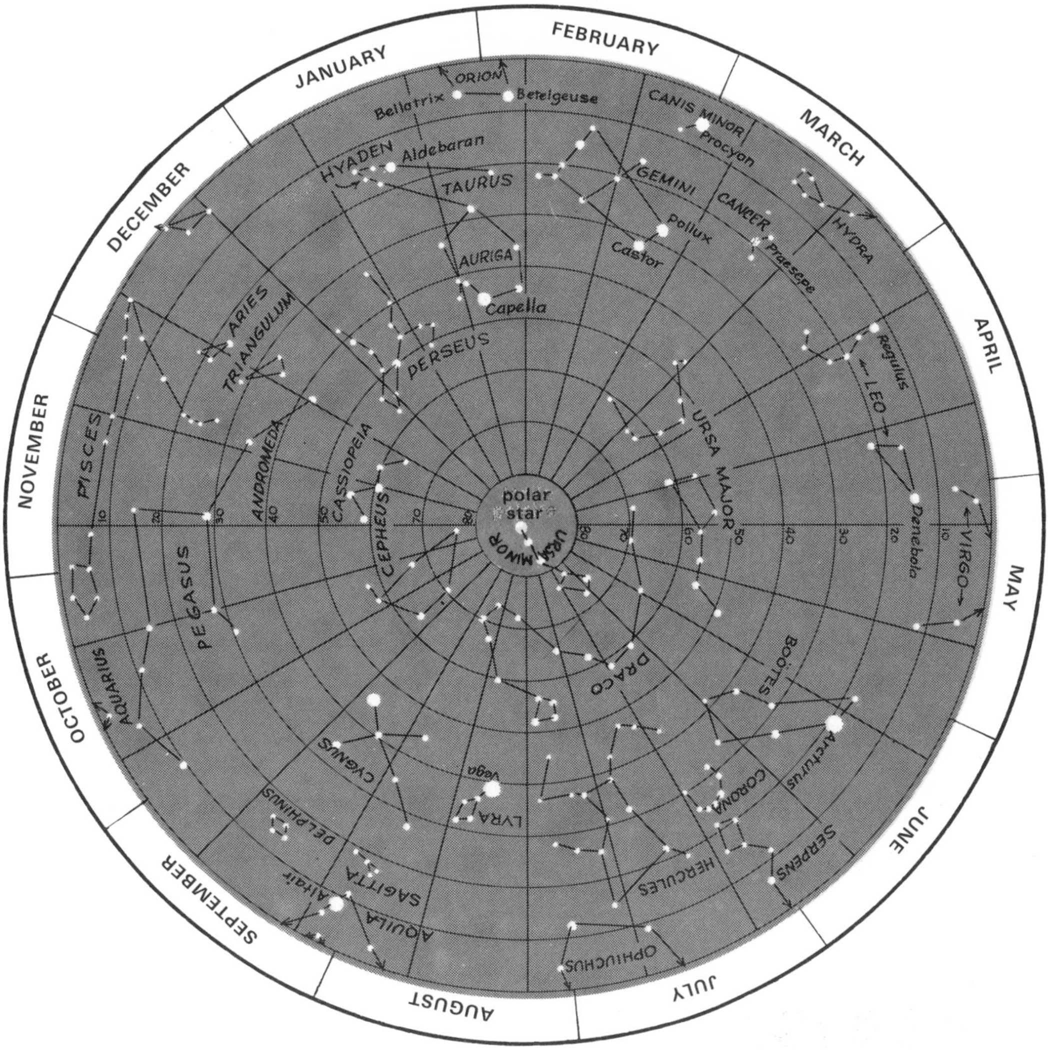

Map of the northern hemisphere.

What is astology?

During the Middle Ages there were a number of people who took a serious interest in the sky. But they made few discoveries because they were concerned not so much with astronomy proper as with astrology, and the belief that men's destinies are determined by the movements of the stars. The astronomer and the astrologer both investigate phenomena which are not observable in everyday life or with the naked eye.
For the astrologer the paths of the Sun, the Moon and the planets are limited to a small zone of the celestial globe. This zone is divided into twelve sections which represent the signs of the *zodiac*. Each of them bears the name of a constellation and is crossed by the Sun once a year.

Why isn't the solar system subject to change?

The Sun's position in the zodiac on the day and at the time of a person's birth thus, according to astrology, determines his character and the course of his life. Copernicus did not agree with the opinions of his contemporaries on the movement of the stars and he held that the planets described a circular trajectory around the Sun. Some sixty years later Galileo upheld the same views. In 1609 Kepler discovered that the planets' paths around the Sun were not circular but ellipsoidal. The Englishman Isaac Newton also explained why the planets followed these trajectories, and why the system never altered. He found that every particle of matter attracted others and he called this force of attraction *gravity*.

Above: Nicolaus Copernicus, a Polish philosopher, astronomer, lawyer, doctor and monk. He studied the planets and calculated their precise location and distance from the sun. This enabled him to establish that they revolve around it.

Planets and Comets

The planets and comets belong to our Solar System. A planet is a heavenly body which revolves around the Sun, and the Earth on which we live is one of the nine planets. Comets are composed of small solid particles, and have very eccentric orbits.

Above: Johannes Kepler, a German astronomer who lived from 1571 to 1630. In 1609 he discovered that the planets' orbits were ellipsoidal, thereby improving on the universal system of Copernicus. He maintained that the nearer the planets were to the sun the faster they travelled. He was also the first to state that heavy bodies exert a mutual attraction.
Below: The planet Saturn, the largest after Jupiter. It's also the most distant planet that can be seen with the naked eye. The path is describes is approximately 1,424 million km from the sun. Composed of gas, it's more than nine times as big as the Earth. Its most striking features are the three flat rings encircling it, two of which are luminous.

Can planets emit light?

If we could see a very long way we'd notice that the ball of fire which is the sun is surrounded by small luminous spots. These are the planets, which do not themselves emit light but which reflect the light of the sun. The nine planets, in the order of their distance from the sun, are Mercury, Venus, Earth, Mars, Jupiter, Saturn, Uranus, Neptune and Pluto. Four of these planets, Mercury, Venus, Mars and Pluto, resemble the Earth in their general appearance and dimensions. By comparison with the Earth the four others are giants, and are made of much lighter matter. These are Jupiter, Saturn, Uranus and Neptune.
Many astronomers think that Pluto was once a moon of Neptune that escaped from its orbit and became a planet instead.

How do the planets move?

The Greeks called the planets wandering stars and were unable to understand how they moved. But in fact the Sun's family behaves in a very orderly way, each planet keeping to a regular path.
All the planets move around the Sun in the same direction, simultaneously rotating about their own axes. The axis is an imaginary line which passes through the centre of the planet from one pole to another. Although we're unable to verify it in the case of certain planets, all the signs are that they do in fact rotate about their axes in the same way as the Earth. (Uranus is a special case: it has tilted, and its north pole is pointed towards the centre of the sun.)
The Sun also rotates about its axis, but more slowly than some planets. It takes 25 days to complete a rotation, whereas Saturn takes 10 hours 14 minutes, Uranus 10 hours 49 minutes and Jupiter 9 hours 50 minutes. However on Venus the axial rotation period is 243 days. And since it completes a revolution round the sun every 225 days, a day on Venus is, in fact, longer than a year.

How were asteroids discovered?

The eighteenth century German astronomer Bode demonstrated how to calculate approximmately the distances between the planets and the Sun. He discovered that Jupiter (the fifth planet from the Sun) was travelling in an orbit in which, according to his calculations, the sixth planet ought to have been. So for several years efforts were made to find a planet between Mars and Jupiter.
In 1801 a small celestial body was duly discovered and given the name of Ceres. It has a circumference of 770 km and consists chiefly of rock. Several million of these small celestial bodies, called asteroids, were later discovered in the same region. The orbits of 3,000 of them have so far been plotted.

How was the solar system born?

Once it was known that the planets revolve around the Sun, people began to ask various questions. How was the Solar System born? When did this occur? Are there similarities between solar matter and the matter of which the Earth and other planets are composed? Astronomers have made many discoveries with the aid of scientific instruments. By examining the light of the Sun and planets they've established that no matter exists in any part of the solar system which cannot be found on the Earth.

It therefore seems very likely that the Sun and planets came into being at the same time, that everything began five thousand million years ago with a cloud of whirling gas. This whirling made the mass of gas more compact and the force of gravity attracted ever more matter on to the spinning mass. An immense globe thus developed at the centre, rotating with increasing speed. The masses of gas farthest from the globe, set in rotatory motion by the force of attraction, formed a flat ring. Further whirling or *vortices* arose in this ring and attracted additional gaseous masses which progressively agglomerated, and formed small globes. These newly formed globes were to be the planets.

Above: **Halley's comet. This is the best known of the comets and is named after the English astronomer Edmond Halley. In 1682 he discovered a luminous heavenly body which he predicted would reappear in 1758. This turned out to be correct, and it was calculated that the comet took 76 years to complete one orbit around the sun. It was seen for the last time in 1910 and will therefore reappear in 1986.**
Below: **The planets of the solar system in descending order of size: Jupiter, Saturn, Uranus, Neptune, Earth, Venus, Pluto, Mars and Mercury.**

The Moon

Our nearest neighbour in space is the Moon, which moves in orbit around the Earth. It was the first satellite known to man and is one of the heavenly bodies which do not emit light of their own.

What is a satellite?

In recent years everyone has become familiar with the word satellite. The first one known to man was the Moon, but man later sent his own satellites into orbit around the Earth and other heavenly bodies. The first artificial satellite was launched by Russia in 1957. The planets are satellites of the Sun and the Moon is the Earth's satellite. Other planets have satellites of their own, but none of them is as big in relation to its mother planet as the Moon is to the Earth. The Moon's diameter measures 3,476 km, about a quarter of the Earth's

Above: An illustration from Jules Verne's book _Voyage Around the Moon_. This French writer lived from 1825 to 1905. From 1863 onwards he wrote 'scientific' novels which earned him a worldwide reputation. These early works of science fiction were eagerly devoured by large numbers of readers. Verne described with great imagination events which he thought would happen in the future and which have actually occurred in the twentieth century.
Below: The Moon, our nearest neighbour, can be seen at night. Fragments brought back by space capsules have enabled scientists to establish that it's composed of rocks and dust. Its surface consists of high mountains and innumerable craters, the latter being remains of volcanoes which existed before the Moon had cooled. But some of the craters were made by meteors crashing on to the Moon at high speed with no atmosphere to slow them.

Why do we always see the same face of the Moon?

The Moon rotates once about its own axis in the same time as it completes an orbit around the Earth. This means that we shall only ever be able to see one single face of the Moon. Why is that? Take for example a bottle of lemonade, with a label, to represent the Moon and a bottle of milk to represent the Earth. Turn the bottle with the label around the bottle of milk so that the label is always turned towards the bottle of milk you do this, you'll find that in order to do it you'll have to turn the bottle of lemonade slightly and that it will have to turn once about its own axis before completing a revolution around the bottle of milk. However, although we see only one side of the moon we know from photographs what the other side looks like. The first photographs of the far side of the moon were taken in 1959 by the Russian lunar probe, Lunik III.

Why does the Moon seem to change its shape?

Seen from the Earth, the Moon appears to change its shape. First of all we observe no more than a slender quarter, but each night it grows until a full round moon is visible. This then becomes smaller and smaller, and finally disappears entirely. These apparent changes in the Moon's form are called phases and it takes twenty-nine days to go through them all. Our modern calendar is based on these lunar periods.
In fact the Moon doesn't change its form, but remains a sphere all the time. The light which it seems to emit is really the Sun's light reflected on its surface and sent back to the Earth. If you take a spherical object, for example a ball, and shine your torch on to it in a dark room, you'll find that half the ball is illuminated and the other half remains dark. The same

Opposite: **The first man on the Moon. The launching of manned spacecraft by the Americans and Soviets has enabled a large amount of information to be obtained about the Moon. One of the great moments in this lunar exploration was the launching of Apollo 11 from the John F. Kennedy Space Centre at Cape Canaveral, then Cape Kennedy, at Houston in Texas on the 16 July 1969. The members of the crew were Neil Armstrong, Michael Collins and Edwin Aldrin. After a successful voyage they landed on the Moon near the Sea of Tranquillity and Captain Armstrong became the first man to set foot on lunar soil.**

applies to the Moon and other planets. The moon is always half in sunlight and half in darkness. We can only see the part turned towards the Sun and we often don't see even this half-moon in its entirety. Like the Moon, the Earth is illuminated by the light of the Sun and it is the Earth which lights up the dark portion of the Moon.

What do we know about the Moon?

The Moon consists of rocks which hardly differ from those found on Earth, and in fact they must share a common origin. Before lunar probes and astronauts landed on the Moon we already possessed a large amount of information about the lunar surface. Powerful telescopes enable the moon to be observed in detail, just as though it were no more than 300 km from the Earth. Scientific observation is concentrated mainly on that part of the Moon turned towards the Earth. The far side has been photographed with the aid of lunar probes and space capsules, so we now have accurate maps of the entire surface of the Moon.

The Moon has no atmosphere or vapour circle, so it is not surrounded by a layer of air like the Earth. This is why the Earth is always dark when seen from the Moon, even when the Sun is shining.

Although much is said about the Moon's 'seas' there is, in fact, no surface water on the moon. These 'seas', most of which are on the side of the Moon facing Earth, are plains of solidified lava. The daytime temperature on the Moon reaches about 130°C, and at night can fall to as low as −150°C.

Influence of the Moon

The Moon exerts a considerable influence on the Earth. For example, its action is the primary cause of the tides, making the level of the sea rise and fall periodically by its gravitational force. This phenomenon can generally be observed once or twice a day: the sea approaches (high tide), then recedes (low tide). The biggest tides occur when the Moon's attraction is combined with that of the Sun.

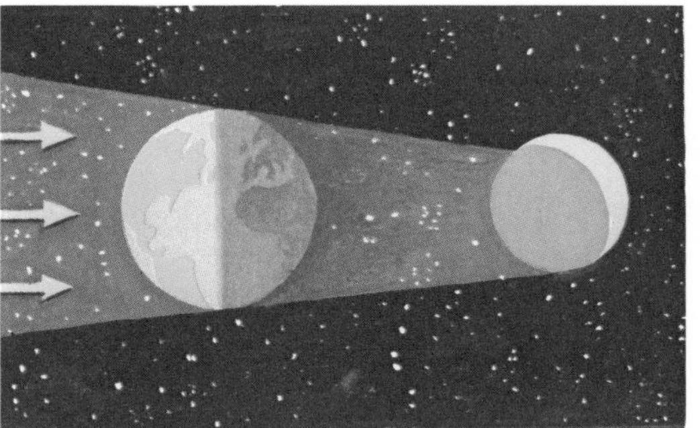

Opposite: **One of the Moon's phases. The three arrows represent the Sun's rays illuminating half the Earth, while the rays which pass beyond the Earth light up part of the Moon. The rest is in darkness because the Sun's rays are stopped by the Earth. When the Moon is on the Sun's side we cannot see it because the illuminated half is facing away from the Earth. This is called the new Moon.**

The Earth's origins

The Earth is the only known habitation of men, animals and plants. We haven't yet discovered whether other planets are inhabited by living beings. But a whole process of evolution was necessary before life appeared on Earth.

Above: **Fossils are hardened remains of plants and animals, or else impressions of them. These souvenirs of the past tell us a lot about the Earth's history and the species which used to exist. The earliest known form of life dates from about two thousand million years ago.**

Below: **Marl is produced by a deposit of mud, fine sand and remains of shellfish in briny water. This deposit hardened and combined with limestone. Peat is formed by plants and is combustible.**

How did the Earth originate?

Scientists tell us that the Earth, Sun and other planets in the Solar System existed some 100,000 million years ago in the form of an immense cloud of cold particles of dust whirling in the void of the Universe. These particles were gradually attracted by each other and began to form an enormous spinning disc. The force of this motion caused the disc to split up into several rings and the small particles started to burn. The Sun formed at the centre of the disc.

Other particles formed hot balls of gas and molten matter, which then began to cool and condense (like the change from vapour to water) and finally assumed their solid form. We don't know exactly when the Earth, Mars, Venus and the other planets were born in this way, but it would seem to have occurred about four to five thousand million years ago.

What is the Earth like inside?

If you were to cut a baseball through the middle you'd see that it consists of a core of hard rubber enclosed in several solid but less hard layers and a thin outer covering of horse hide. The Earth's composition is similar to that of the ball. The hard outer layer of stone is called the Earth's crust and is 15 to 50 km thick, which is much thinner in relative terms than the covering on the ball. It makes up less than one per cent of the volume of the earth. Beneath this crust is a second, thicker layer called the Earth's mantle. Although composed of hard rocks, mainly the volcanic rock peridotite, the mantle can become deformed and change its structure when subjected to pressure. It is thought that the upper layers are cooler than the lower layers.

Finally, this mantle encloses the core, which consists of two parts, the outer and the inner core. Both are composed of metal, with a predominance of iron, the outer core being molten and the inner core solid. The temperature here reaches 8,000°C. The distance from the Earth's surface to its centre is 6,400 km.

Earthquakes have enabled us to deduce a number of facts about the internal composition of our planet. Several thousand tremors occur every year in various parts of the world, producing shock-waves which penetrate to the very centre of the Earth. The force of these waves depends on the types of rock through which they have to pass. When they re-emerge at the surface they're registered by a seismograph. Scientists can determine the Earth's composition by calculating their speed and force, the distance covered from their point of departure, the depth they reach before re-ascending and the time taken to cover this distance.

Left, above: **The Alps are a chain of mountains running from east to west in the heart of central Europe. If we could make a section through them we'd see that the layers of rock are broken, folded or crumpled. Some of them, now several thousand metres above the sea, once formed part of the sea-bed. We know this from the hardened remains of marine animals found in the rock of the highest summits. Mountain chains rose slowly out of the sea and were subjected to different kinds of erosion, such as that caused by rapid-flowing mountain rivers and glaciers. The Alpine chain is still relatively young, a fact revealed by its sharp peaks and deep, steep-sided valleys.**

Left, below: **A river in Scotland. The Scottish mountains were formed a long time ago and their summits began to be weathered and eroded much earlier than those in the Alps – often by powerful torrents which carried away huge quantities of debris. We know they are old from their rounded, eroded peaks and debris-filled valleys.**

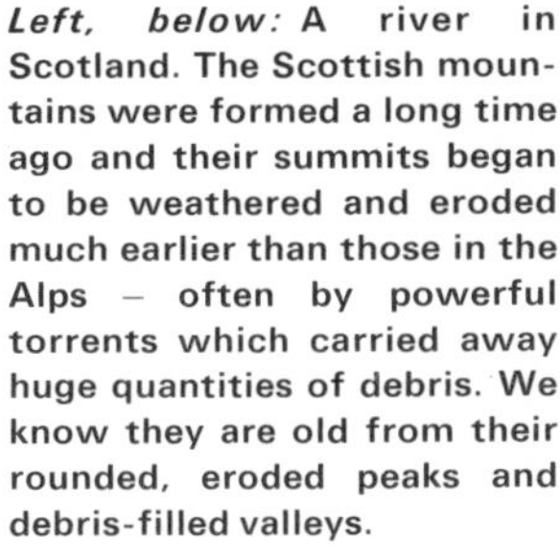

How can we reconstruct the earlier appearance of the Earth?

The Earth, it seems, looked very different a few thousand years ago. A land bridge probably joined northern Europe to Greenland, and Spain to the east of the United States. Later, Africa, Australia and America were formed into a single continent. Unbroken forests of gigantic ferns covered regions now separated from each other by thousands of kilometres of sea. In the Ice Age the British Isles and southern Sweden were joined to the European continent. At that time the North Sea and the English Channel were no more than an enormous swamp. The Thames was a tributary of the Rhine and the two together formed a single gigantic river. It was also possible to go on foot from Siberia to Alaska over a land bridge above the Bering Strait. This is said to be the route by which both prehistoric Asian man and the mammoth arrived in America.

What's an earthquake?

From time to time the Earth begins to tremble, rocky masses break up and come crashing down mountains, fissures occur in the Earth's surface, and houses, villages and whole towns are destroyed. Why? The Earth's thin crust is made up of different layers of rock, which although of varying kinds are mostly hard. These rocks are subject to constant pressure, both from the layers above and from the forces originating at the Earth's core. This pressure makes the layers bend, and they sometimes break in the same way as a stick will snap if you bend it far enough. The sudden jolt produces a tremor in the Earth's crust and an earthquake takes place. The point where the earthquake begins is called the focus; from here the vibrations spread out in all directions. Seismographs enable earthquakes to be registered thousands of kilometres from their point of origin.

The Air

The Earth is surrounded by an atmosphere. Without this atmosphere life would not be possible, because the atmosphere contains oxygen. It also protects us against over-low or over-high temperatures.

Above: Henry Cavendish, an English chemist who lived from 1731 to 1810. He demonstrated that water is composed of hydrogen and oxygen, and was the first to determine the composition of air.
Below: This windmill is one of the oldest mills in Holland. Its sails turn on an axle or shaft. Mills of this kind were used for grinding corn or as oil crushers. They were also widely employed in the west of the Netherlands for draining lakes.

Right: A cloud is a condensed mass of fine droplets of water or frozen particles. This photograph shows clouds in loosely scattered formation.

What are clouds?

The atmosphere is made up of several layers, and most cloud is located in the lower layer up to a height of 10 km. Above the polar regions clouds rarely exceed an altitude of 8 km; in tropical zones they can reach 18 km.

Water can exist in a variety of forms: as a gas, a liquid or a solid. Water in a gaseous form is called vapour. The water in taps, streams and rivers is liquid. Solid water takes the form of snow, hail or ice. It's water which is at the origin of clouds.

The air we breathe contains fine droplets resulting from the evaporation of water in the sea and on land. The colder the air, the more these droplets of vapour condense and become heavy. Every cloud of water and ice is thus caused by the cooling of a certain quantity of air (nitrogen and oxygen). Like the gases which constitute the air, vapour is invisible; even in considerable quantities it remains transparent. This transparency only diminishes when bigger droplets form, with the result that the sky changes colour at the horizon, becoming bluish-grey or even grey. At this stage we speak of a cloudy sky or haze. If there is a further decrease in transparency we call it mist, and when visibility is reduced to a hundred metres or even less we're contending with fog. Fog is a cloud of water just above the Earth's surface.

Different types of cloud formations can be identified and used to forecast weather in the immediate future.

What's condensation?

The moment at which vapour is transformed into drops of water is called the condensation point. At a low temperature water actually forms crystals of ice, and for this the temperature has to be below –10°C or sometimes below –15°C, depending on the particles of dust which are present in the air and which warm it. Most clouds are made up of frozen drops of water, which means that their temperature is below zero.

Warm air can hold more moisture than cold air. Therefore when a region of warm air is forced upwards, and is cooled, the temperature falls, and some of the water vapour must condense out – either as ice crystals or as water droplets.

Why does air rise?

Air rises for two reasons:

1. Local warming of the air. When warmed, air masses expand, which makes them become less dense. They will therefore weigh less than the surrounding air masses, and so they begin to rise.
2. The presence of a mountain. When horizontal air strata encounter an obstacle such as a mountain, a thick layer of clouds forms on the side from which the wind is coming. The air rises up the slope, cools, the vapour condenses and it begins to rain. This can sometimes last for hours on end. If the air reaches the mountain's summit, it passes

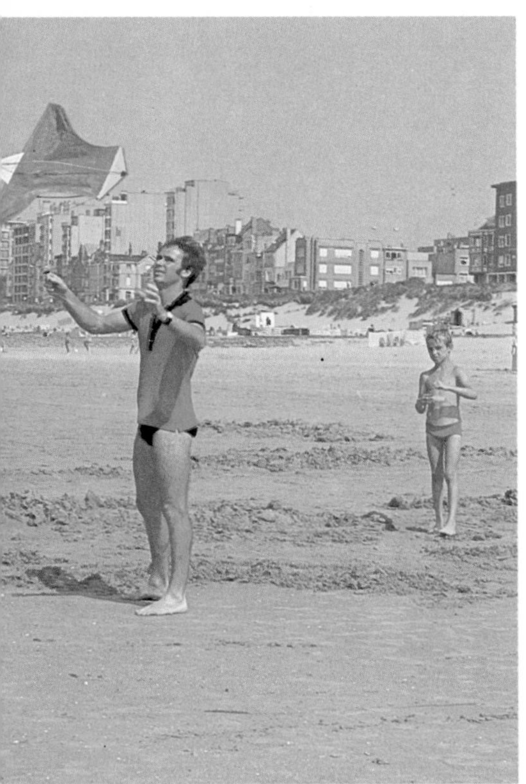

Above: Wind is caused by displacement of air following variations in atmospheric pressure. Over the sea it generally blows uniformly from the same direction, but can change abruptly on the coast. The wind needs to be fairly strong to make a kite fly.

over and comes down again: the clouds disappear and it stops raining.

What makes it rain, snow and hail?

The rain reaching the Earth is part of a natural cycle. Some evaporation occurs wherever there is an area of water, for example a lake or ocean, and this causes condensation in the atmosphere. The higher the temperature at ground level, the greater the degree of evaporation. Above deserts, where there is little moisture in the ground, and above the polar regions, however, evaporation is insignificant. The ground in the polar regions consists mainly of frozen water, and large masses of snow and ice; the temperature is very low, so there's hardly any evaporation.

When the water vapour resulting from evaporation cools, it becomes water again and a cloud forms. As we've already said, a cloud is made up of a large number of little drops of water, most of which acquire a diameter of no more than 0.005 mm. Drops of this size are exceedingly light and float about in the cloud, falling at less than 30 cm per second. Since rising air generally moves at a speed of several metres per second, these little drops will never reach the ground. They simply evaporate before getting there. Over northern and central Europe, drops of rain start off as thawed crystals or melting snow. In winter, when temperatures are below zero, these snow crystals are heavy enough to reach the ground and they do not melt to form rain. It sometimes also happens in winter that a warmer layer of air is situated between two layers of cold air. The snow in the upper layer of cold air then turns into rain before becoming frozen once again. In this case the drops fall in the form of hailstones. As a rule, however, hailstones aren't formed in this way, but develop in rainclouds of enormous vertical depth. The hailstone's core consists of granular snow, an agglomerated mass of snow crystals. As it falls, this generally encounters layers of colder water and consequently becomes coated with ice.

Top: Making use of wind. A parachutist uses the air to slow his descent to the ground with a parachute.
Centre: A sailing-boat is moved by the wind blowing in its sails.
Bottom: Air pollution. Industrial exhaust gases and residual gases can be harmful to man and to plants if expelled into the air.

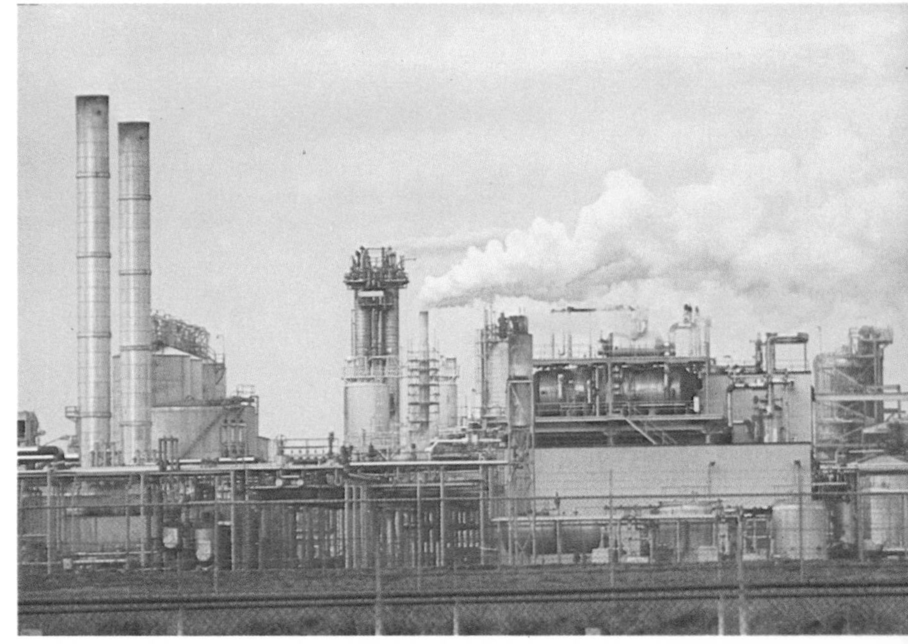

Water

Two-thirds of the Earth's surface is covered in water. Below the surface of the oceans, the sea bed is not smooth, but has deep valleys, and mountains which are higher than those on land.

Above: **A well in the desert. A desert is a region where very little rain falls. Inhabitants of desert areas sink wells wherever they can.**
Right: **A ditch in the Netherlands, dug to allow excess water to flow away. The water often reaches the level of the surrounding terrain.**
Below: **The sea around the Japanese coasts contains abundant fish because of the warm and cold currents which meet on the east coast. The cold currents have a high oxygen content and the region is also rich in plankton.**

Why is sea-water salty?

The oceans are like enormous ponds filling cavities in the Earth's crust. Together with the seas they contain 97% of the Earth's water. The remaining 3% is fresh water: lakes, rivers and atmospheric vapour.
Sea-water is salty because rivers dissolve the salts they collect in the mountains and carry them down to the ocean. When water evaporates on the surface, the salts remain. Over millions of years the salt deposit has reached a level which makes it impossible to drink sea-water.

Why are there waves?

Ocean waves are caused partly by the wind. High tide and low tide can be compared to

huge, slow-motion waves. They're caused by the gravitational force of the Sun and the Moon, so that the water ebbs and flows twice a day. On ocean coastlines the tides can bring about differences of several metres in the water level, but the water in inland seas moves very little and tides are hardly noticeable.
The ocean water moves in currents, some of which arise on the surface as a result of strong winds blowing from a single direction. Cold currents flow through the oceans far below the surface, often moving in the opposite direction from surface currents. Others describe circles from one side of the ocean to the other, returning to their point of departure. These are caused by the Earth's rotation.
There are four big oceans, the biggest of which is the Pacific. The others are the Atlantic Ocean, the Indian Ocean and the Arctic Ocean, which is around the North Pole.

How do rivers develop?

Water also exists on the mainland. When a

Right: A flood. In 1953 there was serious flooding in the south-west of the Netherlands, causing the deaths of 1,800 people as well as a great deal of other damage. The disaster was due to a violent storm on the coast accompanied by an exceptional tide. The dykes, unable to contain the water, burst at several points. To prevent such a disaster occurring again, the Delta plan was put into effect. This involved the construction of large barrages wherever the sea formed wide bays. While providing additional security, these barrages also act as bridges linking the different islands. Two waterways are open to shipping: the Westerschelde to and from Antwerp and the north-west canal to and from Rotterdam.

heavy shower of rain falls on a mountain, the water flows quickly down its slopes and forms little streams. When these streams reach the bottom of the mountain, they will join together to produce a wide river valley, through which, since the valley is less steep than the mountainside, the water will flow more slowly. The river will be wider and more shallow.

The water now begins to deposit all the pebbles and soil which it has carried with it. Often these little stones and sand gradually form an obstacle in the river's path, so that the water is diverted and begins to gouge out another bed in which the various débris will again be deposited. The water will then change direction once more and a series of serpentine bends will develop.

What causes floods?

Sometimes a large quantity of rain falls in a short time, or else it rains steadily for days on end. After downpours of this kind rivers may no longer be able to contain the water between their banks. They then start to overflow and flood the surrounding land.

These floods can be highly destructive. Sometimes the fertile layer of soil is carried off by the water and the rest of the soil remains uncultivatable for several years. Buildings, parts of towns and even whole villages are swept away by the current and large numbers of people and animals are drowned. Sometimes dams are built to prevent flooding, but these are always expensive, and can be very difficult projects.

Floods can occasionally prove beneficial. This is the case in Egypt, where the Nile overflows every year. During the spring very heavy rain falls in central Africa. When the water gets to the lower reaches of the Nile the land is flooded. As a result, a layer of silt is deposited on the desert soil every year and the Egyptians are able to cultivate cotton, fruit and corn there.

Opposite: The Niagara Falls. The Niagara River joins Lake Erie and Lake Ontario, the difference between their levels being a hundred metres. The falls are 32 km from the river's source and 47 m high. An island in the middle of the river divides it into two branches. Most of the water passes over the Horseshoe Falls into Canada. The water at the bottom of the falls flows so gently that in winter it begins to freeze.

The Land

A third of the Earth's surface is not covered by water. Various influences including weather and erosion have resulted in a wide range of different landscapes.

How does a landscape develop?

Nature is constantly changing under the influence of erosion. Assaulted by glacial rivers, powerful ocean waves, hard frosts and torrential rivers, mountain ridges were transformed into undulating plains over a period of several million years. Huge rocks were worn away to form sand and mud. As soon as a mountain was created the weather began to act on it. The result was a wide variety of different landscapes.

Millions of years ago, much of the Earth was covered with snow. The snow changed the landscape in many ways before finally melting. In some places it wore away (eroded) the rock, and in others it deposited material. Glaciers (slow moving masses of snow frozen into ice) gouged out deep valleys, which later filled with water. Examples are the Norwegian fjords, and the lochs of Scotland.

Looking at a parched and arid expanse of desert, you immediately see that it contains little life. There may be a scraggy bush or prickly cactus somewhere in view, but no other vegetation will survive on such sandy, rocky soil.

In places the strong, dry wind has eroded the sand and other softer materials off the rocks and produced bizarre shapes. In daytime the sky is bright and clear, the sun burning-hot. When the sun finally sets, the temperature can drop very low.

We've already seen how wind and water modify the Earth's surface. The wind's influence is practically as great as that of water. In desert regions it moves the sand from one place to another, sometimes hurling it against the rocks. These gradually become weathered, the softer portions disappearing first and leaving the harder rock standing. Swept by wind and sand, they often turn into veritable sculptures.

Top left: **In a region of low rainfall, the ground dries out in the hot sunshine and begins to crack.**
Opposite: **A mountain ridge in the Vosges. This mountainous region to the west of the Rhine in north-east France was formed a very long time ago. Its appearance has been transformed by wind, water and glaciers.**

Above: **This rock was broken off by the ice. A glacier is like a river of ice which slowly moves down a mountainside. Carving out its own bed, it takes with it everything in its path. The glacier which once covered the northern Netherlands carried rocks as far as Scandinavia. These rocks were used to make the dolmens (tombs) of the ancient inhabitants of Drente.**

Have some landscapes been modified by man?

Man also plays a large part in modifications to the appearance and quality of certain regions. Unfortunately his intervention has often had tragic consequences.

Part of Texas and Oklahoma, for example, was once covered in lush grassland. Firm roots retained the humidity in the soil, and in dry periods the grass survived and the soil was always fertile. But farmers began to plough the land so that they could sow and harvest corn. Then, between 1930 and 1940, there was a long period of drought. Harvests were disastrous. The deep roots of the grass would have retained the soil, but because the grass had been ploughed up the soil was simply swept away in dusty clouds by the strong winds. For several years the region no longer produced anything and the majority of farmers had to leave for other regions.

On the other hand, man has sometimes also modified a landscape to its advantage. When the first inhabitants of the United States reached the west coast, California was essentially a desert region. The farmers managed to make it fertile by digging channels which brought water from distant rivers.

What rocks make up the Earth's crust?

The Earth's crust consists of three different types of rock:

a) *Magmatic, or igneous, rocks.* These are the oldest of the world's rocks. They came into existence several thousand million years ago and are derived from magma (a hot molten substance which surged up out of the depths of the Earth) at the time when the Earth was cooling. From these, two other types of rock were formed – a sand and a variety of soil produced by erosion. The largest part of the Earth's crust is made up of igneous rocks. The two principal igneous rocks are granite and basalt. Granite is found all over Norway and is used chiefly in building because of its durability and resistance to the effects of weather. The edges of pavements are often made from it for the

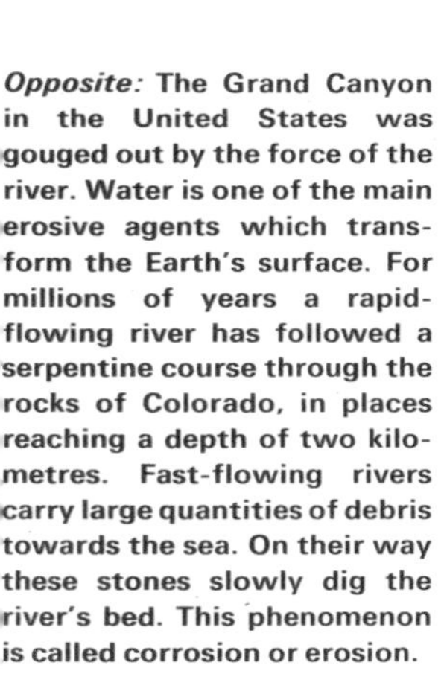

Opposite: **The Grand Canyon in the United States was gouged out by the force of the river. Water is one of the main erosive agents which transform the Earth's surface. For millions of years a rapid-flowing river has followed a serpentine course through the rocks of Colorado, in places reaching a depth of two kilometres. Fast-flowing rivers carry large quantities of debris towards the sea. On their way these stones slowly dig the river's bed. This phenomenon is called corrosion or erosion.**

Below: **The River Amazon in Brazil flows through a thick virgin forest, reaching a width of 10km in several places. Its flow rate depends on the rainfall, which causes big differences in the water level.**
Bottom: **A mountain river. The glaciers at the tops of mountains only move a few centimetres per day. But the further they descend, the higher the temperature becomes. Finally the ice begins to melt.**

same reason. Its colour varies: white, grey, green, pink or red.

Basalt is the most common form of lava (rock formed from magma thrown out by volcanoes. While cooling, it acquires the form of a prism with five or six faces. It is widely used in the construction of dykes and causeways, and is employed in powder form in the building of roads. Its colour varies from dark grey to black.

b) *Sedimentary rocks.* These were produced by erosive substances such as sand, gravel and mud being deposited at the bottom of the sea several million years ago. The enormous pressure of overlying substances hardened them into solid rock.

The best-known sedimentary rocks are sandstone, limestone and slate (hardened clay).

c) *Metamorphic rocks.* These originated as sedimentary rocks and their structure and mineral content were transformed by high pressure and the temperature of the Earth's crust. The best-known metamorphic rocks are marble, schist and quartzite.

Marble, for instance, is a derivative of limestone and is often used for monuments.

Schist is the result of a transformation of slate and clay. It is easily divided into small slabs with smooth, flat surfaces. Its main use is for roofing.

Quartzite is very similar to sandstone, from which it is in fact derived. But whereas sandstone is relatively soft, quartzite is one of the hardest rocks. When a mass of quartzite appears on the surface it forms a sheer cliff because the softer rocks around it disappear as a result of erosion.

What are the least common rocks?

There are many other less common rocks.

Asbestos, for example, is a type of metamorphic rock with long silky fibres. These fibres are interwoven and compressed to give a fire-resistant material which is used for brake linings and non-inflammable clothing.

Flint was used by Stone Age man for making tools: axes, knives and arrow heads. Conglomerates are strange-looking rocks which were often formed in river beds.

Pebbles, sand and pieces of rock sometimes combine with other minerals to give a solid aggregate. The original pebbles and little stones can still be recognized. This is known as natural concrete.

Pieces of petrified wood are sometimes found among the pebbles on a river-bed. This is not in fact real wood turned into stone. So what has occurred? Several million years ago trees fell into the mud at a point where the water in the mud had a high content of silicic acid. This water penetrated the ligneous cells and when the wood began to rot each cell was replaced by flint. As a result the rock continues to resemble the original wood, but is harder.

What are the different kinds of landscape?

Regions lying at an altitude of up to 200 metres above sea level are generally described as *plains*. An eminence rising 200 to 500 metres above sea level is classified as a *hill*. From 500 to 1500 metres we speak of a *chain of low mountains* and above 1500 metres of a *chain of high mountains*.
An atlas indicates the different types of landscape. A map of Europe shows that more than half (about 60%) of the continent consists of plains: western France, northern Belgium, the Low Countries, Denmark, northern Germany, Poland and Russia. 24% of its surface is taken up with hills, merging progressively into more mountainous country. This sort of landscape is found chiefly in the north of France, the central portion of Germany and Great Birtain. The chain of low mountains covers 10% of Europe's territory.
Finally there is the 6% of high mountains in Scandinavia, the south of France, Spain, Italy, Switzerland, Austria, southern Germany and the U.S.S.R. Europe's highest summit is Mount Elbrus (5,633 m) in the Caucasus.

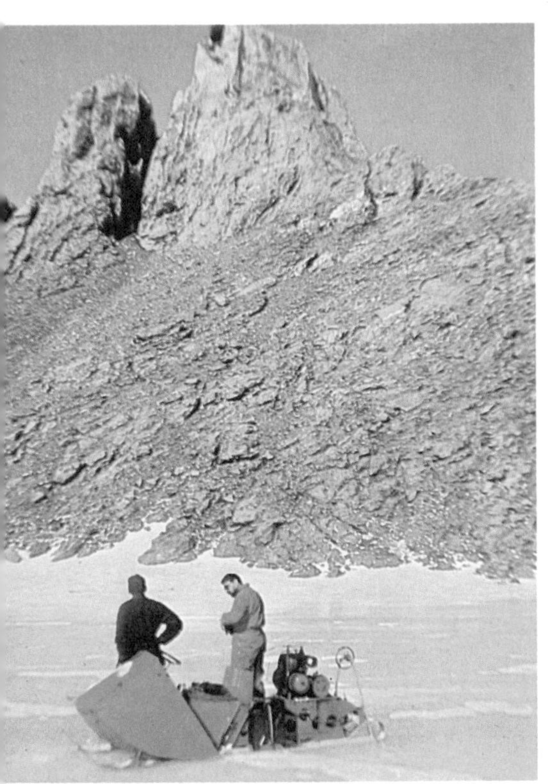

Mountains are a result of folds in the Earth's crust. You can get some idea of this phenomenon by pushing the two opposite ends of a thick table-cloth towards the centre, making folds. The vertical folds in the layers of rock can often be seen. A mountain formed in this way is called a folded mountain. The areas between the folds are valleys. Other mountains are formed when large areas of the Earth's crust slip, due to faults in the rocks, leaving vast expanses of high land still standing. These are known as block, or table mountains.

Top: **A steppe in Kenya with zebras and antelopes. Steppes generally take the form of treeless, grassy plains, with scattered trees appearing where they merge into savannah.**
Above: **Mountains sometimes break up the desert's sandy expanse.**
Left: **The temperature in Antarctica never rises above zero centigrade. The layer of ice is roughly 3000 m thick. Antarctica is larger than either Europe or Australia, but it was not discovered until 1819. The exlporer Captain Cook, who died in 1779, correctly surmised its existence.**

Above: Salt production. Salt water is directed into a shallow basin near the sea. Warmed by the sun, the water evaporates and leaves the salt. Salt can only be produced in this way in a warm climate, as in the south of France.

Below: Modern equipment is being used increasingly for drilling in rocky ground, either to extract rock or to build tunnels for motor traffic through mountains.

Rocks and minerals

The earth (plains, mountains, sea-bed) consists almost entirely of rocks and minerals, of which a wide variety is distributed unequally around the world. Some are common, others rare.

Why do we study rocks and minerals?

Life in the twentieth century is influenced by many technologies. Each day sees the appearance of new inventions, every one of which would be unthinkable without the utilization of rocks or minerals. The most common mineral is water. A certain quantity of water is to be found everywhere, and the oceans, rivers and lakes alone cover two-thirds of the Earth's surface. Sea-water itself contains other minerals in a dissolved form; salt, for instance, you can taste. Minerals and rocks are used in the manufacture of many products. Glass for example, is derived from sand, even though it may not look like it. Metal is obtained from ore extracted from the ground. So it's interesting to study minerals and rocks to find out what they're made of and what they can be used for.

Minerals and rocks have always been indispensable to man, who in primitive times used stones (flint) for making tools and weapons. In various parts of the world he began to work metal, starting with bronze. The Bronze Age in western Europe lasted from 2000 to 800 B.C., when man discovered iron. The Iron Age extended down to the beginning of our own era, but iron ore is still important today.

What is rock?

Rocks are composed of minerals, and most of them contain several different kinds. But clear sand is composed of a single mineral, quartz. Rocks can be of different colours (red, yellow, blue, green, white, grey or black). Why are they so diverse in their composition?

The diversity is due to the fact that rocks originate in different ways. New ones are still being formed today. Certain parts of the Earth's crust are affected by subsidences which discharge bubbling hot magma from far down inside the Earth. This phenomenon is commonly known as a volcanic eruption. When it has cooled, the magma solidifies into magmatic rocks, forming a cone (or volcano) and a large crater.

Other rocks are forming several metres below the Earth's surface.

What is a mineral?

A mineral is a chemical element or a combination of chemical elements. Anything which is not vegetable or animal is mineral. Most minerals are solid, but some, such as water, mercury and petroleum, are liquid. Water is composed of two elements, oxygen and hydrogen, while petroleum is a combination of several elements. Other important minerals are clay, limestone, salt,

Top left: Limestone is a sedimentary rock hardened by the pressure of the layers above.
Top right: Schist is a sedimentary rock formed by the superimposition of small, very fragile sheets pressed on to one another.
Centre: Marble is a metamorphic rock derived from limestone.
Bottom: Smoky quartz, the mineral from which white sand is formed. Rocks develop by a clearly defined process. Isolated stones can produce a sedimentary rock by compression. Heat and pressure then turn this sedimentary rock into metamorphic rock.

gypsum, iron, copper, gold and silver. Scientists tell us that there are about two thousand different kinds.

Precious minerals are found in many parts of the world. If there is enough of a certain mineral to justify systematic exploitation, mines are sunk. Certain strata are located on the surface, but more often, the mineral-bearing rock lies far below and requires subterranean mining. The mineral extracted from an iron mine is called iron ore. The word 'ore' is used for all minerals from which metal is extracted. The pure metal must be separated from the ore, before it can be used.

Very often, several different kinds of ore are found next to one another: lead ore and silver ore, for example, frequently exist together. Precious stones such as diamonds and emeralds are also worth the expense of mining. But not all minerals are extracted in mines. Some, like cooking salt, are taken from the sea. Cooking salt is also found in deep 'columns' and is then known as *rock salt*.

Of which minerals are rocks composed?

Granite, for instance, is based on three different minerals: feldspar, quartz and mica. These three are called rock-forming minerals.

The most common is feldspar, which is in fact a collective term for a whole range of feldspathic minerals. Although these closely resemble each other, their chemical composition varies. They also determine the rock's colour.

Below: Limestone cliffs on a Danish island in the Baltic Sea. This coastline is characterized by very steep cliffs and the beaches are only visible at low tide. Cliffs of this type are found at Calais in France and at Dover and Beachy Head in England, where they are even more precipitous because of the force of the waves.

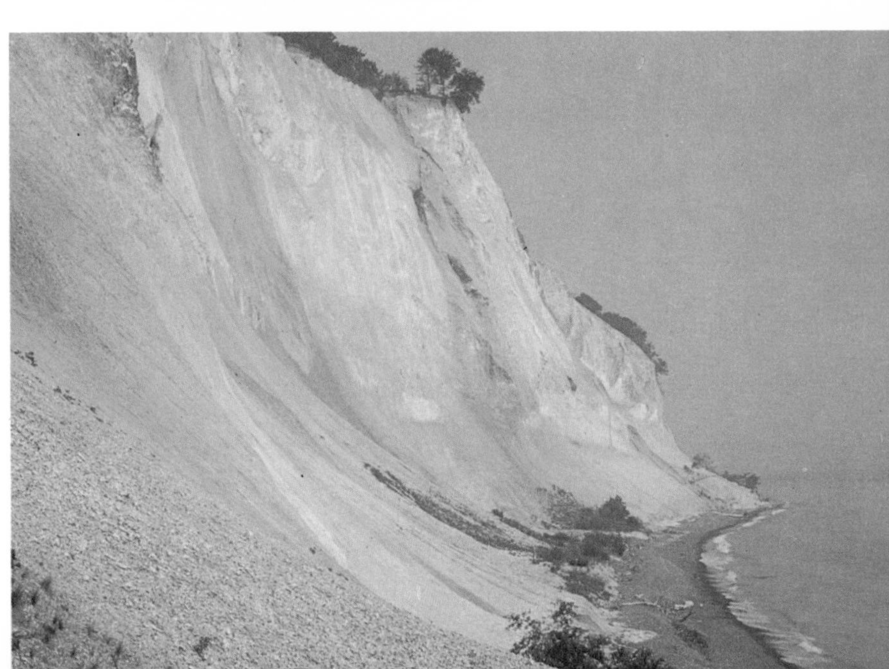

Sources of energy

Deep inside the Earth are precious reserves of ores and energy. But these reserves aren't inexhaustible. Fuels such as coal, in particular, are relatively rare, and are being rapidly used up.

Top: **Drilling derricks are found where oil prospecting is in progress.**
Above: **An oil refinery (cracking plant) near Pernis. Cracking is the process by which oil is transformed into petrol, kerosene and other products. Oil is also one of the basic materials used in the making of plastics, fertilizers, medicines, asphalt and insecticides. It can be detected, and its distance below the earth measured, by using a seismograph. When oil is struck the derrick is removed and the oil well is plugged with a series of valves.**

Why do we need energy?

Energy is required before anything will work. We require a form of energy ourselves in order to live. This is derived from the sun, and from air, food and water.
Modern industry would be unthinkable without oil, electricity, natural gas, coal or running water. You need energy to go to school by bicycle, to make a wireless work, to run a motor-bike or to light a room.
Energy is obtained by pedalling in the case of the bicycle or from an engine in that of the motor-bike. Energy is the faculty of performing work.

In the old days energy was provided solely by men and animals. A man pulled his cart himself or trained a dog to do it. Ploughs were drawn by horses or oxen. This kind of energy is called mechanical energy. Later, man began to harness the power of running water and wind, using water wheels and windmills to provide motion. And today we possess other sources of energy such as coal, oil, natural gas and nuclear power. Energy of these types is released in different ways. It can supply heat, which is turned into motion by the current (steam engine, steam turbine). A steam turbine or running water can drive a dynamo. In this way we obtain another form of energy called electricity. Oil and gas can also release energy by explosion, to form heat, which is a form of energy.

Below: **Electricity being produced with the aid of a windmill, a method which can only be used in relatively flat regions where the wind blows regularly and in strong gusts. This technique was used for producing electric current before the discovery that electricity could be made with coal.**
Bottom: **A dam in Japan. The levels of the rivers in this mountainous region vary so much that they're unusable for navigation. But the force and speed of their currents make them ideal for producing hydroelectricity.**

How did sources of energy develop?

Several times in the Earth's history, portions of sea were cut off from the rest of the ocean by a kind of shelf. The water at the surface contained a large number of living organic particles, but plants and animals were unable to survive in either deep or stagnant waters. The sea-bed was carpeted with decomposing matter: dead plants and animals from the surface which were deposited there. Gradually accumulating, they formed thick layers of organic matter subsequently covered over with sand and clay brought from the mainland by the rivers. In the course of millions of years these remains of plants and animals were transformed into strata of oil, gas and coal.

How did coal originate?

Coal, a traditional source of energy, is generally found deep down below the Earth's surface.

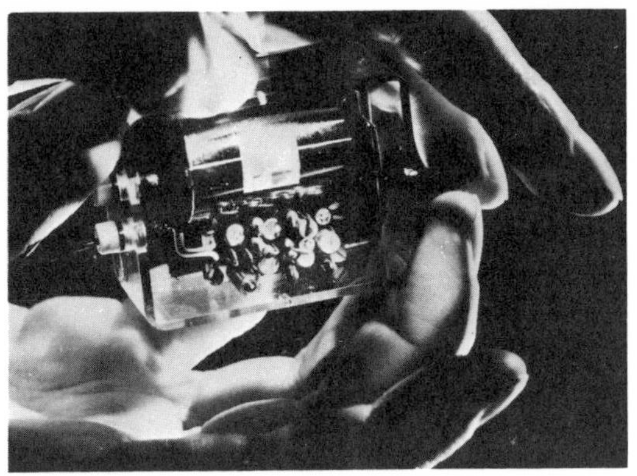

What is an 'alternative source of energy?'
This is a source of energy which is inexhaustible but can only produce a limited quantity in a certain time. Alternative sources include wind, running water, tides (high and low tide), direct insolation, human and animal muscular energy, and atomic energy. Big efforts are being made to develop these to meet the ever-growing demand for energy, because the sources we use at present are only going to last for a limited time.

Long ago, large quantities of dead tropical plants and trees were deposited at the bottom of swamps, where they rotted and became covered with mud and silt. Under the pressure of many layers of deposits this mass gradually solidified and formed rocks. But tree ferns and mosses, instead of rotting, turned into layers of black, crumbly coal because of the influence of various chemical processes.

Where does oil come from?

Oil, which is harder to find, resulted from the decomposition of organic matter deposited at the bottom of the sea millions of years ago. It is located in moderately folded substrata where it impregnates porous rocks such as sandstone, and is generally accompanied by salt water and natural gas. Deep wells have to be drilled to extract it. When the stratum has been reached the oil surges up under pressure from the gas; otherwise it has to be pumped. It's then transported by means of pipelines (on land) or tankers (be sea) to refineries where it's treated and turned into various different products.

Oil has become one of the main fuels in our modern industrial society. This is why we're so dependent economically on the petroleum-producing countries.
Substantial exploitation of natural gas began after the Second World War. The best-known British fields are under the North Sea.
Large quantities of electricity are obtained from hydroelectric power stations, in which falling water drives turbines and these in turn rotate generators.

What is nuclear energy?

This new source of energy is being used more and more. Nuclear or atomic energy is obtained from a chemical reaction involving uranium, an ore mined in parts of Europe. The energy produced by this can be used for feeding electric power stations.

Top left: **This little device is used in the treatment of heart diseases. It is powered by nuclear energy.**
Above: **This house is heated by solar energy. The heat of the sun accumulates after being caught by the plates set in the roof.**

Above: A geyser in Yellowstone National Park, U.S.A. This park contains a hundred geysers and three thousand sources of hot water. The most famous of the geysers is Old Faithful which erupts every sixty-five minutes, throwing up a column of water forty metres high. Each time, fifty thousand litres of water are hurled into the air.
Below: Fujiyama, Japan's sacred mountain, whose summit is always white. Situated on the island of Honshu, Fujiyama is an example of a conical volcano. But it has long been extinct, its last eruption having occurred in the year 107 A.D. Japan has two hundred volcanoes, of which seventy are still active.

Volcanoes and Geysers

A volcano occurs at a point where the Earth's crust is thinner than elsewhere, and rocks, liquids, gases and solid materials are able to surge out above the surface from far down inside the bowels of the Earth.

How do volcanoes develop?

Rock strata forming the Earth's crust are subjected from below to such a high temperature that they begin partially to melt. This mass of molten rock is called magma and discharges gases which are so highly compressed that at points where the Earth's crust is weaker or already cracked they are released, causing explosions and hurling up quantities of lava (magma). This is a volcanic eruption.
When lava emerges above the Earth's crust it cools and solidifies. After a time a cone of increasing height forms around the centre of the eruption. It is called a crater. This is how a volcanic cone develops.
A volcano sometimes remains in a state of eruption for several years on end. During this time, clouds of smoke and ashes escape from it and lava flows over its slopes. When enough gas has been released to diminish the subterranean pressures, the eruptions stop. The lava cools inside the cone and the breach in the Earth's crust closes up again. After a number of years the pressure of gas may become too great again. The solidified lava in the cone then bursts and the volcano begins to erupt once more. In the course of history, volcanic eruptions have caused enormous damage. For example, when Vesuvius erupted in 79 A.D. the town of Pompeii was buried beneath the ashes.

What are geysers?

Geysers, which in many respects resemble volcanoes, are sources of boiling water that gush out at regular intervals. Their existence is due to the Earth's internal heat and they occur only in regions where there has been recent volcanic activity. Water on the surface penetrates into the rocks through fissures which act as natural water-ducts. Having sunk very deep it begins to boil under the influence of the subterranean heat. The steam causes an increase in pressure and the water is then hurled up to the surface with steam pouring through the same ducts, producing a magnificent fountain when they emerge. The process is continually renewed. Geysers are to be found in three places: Iceland, New Zealand and the western United States, in Yellowstone National Park. Here the geysers are more numerous and spectacular than anywhere else, the most famous one being Old Faithful whose boiling water gushes out at intervals of about an hour, reaching a height of

Opposite: A volcanic eruption in January 1973 on Heymaey, an island off the Icelandic coast. The photograph reproduced on the right-hand column of page 28 was taken on the evening of the eruption.

36 m. Geysers have been known to sport fountains of over 300 m.

The geysers in Iceland are put to good use as a source of hot water which provides central heating for the inhabitants of the capital, Reykjavik. The hot water also enables greenhouses to be heated inexpensively, so that in spite of their arctic climate Icelanders are able to go in for horticulture and even cultivate bananas, which will normally only grow in tropical climates.

How do we recognize volcanic traces and where can we find them?

There are many remains of old volcanic eruptions:

1. Volcanic cones (summits of extinct volcanoes). This type of volcanic feature is found along the Rhine in Germany, and in the Auvergne mountain region in France.
2. Lava soil. Because of its high mineral content eroded volcanic matter can be very fertile and beneficial for agriculture, as in Italy and Japan.
3. Volcanic lakes. These are craters formed by a single eruption, which were subsequently filled with water. Lakes of this kind exist in the Eifel region in West Germany.
4. Mineral springs. Gases mix with the water under the surface of the Earth and subject it to pressure, producing mineral wate, which can be purified, bottled and sold. Such springs are found at Vichy in France, and also at Bath, in England.
5. Vapour-holes or fumeroles. Gases sometimes pour out directly. This frequently happens in underground caves, for instance in the Dogs Cave at Naples which discharges harmful toxic gases. Being heavier than air these gases remain at ground level and are therefore dangerous only to small animals.
6. Volcanoes without any external structure. Molten rock escapes through a long crack, so that the lava spreads over a large area and solidifies into basalt. This rock is used for building dykes and causeways. In its natural state it takes the form of hexagonal prisms which need only to be cut lengthwise.

Below: Pompeii was buried beneath the lava of Vesuvius in 79 A.D. Deadly gases and a deluge of ashes, hot water and mud rained down on the city. The inhabitants died of asphyxia, many of them buried under the ashes in their own homes. The victims numbered about two thousand. Herculanum, a town not far from Pompeii, suffered the same fate. The cloud of volcanic vapour condensed into a shower of muddy rain which covered the buildings.

Weather and climate

The weather is a daily topic of conversation. This is hardly surprising when we consider how changeable it is in our part of the world and how much of our daily life depends on it.

What is weather?

Under the influence of solar energy the layer of vapour surrounding the Earth is transformed into a gigantic meteorological machine. The sun heats both the air and the Earth; in the desert, where there are no trees to give shade, the temperature of the ground can reach 65°C. In summer the sun's heat causes large quantities of water to evaporate from rivers, lakes and seas, forming clouds. The heat at the Equator is much stronger than at the Poles. Hot air expands and rises. Cold air descends. Meteorologists can predict what kind of weather we are likely to have and weather forecasts are given on radio and television every day.

What is meant by the climate?

When we refer to the climate we're not thinking of day-to-day variations in the weather; we take the meteorological data relating to a period of up to thirty years and the climate is the average weather in a particular region during this period. There are several sorts of climate, each with its own characteristic features.
The climate affects the type of vegetation which is found in the region, and the crops which will grow, and even the kind of animals which live there.
The type of climate in a given region depends on a number of factors:

1. In what part of the world is the region situated? Near the Equator, the North Pole or the South Pole, or somewhere in-between? It is very warm near the Equator, but extremely cold near the poles.
2. Is the region by the sea or inland? The sea may bring more wet weather.
3. What is the prevailing wind? This may bring hot or cold weather, rain or snow.
4. If the region is by the sea, are there any warm or cold ocean currents nearby? These will affect the temperature of the area.
5. Is the region high or low? The higher the altitude, the lower the temperature.

Let's examine these five points more closely. At midday the sun stands vertically above

Top: **A typical winter scene. The trees are bare, having lost their leaves in autumn. The ground is covered with a thin layer of snow.**
Above: **Trees in autumn. First of all the leaves change colour, turning yellow, red or brown. Then they begin to fall.**
Opposite: **A barn in summer. The harvest is over, the corn threshed. Straw is stacked in the barn.**

the Equator. If we move from the Equator towards the North or South Pole the sun's rays become more oblique. Now, if its rays are vertical the sun gives more heat. If they're oblique they warm a wider area of the Earth's surface, but with a lesser degree of intensity.

In winter the sea is warmer than the land. During the summer it's the other way round. This is because the sea takes much longer to heat up and cool down than the land. The land may become warm very quickly, but this heat is lost more quickly as well.

In Europe, the sea plays an important role during the winter owing to a warm current in the Atlantic Ocean which flows along the European coastline. (A warm current is one whose temperature is higher than that of the surrounding water.)

The greater the altitude, the colder it gets: at a thousand metres the temperature is 6°C. Wintertime in Sweden is very cold, but the weather on the Mediterranean coast of Spain at the same season is much milder.

What are the different types of climate on our continent?

Our continent is characterized by several types of climate:

a) The *maritime* climate, mainly in the west and north-west of Europe. This climate is influenced by the Atlantic Ocean. Temperatures are not too high in summer and not too low in winter.

b) The *continental* climate predominant in the north-east, east and south-east of Europe and characterized by hot summers and cold winters. Rain falls chiefly in summer.

c) The *Mediterranean* climate around the coast of the Mediterranean Sea. The weather in summer is very hot. Winters are mild with a certain amount of rain.

d) The climate of the *tundra* is characteristic of northern Europe (northern Russia). Summers are very short but hot, winters very long and very cold.

Below: **The African steppe. Trees are rare because of the arid climate and animals are often unable to find shade from the sun. This dead animal, which looks like an antelope, was probably ill or died of thirst. Now it's fallen a victim to vultures, the notorious birds of prey. Carcasses of dead animals always disappear in no time at all because they form the staple diet of these predators.**

Europe

Europe is the smallest of the continents and also one of the oldest. It forms a single land mass with Asia.

The European continent is contained between the Atlantic Ocean in the west, the Arctic Ocean in the north, the Ural Mountains in the east and the Mediterranean, the Caucasus chain and the Caspian Sea in the south. After the Second World War the eastern part of Germany and Poland, Czechoslovakia, Hungary, Yugoslavia and the other countries in the east of Europe were formed into what is known as the Eastern Bloc.

The European continent can be divided into four principal geographical areas – west, north, east and south – each characterized by a particular climate.

Western Europe enjoys a temperate climate, while the northern climate is that of the tundra. The Mediterranean coast has a so-called Mediterranean climate and the countries of eastern Europe a continental one.

Western Europe

Western Europe experiences a large amount of precipitation in the form of rain or snow all through the year. As a result its rivers are usually filled with an abundant quantity of water. Long periods of frost in winter are rare and generally occur only once; they are always caused by a wind blowing from the east. The prevailing currents of air in this part of Europe are humid ones from the Atlantic Ocean in the west. In the coastal regions of the Mediterranean the winter and autumn are milder: the trees are always green because they keep their leaves in winter. The highest peaks in the Alps and Pyrenees are always covered with snow – perpetual snow as it's commonly called. In northern regions the summer

Top left: This English village snuggles by the river amongst gentle hills. _Centre left:_ The Thames and the Houses of Parliament. Big Ben can be seen near the bridge. _Bottom left:_ A typical Dutch scene: a bridge over a canal. The arched shape of the bridge allowed the boats which used to carry milk to pass underneath. _Right:_ The _Grand Place_ of the Flemish town of Furnes with its magnificent sixteenth and seventeenth century buildings. The modern cars are a striking contrast to the old buildings.

Left: The medieval town of Rothenburg on the Tauber (Germany). The town walls are well preserved.
Below: The German town of Montjoie, the oldest part of which dates from the fifteenth century. The half-timbered houses were built mainly in the sixteenth and seventeenth centuries.

along the coasts is never as hot and the winter never as cold as in areas further inland. This is due to the effect of the sea.

The countries of western Europe are very diverse, with each nation having its own special characteristics. Because of the variations in geology and soil type a wide range of agricultural activities can be carried out. Some areas are very fertile while others are suitable only for sheep farming.

This part of Europe has been ravaged by numerous wars, both great and small. It has nevertheless continued to exercise considerable influence on world history, and art and science have always flourished there.

In 1957, France, Belgium, the Netherlands, Luxembourg, West Germany and Italy formed a union called the E.E.C. (European Economic Community). Subsequently, Great Britain, Ireland and Denmark also joined. The aim of the E.E.C. is common administration of the different countries' economies, and it is also hoped that gradual progress can be made towards political union.

The most important industrial region of Western Europe lies within a funnel-shaped area. Starting from Basle we can draw a line northwards through the plain of the Upper Rhine via Frankfurt and the Ruhr to Hamburg and Bremen. The other branch also begins at Basle and passes along the French bank of the Rhine through the industrial towns of northern France and across the English Channel to London and the British Midlands.

The Rhine and its tributaries flow across the west of Europe draining an area of 196,000 square kilometres. It is the continent's main river for inland navigation and is connected to all Europe's big navigable waterways by a vast network of canals. The source of the Rhine is in the St Gotthard mountain region.

France is well placed geographically, with three seas washing its coasts and surrounded by countries with advanced economies. Its subsoil produces iron ore. It has several natural frontiers – the Pyrenees, the western Alps, the Jura chain and the Rhine – but is open to the north, which is where all its invaders have gained access. The heart of the country is the Parisian basin, which was once an inland sea.

Below: A florist's in Salzburg, Austria. Note the plaits of dried flowers.
Bottom: A farm at the eastern end of Burgenland in Austria. This part of Austria is covered by plains resembling the Hungarian steppe. Once a region of heather and grass, the land is now predominantly arable.

Right: Switzerland. Refuges like this are common in the Alps. They're used as shelters by mountaineers and hikers.

It is now an undulating plain of limestone soil crossed by the River Seine. At the point where this region meets the English Channel we find chalky cliffs. Brittany and Normandy are ancient regions in which the mountains have undergone substantial erosion and reach a maximum height of only some four hundred metres. The Massif Central, which is a plateau region in the south of central France, has volcanic features: sources of warm mineral water (Vichy), extinct cones (Puy de Come) and volcanic lakes. Most of the Massif Central consists of granite; in the south the soil is more chalky and the River Tarn has carved out deep valleys. France is primarily an agricultural country and farmers generally own their land. The main products of the north are corn, potatoes and beet, and viticulture (grape-growing) plays an important role in several regions. France produces cars of international renown: Peugeot, Citroen and Renault. It is also famous for its porcelain (Limoges). The Caravelle is a French aircraft built at Toulouse. But the country lacks energy resources, having insufficient reserves of coal and oil. Natural gas is found in the Lacq region, and in the south-east the main source of energy is hydro-electric power. The largest industrial city is Paris (although firms are now being encouraged to move out of the city), and the principal port Marseilles. Other big ports are Le Havre, Nantes, Saint-Nazaire and Bordeaux.

Northern Europe

A large part of northern Europe is quite scarcely populated because much of the landscape consists of lakes and mountains.

Below: The Eiffel Tower in Paris. It stands three hundred metres high and takes its name from the engineer, Gustave Eiffel. The tower was one of the curiosities of the World Exhibition of 1889 and is now used as a radio station.
Right: The Palace of Versailles was built for Louis XIV, and the kings of France made it their residence from 1676 to 1789. Its many rooms are now open to the public as a museum. The treaty which ended the First World War was signed here.

Left: A Lapp family. These people live in the northern parts of Norway, Sweden and Finland, and on the Kola Peninsula in the Soviet Union. The Lapps are the smallest racial group in Europe and live mainly by breeding reindeer and by fishing.

It includes countries such as Norway, Sweden, Denmark, Finland and Iceland. The Norwegian landscape is characterized by mountains of granite with high, barren plateaux (fjelden) and long narrow inlets (called fjords) along the coast. Sweden has many rivers and waterfalls. Iceland is the land of geysers, volcanoes and glaciers. Finland is dotted with thousands of lakes. Denmark is a country of plains. The coastal regions of Denmark, Norway and southern Sweden enjoy a maritime climate due to the proximity of the Atlantic Ocean. The rest of Sweden and Finland has a continental climate. Denmark, Norway and Finland suffer from a marked shortage of ores, but the mineral strata are near the surface in this region because it has undegone substantial erosion. Iron ore is mined in Sweden, in the Kiruna region, and timber is also an important natural resource. In Finland the forests are the main source of revenue. Norway depends chiefly on fishing and allied industries. Denmark's economy is centred round cattle breeding and dairy products.

Eastern Europe

Between West Germany, the Urals, the White Sea and the Aegean Sea are the communist states: East Germany, Poland, Czechoslovakia, Hungary, Yugoslavia, Albania, Rumania, Bulgaria and the Soviet

Above: A Swedish village. Sweden is a very prosperous country covered in forests. Its sub-soil is rich in ores: iron, lead and zinc. The main source of energy is hydroelectricity.
Left: The Sognefjord is Norway's longest fjord (175 km). This landscape was formed in the Ice Age, when glaciers descended from the mountains along the beds of rivers, gouging out U-shaped valleys as they advanced. When the ice receded twenty thousand years ago, water from the melting glaciers raised the level of the sea by about ninety metres. This sudden change in the water level caused flooding in low-lying regions, coastal valleys and small creeks. Transport in these parts is mainly by water.

Above: **A Rumanian family.**

Right: **Red Square in Moscow. St Basil's cathedral became a museum after the revolution of 1917.**

Union (Russia). In these countries the good of the state is the supreme goal and the whole economic structure is accordingly different from that in Western Europe. These states are known as the Eastern Bloc.

The Alps come to an end in the Vienna Woods. To the north of the river port of Bratislava in Czechoslovakia you can see the first crests of the Carpathians, which reach their culmination at 2,663 metres in the High Tatra mountain group. These chains extend eastwards, then turn south-east towards Rumania. In central Rumania the range curves round to the west in the direction of the Transylvanian Alps. Then, at the point where it rejoins the Danube, it forms a very narrow valley called the Iron Gates. South of the Danube the mountains again extend eastwards, dividing into two ranges: the Balkans in Bulgaria and the Rodopi Planina in southern Bulgaria and northern Greece. The Carpathians constitute an important climatic barrier between the continental climate of eastern Europe and the temperate maritime climate. They also form a kind of watershed. To the south of the mountains the water flows toward the Danube. To the north the rain and snow end up on the one hand in the Baltic Sea by way of the Oder and the Vistula and on the other hand in the Black Sea via the big rivers in the south-west of the Soviet Union. In the north are wide plains interspersed with a few mountains. In the south is Yugoslavia, a mountainous country. Hungary is an extensive plain with only a few mountains; the Hungarian plain is called the Puszta. Rumania has both mountains and broad, fertile plains: these are found in the valley of the Lower Danube. This region is called Wallachia, and is Rumania's main agricultural area.

The main river of this area is the Danube, which is the longest in Europe apart from the Volga. The major cities are found along the Danube.

Eastern Europe is the cradle of the Slavonic languages. However, the Rumanians speak a Latin language like the French and Italians, and most of the population are Roman Catholic. Yugoslavia is unusual from the religious point of view, having three different religious groups: Orthodox, Roman Catholic and Islamic. The Turks, who came chiefly from central Asia, exercised a considerable influence on this part of Europe. In the nineteenth century eastern Europe and the Balkans were the theatre of numerous conflicts involving four main powers: Germany, Russia, Austria–Hungary and Turkey. Since then this part of the world has been constantly torn by wars. The power of the east European countries diminished greatly during the First World War. After the liberation which followed the Second World, German domination was replaced by Russian domination.

What is the Kremlin?

The Kremlin is the walled part of the city of Moscow. Inside the walls are palaces, churches, barracks and Soviet government buildings. Adjoining the Kremlin is Red Square, frequently used as a parade ground and dominated by two buildings: the Lenin mausoleum and the cathedral.

The Mediterranean region and southern Europe

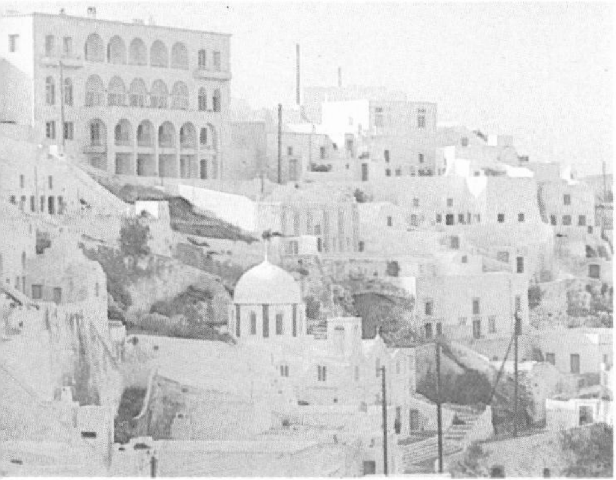

This region is composed of the following countries: Italy, Spain, Portugal, Greece, Malta, the Vatican and San Marino. (The last three states are minute in size.)

Almost all of southern Europe is mountainous and there are only a few plains, such as that of the Po in Italy and the Andalusian plain in Spain. Earthquakes, which have certain features in common with volcanoes, occur to a limited extent all over this area. Volcanoes derive their name from Vulcano, a town near Sicily. One of them, Stromboli, is rather unusual. Situated on an island and reaching a height of 926 metres, it produces an explosion accompanied by a bright flash every fifteen minutes. The highest volcano is Etna (3,274 metres). More than eighty eruptions have been counted so far in this region. One of the biggest was produced by Vesuvius.

The summers in these regions are hot and dry, the winters mild and rainy. Around Rome there are no more than five days of rain in July and August, and the temperature is about 30°C. Not all southern Europe enjoys a Mediterranean climate. Winters are colder in the plain of the Po and in the Apennines, and there's even occasional snow. Spain, on the other hand, is mostly very dry and it has very few trees; instead of prairies there are steppes. Indeed, trees are becoming rare in vast areas of southern Europe, a situation for which man bears much of the responsibility. Whole forests are sometimes felled, and when this happens on the sides of mountains the ground no longer holds. Heavy rainfall sweeps the loose soil into the rivers, creating deposits of mud. The water level becomes irregular and when the rivers are in spate they often flood enormous areas. This still happens today.

In many ways southern Europe is a world of its own: a mountanous region devoid of vegetation or with only occasional thorn bushes. It has extremely dry summers with oppressively hot sunshine, blue seas, and a very different way of life compared with the north side of the Alps. Southern Europe subsists almost entirely on agriculture, but a marked contrast exists between the dry, stony, dusty interior where the land is sparsely populated and the irrigated regions (dry areas watered artificially). Here, where the soil is fertile, they grow wheat, rice, citrus fruits (oranges, lemons, tangerines and grapefruit), olives and other southern fruits (currants and raisins). Southern Europe has only two industrial regions: the plain of the Po and the Andalusian plain. But efforts are under way to establish industries throughout the whole of Italy. Most of their raw materials have to be imported. There is a considerable tourist trade in the coastal towns and cultural cities of southern Europe.

Below: Portugal: a fisherman's wife at Nazare on the Atlantic coast. After cork, fish is one of Portugal's main exports.
Top: St Peter's Square in front of the Vatican. The Vatican covers an area of 44 hectares and has a thousand inhabitants. The square is surrounded by arcades. It is an independent state, within the city of Rome, and was established in 1929. It is ruled by the Pope.
Above: A Greek village, with houses built on the hillside. They generally have small windows to keep out the heat and the sunlight.
Below right: A Spanish village in the Pyrenees. This mountain chain, which reaches a height of 3,404 m, forms the frontier between Spain and France. Sheep-breeding is the main economic activity in the higher regions.

Asia

Asia is the largest and most heavily populated of the continents. The bigest population groups live around its edges.

In all probability it was in Asia that the human race first evolved. Here, too, the main religions grew up: Christianity, Hinduism, Buddhism and Islam. Whole tribes left this vast continent in order to settle in the peninsular regions.

Asia can be divided into four principal areas: western Asia, south-west Asia, central Asia including China, and northern and eastern Asia.

These regions offer marked contrasts. Western and central Asia are very arid, with a predominance of steppes (huge grassy plains) and desert. Southern and eastern Asia are dominated by the monsoon, which brings frequent downpours during the summer months. The original forests have been modified by man to make way for arable land.

The contrasts can also be seen among the population. Western Asia is very sparsely populated and the same goes for all of central Asia with the exception of certain parts of China. South-east Asia, on the other hand, is very densely populated. Here, in a relatively small area, lives almost half the world's population. The land has to be farmed intensively, with two or three crops a year, to provide enough food to support the population.

Above: Alta in southern Anatolia (Turkey). This is a mountainous region with numerous volcanic phenomena: great folds in the earth and solidified lava. It's also extremely dry. Being very poor, the inhabitants dig their homes in the mountainsides.
Below left: The Wailing Wall in Jerusalem, a remnant of the Second Temple, is now incorporated in the city walls. Jews have come to this spot for centuries to lament the temple's destruction.
Below right: A caterpillar tractor laboriously working the desert soil of Israel. This area may be in the process of becoming a kibbutz (collective farm). Before 1948 the Negev was an immense barren desert where Bedouins grazed their sheep, goats and camels. Now part of it has been transformed into a prosperous agricultural region and the operation will continue as long as enough water is available.

Western Asia

The countries of the Middle East include Saudi Arabia, Israel, Jordan, Syria, Turkey, Iraq, Iran and a few small states on the Gulf of Aden and the Gulf of Oman. The area to the south of this region (between the Mediterranean and the Gulf of Oman) is characterized by high plateaux. There are also two big plains, the valley of the River Jordan, which flows into the Dead Sea and is situated more than a hundred metres below sea

Above: A Vietnamese woman harvesting rice, the staple diet in this part of Asia. Rice is still produced manually. Very few machines are used because labour is cheap.
Right: A Persian sabre dancer. This traditional war dance is still performed today.

level, and the plain of Mesopotamia.

The north of western Asia (from Asia Minor to Afghanistan) is a region of high mountains. This is where the largest number of earthquakes occurs, especially in Turkey and Iran. The Arabian peninsula consists mainly of deserts, and steppes have developed in areas where rain falls.

Islam, the Mohammedan religion, originated in Arabia. From here it spread out and conquered most of Asia and Africa.

The population supports itself for the most part by agriculture and rearing livestock. Water plays a role of prime importance, and in arid regions the inhabitants live solely by breeding horses, camels, sheep and goats. As pastures are very poor, farmers have to take their flocks and herds to more fertile regions, and these travelling farmers are called nomads.

Wherever water is present there will be a population to till the soil. Corn was already being grown in Mesopotamia in ancient times. The economy of western Asia and the people's standard of living were changed considerably when oil was discovered in the Persian Gulf, as the oil-producing countries were able to charge very high prices since they controlled such a large proportion of the world's oil. The industries of western Europe and Japan now depend almost entirely on imports from these countries: the Middle East supplies more than half the world's oil. The main producing countries are Saudi Arabia, Iran, Iraq, Kuwait and the Arab Emirates. Britain's North Sea oil finds have been a great help to her economy.

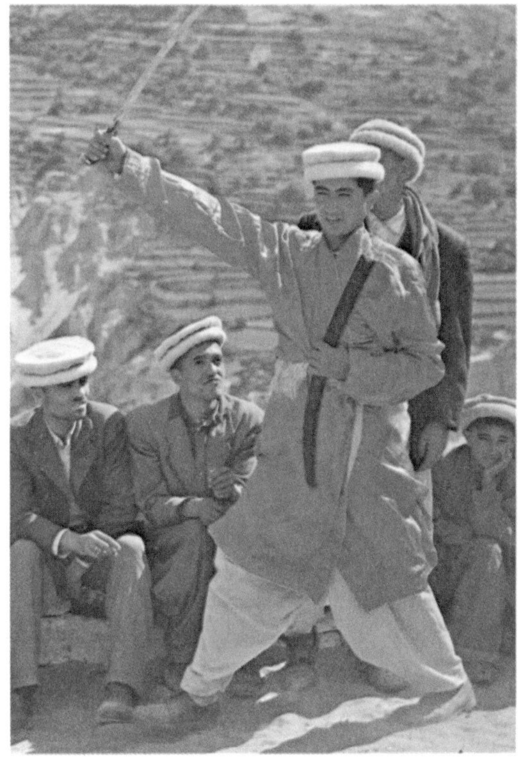

South-east Asia

The coast of south-east Asia is studded with bays and peninsulas. To the east the sea is cut off from the Pacific Ocean by archipelagoes. The eastern side of these archipelagoes (towards the ocean) consists of marine troughs which go down far below the level of the sea-bed. In fact they are the deepest in the world, at some points reaching a depth of over 10 kilometres. Frequent

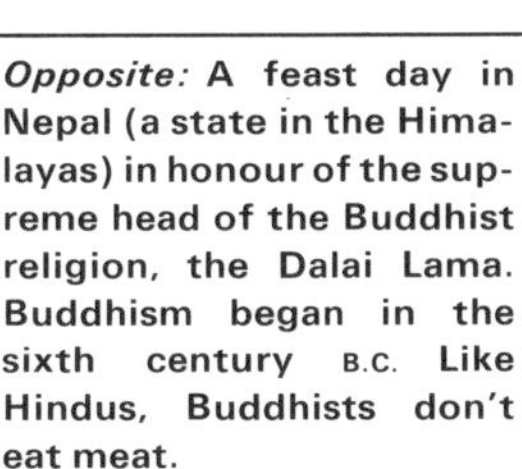

Opposite: A feast day in Nepal (a state in the Himalayas) in honour of the supreme head of the Buddhist religion, the Dalai Lama. Buddhism began in the sixth century B.C. Like Hindus, Buddhists don't eat meat.

Opposite: **India: the town of Benares on the Ganges in north-east India. This is the holy city of the Hindus. Over a million pilgrims come here every year from all four corners of the continent to bathe in the river. According to their religion this water purifies body and soul.**

earthquakes occur on the eastern coast of Asia, especially in Japan and the Philippines. South-east Asia is particularly famous for its monsoons. In summer the wind blows from the sea, bringing large amounts of rain. This is the wet monsoon. In winter a dry wind blows from the continent towards the sea, causing the dry monsoon. This region relies above all on agriculture, so rain is of capital importance. If the rains come too late the crops dry up. If it rains too long, floods occur in low-lying areas.

A brilliant and original civilization was already flourishing in China and western India before the Christian era. At this time there was as yet little contact between Europe and the Far East. It was only at a very late stage that a few Europeans came to explore these regions. One of them, the Venetian Marco Polo, spent many years in the East around 1300. Thereafter, Indian products gradually began to appear on European markets. They reached Europe by way of the Levant – the eastern coast of the Mediterranean – and were transported either by caravan along the main trade routes or else by sea. These products were introduced into western Europe by Venetian and Genoese merchants. The Portuguese played an important role in the discovery of maritime routes to India. Much of the area is covered with forests, and rubber and teak are exported to other countries.

Most of the population belong to the Mongol race.

Hinduism and Buddhism are the most wide-

Opposite: **Indonesia, a former Dutch colony, now an independent republic. The population's staple diet is rice. The flooded paddy fields are ploughed to aerate and mould the mud, then the rice is sown. The farmer here is using a primitive plough drawn by a pair of buffaloes.**

Above: **Two symbols of the Japanese archipelago: a geisha girl (professional social entertainer) in her kimono, and a Japanese car. Large numbers of cars are exported to Europe.**
Right: **The famous Wall of China, built to protect the empire from Mongol invasions. 2,450 km long, it's regarded as one of the world's greatest structures.**

spread religions. Islam predominates in Indonesia, Pakistan and Bangla Desh. The inhabitants of the Philippines are mainly Roman Catholic.

Central Asia

Much of this region was under western domination up to the Second World War.
The population of this part of Asia, except for the Japanese, lives mainly on agriculture. Rice, the staple food, is generally planted by hand because labour is inexpensive in these overpopulated regions.
Importance is also attached to the cultivation of products for commercial use (rubber, tea, sugar, cotton). These are either exported or employed in industry, where they serve as raw materials. Buffaloes and zebus are used as beasts of burden.
The inhabitants of the coastal areas and islands make a living primarily from fishing. Coal and iron ore are mined in China and India, and oil has been found in Indonesia. Malaysia is the world's biggest tin producer. The industrial boom in this part of the world is having repercussions on other continents. The fact that wages are very low there means that goods can be manufactured at lower cost than in Europe and America.
China is one of the biggest countries in the world after the Soviet Union, being equal in area to the United States. It takes in the high plateaux of central Asia and has an estimated population of eight hundred million. China has a number of large cities, and its capital city is Peking. Chinese civilization is one of the most ancient in the world.

Northern and eastern Asia

This region comprises the Asian part of the Soviet Union and Mongolia. It consists basically of a plain covered by immense forests of birch and pine, with endless deserts (including the Gobi desert) and lakes. The sub-soil of the Soviet Union is extremely rich, containing some of the largest of the world's reserves of coal, peat, oil, natural gas and ores. The biggest oil fields are between the Volga and the Urals and in the Caucasus mountain range. The Urals are now an industrial area.

Right: **Hong Kong is a British colony on a number of small islands at the mouth of the Canton River. It's the main port opposite the Chinese coast.**
Below: **Thai girls dancing in traditional costume.**

Africa

Like Europe and Asia (Eurasia) Africa is part of the Old World. Much of it consists of former European colonies. Many countries in Africa are now self-governing and Africa is playing an increasingly important part in world affairs.

Above: Women at a well in northern Africa. The well is the daily meeting-place. Most houses in north Africa are without running water and the women go to fetch their day's supply at the well. Water can be found in practically every desert, usually fairly deep underground. Deep wells are sunk in the search for water, which is hauled up in a bucket.

Below: The Tuareg, the aristocrats of the Sahara, are generally dressed in blue. The dromedary, sometimes called the 'water-vessel of the desert', is extremely important to these desert tribes. It can drink a hundred litres of water in a single draught and then go for four days without drinking (even longer in winter). It's an ideal animal for the desert, providing milk, meat and wool. At one time it was also the sole means of transport. Merchants gathered in caravans and crossed the desert from one oasis to another on their dromedaries.

What are Africa's main physical features?

Africa, the world's largest continent after Asia, is situated between the Atlantic Ocean and the Indian Ocean. The distance from its northern extremity on the Mediterranean to its southern extremity, the Cape of Good Hope, is 8,000 kilometres and it covers an area of 30,000,000 square kilometres. It is as big as the United States, western Europe, China and India together. This gigantic continent is shaped roughly like a question mark. A hundred years ago, most of it, except for the coastal regions, was still entirely unknown. Many people tried to penetrate its secrets, but exploration was made difficult by the climate and the fact that the coast had neither bays nor peninsulas. It was very hard for ships to cope with the powerful waves and find suitable berths along its shores.

African rivers, too, are not easily navigable. Before reaching the sea they descend from far above through many waterfalls and rapids. On land, roads were practically non-existent. In certain regions, deserts of stone and sand stretched for several thousand kilometres under an oppressively hot sun. In other parts virgin forests presented an almost impenetrable obstacle. Even where it's possible to land on the coast the way inland is sometimes barred by rocky crags or swamps.

Africa is full of contrasts. At its centre is an immense jungle, a dense mass of trees and plants which can only be crossed by way of primitive tracks or by river.

There are several layers of vegetation. The branches of giant trees form a kind of roof foliage above smaller ones growing below, and there are many climbing plants and vines (called lianas) which cling to the branches of these trees, and grow round them. The floor of the forest is covered with dense bushes and young trees.

Around this jungle is the savannah, an immense, undulating plain covered with high grass, bushes and scattered trees. As you get nearer to the desert the trees become increasingly rare: soon only short grass and small bushes can still be seen on the horizon. This is the habitat of Africa's principal wild animals: antelopes, zebras, giraffes, elephants, lions and rhinoceroses. To the north of the equator the savannah stretches over the Sudan. To the south it forms the South African *veld.*

South and west of the veld is a very dry region: the Kalahari desert. But the Kalahari is small compared with the Sahara, the world's largest desert, which stretches over 5,000 km from east to west in the north of Africa and separates north Africa from the rest of the world. The country to the south of the Kalahari desert closely resembles northern Africa, with fertile fields and green mountains. Two-fifths of the continent is covered with prairies, almost one fifth with forests. All the rest is desert. Remarkable things can be seen in these vast areas of virgin forest, savannah, desert and coastal terrain.

Kilimanjaro (6,000 metres) and Mount Kenya (5,200 metres), for example, are covered in perpetual snow at their summits even though they are both very close to the equator.

Not far away is the deep East African Rift Valley, which runs from north to south over several thousand kilometres and features a succession of lakes and craters. Large rivers flow through the heart of Africa, first crossing swampland and virgin forest very slowly for hundreds of kilometres. Then, as the water reaches lower-lying areas, it begins to flow more rapidly. Some of the rivers form waterfalls as they descend from higher ground. This is the case with the Zambesi, which is completely impossible to navigate.

Which is the longest river in Africa?

The longest river in Africa and in the world is the Nile, which flows for 6,680 kilometres. In fact the Nile consists of two rivers: the White Nile which descends from Lake Victoria and the Blue Nile which rises in Lake Tana. The two join up at Khartoum, then flow across the Nubian desert towards the Mediterranean. In Egypt the Nile grows to a width of several kilometres. After Cairo it splits up into several branches which together form a delta.

The second longest river in Africa is the Congo, at 4,670 kilometres. At certain points it too is extremely wide.

Top left: A street scene in Tunisia, very different from the streets of Europe. The people wear long robes and the houses are low with flat roofs. The windows are no more than little slits in the walls to prevent the burning sun from penetrating inside.

Top right: A Tunisian mosque. The mosque is the Moslems' church. During the hours of prayer (five times a day) the faithful kneel down and bow themselves towards Mecca, the holy city. Moslems call their god Allah and follow the doctrine of their prophet Mohammed who lived from 570 A.D. to 632 A.D.

Opposite: Different peoples of Kenya. Central Africa is inhabited mainly by negroes: Sudanese in the Sudan and Bantus in the south.

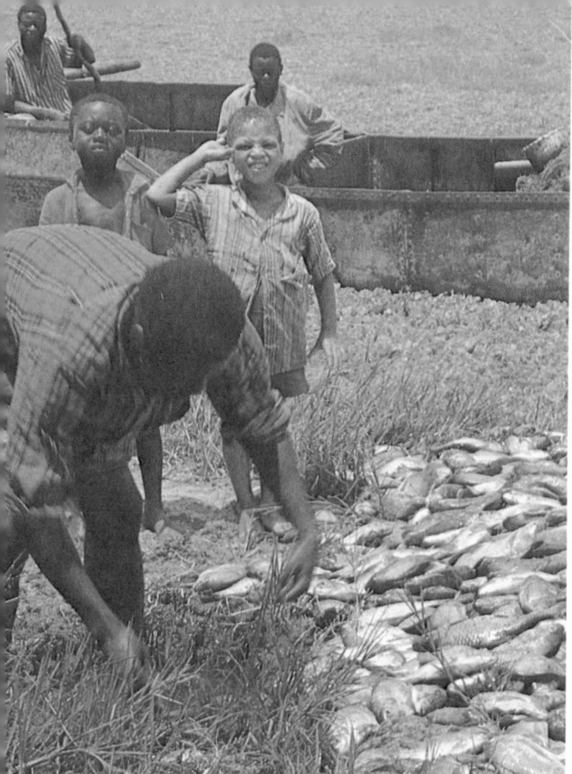

The Niger is 4,185 kilometres long. Year after year, explorers tried to follow its course, believing that it flowed westwards in the direction of the Atlantic Ocean. In fact it rises in the mountains 320 kilometres from the Atlantic, flowing north towards the Sahara. Around Timbuktu the Niger's floods enable rice and cotton to be cultivated. The river then turns southwards through Nigeria and flows into the Gulf of Guinea, forming a delta. The first European to see the Niger was the Scotsman Mungo Park.

The Zambesi (2,600 kilometres long) constitutes a natural frontier between Zambia and Rhodesia. Near the town of Livingstone the Zambesi forms the famous Victoria Falls. The river has been dammed for hydroelectric power at the Kariba Gorge 320 kilometres downstream from the falls.

The biggest river in southern Africa is the Orange (2,100 kilometres long), which flows into the Atlantic Ocean. For a time it passes through the Kalahari desert, where its bed is frequently dried out except in the rainy season. The Orange River is useless either for navigation or for irrigation.

What are Africa's islands?

A number of islands are to be found off the African coast. Madagascar is situated in the Indian Ocean near the southern coast of Africa. 1,600 kilometres long and 550 kilometres wide, it's the fourth largest island in the world after Greenland, New Guinea and Borneo. It is very rugged, with a moist and tropical climate in the east. Coffee, vanilla, pepper and cloves are grown there.

The island of Zanzibar covers an area of 2,500 square kilometres and lies a short distance off the coast of Tanzania. It's the world's biggest producer of cloves.

The Gulf of Guinea is also dotted with a few small islands which are the peaks of former volcanoes. These include Fernando Po, Sao Tome and Principe which have cocoa and coffee plantations.

The Cape Verde Islands off the west coast of Africa are also of volcanic origin. Although very barren, they have a pleasant climate and attract large numbers of tourists. They serve as a port of call for ships sailing to South America. Transatlantic liners also cross near the Canary Islands. The Azores and Maderia to the north are further from the coast. Madeira possesses an abundanant and varied flora, and the terraced gardens on the hillsides are full of exotic fruit and flowers. Its grapes produce the famous Maderia wine.

Opposite: **Zaire, formerly the Belgian Congo. Lake Edward in the north-east of Zaire contains abundant supplies of fish. These fishermen seem content with their catch.**
Below: **A Ndebele village in southern Africa. Woman and child in traditional costume.**

Below: **Zaire: a typical landscape in Kivu province. Towards the east the ground rises in terraced stages, forest giving way to savannah. In the foreground, huts covered with leaves.**

What peoples inhabit Africa?

Northern Africa has a long and eventful history. Its earliest inhabitants were the Berbers, but other tribes also came to settle here. In the sixteenth century B.C., groups of Phoenicians established colonies in what is now Tunisia.

Later the city of Carthage, founded in about 850 B.C., became the capital of an empire which took in most of northern Africa and Spain. In the seventh century A.D. this territory was conquered by the Arabs on behalf of Islam and the population speaks Arabic to this day. Northern Africa now comprises Morocco, Algeria, Tunisia, Libya and Egypt. The region consists of high plateaux and mountain chains, some of whose peaks are covered with snow in winter. In regions with rainfall the fields produce good harvests. The further away from the coast you move towards the south, the more barren the soil becomes. Forests are succeeded by small bushes (*maquis*) and dry grass, followed by the desert with an occasional oasis. The Arabic word *sahara* means 'empty': the Sahara Desert is an empty area covering some nine million square kilometres. This region of sand and stones stretches from the Atlantic Ocean to the Red Sea. The Tuareg are a very strange desert tribe: no-one knows where they come from. It seems they are descended from the Berbers, who took refuge there. They are nomads, a wandering people, and they live in leather tents.

In dry regions the inhabitants breed sheep, goats, cattle, horses and camels. On the coast, fishing is the main industry. Morocco has factories in which sardines are tinned for export. The country is poor in minerals, but there are deposits of phosphates.

After the discovery of oil in the desert in 1956, derricks soon began to sprout up and pipelines were laid to take the oil to the coast. The sub-soil also contains large quantities of natural gas.

West Africa is an interesting region. During recent years it has undergone rapid development which has highlighted the contrasts between the new world and the old. About a thousand years ago this region already consisted of states such as Ghana, which went through a glorious period around the year 1000 A.D. West African men now usually wear European clothes, but the women often retain their traditional garments.

South Africa is a republic in which 80% of the population are Bantus. The white Afrikaners, dscendents of Dutch colonists, constitute a minority. The most fertile provinces are the Cape Province and Natal, where the Europeans have settled. By settling on these coasts they were able to control the maritime route from Europe to India.

Above: **This is the type of vehicle now used for safaris (hunting expeditions) in east Africa. Safaris are very often harmful to wildlife and endanger rare species.**
Below: **A market in Kenya. Vendors sit on the ground, their wares spread out beside them.**
Bottom: **Johannesburg in South Africa. More than half the world's gold is mined in this region.**

North America

North and South America situated between the Atlantic and Pacific Oceans, together make up what was known as the New World.

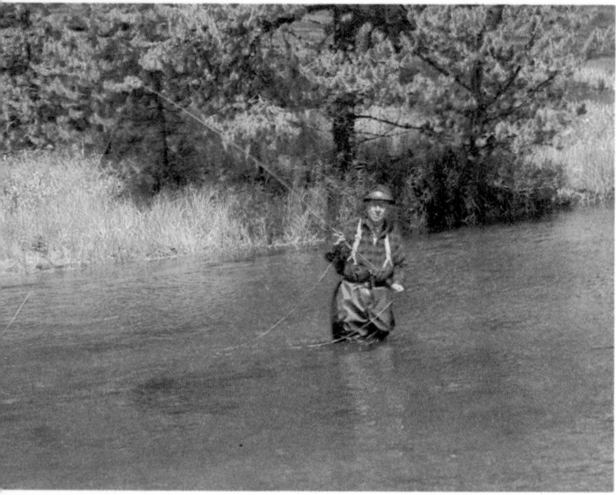

Above: **Canada is the world's biggest exporter of fish: both its Atlantic and pacific coasts have abundant supplies. Fishing alone employs 90,000 people and allied industries provide work for a further 20,000. 44% of Canada's fish products come from British Columbia. The main types are salmon, cod, herring, lobster, and sardine.**

Below: **Huron Indians in their traditional costume. This tribe used to inhabit the south-east of Canada and cultivated wheat. The name Indian is incorrect. It was given to the natives by white settlers who thought they looked like the inhabitants of India.**

Why is America called the 'New World'?

In the fifteenth century the existence of America was as yet unknown. Norsemen had landed in Newfoundland and Labrador in about 1000 A.D., but no-one attached importance to the event. Then in 1492 Christopher Columbus tried to find a new route to India by crossing the Atlantic Ocean in a westerly direction. But he miscalculated the distances and on reaching some islands (later to be known as the West Indies) thought he had arrived in Asia. It was only after his death that people realized he'd discovered the 'New World'. America took its name from the explorer Amerigo Vespucci who described it in the letters he wrote about his expeditions.

The North American continent comprises only two countries, in contrast to Europe with its many smaller states. English is spoken in the U.S.A. and Canada, and French is the main language in the Canadian province of Quebec.

Who were the first inhabitants of North America?

Before the arrival of Europeans, the whole of America was populated by Indians except for the extreme north, where thousands of Eskimos lived. The European conquests had dire consequences. The populations of several islands in the West Indies were completely exterminated. In other places the number of Indians diminished appreciably and the survivors had to live in difficult conditions. The original population of North America has almost disappeared. Driven from their territories, the Indians were compelled to re-settle in barren regions. Many died of infectious diseases imported by the white people. Others living in the prairies (steppes) were no longer able to find enough food.

Those Indians who survived were placed in reserves, where they had to learn the language, religion and way of life of the white man. At present their numbers are beginning to increase slightly.

The number of Eskimos inhabiting the northern regions is now limited. They live by fishing and by hunting seals, whose skins they use to make clothes, tents and kayaks (a sort of canoe for hunting).

Most of the present population of America is descended from European colonists. But when workers were needed for the plantations in the seventeenth and eighteenth centuries, large numbers of negroes were imported from Africa. When slavery was abolished these negroes continued to live in America. This is why the population is made up of such a wide variety of races and cultures.

What are North America's main physical features?

In the west of North America is a vast mountainous region – the Rocky Mountains – enclosing extensive high plateaux: the Colorado Plateau and the Great Plains. Rivers such as the Colorado have carved out deep valleys with steep sides, like the Grand Canyon, in a process which took one and a half million years. Volcanic phenomena are present too: active volcanoes in Alaska and geysers in the Yellowstone National Park. Earthquakes sometimes occur along the coast: San Francisco, for example, was completely destroyed at the beginning of the twentieth century. The east of North America is dominated by the Appalachians, a mountainous area with substantially eroded crests. A great plain traversed by the Mississippi and its tributaries stretches between the Rockies and the Appalachians. The five great lakes on the border between Canada and the United States were formed by ice. They are not all at the same altitude: there is a difference of a hundred metres, for instance, between the levels of Lake Erie and Lake Ontario which are joined by the Niagara River. Here are found the famous Niagara Falls.

Much of Greenland is still covered in ice.

North America is less densely populated than Europe. The forests which used to cover the east of the country have been uprooted to make way for cultivation, and the grass of the prairies has been replaced by maize and wheat. Canada and the United States are big corn producers. The original vegetation, though, has been retained in places where the populatpon is less dense: the northern tundras, for example, and the deserts of the west. Only small patches of desert have been turned into arable land, in the few places where water could be found. The fir woods of Canada have been spared and this country exports a large quantity of wood. After the declaration of independence in 1776 by the thirteen British colonies the United States expanded to the Pacific coast. The country covers an area practically equal to that of Europe. There are now fifty states, including Alaska and Hawaii.

Above: **George Washington, first President of the United States. The federal capital of the U.S.A. was named after him.**
Below left: **The Statue of Liberty in New York harbour is the American symbol of freedom.**
Below right: **Manhattan, the heart of New York, on the Hudson River. Here are the headquarters of the big banks and leading companies.**

Who are the present inhabitants of the United States?

In 1790 the United States had four million inhabitants. Today there are more than two hundred million, an increase due mainly to immigration. Most of those who went to settle there in the nineteenth century were Europeans. Considerable unemployment existed in Europe at this period, and America offered many opportunities for work. To begin with, the immigrants came from western Europe; then, after 1880, they started

Opposite: Monument Valley in the U.S.A. is a wonder of nature: rocky edifices towering out of the arid expanse of the Great Desert. The wind has sculpted them into high, tapered peaks that have served as a background in many a western. This is the territory of the Navajo Indians, who believed the rocks were inhabited by spirits.

arriving from the south and east as well, the majority being Italians and Poles. Between 1880 and 1914 an average of 2,000 people landed in the United States every day. It was feared that this invasion might put excessive strains on American society, so laws were passed to limit immigration. The unity of the American people was thus preserved. New arrivals, for the most part young people, adapted themselves to their environment and began to learn the language. The population grew rapidly. Initially most immigrants settled in the east of the country, but increasing numbers later went to the mid-west and west. The north-east is still the most heavily populated region of the United States.

New York with its eight million inhabitants is the principal city of the U.S.A. Counting the suburbs, its total population is thirteen million. The capital city is Washington, D.C.

Below left: Arizona, the home of the Navajo Indians. When they settled here these Indians lived on wild fruit and the spoils of hunting. Today they cultivate the soil and breed livestock. Their houses, called *hogans*, are hardly more than primitive shelters.

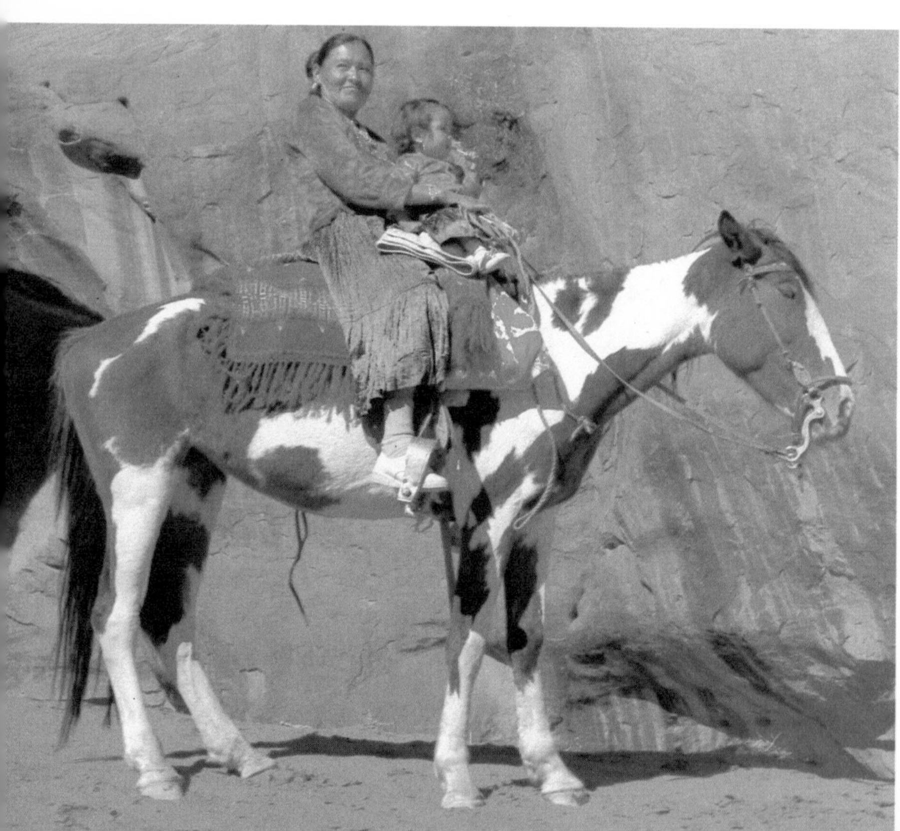

How do Americans make a living?

New York is an important centre of commerce and transport, having begun as the main destination for sea routes across the Atlantic Ocean. It's also important industrially. The principal products manufactured there are clothing, foodstuffs and domestic accessories. The headquarters of the United Nations are in New York.

The United States possesses an enormous wealth of resources. Huge tracts of land are given over to agriculture. The sub-soil has an abundance of mineral ores and there are plentiful sources of energy: oil, natural gas, coal, hydro-electric power, uranium. The rural working population is declining, as in Europe.

Agriculture, though, still plays an imortant role and large numbers of people make a living from it. The main crops are wheat, maize, tobacco, cotton and soya beans. Maize is used chiefly for fodder. Large quantities of citrus fruits are grown in California and Florida: oranges, lemons, grapefruit and tangerines. In the west, livestock breeding is organized on a large scale, with farms covering thousands of acres. Cattle are reared for meat and hides, sheep for wool (in Texas). Dairy farms are located near the big towns, and horticulture is also fairly widespread.

One of the biggest problems is soil erosion. Tree clearance on high ground and poor agricultural methods have had very dire consequences.

The sub-soil abounds in mineral ores. The search for oil began in the mid-nineteenth

Below: Disneyland in the U.S.A. Walt Disney is famous as the creator of the world's most popular cartoon films. He later made an even greater name for himself with his films about strange tribes and wildlife.
Right: The cable car in San Francisco. No town in the world has such steep streets as San Francisco. This tram is in fact a funicular.

century when the first wells were sunk in Pennsylvania. Today oil is extracted in twenty-five states. But industry, motor traffic and heating now require such large quantities that oil also has to be imported.
Coal seams are thick and located just below the surface, so the cost of mining is lower than in Europe. Oil and natural gas also serve as raw materials for the chemical industry. Large amounts of iron ore are mined near Lake Superior. The main industry is iron and steel.
The motor-car industry is based in several cities, the main centre being Detroit with big factories belonging to Ford and General Motors. Los Angeles is renowned for its aircraft industry, Chicago for meat canning.
Foreign trade is very important and American products are sold throughout the world. Primary imports are iron ore, copper ore and bauxite for use in the aircraft industry. The main suppliers are Jamaica and Surinam. There is free trade between all U.S. states, whose frontiers do not present any hindrance in this respect. River transport is insignificant. But the Great Lakes carry heavy traffic which connects up not only with domestic commercial routes but also with Canadian ones. The St Lawrence Seaway is navigable by ocean-going ships. The Panama Canal in central America joins the Atlantic to the Pacific.
Canada's chief source of revenue is the processing and export of wood in all its forms, and exports of agricultural

machinery. The north of Canada is one enormous expanse of plains and forests, and the northern extension of the Rocky Mountains runs up the western side of the country. The central and eastern regions are very important for agriculture. Most of the country's industry is concentrated in the east, to the south of Montreal, which is one of the largest seaports in North America. It is situated on an island in the St Lawrence River, and has miles of docks and warehouses to handle all the traffic from the Great Lakes. It is an important centre for exports, as it links the Lakes with the North Atlantic ocean routes.

The capital city of Canada is Ottawa, which is situated on the Ottawa River, on the border of Ontario and Quebec. Paper milling and wood working are the main industries.

The Grand Canyon in the state of Arizona. Differently coloured rock strata show up very clearly the horizontal sedimentation. The Colorado River has carved out this valley down to a depth of 2,000 m, the river itself being ninety metres wide and from four to thirteen metres deep. Big hydroelectric stations and dams have been built downstream from the Grand Canyon. The most important of these is the Hoover Barrage, whose water is used to irrigate 800,000 hectares of land. The Colorado is of no great value for commercial navigation and consequently attracts tourists from all over the world. It flows into the Gulf of California.

Central America and South America

South America comprises what are called 'developing countries'. Big contrasts exist between the old and the new way of life, between poverty and wealth. Wealthier countries give some aid to South America, but a great deal of poverty still exists.

Above: **Simon Bolivar, hero of South America's liberation. Bolivar lived from 1783 to 1830 and fought mostly against the Spanish armies. The state of Bolivia was named after him.**

Where is South America?

It is often thought that South and North America form a single continent. If you look in the atlas you'll find that in fact they are joined only by the isthmus of Panama, which is crossed by the Panama Canal.

South America is 7,500 kilometres long and over 5,000 kilometres wide. All the countries in it are republics.

Three quarters of South America lies within the Tropics, but the rest of the continent extends so far south that the southernmost point, Cape Horn, is only 1,040 kilometres from the Antarctic.

The continent is divided into three big regions: a chain of high mountains in the west, a chain of low mountains and plateaux in the east, and a central plain.

South America has a population of 170 million. Certain regions are very densely populated and the number of inhabitants continues to grow. Population distribution depends on the climate, soil and vegetation: the majority of Brazilians, for instance, live on the coast. The Atacama Desert in the Chilean Morte Grande is very poor and barren, more or less uninhabitable. The same goes for the Andes, whose peaks are perpetually covered in snow, and for the Amazon basin with its hot, humid and impenetrable virgin forests. Many people are attracted by the arable regions of central Chile and by the fertile pampas (steppes without trees or bushes) in Argentina.

In most South American states the gap between rich and poor is very great. Some regions are extremely wealthy, while in others the people have only just enough to live on.

Who were the original inhabitants of South America?

The original inhabitants of South America were the Indians, who are thought to have come from Siberia ten thousand years ago, by crossing the Bering Strait.

The several hundred different Indian tribes were decimated by their European con-

Below right: **La Paz, capital of Bolivia, is situated at a height of some 3,700 m, dominating a valley with a very cool climate. It's the centre of an important mining region which produces mainly tin and oil.**

Below left: **Poverty is common in Central and South America.**

Left: Aztec Indians in traditional costume. The Aztec empire came to an end in 1520. When the Spaniards arrived in Latin America they settled in Mexico and Central America. The diseases they brought with them coupled with the cruelties they inflicted, caused a sharp decline in the Indian population up to the nineteenth century.
Right: Mexico, the floating gardens of Xochimilco.

querors. The survivors were assimilated into the white and black population.

Many South American Indians still live as they were taught by their ancestors: small groups can be found in the Gran Chaco valley in the west of Paraguay and also in northern Argentina, where they lead a nomadic existence. These Indians hunt, fish and gather roots and berries. Some do a little farming.

In the dense forests of the Amazon basin which have not yet been penetrated by settlers, one can still find primitive tribes who live by hunting and trapping fish.

An important Indian civilization was that of the Incas, whose empire stretched from what is now Ecuador to Peru and central Chile. Pizarro conquered it in 1532.

The Incas cultivated fields and terraces on the sides of mountains, irrigating them by means of special ducts. They bred llamas and exploited mines. Their chief god was the god of the Sun, but they also worshipped many others – often more ancient – such as Mama killa, the goddess of the Moon. They didn't know how to write. The Mayas of Mexico, on the other hand, used hieroglyphs but were unacquainted with the

Opposite: Brazil: Carayas fishing. These Indians belong to the Tupi tribe and live chiefly in regions of virgin forest. They live by agriculture, hunting and fishing.

Brazil: a Makir, an Indian from the region watered by the River Parana.

wheel – a very basic instrument.
Christopher Columbus had reached the West Indies in 1492; in 1498 he landed on the South American continent. Some years later the Spaniards and Portuguese set out simultaneously but independently to conquer it. In fact the fate of these countries had been sealed well before the arrival of the Spaniards and Portuguese. By the Treaty of Tordesillas signed in 1494 with the Pope's approval, Portugal had obtained the eastern part and Spain the western part. The Spaniards invaded the country as military conquerors with the aim of taking its gold and establishing their own supremacy. The Portuguese, by contrast, came as merchants. For them, South America was a stopping-point on the route to the east. The colonial period lasted about 350 years. The Indians were unsuited to working in the plantations, so black slaves were imported from Africa. When slavery came to an end in the nineteenth century, large numbers of Hindus came to work in South America. The present population consists of a mixture of many different races.

What are South America's main physical features?

South America is very mountainous, with the Andes stretching from north to south over a distance of 8,500 kilometres. Their peaks reach heights of 6,000 to 7,000 metres. On the Pacific side the mountain range extends right up to the coast. Roads and railways are often very steep and very high, and most of the passes are at enormous heights. Rivers on the west of the Andes flow into the Pacific Ocean and have many waterfalls and rapids.
Most of the population prefer to live in the mountains because the climate is pleasanter. The plains are too hot. The valleys are very densely populated and agriculture is almost the sole means of making a livelihood. Quito is an Indian city whose inhabitants grow potatoes and maize and live in very squat houses of a greyish-brown colour built of large clay blocks dried in the sun. They have no windows and hardly any furniture. The Indians wear black clothes with a shawl to protect them from the wind. Their staple food is maize. The mountainous state of Columbia possesses numerous banana plantations on the coastal plain of Santa Marta. Livestock breeding predominates in the hot, dry plains. The famous coffee plantations are at a height of 1,000 to 1,800 metres to the west of the city of Bogota.
The orchards on the mountainsides produce oranges, pears, peaches and pineapples.
The central part of South America is a vast lowland area which extends across nearly the whole width of the continent. Through this flows the Amazon River. There are many tributaries flowing into the Amazon, and one area is covered by dense tropical rain forests.

The Republic of Chile stretches like a thin band along 4,300 kilometres of the west coast, the highest peaks of the Andes constituting its eastern border. To the north, at a height of 3,000 to 4,000 metres, is the Atacama Desert, covered in salt. Central Chile is rich in minerals, especially saltpetre, which is used for making fertilizers, iodine and explosives. Large quantities of copper have also been found there.
Off the southern tip of South America there is a group of islands called Tierra del Fuego (Land of Fire). It was named by the explorer Ferdinand Magellan. The cold, humid climate prevented the Fuegians in the south from making fire. When at last they succeeded they tried to preserve the flame, taking it with them from one island to another in their boats of bark. The most important region is around the capital, Santiago.

Below: The Rio Negro, whose banks are very steep. As there was no room to build houses along the riverside, they were constructed on piles above the water.

How do people live in South America?

Farmers live in huts with walls and floor of clay and a roof made of straw. The region of the haciendas consists mainly of prairies.
Argentina's agriculture and stock farming are the most flourishing in South America, but the sub-soil contains no metal. The country's wealth is in the pampas. Argentina is known primarily for its livestock breeding, but corn is also grown. The main market outlet is Buenos Aires.
Uruguay is a small country whose economy depends largely on livestock. Its principal exports are meat and meat-based products.
Brazil is the biggest of the republics and its capital, Brasilia, is the world's most modern city. It's situated on a high plateau 1,000 kilometres from the coast. To begin with, houses of corrugated metal were built for the workforce. When Brasilia was completed in 1960 these houses were left because the workers were unable to pay the rent on the modern buildings. The central plateau of Brazil was very sparsely populated, with most of the towns and farming areas grouped along the coast, because the climate of the interior was very poor and unfavourable for farming. Brasilia was built partly to attract more people to the interior.
The Amazonian plain is also part of Brazil. Whole regions are covered in thick, humid, hot, virgin forest. The river Amazon flows through swampy forests with palms, rubber-trees and mangroves.
The extremely humid climate means that there are very few inhabitants.
South America is rich in natural sources of energy. The ground contains large quantities of copper, gold, iron, lead, silver and oil (in and around Lake Maracaibo). The various countries for the most part export raw materials and monoculture products such as coffee or bananas. There is as yet only a limited amount of industry.
In the north of Central America is Mexico, a barren region consisting essentially of deserts.
A little industry is found in the suburbs of Mexico City and along the east coast. Tourism is one of the main sources of revenue. The other countries of Central America are very poor. Most of the population are Indians.

Left: **An Argentinian *vaquero* (herdsman) watching over herds belonging to one of the big farming estates or *estancias*.**
Top right: Peru, a state in the Andes. A Pirac Indian and his daughter in traditional costume.
Bottom right: **The Incas lived in the Andes from the twelfth century onwards. Theirs was the only great Indian state in South America. They invented more advanced weapons and evolved superior military tactics which enabled them to conquer the other tribes. At their capital, Cuzco, they built temples and palaces and laid out parks, sports grounds and road systems. Their goldsmiths fashioned beautiful works of art. This photograph shows the treasure of Atahualpa.**

Top: New Zealand: a young Maori girl. The Maoris live on the North Island and are famous throughout the world for their wood sculptures, dancing and music. Today they tattoo themselves only rarely. They left Polynesia to settle on this island in about 1350 and now make up no more than 6% of the total population. Most of them wear European clothes.
Above: New Guinea: a Papuan of the plateaux in traditional costume. The mountain dwellers in particular have had little contact with the Western world. The majority of Papuans live on the coast.

Oceania and Australia

Oceania comprises all the islands of the Pacific Ocean except Indonesia, Japan and the Philippines.

What are Australia's main physical features?

Australia is the world's smallest continent and has no borders with other countries. Most of it is covered in undulating plains, the central region being more mountainous. The highest point is Koscinsko (2,230 metres). Along the eastern coastline runs the Great Barrier Reef, while the west coast is composed of a series of plateaux. The population is thinly and very unequally distributed: out of a total of twelve million, about five million live in Sydney and Melbourne. Vast areas are completely uninhabited. Northern Territory, for example, has an extremely sparse population owing to its desert soil and arid climate. But the fact that its inhabitants are few and far between doesn't mean that Australia is unimportant. On the contrary, it plays a significant role in the world. Economically it's a very advanced country, producing large quantities of wool, wheat, meat and mineral ores which are sold on the world market.
Australia is situated south of the Equator. The north of the country has a tropical climate with monsoons and the rain falls in summer (January). The south of Australia and its east coast enjoy a Mediterranean-type climate, with rainfall in winter (July). The climate in the centre of the country is very dry, which explains the vegetation.

Who discovered Australia?

This continent was discovered very late in history. The old sea route from the Cape of Good Hope to Java passed near the Australian coast and the Dutch eventually landed in the west of the country, which they found very inhospitable. This region offered little of interest and seemed unsuitable for colonization. In 1462 Abel Tasman circumnavigated Australia in his sailing ship and discovered that it didn't belong to a big 'southern land', as had been thought. James Cook, an Englishman, landed on the fertile south-east coast in 1770 and claimed it on behalf of the King of England. The continent was inhabited by people of small stature and with brown skin, the Australian aborigines. They were few in number when the Europeans arrived, used no metals and knew nothing of either agriculture or livestock breeding. A race of nomads, they lived by hunting and gathering, their only weapon being the boomerang. They had no tents, but instead used windbreaks to protect themselves from the wind. The coming of the Europeans drove the aborigines back into the infertile regions, where little sustenance could be found.
The British originally used Australia as a convict settlement. But gold was discovered there in about 1850 and from then on the country attracted large numbers of colonists, who lived as farmers and livestock breeders and who established towns. Much of Australia is suitable for large scale sheep farming.

What other islands belong to Oceania?

Oceania also comprises the two islands which make up New Zealand, as well as New Guinea and three groups of islands in the Pacific Ocean: Polynesia (many islands), Micronesia (small islands) and Melanesia (black islands). The small, high islands are of volcanic origin; the low ones, called atolls, were formed from coral.
The climate is greatly influenced by the sea, and many of the islands are hot and humid. Melanesia (which includes New Guinea) is inhabited by a race of black-skinned people numbering about three million. Micronesia has roughly 100,000 inhabitants who have greater affinities with Europeans. Polynesia consists of the famous islands of Hawaii, Samoa, Tonga, Tahiti and Easter Island.

The Polar Regions

The polar regions are inhospitable territories around the North and South Poles. Certain explorers have gone there for the glory of their country. Others thought that the results of their explorations could be of scientific interest.

Above: **Roald Amundsen, the Norwegian explorer who was the first to reach the South Pole with his expedition in 1911.**

Who was the first explorer of the polar regions?

The Ancient Greeks were convinced that Norway was at the end of the world. A scholar called Pytheas claimed to have been even further and was the first man from the civilised world to have witnessed the midnight sun. He was the first to venture into the polar regions, in about 325 B.C.

Several centuries later the Vikings set out into unknown waters. The colonization of Iceland in about 870 A.D. was the first step towards the discovery of North America. Eric the Red discovered the route to Greenland and his son Leif reached the coast of America. In the eleventh century A.D., Ottar, captain of the Vikings, navigated along the coast of Norway to the North Pole. He was the first traveller ever to venture into Arctic waters. In 1596 Willem Harentsz set out to explore the north-east passage.

Following the expeditions of the Danish captain Bering in the service of Russia in about 1730, other navigators began to explore these regions, gathering information about the islands, ocean currents and movements of the ice barrier. The feat was finally accomplished towards the end of the nineteenth century. The Swede Nils Nordenskjold sailed from Sweden in 1878 in his ship the Vega and headed for the North Pole. In the spring of the following year the ship freed itself from the ice, passed through the Bering Strait and arrived in the open waters of the Pacific Ocean. Amundson also succeeded in making the passage, but the achievement had no practical value. Although numerous explorers tried to reach the Pole, the American Peary was the first to do so, in April 1909.

Robert Scott, an Englishman, had launched an expedition to the South Pole in 1902, but had abandoned the struggle 400 nautical miles from the Pole and returned home. Meanwhile, Amundsen was preparing his own trip very thoroughly, procuring sledges, skis and dogs. The expedition began in 1911 and after three months the group reached 90° latitude south. The South Pole had been conquered. Scott returned in 1912 for a second attempt. He was better prepared than the first time, but his men succumbed to a variety of illnesses and he had to postpone the endeavour. He reached the Pole a few weeks after Amundsen's expedition. The two base camps were located on either side of the Ross Sea, named after the explorer who discovered it in 1841.

Bottom left: **The Eskimos of the north travel in kayaks, small boats pointed at both ends with room for one or two men. They are made of wooden frames covered with sealskins. (Sealskins are also used for clothing.) Kayaks are waterproof and the Eskimos can make long voyages in them. They are also very light and can easily be hauled on to the ice.**

Bottom right: **An Eskimo family. Eskimos are small and have dark hair and the slit eyes of the Mongol race. Their family life is highly disciplined and they're among the most hospitable people in the world. They live in houses of ice, called igloos. The Eskimos of the Pole are the most primitive of all.**

Nature

These days there are few newspapers that don't carry a nature column. Quite often these articles are alarmist in tone, but they do make us think about the relationship between man and nature.

Above: An owl returning from hunting with a mole in its beak. Life consists of a vast natural cycle. Plants grow with the help of nutrients which they draw from the soil. They are eaten by animals, which are eaten in their turn by men and other animals. So life goes in a full circle.
Below: **Beetles make small round pellets out of the dung of other animals and lay their eggs in them.**

What is nature?

This isn't a very easy question to answer, because nature is an extremely wide concept covering everything existing in the universe that hasn't been made by man – the land and the seas, trees and flowers, fishes and birds, the mountains and the desert, the air and the rain, thunder, lightning and volcanoes – and also man himself. Nature includes the entire earth and the powerful energies hidden in its depths, and also the sun, moon and planets, all of which obey natural laws.

How is nature divided?

To get a clear picture of nature we can draw a line between inaminate, or lifeless, nature and the living world, or biosphere. Inanimate nature includes the mountains, oceans, air, clouds, volcanoes and storms, as well as the energies active in the centre of the earth.

Does nature ever change?

The whole of nature is changing every moment of the day. Alterations in the natural environment, such as the sea and the mountains, only happen very slowly, while living things change at a fast rate. Flowers and plants can grow very quickly indeed. One way or another, a careful observer can always spot something in nature in the process of changing.

At the same time, the action of natural forces is continuous: in the long run the sun, rain and wind bring about the erosion of the most solid rocks. The gravitational forces of the moon and the sun give rise to the daily tides, and a perpetual wind stirs up the waves.

The biosphere, too, is constantly undergoing changes. Animal species adapt to the changing conditions of the environment; if they don't, they gradually die out. Any change in climate or food affects living things. This progressive adaptation of life to the environment is called 'evolution'. It was the English naturalist Charles Darwin who first put forward the theory of evolution in the nineteenth century, and it upset many people's ideas.

How did Charles Darwin make his discovery?

In 1831 Charles Darwin, then a young student of geology and botany, joined a round-the-world voyage on board the *Beagle* as a naturalist, and took this opportunity to pursue his own research. He visited the Galapagos Islands, a series of islands quite widely separated from each other. On each one he observed some species that didn't appear on the other islands of the archipelago. For example, on each island he came across a

Left: The mole is an insectivore with dark brown fur, who digs tunnels and chambers to live in. He helps farmers by eating up lots of insects and harmful grubs and by aerating the earth with his tunnels, which improves the physical properties of the soil. However gardeners are not so keen on moles because they also eat worms, which are very useful, and leave their mole-hills all over lawns. In the photo opposite you can clearly see the mole's fore-paws which are specially adapted for digging.

different species of finch. On his return to England he re-read closely the notes he had carefully recorded every day in his notebook on board ship, and at the end of many years of thought and study he came to the conclusion that the whole of nature was evolving. According to Darwin's theory, the strongest and most intelligent species are those most capable of adapting themselves to changes in the environment, and they can pass on to their descendants the characteristics which best help them to survive. Many people thought Darwin's theories contradicted the Bible and were therefore unwilling to accept them.

What is man's place in nature?

We can think of nature as a pyramid, with the mineral kingdom as its base; then, going upwards, the vegetable kingdom, and next the animal kingdom, in a series of levels corresponding with different levels of development. Man, being the most highly developed form of nature, would come at the top of such a pyramid.

Man can in fact adapt to all kinds of different environments, and is able to stand up to the most extreme conditions – take the Eskimos, for example. Man also has the ability to make use of nature to serve his own ends – which is why he had sometimes been called 'the lord of creation'. He cultivates the plants he needs and rears animals, either for food or to help him with his work. He also knows how to transform natural energy into power for domestic use. Now that supplies of coal and oil are threatening to run out, people are looking for new and different ways of providing energy. They are looking at sunlight and at the wind and the waves, for these are inexhaustible sources.

Man has succeeded, too, in splitting the atom and harnessing the energy liberated in the process. However, the production of nuclear energy for domestic and industrial purposes raises all kinds of theoretical and political questions which human reason and intelligence must try to solve.

Again, it is only man, among all nature's creatures, who has been able to use his intelligence, and the resources around him, to discover what happens outside his own environment – below the oceans, in the air, and on the planets.

Charles Darwin (1809–1882): an English naturalist who wrote a number of books after a voyage to South America and the Galapagos Islands. His most important book is *The Origin of the Species by Means of Natural Selection*, in which he describes his theory of evolution. Although his theories were revised later on, Darwin was the first scientist to advance the idea of natural evolution.

The Balance of Nature

The balance of nature is a vitally important issue. All living things are distributed among a vast number of specific geographical areas, and the various forms of life within each area are linked by close ties of interdependence. This means, for example, that when the plants which one group of animals lives on becomes scarce, the animals, too, will tend to diminish in number.

What is a territory?

By territory we mean an area which the male of a species takes over so that he can settle there with his female partner and bring up a family, and which he defends against intrusion by rivals of the same species. Birds mark out their territories by singing, and some animals stake out boundaries with the help of special substances like urine, droppings or strong-smelling secretions.

Why do birds and animals defend their territories?

A very long time ago there was enough room for all animals to live together in harmony. But little by little the animal populations grew, food became scarcer, and a struggle for survival began. The factors which determined how many and what kind of animals could live in any one area were strength, cunning, and the type of food they needed.

What is the relationship between predators and their prey?

Numerous connections build up between predatory animals and the prey they live on, and these tend to maintain the balance of nature. Thus, when a particular animal population grows, the numbers of the predatory animal living off it also begin to increase, until they have reached the maximum that can be fed. So we can say that predators go on multiplying until there is a food shortage. If their numbers started to decrease, their prey would tend to grow in number. The whole process works towards maintaining the natural balance.

Above: **Man has an ever-increasing need for timber for building and paper-making. To satisfy it he has had to cut down enormous stretches of forest, resulting in the destruction of the animals in these habitats.**
Below: **Large numbers of seabirds live along our coasts. An oil-tanker running aground and polluting the sea with its cargo is a real catastrophe for them.**

Who causes the worst disturbances in the balance of nature?

Man does. Enormous stretches of forest-land have been stripped of trees for timber, destroying natural habitats and leading inevitably to the extinction of many animal species living there. Huge areas of land formerly inhabited by a very large number of animals have also been cleared to make way for agriculture and the building of farms and factories. And man's destructive activities take effect in many other ways, to the detriment of the balance of nature. Factories empty all kinds of industrial waste into lakes, rivers and other waterways, resulting in the destruction of plants and living creatures in and around them. After detergents have been used in the household they nearly always end up polluting river-water and

Left: The quality of the air we breathe is of prime importance for the balance of nature. Factories are a big source of air pollution. Cars and domestic heating systems also contribute a great deal to pollution. The exhaust pipes of cars, for example, give off a lot of carbon monoxide, which is very dangerous to the health of living creatures.
Below, left: This owl is dying after eating mice poisoned with D.D.T. The mice absorbed the poison by eating plants which had been treated with D.D.T. as an insecticide.
Below, right: The Colorado beetle comes from the U.S.A. It was accidentally brought to Europe, where it became a potato pest. To get rid of these beetles man sprays the potato plants with liquid insecticides.

making it unfit for animal and plant life. Consider, too, the pollution caused around us by, for instance, cars and aeroplanes – developments that are an accepted part of life today. Man must learn to use his unique abilities to combat the ill effects of his progress.

Man has also disrupted the biological balance – on purpose or accidentally – by artificially introducing animals into environments where they don't belong. For example, the importation of rabbits into Australia threw the natural order completely out of balance. The rabbits, with no natural enemies to stop them, rapidly multiplied and could soon be counted in their millions. It wasn't long before these pests had laid waste the rich grasslands of the Australian continent, destroying the roots of trees, devouring shrubs and leaving nothing behind them but dusty deserts from which all trace of vegetation had disappeared. In an effort to check this plague, foxes and ermines were also introduced, but in the end these caused more harm than good by destroying many species of birds and marsupials.

THE TORREY CANYON DISASTER

On 18 March 1967, a fine, bright day, the giant oil-tanker *Torrey Canyon*, loaded with 117,000 tons of crude oil, ran into the Seven Stones reef to the north east of the Scilly Isles. A number of holes were pierced in its tanks, and thousands of litres of oil poured out into the sea. Following a storm the ship broke in two and a total of 90 million litres of crude oil escaped, reaching the coasts of Brittany and Cornwall. This disaster caused the death of thousands of sea-birds.

Carl von Linné (formerly Carolus Linnaeus, 1707–1778) was a Swedish doctor and botanist. He formulated a way of classifying plants and animals, by giving each one a name consisting of two words, the first standing for the *genus* (or family) and the second for the *species* (different kinds of plant or animal within the same genus). These names are still used today.

The Plant Kingdom

It is impossible to imagine life on earth without green plants. They help to provide us with food and with the oxygen we need.

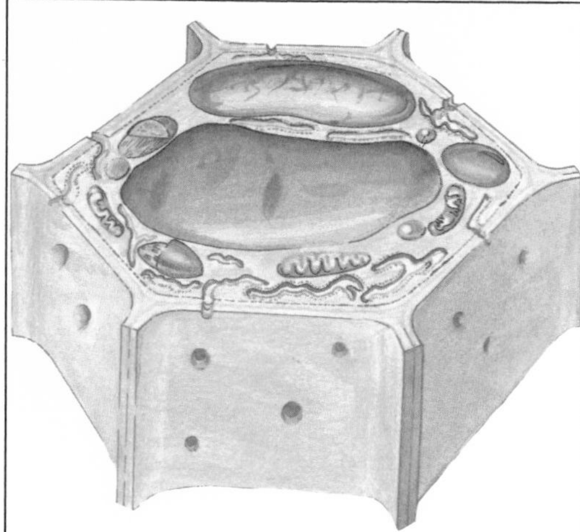

The cell of a plant consists of very strong outer walls and the contents of the cell proper. Around the inside of the cell walls is protoplasm, a substance rather like frog spawn or the raw white of egg. In this protoplasm can be seen particles of chlorophyll if the plant is green, and particles of another colour if the cell belongs to a flower. The most important part of the cell is the nucleus, which is also found in the protoplasm. The nucleus regulates the whole life process of the cell. In the centre of the cell is a small pocket filled with liquid.

CLASSIFICATION OF THE PLANT KINGDOM

Plants are divided into lower plants and higher plants. Lower plants are very simple; they have no root, stem or leaves. They are unicellular (bacteria), or thread-like (seaweeds and moulds).

Higher plants have roots, stems or trunks, and leaves. They are divided into two groups, cryptogams (plants which have spores and no flowers) and phanerogams (flowering plants).

Cryptogams have no flowers but reproduce by means of spores. Ferns, mosses and horsetails belong to this branch of the plant kingdom.

Phanerogams have flowers which produce seeds. They include gymnosperms, whose seeds are not enclosed in receptacles, such as conifers; and angiosperms, whose seeds are enclosed in an ovary, such as deciduous trees and herbaceous flowers. Angiosperms are in turn divided into monocotyledons, which have a single cotyledon or seed-leaf, and dicotyledons, with two cotyledons.

You can see this in chart form, below:

Lower plants
- Seaweeds (green, brown, red and blue seaweeds)
- Fungi – moulds, mushrooms, toadstools, and varieties of yeast bacteria

Higher plants
- Cryptogams (spore-bearing plants), mosses, ferns, horsetails
- Phanerogams (flowering plants)
  - – gymnosperms (conifers)
  - – angiosperms, which are further divided into
    1) Monocotyledons – including palm-trees, bamboos and grasses
    2) Dicotyledons – deciduous trees and most leguminous and herbaceous plants.

What are the different parts of a plant?

If we look carefully at a flowering plant, we can see that it is made up of five very important parts: the root, the stem, the leaves, the flower and the fruit. The root is in the soil; its role is to support the plant and also to draw up water and mineral salts from the soil in order to feed the plant.

The stem (or trunk, in the case of a tree) grows above ground. The leaves grow from it and it also acts as an internal transport system, carrying the nutrients which keep the plant alive.

The leaf takes in sunlight, which is essential for growth, the flower encloses the reproductive organs from which the seeds and fruit grow.

Can green plants make their own food?

Green plants have one very remarkable characteristic: because they have a colour-

Above: **Johann Gregor Mendel (1822–1884) was an Austrian monk whose experiments with sweet peas led him to discover the principle of the transmission of hereditary factors in plants. The laws of heredity which Mendel established as a result of his experiments are called 'Mendel's laws'.**

Below: **Every year a layer of new, light-coloured wood grows inside the tree, between the bark and the heartwood, the hard wood in the middle. The new wood is called alburnum or sapwood. In the spring when there is most sap rising, large, thin-walled veins appear in the tree-trunk; they act as an internal transport system for the sap.**

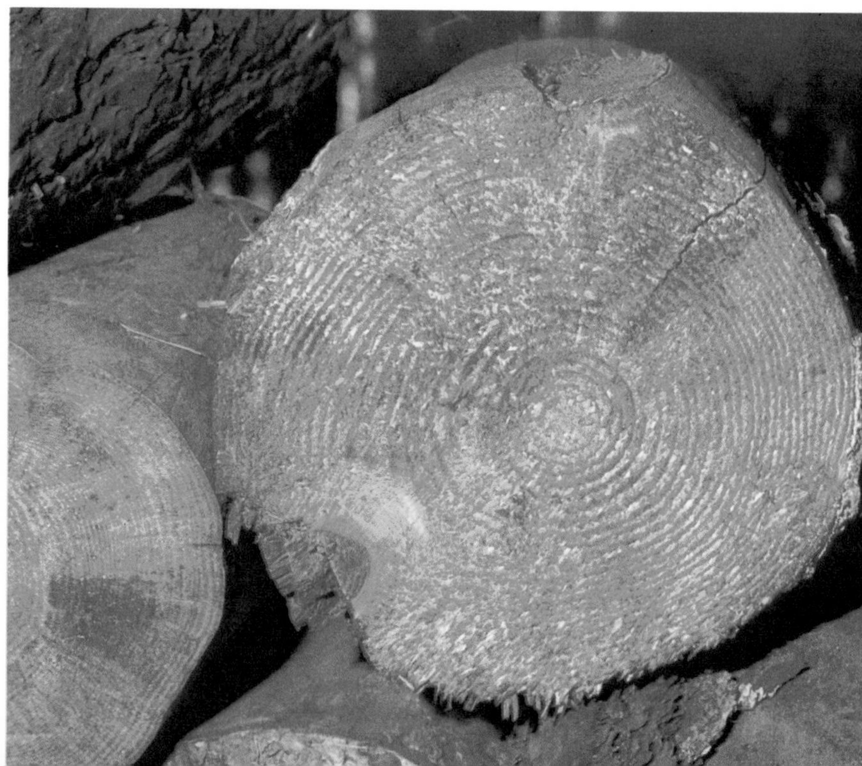

Right: Mushrooms are cryptogams with no chlorophyll, so they can't manufacture their own food.

ing substance known as chlorophyll they are able to manufacture their own sugar. This sugar, which is also called glucose, feeds the plant. To make it the plant needs two basic ingredients – water and carbon dioxide.

The water is taken up from the soil by means of the tiny root hairs on the plant's roots, and is carried upwards by the stem to the leaves. Carbon dioxide is a gas which exists in the air in very tiny quantities. It gets into the plant through minute openings in the leaves, called pores.

These two basic ingredients are turned into glucose in the chloroplasts which contain particles of chlorophyll and are found in each of the leaf's cells. Energy is needed to complete this process, and the plant obtains this from sunlight.

We call this process *photosynthesis*; *photo* comes from the Greek word meaning light, and *synthesis* means putting together or combining. In addition, in manufacturing the glucose the plant gives off oxygen, a gas which is essential to the life of human beings, animals and plants. Because of this, whenever a very large area of vegetation is cleared there are serious repercussions to surrounding life forms.

You can see, of course, that only green plants can manufacture their own food, since it cannot be done without chlorophyll. In the same way, it is obvious that they can only do this during the day, since there is no sunlight at night.

Cross section of a flower

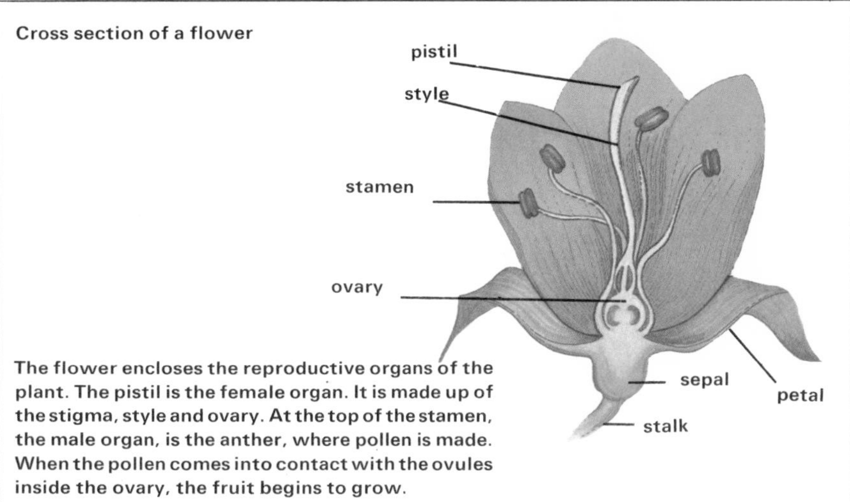

The flower encloses the reproductive organs of the plant. The pistil is the female organ. It is made up of the stigma, style and ovary. At the top of the stamen, the male organ, is the anther, where pollen is made. When the pollen comes into contact with the ovules inside the ovary, the fruit begins to grow.

How does a flower become a fruit?

In the centre of a flower you will find a number of little filaments called pistils and stamens; these are the reproductive organs of the plant. The pistils, or carpels, are the female organs and the stamens the male organs.

The pistil is made up of three parts: the top part is the stigma, the middle is the style and the bottom part is the ovary. Inside the ovary is a multitude of tiny seeds containing the ovules.

The top end of the stamen, which looks like a little knob, is called the anther. It is here that the tiny grains of pollen are made which scatter when they are ripe and are carried away by the wind or by insects. When the pollen falls on to a stigma, pollination takes place. The grains of pollen pass down the style into the ovary where they combine with the ovules inside. This process of fusion is called fertilization. After fertilization the ovule starts to grow until it becomes a seed or pip. The ovary surrounding it also ripens into a fruit or berry.

Below: The iris is a member of the *Liliaceae* family.

Above: **The banana is a tropical plant with big leaves measuring up to 3m long and 1m wide.**
Below: **Conifers have small, needle-shaped leaves which store water.**

How do plants grow?

We have seen how a fruit grows from a flower. When the seeds are planted in the ground they begin to germinate, then to grow into a new plant. The seeds grow after fertilization, when a male grain of pollen fuses with a female cell, the ovule. When fertilization takes place, this is described as sexual reproduction. But some plants don't have seeds – so how do they reproduce themselves?

Such plants reproduce by means of asexual (non-sexual) reproduction, that is, without the process of fertilization. There are several ways in which this can happen. Bacteria, for example, are unicellular plants: this means that they are plants which consist of a single cell; they multiply by dividing themselves in two, so that two new cells are created, each of which will grow into two full-sized bacteria. In favourable conditions bacteria can split themselves up like this every twenty minutes. Even if there were only a single bacterium affected, after three or four hours there would be many hundreds of bacteria. So you can imagine the situation if thousands of bacteria are multiplying at the same rate.

Some of the common weeds growing in ditchwater are thread-like plants, which can reproduce themselves without fertilization; one of the threads of which they are composed detaches itself from the rest and begins to grow all by itself.

Mushrooms produce special cells called spores inside their caps; these spores come into being without fertilization taking place. When they fall to the ground, new mushrooms begin to grow.

We have just seen that plants which don't have seeds reproduce themselves asexually. However, this doesn't mean that all seed-bearing plants always reproduce sexually. Tulips, for example, have ovules inside their flowers, but are propagated in an asexual fashion – underground, by means of their bulbs. Strawberries, too, are reproduced asexually by means of underground stolons, or runners.

Finally, there is an artificial means of asexual reproduction much used by gardeners. You probably know how house-plants can be made to grow from cuttings. These cuttings grow into plants from which more cuttings can be taken in time.

What are saprophytes and parasites?

We said a little earlier that green plants can manufacture their own food because they contain chlorophyll.

Moulds, fungi and bacteria, however, don't contain chlorophyll, so their needs have to be met in other ways. In autumn when the leaves are falling from the trees, you can find a great many mushrooms. Mushrooms are fungi, and don't contain chlorophyll. Most of them are fed by the waste products of trees – dead leaves and twigs. From these they extract all the nutrients they need, and what is left over goes back into the soil to feed the trees.

Many varieties of bacteria also live on waste matter, which makes them very useful. What is much less pleasant, however, is when these plants regard our own food as waste matter. We all know about bread getting mouldy, fruit and vegetable going rotten, milk going sour – all these are the work of different kinds of saprophyte. It must be acknowledged, though, that moulds and fungi do much more good than harm. They not only clear up a lot of rubbish; they can also be used in the preparation of a wide variety of products. Yeast, for example, is a fungus used in making bread and in the manufacture of various alcoholic drinks. Bacteria also play a part in the making of yoghurt and cheese. And penicillin is produced from a mould. Plants which feed on dead organic matter are known as *saprophytes*.

As well as saprophytes there are other plants with no chlorophyll, which we call parasitic. They don't live on waste matter but attach themselves to other plants, animals and even humans, or live inside them. Mildew is a kind of mould which covers the leaves of plants with a whitish coat and sucks nourishment from the leaf-cells.

Some plants make no food of their own – broomrape and toothwort attach themselves to the roots of other plants and live entirely on the nourishment they derive from their host.

Other plants are semi-parasitic. Mistletoe, for example, sends suckers into the wood of a tree. The tree supplies the water and minerals, and the mistletoe's leaves – which *do* contain chlorophyll – carry on the process of photosynthesis in the usual way. The host tree is not seriously affected.

Left to right and from top to bottom:
Rubber tree: **Rubber is made from latex, the milk liquid which is tapped from this tropical tree.**
Palm tree: **Palm trees are found in the tropics and other hot regions. They have leaves in the shape of feathers or fans.**
Strawberry: **The strawberry reproduces itself asexually by sending out runners into the soil around it.**
Cactus: **A plant growing in dry, rocky areas, which is able to lay down its own water supply.**
Flooded rice-field: **Rice-fields are heavily watered while the young plants are growing. Once the crop is mature, the water is allowed to run away.**

The Animal Kingdom

Animals are living creatures, which means that they are organisms whose behaviour and processes prove that life is present — they breathe, grow, reproduce, digest and have senses. They are distinguished from plants chiefly by their feeding methods, by being able to move, and by not having cellulose in their cell walls.

What is the difference between a plant and an animal?

The lives of all independent living creatures are subject to a great number of internal processes and to the influence of the environment they live in. It is clear that in general animals are rather more independent in relation to the environment than are plants. Thus animals are capable of adapting to lowered temperatures; in cold weather many of them grow a thicker coat of fur or feathers. Others survive the winter by hibernating: some mammals fall into a state of torpor very like sleep during the winter months, while their circulation, digestion and respiration slow down considerably. In this state of hibernation they are close to unconsciousness. Often if there is a mild spell during the cold season the hibernating animals will waken until the cold returns.

Many invertebrates (like some insects) survive very cold or very dry weather — which demand the same sort of adaptation — by spending part of their lives as an egg, completely protected from frost and drought.

Below: Sea anemones, which look like beautiful, open flowers, are actually marine animals. They can be found clinging to rocks along the seashore. They use their tentacles, which form a kind of crown around the mouth, to trap food.

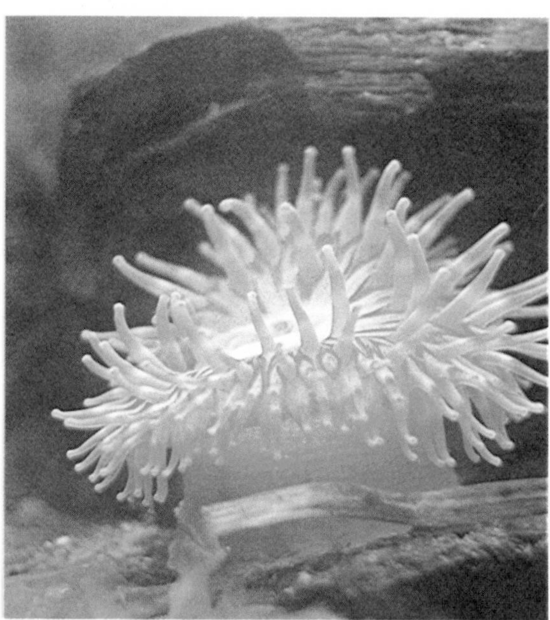

Below: This illustration shows a piece of sandstone. It comes from very old layers of rocks originally formed by the compression of sand under the sea, but which can now be found far inland. These rocks tell us a lot about the history of the earth. Pieces of sandstone like this can be found in various parts of the British Isles and northern Europe. In this one you can clearly see the spiral form of a snail-shell, high up in the centre, while impressions of sea-shells are also visible in several places. You can also find fossils of paw-prints and animal droppings in sandstone.

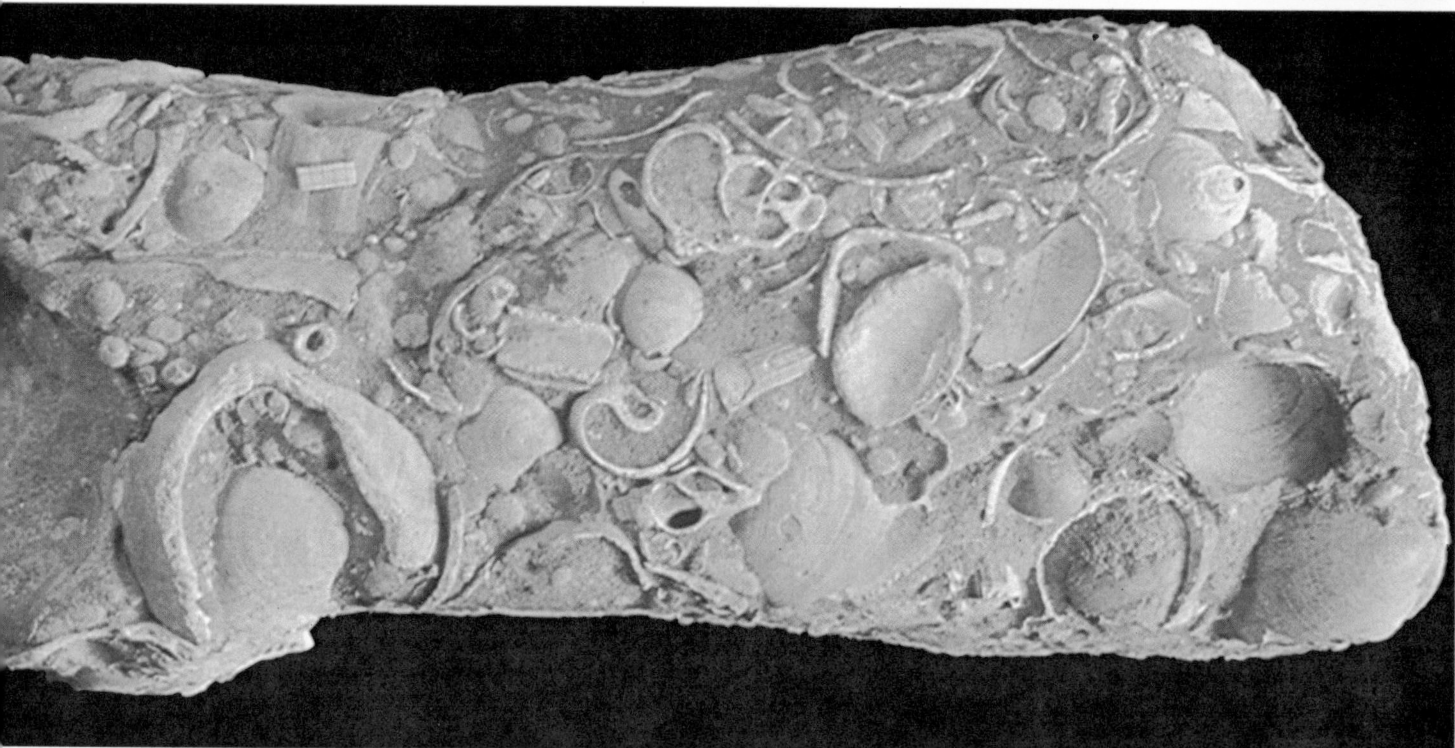

Left: The aurochs, or primitive bison *(Bos primigenius)*. Pictures of this animal, which was almost as big as an ox of today, are found on the walls of prehistoric caves in France and Spain. The horns of our cattle today are very small in comparison with the aurochs's horns, which were about 80cm long and looked very menacing. The aurochs is considered to be the ancestor of today's farm cattle. It died out in Europe around 1600.

Plants, however, also have ways of protecting themselves; in winter they close their pores and let their leaves fall. The great difference between *green* plants and the animal world is that the former are able to use sunlight to manufacture their own food, whilst the latter rely on the green plants, or other animals, for their source of food.

Are there any organisms which are both plant and animal?

In the biological world we find some creatures which have both plant and animal characteristics, so that it is impossible to say exactly which category they belong to. In the plant kingdom, as in the animal kingdom, there are some beings which are definitely plants because they can make their own food from minerals thanks to the action of sunlight on the chlorophyll in their cells, but which also have rudimentary eyes with which they can *see* light – as animals can. These organisms are very tiny.

CLASSIFICATION OF THE ANIMAL KINGDOM

A species identifies an animal exactly. The most commonly accepted biological definition of a species is that it is a group of animals which form a viable breeding unit. Different levels of animal identification include the species, the genus, the family, the order, the class and the phylum.

A. **Invertebrates.** Animals with no backbones, spinal cords or skeletons.

1. **Protozoans.** Consisting of a single cell, they are so tiny that you need a microscope to see them properly. Unicellular creatures are traditionally classed within the animal kingdom.
2. **Coelenterates.** Consisting of a single body cavity with a mouth, they take in food captured with the help of their stinging cells. Aquatic.
3. **Platyhelminthes.** Flat worms. These are primitive worms, very often parasites of other animals, the best known being the tapeworm or taenia.
4. **Nemathelminths.** Round worms. They are made up of a series of clearly visible rings, like the earthworm.
5. **Crustaceans.** Examples are crabs and lobsters.
6. **Insects.** The class of animal with the biggest number of orders and species. They have bodies divided into three segments, and six legs, and they go through metamorphosis.
7. **Arachnids.** Spiders. These are classified with the two classes above in the group of *arthropoda (*arthropods). Spiders have eight legs and no wings.
8. **Molluscs.** These soft-bodied animals have to live in a moist environment; they need the lime in the soil to build up their shells.
9. **Echinoderms.** They also extract lime from water, but it goes to form spines. Echinoderms are always built on symmetrical, circular lines. Examples are sea-urchins and starfish.

B. **Vertebrates.** All vertebrates have a skeleton comprising a minimum of a skull and vertebral column. The vertebral column or spine holds up the skeleton and protects the spinal cord.

1. **Fish.** These beautiful animals live in water and are provided with fins.
2. **Amphibians.** These can live both in and out of water. Their hairless, soft, moist skin contains a large number of glands which secrete a sticky fluid. They breathe mainly through the skin, and go through metamorphosis.
3. **Reptiles.** Like the two previous classes, this class is composed of animals whose temperature is related to the environment they live in. They lay eggs on land.
4. **Birds.** Warm-blooded animals, covered with feathers, winged, and with hard beaks.
5. **Mammals.** This class includes the most highly developed animals, including man. Many biologists believe that evolution has not come to an end with man.

Unlike most other animals a great deal is known about the evolution of the horse over the centuries. Fossils have been found of many of the intermediate stages, so that we can trace the struggles of the first little primitive horse *(Eohippus)* to become the horse we are familiar with today *(Equus)*. *Eohippus* was the size of a fox and had four toes, while today's horse has a single toe in the form of a hoof. Bucephalus, the charger which belonged to Alexander the Great, had three toes, a throwback to *Pliohippus* the immediate ancestor of the horse. The small horse which came before it *(Mesohippus)* also ran about on three toes.

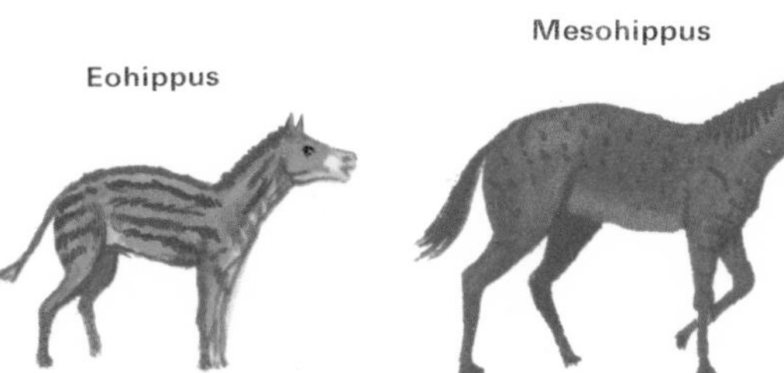

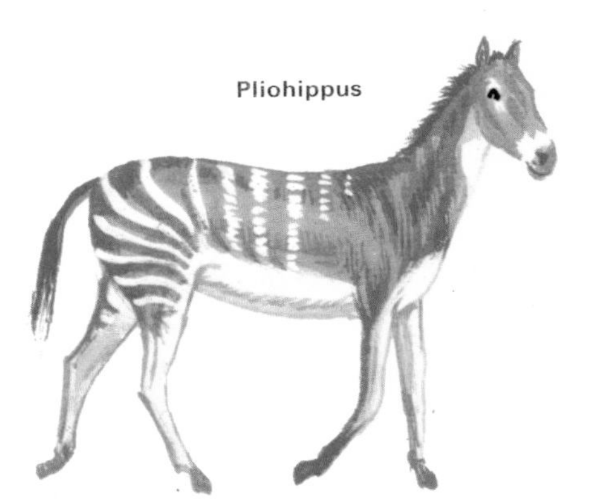

Top: The giraffe, with its long legs and neck, is the tallest animal in the world; male giraffes can be nearly 6m tall. These days they are found only in Africa. They eat greenery and have long tongues which they can stretch out a long way to get at the leaves on the top of trees. Their favourite food is acacia leaves. Surprisingly, their long necks contain only seven vertebrae – the same as in humans – each one very long.

Above: The fennec is a kind of fox, living in the dryest, hottest regions of Africa, Arabia and the Sinai desert. It is the smallest of the foxes and has the longest ears, which are also very sensitive. Its prey is hard to find, and it has to have very good hearing to be able to catch it. It is also thought that the size of its ears is an adaptation to life in a very hot, dry climate; a lot of heat is lost through them, which helps their owner to keep cool. By contrast, the white fox who lives in the frozen north, has very small ears covered in thick fur, which definitely protect it against heat loss.
The fennec is 35 to 40cm high; its ears alone are 15cm long. It is carnivorous (meat-eating); for food it hunts scorpions and insects in holes in the ground and under stones, and it also catches snakes, lizards and mammals, which it kills with a swift bite at the neck. It takes in enough moisture for survival by consuming the body liquids of its victims. It also escapes from the worst midday heat by staying in the shelter of its earth.

Mammals

Mammals are the animals we are most familiar with. Many species can be useful to human beings, and man has made these into domestic animals, pets and beasts of burden.

What is a mammal?

The chief characteristic of mammals is that they suckle their young. After their birth the babies drink the milk which is secreted from their mothers' teats. Mammals are fully formed at birth. Before being born, the baby mammal grows inside its mother, in the womb. Here it is nourished by the placenta. Large blood vessels going through the placenta carry food from the mother to the baby and take away the waste products. The time which the baby takes to grow inside its mother is called the gestation period, and this is different for every animal.
At birth the young mammal cannot yet fend for itself. Its mother looks after its needs by giving it her milk which is secreted through the teats. The teats, and the mammary glands which produce the milk, are found on the mother's chest or abdomen.

Above: Dolphins are carnivorous sea mammals. **Below:** The cow, like most female mammals, is equipped with milk-producing glands; in cows they are called udders.

Do mammals have any other characteristics?

We've already seen two: the babies are born fully formed and they drink their mothers' milk.

In addition, all mammals except whales and dolphins have skin covered with hair or fur. Bats – the only mammals that can really fly – have short fur. Mammals are also provided with important glands, like sweat glands, salivary glands, etc.

Another characteristic of mammals is that they have a more or less constant body temperature. They are called warm-blooded, with temperatures ranging from 35°C (in hedgehogs) to 39°C (in rabbits and cattle). Human body temperature is about 37°C.

Other important features are that they need air and breathe with lungs (mammals who live in water have to surface from time to time in order to breathe), and they have a fully developed nervous system.

How do mammals differ from other animals?

They have warm blood, which is taken care of by the heart and which helps to regulate their temperature. In mammals the heart consists of four clearly divided chambers, two auricles and two ventricles.

In most mammals the brain is well developed, so that some species – like anthropoid apes and dolphins – are highly intelligent. Mammals are also distinguished by the way their teeth are adapted to the different kinds of food they eat. Some mammals have milk teeth which drop out and are replaced by a second growth; in others, one set of teeth keeps on growing throughout their lives.

All mammals have joints, where two or more neighbouring bones meet to form a movable hinge. Their bones are hard and strong, which enables some of them to be very big. Most mammals, including the giraffe, have seven cervical vertebrae forming the neck part of the vertebral column. Exceptions to this are the sloth and the sea-cow, which have more. Reptiles and birds often have many more.

Above: The birth of a mammal. At birth, the young look like the adults. Baby deer and other hoofed animals are able to run at a very early stage, and can follow their mothers. The coats of many young mammals have different markings from those of the adults; this is called camouflage, and helps them to hide. In other mammals the newly-born babies are completely helpless, and their parents build nests or burrows to give birth to them.

Can mammals be found everywhere?

Yes – not only living on land, but also underground, like moles and some varieties of mice, while members of some orders are very good at living in water. They come on to dry land to give birth to their young or to rest, but they catch their food in the water.

Cetaceans – large, fish-like mammals such as dolphins and whales – never go on dry land; that would be the death of them. Their young are born in the sea.

Another order has taken to the air – bats, which have remarkable flying abilities.

ORDERS OF MAMMALS
Monotremata (monotremes). The duck-billed platypus and the spiny anteater.
Marsupiala (marsupials). Kangaroos, koala bears, etc. The babies are very tiny at birth, and live for some time in the mothers' *pouches*.
Insectivora (insectivores). Moles, hedgehogs, shrews, etc. Mainly nocturnal; some of them live underground.
Chiroptera (bats). They have a membrane stretched between the digits (fingers) of their forelimbs and their hind limbs which enables them to fly. Nocturnal.
Dermoptera ('flying' animals). Flying squirrels, etc. They have a flange of skin along the sides of the body between the fore and hind legs. Nocturnal.
Primates. Humans, lemurs, North American monkeys and anthropoid apes. The most highly evolved mammals.
Edentata (edentates). Anteaters, sloths, armadillos. They have no incisors or canine teeth. Anteaters have no teeth at all. Many are nocturnal. Found only in America.
Pholidota. Pangolins, or scaly anteaters. Covered in hard scales interspersed with hairs. No teeth. Live on insects, which are ground up fine by horny growths in their stomachs. Nocturnal.
Leporidae. Family belonging to the rodent order (see below). Agoutis, hares, rabbits. Long ears and long hind legs.
Pinnipedia (pinnipeds). Seals, sea lions, walruses, sea-elephants. Completely marine animals, with streamlined bodies. They eat fish, swallowing them whole.
Carnivora (carnivores). Flesh-eating animals, the cat and dog family, bears, weasels etc.
Tubulidenta (tubulidentates). Long narrow snout, large donkey-like ears, very mobile tongue. (Aardvarks.)
Cetacea (cetaceans). Toothed whales, and whales with whalebone plates. Completely aquatic.
Perissodactyla (perissodactyls). Equidae. Horse, donkeys, zebras, rhinoceroses. Feet reduced to one toe.
Artiodactyla (artiodactyls). Hippopptamus, pigs, ruminants. Feet reduced to two toes.
Sirenia (sirenians). Sea-cows, dugongs. Tapering bodies, with a large caudal fin.
Hyracoidea. The hyrax, or coney. Resemble marmots. Live among rocks.
Proboscidea (roboscids). Elephants. Nose elongated into a trunk.

Above: **Kangaroos are marsupials. At birth the baby kangaroo is very tiny. Life in its mother's pouch is an extension of life in the womb.**

Flying squirrels don't really fly, but stretch out the flange of skin and fur between their front and back feet, so that they can glide from tree to tree.

Mammals are found in all parts of the world. Some maps or planispheres show the areas where only certain mammals can be found. On a map like this you can see, for example, that the largest number of marsupials are found in the regions comprising Australia, Tasmania and New Guinea.

However, it is very difficult to mark out exactly the territories naturally inhabited by particular animals, because humans make life very precarious for them. In the old days there used to be lions and bears in Europe, and tigers used to be found in the north of European Russia.

When we study their habitation zones, we can see that the only reason some animals are not more widespread is that some great natural obstacles have prevented them from travelling further. These are high mountains like the Himalayas, the oceans, deserts like the Sahara, and the climate. It's the climate, above all, that makes adaptation necessary.

Left: **Baboons are aggressive animals who live in troops. Usually a mother baboon has just one baby at a time. For the first five weeks she carries it about, hanging on to her belly. Later, she carries it on her back.**

How have mammals developed their way of life?

If we look at how mammals are classified, we can see that there is a number of orders, each of which lives on a particular kind of food. Insectivores and carnivores eat flesh; ungulates, or hooved animals, eat grass. Insectivores have sharp teeth so that they can pierce through the insects' hard exterior. Herbivores, on the other hand, have molars designed for munching grass. Edentates have no teeth, or only half-formed ones, but they don't need teeth. Most of them have long, sticky tongues which they use to trap ants and termites.

The choice of food determines the animal's way of life; the sense organs and feet also have to be adapted accordingly. So lions and tigers have claws, while anteaters and moles have forepaws they can dig with. The Asian tiger, the African lion and leopard and the American puma have a number of similar features, as do the wild ox in Asia, the European bison and the African Cape bison. This is because animals which eat the same kind of food are adapted to life in very similar ways.

Water animals have adapted themselves in other ways. They have streamlined bodies, and paws which have taken on the shape of flippers with the paw-shaped bones inside. Water is their element, and on dry land they become clumsy. The sebaceous glands in their skin play an important part in keeping their fur water-proof. Under water they can close up their nostrils. Cetaceans have 'nostrils' in the form of air-holes on their backs.

We can get a better idea of what is meant by 'adaptation' if we study the same species of animal living in different climates. For example there are three known types of fox: in the far north there is the white fox, which has small ears; our own foxes have quite big ears; and the fennec, a type of fox which lives in the desert, has very large ears indeed. Why such a difference in ear size? It's a method of regulating the body temperature. Another thing to note is that species which belong to the same family but live on different kinds of food are adapted in different ways. The white rhinoceros, which browses grass, has a long neck, while the black rhinoceros has a short neck because it eats the leaves of shrubs.

Other examples of adaptation are colour and

Above: The hedgehog is insectivorous. He uses his snout to dig insects out from under leaves and moss. He comes out at night. Hedgehogs are armed with prickles; in addition, they have a circular muscle which goes round their body. When they are threatened, this muscle contracts and the animal turns himself into a little prickly ball. Even foxes steer clear! In winter, hedgehogs find a sheltered place to sleep in. Their body temperature goes down to a few degrees below 0°C. If the weather gets too cold for them, they wake up and warm themselves by moving about.
Left: Like the hedgehog, the mole eats insects. He lives underground and is almost blind, but has a very keen sense of smell. His front paws are set at a sideways angle to his body to make digging easier. The paws have a crescent-shaped bone called a displaced carpal. The mole digs burrows and connects them up with a number of tunnels.

markings. In the jungle it's difficult to see the tiger or his striped coat. The same thing applies to deer who live in woods and forests. Young deer often have different markings from the adults because they are smaller and closer to the ground. Young wild boars have striped coats. There are many other similar examples in the animal world.

Do all mammals live in groups?

There are some animals which live alone. Others live in groups, and are called 'social' animals. There are several kinds of groups, from the very large to the quite small. Large groups are usually called herds. Up to 10,000 animals have been counted in a single herd.

Smaller groups are often given different names: we talk about a pride of lions and a troop of monkeys.

Animals who form large herds, particularly the herbivores, nearly always live in open spaces. Zebras, gnus and gazelles, for example, can be found in large herds. Elephant herds can include up to 100 animals.

Carnivorous animals tend to be more solitary because they do not often find sufficient numbers of their prey to support a group. Only when there are large herds – as on the grasslands of Africa – is it possible for a group of carnivores to kill enough for their needs.

What is the use of the group?

In wide open spaces where animals are easy prey for flesh-eaters, the individuals find safety in numbers. Only the weaker and older members get caught. Some animals protect each other when the herd is attacked. The biggest ones place themselves round the outside and protect the younger ones, who stay in the middle.

Some beasts of prey who live in open spaces, like the African grasslands, form groups – these include lions, cheetahs and hyenas. These groups are never very big, and their members help each other to hunt. Generally speaking, members of the cat family are not social animals – lions are the only truly social cats – but those of the dog family are. In the cold regions of the northern hemisphere there are large herds of reindeer. Rodents can also form large groups – Alpine marmots, for examples, and Norwegian lemmings.

The composition of groups varies a great deal. Sometimes they consists of males

Above: **The rabbit is a rodent with big ears and a small tail. His front teeth, both upper and lower, are long and edged like chisels. They go on growing all the time, because they wear out as the animal gnaws his food. Rabbits live in burrows. At dusk they come out to feed on roots and plants. They originate from the Mediterranean area, and are very prolific.**

Opposite: **The squirrel is a rodent. His sharp claws help him to live in the trees. Squirrels are found mainly in coniferous woods and forests. They hibernate.**

Below: **The raccoon lives on insects and fruits, and is also very good at catching fish. That may be how he acquired his habit of 'washing' his food before eating it.**

only, sometimes of females with their young, and sometimes of one male with several females, as with walruses. This last kind of group is called a harem.

Do all groups have leaders?

No, not always. Sometimes the link between the group members is a very loose one. However some groups do have a leader – sometimes a female one. We can study leadership best among monkeys. Baboons who live in the savannah form troops of between twenty and eighty members. The leader is the strongest male. If some difficulty crops up which he can't manage on his own, some of the other males will get together to deal with it; but the leader takes his place again immediately afterwards. The females are subservient to the males, but they also have a hierarchy among themselves. Females with babies have a special position.

Baby baboons are first of all carried about hanging on to their mothers' bellies; then when they get bigger they ride on the mothers' backs. The strongest males, the females and babies travel in the middle of the troop. On the outside are the young

Above: **The lion lives on open grasslands, and the male is said to prefer sleeping to hunting. Lions live in groups called prides, and only hunt when they're hungry – and then it's the lionesses who do all the work! The cubs have spotted coats which act as camouflage.**

Opposite: **The polar bear lives a solitary life on the ice-floes of the Arctic, patiently hunting seals. He has adapted remarkably to icy conditions. He has a thick layer of fat, a heavy coat, and 'snow-boots' – the soles of his feet are furry, so that he can't get stuck in the snow or slip on the ice. The babies are born in crevasses, or holes dug in the snow.**

Above: Zebras live in family groups, with one stallion to about ten mares. Several families form a herd.
Below: Wild asses are very like donkeys, and live in the desert. Like camels, they lose a lot of moisture but can also absorb a great deal at a time. Thanks to nature reserves they are able to live in freedom.

baboons and the weaker males. It's their job to give the alarm if there's any danger. The strongest adult males then form a defence.
Baboons eat roots, bulbs, fruits and even insects and snakes. Hamadryas, or sacred baboons, divide their troops up into smaller bands to hunt for food, each one including a male and several females. The young males form a band of bachelors. The males have to learn strict obedience to the females, or else they are punished by being bitten on the neck, which is painful, though it doesn't do them any real harm.
Chimpanzees live in forests in smaller groups of about sixty. They have no leader, but the group shows respect to the older males. Chimpanzees find their food at ground level, but live in trees, in nests made out of branches.
Gorillas live in small bands consisting of one male and several females; they live mainly on plants. At night they sleep in nests built either in trees or on the ground. Gorillas look very dangerous: a big male can often be over 1.7 m in height. But they are completely harmless and don't like fighting. At most the male will put on a show of ferocity by beating his chest.
Orang-utans live in small bands in the forest.

Below: Springbok belong to the large antelope family. They are delicately-built animals with curving, lyre-shaped horns. Antelopes are famous for their speed. They are ruminants: they eat grass very quickly and then go and chew the cud in peace.

They eat vegetation and insects, and need a lot of moisture. We don't know very much about the habits of these monkeys because it isn't easy to keep track of them in the thick jungle. Sadly, they are threatened with extinction, and are now protected by law.

Which is the biggest animal of all?

The biggest land animal is a mammal – the African elephant, which weighs 7.5 tonnes. He eats about 300 kg of greenery a day. The *tallest* animal, however, is the giraffe, which can be 5.5 m high. The biggest fresh-water animal is the hippopotamus, weighing 3 tonnes. The hippopotamus is herbivorous and only comes out on to dry land in the evenings. It prefers being in the water where its huge weight is supported. The biggest mammal of all is the blue whale, which can be 33 m long and can weigh as much as 136 tonnes. It seems likely that it is the biggest animal ever to have lived, and because whalers have been hunting it down for centuries, we must take care to ensure that it survives. It is grey-blue in colour and has no teeth; instead it has a series of whale-bone plates, or baleen, inside its upper jaw, and these act as a filter. The whale eats by taking in a large amount of sea-water and then forcing it out

of its mouth so that plants and tiny creatures are caught inside the plates. In this way it can consume 2000 kg of food in a day! It has a 'nostril' in the form of an air-hole on its back, which it can open and close. When a whale comes up to the surface to breathe, you can always see a spout of water, because the air it breathes out is hotter than the air outside and condenses in the colder air. It can't get food down its windpipe because this doesn't open out in the throat, like ours, but at the air-hole.

Smaller whales do have teeth, very simple, conical ones. These whales feed on fish and squid. Dolphins are a kind of toothed whale. Walruses (weighing 1.5 tonnes) are also very large animals. With their two enormous tusks they can prize mussels and oysters from the rocks; they are also excellent weapons.

And the smallest mammal? This is the Etruscan shrew (*Suncus etruscus*), which is very like other kinds of shrew both in looks and habits, but measures only 4 cm plus another 3 cm for the tail, and weighs only 2 g. The shrew is found in dry places around the Mediterranean, and in North Africa. It is so tiny that it would be able to fit into a beehive, using the entrance made by the bees!

Above: **The elephant is the heaviest land animal. He feeds on leaves and branches, and destroys a lot of trees. There are two kinds of elephant, the African and the Indian. The African is the bigger and the more difficult to tame. Indian elephants are smaller and can be trained more easily.**

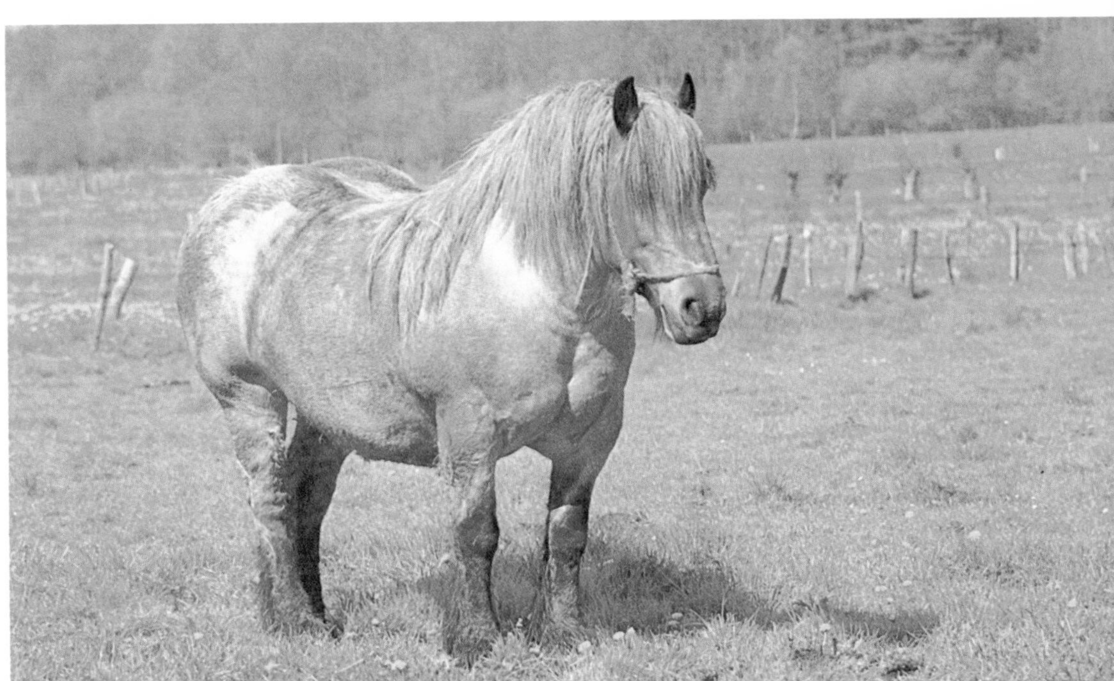

Above right: **The horse is a perissodactyl. The one shown here is a carthorse. Riding horses are more more finely built, and include thoroughbreds. The horse is one of the oldest of domestic animals, and is often called a 'noble beast'.**

Below right: **The warthog is a large, grey-brown animal which lives in the southern Sahara. Its canine teeth have grown outwards and are curved up to form tusks. At night it sleeps in a burrow, which it enters backwards. Warthogs may live singly or in small bands, and they eat bulbs, tubers and grass. They love rolling in mud. They have quite a high temperature – 38.9°C.**

Birds

Of all beautiful living things, birds are among the most fascinating. They often have beautiful and exotic colours, or an amazing ability to camouflage. Some species are wonderful songsters. In addition, they are lively creatures, seldom still for long, and man has always been envious of their ability to fly.

Above: The collared pratincole belongs to the pratincole family. They are graceful birds which nest in colonies on waste land near water. They are found in southern Europe, the south of Russia and Asia Minor. In flight pratincoles look rather like swallows, with their long, pointed wings and black-and-white forked tails.

What was the first bird like?

The fossilized remains of the earliest known bird were found in 1861 in a lime quarry in Bavaria. A second skeleton was found in 1877, and nearly a century later, in 1956, a third was uncovered. The remarkable thing was that all these fossils were lying at a distance of about 15 km from each other. The three skeletons all belong to the same creature, an ancient animal called *Archaeopteryx lithographica* – archaeopteryx for short. This creature must have lived about 150 million years ago. It was almost as big as a magpie, and still had some of the characteristics of its reptile ancestors, including 20 elongated tail vertebrae, three sharp claws on each wing, and teeth in its beak. But despite these features, it was decidedly a bird, for it had a fairly well-developed breastbone, was covered in feathers, and could fly – though not as well as our birds today.

Right: The hedge-sparrow is not actually a sparrow, but belongs to the family of accentors. It has a slate-grey head, breast and throat, and a small, sharp beak. In spring it lives mainly on insects and grubs, and in winter on small seeds.

How is a feather made up?

If you look closely at a feather you can see that the stem down the centre is rigid, but bends very easily at the tip. Indeed, feathers have to be very flexible to operate in the air. Besides the stem – which is called the rachis – the feather is made up of barbs, little silky branches which stick to each other by means of tiny hooks called barbules, making a tight fringe, the vane, down each side of

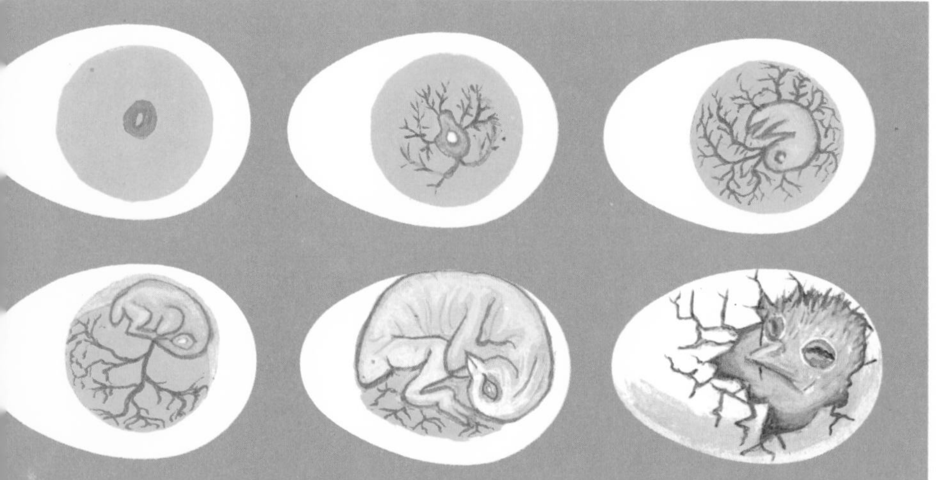

Opposite: An egg is made up of a hard shell with two layers of fine skin directly beneath it, called the first and second integument, which are separated by a layer of air. Beneath the second integument comes the white of the egg, then the yolk, in which can be found a tiny red spot. This is the germinal disc, which will grow into the chick. The yolk is kept in position by two twisted white threads called 'chalazae'. When the mother bird sits on the egg, or when it is kept warm in some way, the embryo begins to grow. The white of the egg is steadily taken up by the embryo, and a network of tiny veins appears in the yolk. In the third drawing the baby bird has grown even bigger: you can make out its tiny head with a developing eye. When the chick is ready to hatch out it gets out of the gg all by itself, by breaking the shell with its 'egg-tooth'.

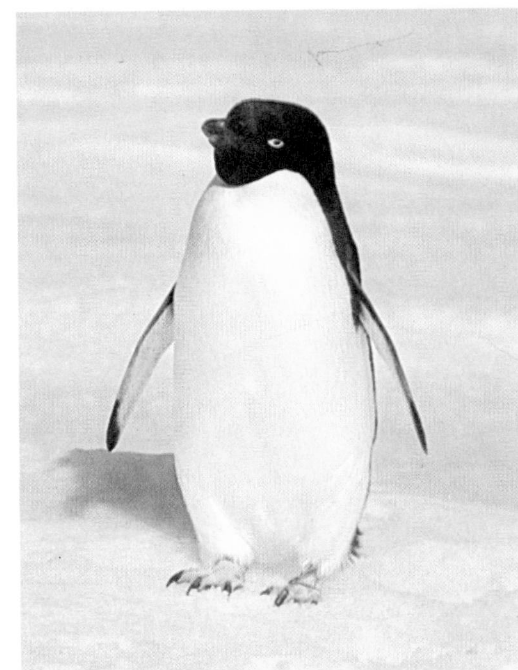

Above: The white stork is one of the largest birds in Europe. It is easily recognized by its long beak and red legs.
Above right: The adelie penguin lives in the southern seas surrounding Antarctica.
Below: You can recognize the blue-tit by the bright blue colouring of its head, tail and part of its wings. In winter it's quite easy to attract it into your garden.

the rachis. If you examine a feather under a microscope, you'll see that the barbules are attached to the barbs in the same way as the barbs are attached to the rachis. All the barbs are equipped with these minute hooks, which interlock with the barbules. In this way the whole feather is supple but very strong.

What are courtship displays?

In the mating seasons male birds go through a series of special routines to attract the females. Some of them sing loudly and exuberantly, and others, like the lapwing, put on wonderful displays of aerial acrobatics. Some show off any particularly bright patches of plumage. The robin, for instance, swells out his bright red breast, and the finch draws attention to the bright bands on his wings.

Are all baby birds alike?

Baby birds can be divided into two distinct groups. The first are blind at birth, most of them have no feathers, and they are completely helpless. All they can do for themselves is open their mouths to beg for food from their parents. They are completely dependent on their parents, who feed them almost non-stop while they are awake, and keep them warm in cold weather. These babies are called nidiculous, which means 'nest-inhabiting'. The birds that nest in our gardens are all nidiculous.
In the second group the chicks come into the world looking like little balls of fluff, with big, open eyes. As soon as they have dried off after hatching they are able to run after their parents and can even swim about – though their parents keep a close eye on them to start with, and warn them at the first sign of danger. These are nidifugous, or 'nest-fleeing' birds, and they include chickens and ducks.

Do all birds sit on their eggs?

No! Take the cuckoo. The mother cuckoo lays an egg in a songbird's nest and leaves it there. The songbird incubates the cuckoo's egg by sitting on it with her own. As soon as it hatches out, the baby cuckoo begins life by pushing all the other eggs out of the owner's nest. Cuckoos are called parasitic

Above: The king penguin is the largest penguin after the emperor penguin. It's about one metre long. The female only lays one egg. There is no nest; the female picks up the single egg on her feet and keeps it warm under a fold of skin in her body.
Right: Unlike the king penguin, which inhabits the Antarctic coastline, the great northern diver lives near the North Pole. On dry land he is encumbered by the fact that his feet are placed very far back under his body.
Below: The great crested grebe is a wonderful diver. His feet are not fully webbed but he has membranes between his toes which he can spread out in order to dive into water with minimum resistance.

birds. There are several species of bird which lay their eggs in other birds' nests.
Another bird which doesn't incubate its own eggs is the mallee fowl which inhabits Australia and the neighbouring islands. It collects dead leaves to build a kind of incubator, which is heated by the warmth of the rotting leaves. Other birds lay their eggs in sand and leave them to hatch out in the heat of the sun. Or they lay them in holes among rocks where the sun shines on them all day long and the warmth is preserved in the rocks at night.
What is important is to make sure that the eggs are kept at the correct temperature. Commercial breeders incubate thousands of hens' eggs artifically and can produce many more chickens than would be possible on a free-range farm.

How is an egg formed?

Inside the adult female is an ovary filled with tiny eggs called ova. When a single ovum has grown large enough the follicle containing it breaks, and frees the ovum. It moves into the oviduct, where it is fertilized by sperm from the male. Next, it reaches the uterus. Finally the egg comes out of the cloaca, a cavity at the tail end of the hen which joins up with the opening of the uterus.
During its journey down the oviduct, the ovum goes on developing. First of all thick, twisted white structures called chalazae form at each end of the fine skin surrounding the yolk, to hold the yolk in place in the middle of the egg. Then the albumen, or egg-white, appears, arranged in concentric layers of protein. Next, fine layers are formed to protect both the white and the yolk inside. Finally, when the egg reaches the uterus it acquires its tough casing, the shell, which is composed of three layers – an inner layer, a spongy layer, and the outer layer called the cuticle.

What are brooding patches?

Eggs have to be incubated, that is, kept warm for a certain length of time until they are ready to hatch out. Most people think that all the mother bird has to do to brood, or incubate her eggs, is to sit on them. However, as feathers don't in fact let much warmth through, most birds have special 'brooding patches' on their bodies, where the heat can get through to the eggs. A brooding patch is a featherless area where the skin is much thinner and there is almost no fat underneath; the surface temperature is increased by an extra supply of blood. When the hen-bird starts to brood she begins by shaking the down feathers off her breast and arranging herself so that the eggs are in contact with the naked part of her skin. When a male bird shares the task of sitting on the eggs, he too has a brooding patch.

Opposite: The common gull is similar to the herring gull, but much smaller. His beak is greenish instead of yellow, and the rounder shape of his head gives him a jaunty look. These gulls usually nest in sandy areas and also in cultivated fields and sometimes even in trees. They have three eggs – sometimes only two – and the male takes equal shares with the female in sitting on them. As soon as they have dried off after hatching, the chicks leave the nest. They are therefore nest-fleeing (nidifugous) birds.

Below: The white pelican is an aquatic bird whose enormous bill has an expandable pouch which he uses as a fishing net. There are seven species of pelican, and all of them are excellent long-distance flyers who can stay in the air for a long time. Sometimes they fly in formation. Some species build their nests in trees, others at ground level, among reeds, for instances. White pelicans often swim in groups to fish, or they catch fish by diving into the water from the air.

What is an 'egg-tooth'?

When a chick is about to hatch out, it has a tough job ahead of it – breaking the egg-shell. Luckily, nature has provided the chick with a special tool, the 'egg-tooth', which is a kind of small, hard bump on the end of its beak. The chick uses it to make a crack round the inside of the shell, just like a glazier cutting glass. Then, to get out of the egg, the baby bird has to push as hard as it can against the round piece of cut-away shell. To help further the chick has a powerful muscle at the back of the neck, which is used to push away the shell and get free. A few days after the chick hatches out, the egg-tooth disappears.

Do birds hibernate?

There is at least one bird which has been known to hibernate, and this curious fact was only discovered in 1946. One day the naturalist Edmund C. Jaeger was on Chuckawalla Mountain in southern California with two companions when they came across a nightjar which was lying under a rock, seemingly quite dead. Suddenly, however, the bird opened its eyes – it was alive, but it was in the resting state of hibernation. For the next four winters this bird was found under the same rock. Tests showed that it would sleep for over 80 days during the winter. There was no trace of moisture when a light was shone in its eyes, and its body temperature was only 18°C instead of the normal 41°. As soon as spring arrived, the bird would wake from its deep sleep and fly away. This bird is called Nuttall's poorwill.

What is meant by a bird's territory?

A bird's territory is an area which it defends against others – especially those of the same species. In many cases defending a territory is part of the search for a mate, such as nest-building and all that it entails. Nest building is a seasonal occurrence. The male bird stakes out a specific area and advertises the fact by singing his song at certain places along his territory. His song is an announcement that he wants a mate; it's also intended as a warning to his rivals that this piece of

Left: The shelduck looks very like a goose. The male has a big red swelling on his beak. These ducks fly with slower wingbeats than other ducks. They often use rabbit holes as nests, but they can also build nests under shrubs, or in the undergrowth on sandbanks.
Above right: The little egret is a kind of heron, with beautiful pure white plumage. It has very long shoulder feathers called 'aigrettes' which make a magnificent lightweight cape. These birds used to be killed for their aigrettes.
Below right: The goshawk is a handsome bird of prey which flies from tree to tree. It swoops down on its victims like an arrow, beating its wings, and carries them off in its talons. The goshawk is a fearsome predator; animals are terrified when they see one.

land is occupied.
Robins have a separate territory outside the nesting season; both male and female robins have territories, which they use as feeding areas.

Which bird holds the record for long-distance migratory flight?

This record is held by the amazing little arctic tern. Like the common tern, it too has a bright red beak, but without a black tip. Terns sometimes come to nest in European estuaries, but most of them breed above the Arctic Circle. When the breeding season is over, which occurs at the end of the northern summer, they leave the pole in order to spend the winter along the coasts of southern Africa. Many of them continue this post-nuptial (after mating) flight as far south as the ice-floes of the Antarctic, where they stay throughout the polar summer. When this comes to an end the Arctic tern returns to its nesting grounds at the North Pole, in a pre-nuptial flight.

How do we classify the birds we see in our own part of the world?

Ornithologists have given the following descriptions to the birds that can be seen in the British Isles and Europe:
Residents: These are species which remain here all the year round, and seldom stray more than a few kilometres outside their chosen territory.
Partial migrants: These are birds which nest and breed in northern Europe, but some of which spend the winter in southern Europe.
Summer visitors: These are migratory birds which only come here in the summer to nest. (Another category of summer birds come here for the summer but do not nest.)
Winter visitors: These are migratory birds which only come here for the winter period.
Birds of passage: These are birds which only fly across our countries in spring and autumn. They nest and breed further north, and spend the winter further south.

Below: The giant fulmar is a species of petrel 80cm long, with a wingspan of up to 2.8m. It is the only petrel which doesn't nest in a burrow but in an open hollow in the ground. These birds nest in colonies on the coasts of Europe and on the islands of the southern hemisphere.

Accidentals: These are birds which have not been sighted in these regions more than 5 times since 1900. They are therefore very rare.
Occasionals: These are species which have been seen here more than 5 times, but intervals of several years have elapsed between sightings.

What is a 'thrush's anvil'?

Thrushes – the songthrush, for example – live on earthworms, and also on slugs and snails. Slugs are easy for them to swallow, but to eat snails they have to remove the shells first. When the thrush has collected several snails, it finds a stone and bangs the snail-shells against it to break them. It's not uncommon to find the remains of ten snail-shells around one of these 'anvils'.

Why do most birds keep their nests clean?

As soon as the babies are hatched, many birds remove the eggshells from the nests. With songbirds, the babies' droppings come in gelatinous capsules. The parents carry away these little packets in their beaks, or swallow them.
Of course, if the droppings were left in the nests they would attract all kinds of germs which would harm the baby birds. In addition, the light colour of the dried droppings would give away the site of the nest to all kinds of predators. So would the light-coloured inside of the eggshells.

Right: The parrot family is extremely large, with over 325 species. The biggest of them is the fantastic-looking, brightly-coloured macaw, which lives in the vast tropical forests of Central and South America. Some of them are nearly a metre in length, if you include most of the tail. They have brilliant plumage in which yellow, blue, green, red and black often make a splendid contrast with the bare white patches on their cheeks. They have extremely large and strong hooked beaks. Their feet are adapted for climbing, with two claws pointing forwards and two backwards. The blue and yellow macaw shown here is one of the most common parrots to be seen in zoos. It can be up to 80cm high.

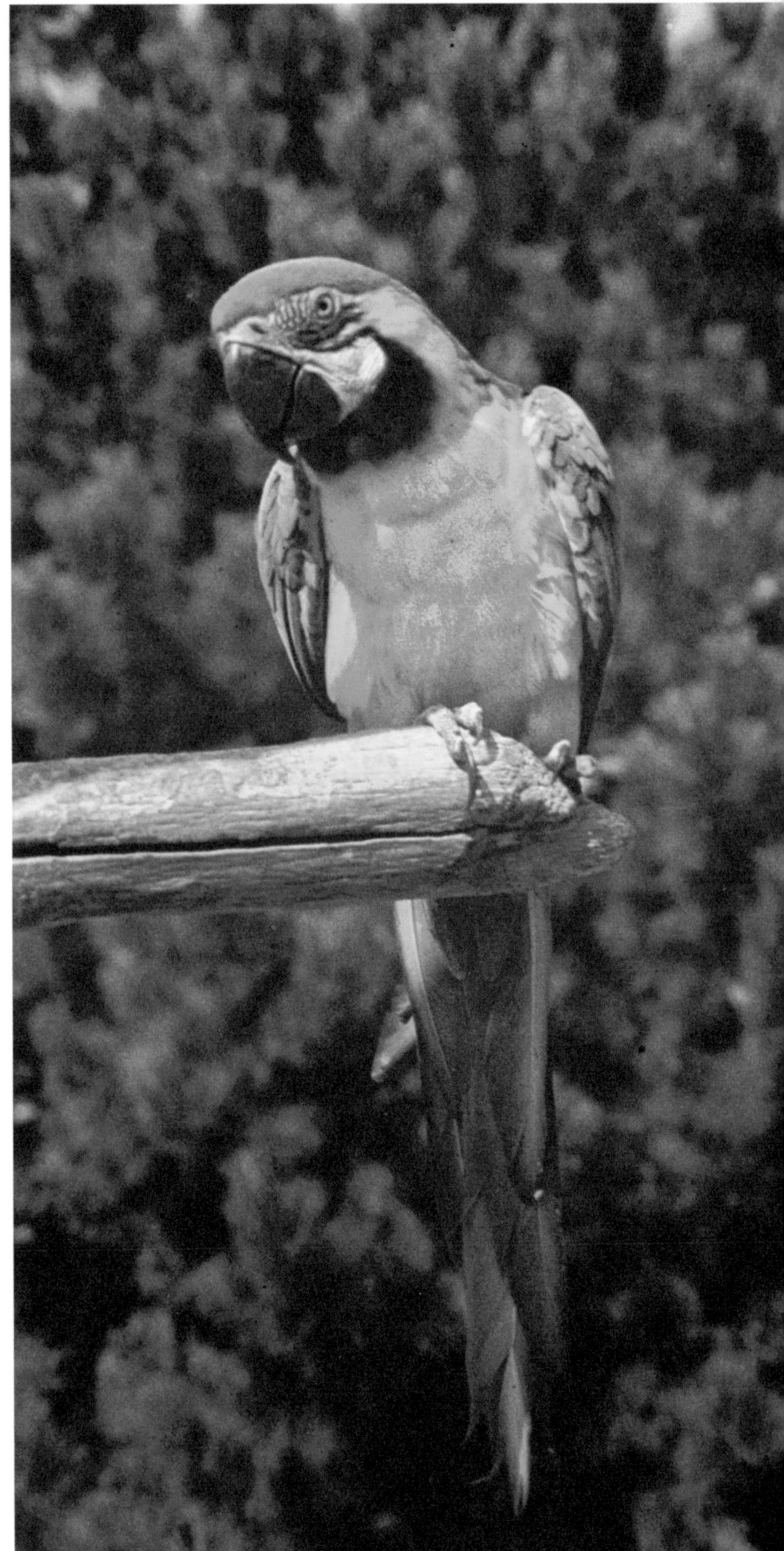

Above: Woodpeckers are the carpenters of the forest. They hammer at tree-trunks with their bills, which are as hard and sharp as steel and shaped like chisels, so that bits of bark fly off the trunks. Underneath they find the insects they feed on.
Below: The great tit is the biggest European tit, about the same size as the house-sparrow. It's always on the hunt for insects and grubs.

Does the wren build only one nest?

The tiny wren is a tireless nest-builder. He weaves about half a dozen nests at the same time, using twigs, lumps of moss, spiders' webs and damp grass. Next, he hangs these basket-like structures on the branch of a pine-tree and invites his mate to make a tour of inspection. When she finds a nest to her liking she moves in to lay her eggs, first lining the inside thickly with down feather. The remaining nests can be used as spares if the hen-bird has to leave the nest of her choice for some reason, such as damage by wind.

Which are the biggest and smallest birds of all?

The biggest bird of all is the ostrich. It can be up to 2.7 m high, and weighs about 150 kg. With its big round body and tiny wings it can't fly, however, but it can run at a speed of over 50 km an hour if an enemy is after it. The heaviest bird that can fly is the mute swan, which sometimes weighs over 20 kg. The bird with the widest wingspan is the great albatross, which comes from the South Sea Islands; in the nineteenth century a very few of these were captured in France and Belgium. When the wings are spread out they measure 3.6 m from top to tip. Runner-up in wingspan, is the Andean condor, a huge South American bird of prey with a wingspan of 3.2 m. The marabou has a wingspan of up to 2.6 m, although some naturalists state that it can be considerably wider.

Humming-birds (also called colibris) are among the smallest kinds of bird. Over 300 species have been counted, living in the humid tropical forests of the Amazon region, Zaire, India and Indochina, as well as several kinds native to high mountain regions, like the Andean humming-bird. This is the largest of the species, measuring 20 cm long. Half of this length consists of the tail. The smallest humming-bird – and therefore the smallest bird in the world – is the tiny bee humming-bird of Cuba, a dwarf species which feeds on nectar from blossoms. It is up to 5 cm long, half of which is accounted for by the body and the rest by the beak and tail. It has a white band between its red breast and the rest of its plumage, which is green. Humming-birds have very long slender bills, which they use to extract nectar, and sometimes insects, from the flowers.

Which bird does the most harm?

The quelea, a small African finch, is by far the most destructive bird. They are grain-eating birds which abound in the African grasslands, and the damage they cause to the cereal crops is all the more serious because they can be counted in millions. They build their nests close together in trees, between 50 and 300 to a tree – sometimes even a thousand – so that at times the branches crack under their weight.

At present it is estimated that there are 100,000 nests to the hectare. Queleas are a real scourge to agriculture, and are especially ruinous to rice crops. Poisonous chemicals have not so far proved an effective way of controlling these pests.

What are the colours of birds used for?

Generally speaking, you'll find more birds with protective colouring living in open spaces than among trees. Plumage is described as 'protective' or 'imitative' when the colouring of the feathers blends in with the bird's surroundings. With this natural means of camouflage the bird can't be seen so easily by its enemies.

The main reason that many male birds are more brightly coloured than female birds however, is that it is the males' way of attracting females for mating. The peacock, for instance, is well known for its attractive fan. Other male birds have attractive mating dances which are meant to attract the attention of the females.

Above left: The crow is really a songbird, although the raucous noise he makes when he sings can hardly be called tuneful. Crows make up for this by being highly intelligent. They build their nests in trees out of twigs, lined with scraps of wool, rags, etc.
Above right: The house sparrow is very fond of people. You'll never find sparrows in uninhabited places. Unfortunately, they can cause a lot of damage.
Below right: The starling shown here has a new coat of feathers after his moult, each feather outlined in a lighter shade. During the winter the light edges wear away, so that the plumage becomes darker, almost black.

Reptiles

By reptiles we generally mean creatures which crawl close to the ground – lizards, snakes, turtles, terrapins, tortoises and crocodiles. They are vertebrates, they breathe air and their temperature varies according to the temperature of their habitat. Most reptiles lay eggs with chalky shells.

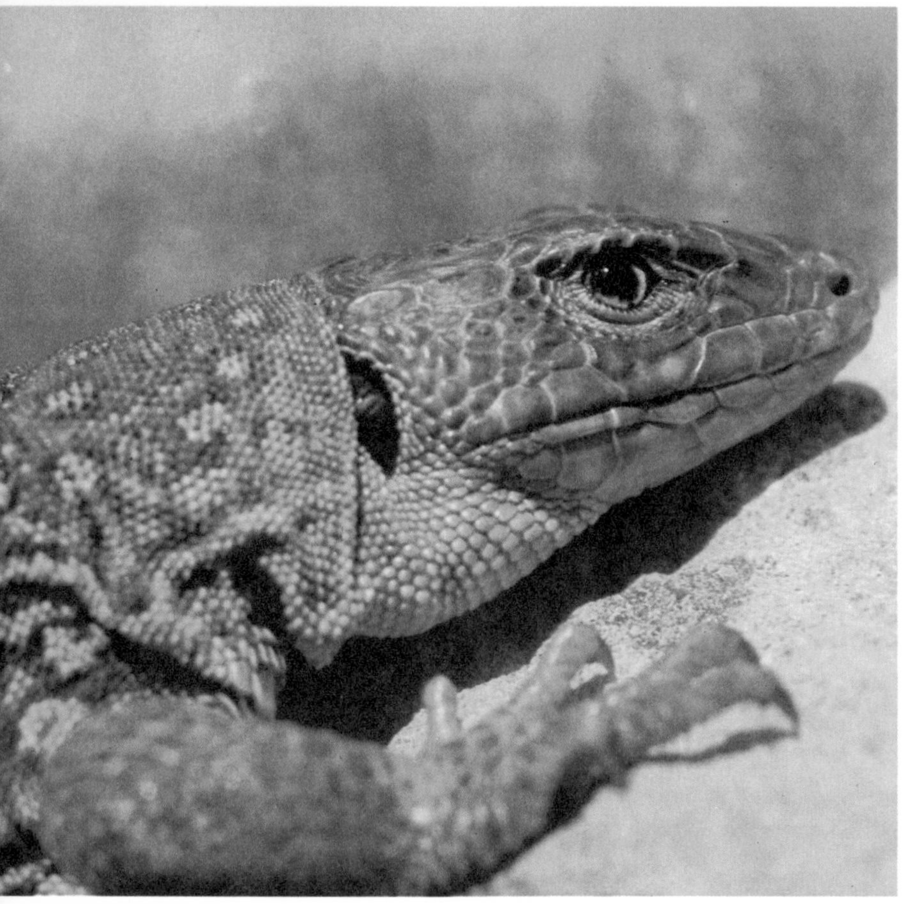

The small photo at the top shows the head of the grass snake, or ringed snake *(Natrix natrix)*. It is still quite common in this country but is now a protected species. It is completely harmless and can be recognized by the yellow markings round its neck. It eats frogs, fishes and insects. The large photograph below shows the head of a green lizard *(Lacerta viridis)*. You can see its clawed toes which help it to run quickly up vertical surfaces.

The ancestors of today's reptiles were amphibians. They were the first creatures to come out of the sea and adapt themselves to life on land, in the mesozoic age, over 200 million years ago. Starting with these primitive creatures, true reptiles gradually evolved and formed the biggest group of animals for over 100 million years. During this period gigantic dinosaurs stalked all over the world.

After this came a period of great changes. The climate, hitherto hot and humid, became more temperate. The damp marshlands dried up, so that much of the vegetation that fed these huge reptiles disappeared. Slowly but steadily these powerful, cold-blooded beasts fell victim to the great climatic upheavals, and died out. The only survivors of this wholesale death were the smaller species, which were better able to adapt to the lower temperature.

Where do turtles lay their eggs?

When the female turtle is nearly ready to lay, she comes out of the sea and heaves herself slowly up the beach, looking for a safe place to lay her eggs. With her four flippers, which help her to swim in the ocean, she begins digging a hole in the ground to make the nest. In a few hours she lays about 100 to 150 eggs. Then, despite her exhaustion, she must find the energy to bury them for warmth and protection.

After laying the eggs, the female turtle slowly crawls back to the sea and swims away. Later, the baby turtles hatch out and have to make their own way to the sea.

The baby turtles' journey is a hazardous one, and many of them never reach the sea as there are many birds of prey which regard them as delicious morsels.

Do reptiles hibernate?

In temperate climates which have warm summers and cold winters, most reptiles spend the winter in a deep sleep, lasting from the end of autumn to the beginning of spring. During this resting period – which is called hibernation – they lie sheltered in a safe place, hardly moving at all unless there is a period of mild weather. When spring returns, they come out to look for food.

Opposite: The Greek tortoise *(Testudo graeca)* is the most common variety of land tortoise, and is distinguished by its round, high-domed shell. Unfortunately it is often captured for sale in markets as a household pet. This should be stopped, because it means that Greek tortoises, which used to be widespread in southern Europe, are fast disappearing.

Opposite: The common iguana is the most typical of its species. It is very large, measuring up to two metres long, of which 45cm is body and the rest is the tail. It belongs to one of the largest lizard families, the Iguanidae.

How does a snake shed its skin?

Since snakes move about by wriggling along the ground, their skin wears out very quickly, and from time to time it has to be replaced. The new skin grows underneath the old one. When it's completely ready, the old skin becomes loosened around the jaws and the snake rubs itself on the ground. Gradually it crawls out of its old coat until it is completely free of it.

Are many reptiles poisonous?

Quite a number of snakes are poisonous, but most other reptiles are quite harmless. Among the 2450 known species of snake, only 175 are known whose venom is fatal to humans. There are only two species of poisonous lizard: the gila monster (*Heloderma suspectum*) which can be found in some American deserts, and the Mexican heloderma or bearded lizard (*Heloderma horridum*) of southern Mexico.

The hundreds of other lizard species are quite harmless. There are no poisonous tortoises, turtles, terrapins, or crocodiles.

How do snakes manage to swallow animals bigger than themselves?

The size and thickness of snakes varies enormously; some are thin like cord, and others – like the python – may be as thick as a man's leg and 10 m long. Yet all snakes can eat prey much bigger than themselves – and they always swallow their prey whole! The Indian, or reticulated, python of South East Asia is one of the largest snakes in the world. It can swallow a wild pig whole, or even a small deer. A case has even been recorded of a python strangling a stag weighing 56 kg and then devouring it. Feats like this are possible because the jaws of snakes are constructed very differently from our own – or even from any other animal for that matter. Our lower jaw is jointed to the upper jaw at ear-level; but snakes have an extra bone linking the ends of the two jaws so as to form a double joint. In addition, the upper

Below: The smooth snake *(Cornella austriaca)* lives in dry sandy places in parts of England, Holland and Belgium. It is less common than the adder and grass-snake. It is a harmless species, and gets its name from its predominantly brown skin, which is covered in smooth scales. Adults are between 50 and 60cm long.

Above top: The European pond tortoise *(Emys orbicularis)* is different in appearance from the Greek tortoise. Its shell is not nearly so humped, and its breastplate is much more flexible than the land tortoise's.
Above, lower photograph: A green gecko (*Phelsuma madagascariensis*). The geckonidae are a family of lizards which are distinguished by being the only reptiles to have a true voice.
Below right: The head of a young American alligator *(Alligator mississipiensis)*. Adult alligators are about two and half to three metres long and live in coastal estuaries in the south-east of the U.S.A. It is a great pity that young alligators are often specially bred to be sold for laboratory experiments.

and lower jaws can completely separate. This enables them to open their mouths very wide indeed.
Snakes swallow their victims whole – fur, feathers, shells, horns and all. Before devouring it, the snake usually kills its prey either by giving it a poisonous bite or by wrapping itself tightly round the victim's body until it stops breathing. The snake's teeth are curved backwards inside its mouth, so that once it has begun to swallow its prey it is difficult to spit it out.

How do lizards break off their tails?

When an animal such as a bird of prey or a carnivorous mammal tries to catch a lizard by the tail, the lizard can make an escape simply by leaving its tail behind! In the middle of its caudal region – the bones which make up the tail – there is a ring-shaped layer of muscle which is strong enough to break some particularly weak vertebrae at this point. In this way the tail detaches and wriggles about on its own to distract the attacker, while the lizard makes its getaway.

Are snakes and lizards useful?

The majority of lizards are actually very useful to mankind. They feed on insects, flies, beetles, grasshoppers, caterpillars and mosquitoes. Many of these insects cause harm to man or his crops. Only two kinds of lizard are poisonous.
Snakes are very fond of rodents. If you think of all the damage done every year by rodents of all kinds – especially to stored food products – you can see that any animal that hunts them down for food is performing a very useful service to mankind. However, it can happen that there are too many snakes in one particular region, and then special measures have to be taken to protect the populations of snake-eating creatures like the mongoose, or the secretary bird which lives in Africa and the Caribbean area.
In Florida in the U.S.A. and in Brazil, in South America, snakes are specially bred for medical purposes. From some snakes we manufacture the antiserum for injections to cure snake-bites.

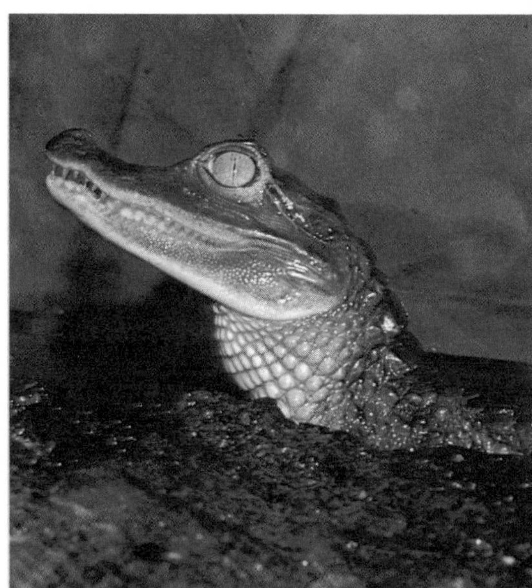

Amphibians

Amphibians are cold-blooded vertebrates which are born and spend the first part of their lives in water, but spend their adult lives both in water and on dry land.

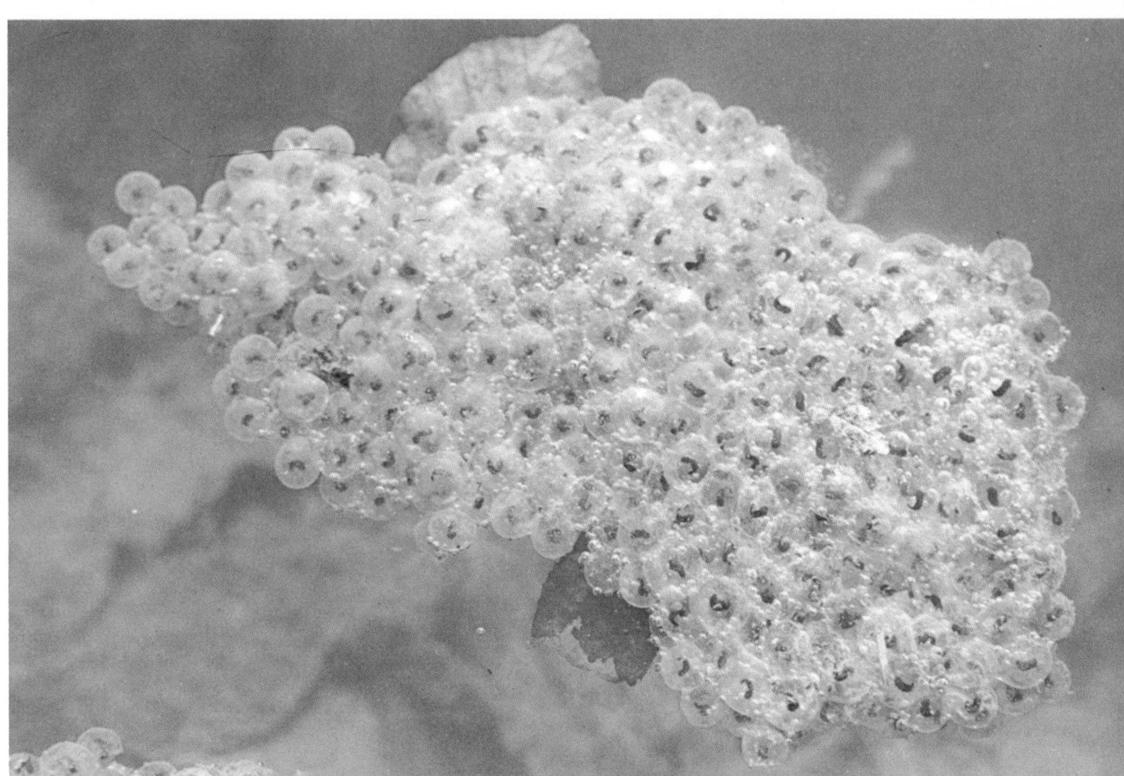

At the mating season the male frogs set up a chorus of croaking, which they produce by puffing out the pouches in their cheeks (see the photograph above).
Opposite: A mass of frog spawn.
Below: The metamorphosis of the common frog.

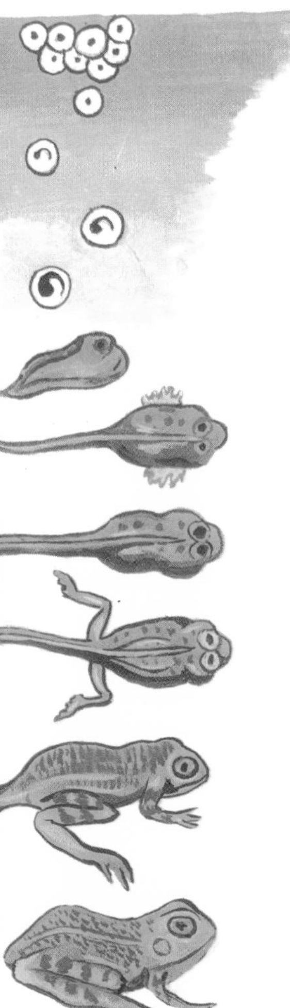

What is the origin of amphibians?

Millions of years ago, when the world was covered in moist swamps and tall fern-like trees grew everywhere, some strange, fish-like creatures came out of the water and ventured on to dry land. These were the ancestors of today's amphibians. Now that they no longer had the water to support them, their fins gradually changed into feet. These would, of course, be more useful for life on land. They had to adapt to land life in another way, too: gradually they had to stop breathing through gills and develop lungs.

How do amphibians reproduce themselves?

In spring, after mating in ponds, the female frogs lay thousands of eggs. These eggs, or spawn, which look like black specks in a jelly-like mass, can be seen round the water weeds at the bottom of the pond. After a length of time which depends both on the species and the temperature of the water, tiny tadpoles emerge from the eggs. To begin with, the young tadpoles have a long tail but no legs. They are able to fend for themselves, however, and they feed on algae – tiny water plants – and microscopic water creatures.

As they develop, their gills and tails start to disappear and they begin to grow limbs. At this point the tadpoles come to the surface of the water to breathe the air with their newly acquired lungs. Once the gills and tails have completely gone, the little frogs emerge to spend their lives near water, venturing back only to lay their eggs.

How many kinds of amphibians are there?

Amphibians are divided into three separate orders: the Anura (frogs and toads, which

have no tails when fully grown); the Apoda (underground amphibians which have no limbs) and the Urodela (salamanders and newts, which have limbs and a tail).
Within these three orders there is a wide range of different species. They vary in size from the Giant Salamander (*Megalobatrachus*) found in China and Japan, which can be up to 1 m in length, to tiny frogs only 1 cm long.

Why do we find more frogs and toads than salamanders?

The main reason we find more frogs and toads than salamanders is because salamanders are nocturnal creatures, and they usually make their homes in dark, sheltered places.

Are there some salamanders with no eyes?

Yes, in the caves of Karst, in Yugoslavia, and in Texas, Georgia and Missouri in the U.S.A., a species of salamander can be found, which is called the olm. This strange creature has no eyes, but despite this apparent handicap it lives very successfully and it can distinguish light from dark by means of organs called light recaptors which are found under the skin. It lives on scraps of vegetation, grubs and small crustaceans. This urodele seems to be remarkably well adapted to its environment.

Are there any other amphibians besides frogs, toads, newts and salamanders?

Yes, there are several other types of amphibian. One such is the gymnophiona, which lives in damp, tropical forests and is also classed as an amphibian. It spends its life completely underground; its limbs have completely disappeared and its tiny eyes can hardly see. In fact it is often mistaken for a kind of worm. Gymnophionae are descendants of the first amphibian to venture on to dry land. They lay their eggs in small streams. When the larvae hatch out they swim up-current in order to continue their growth. But once they are fully grown,

Above: The alpine newt (*Triturus alpestris*) is found mainly in central and western Europe. It is one of the eight European species of urodele. During the mating season the male's orange-red colouring is highly spectacular.

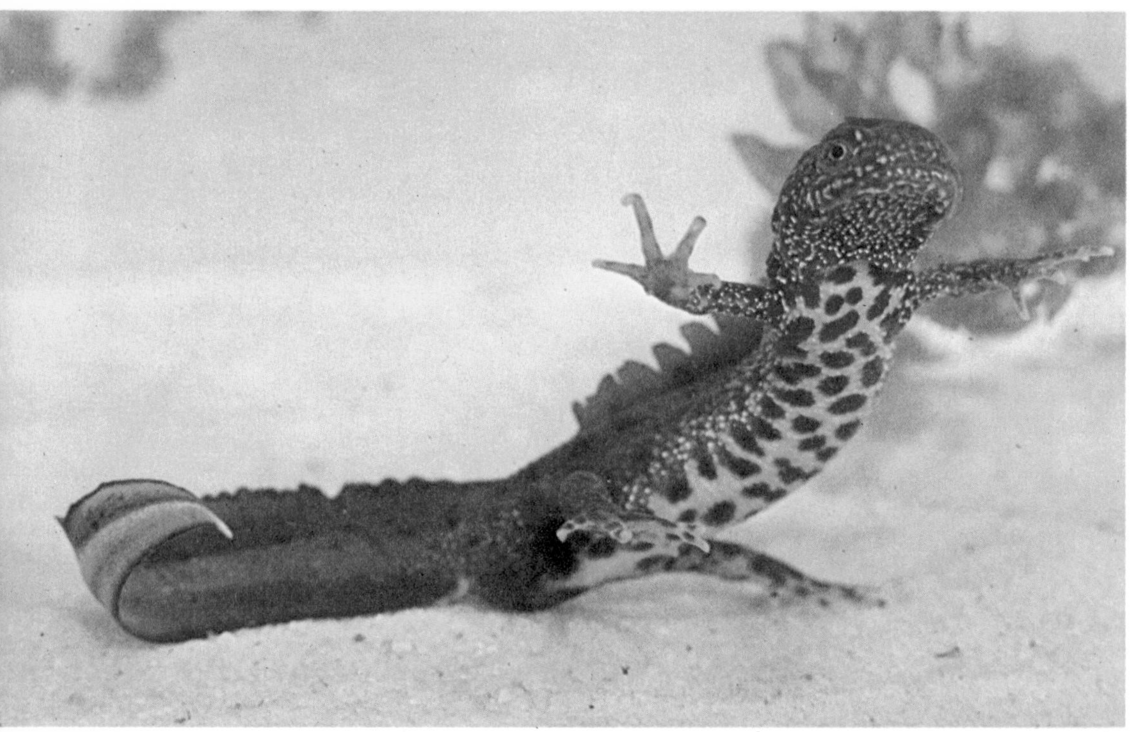

Opposite: The warty or great crested newt (*Triturus cristatus*), common in our part of the world, is quite big – 16cm long. This photograph shows a male in a characteristic pose, spreading out his forelimbs and balancing on his tail to show off his bright yellow stomach to the female. This is an invitation to mate, and the female has to respond by going through a particular kind of dance. Mating can't take place until this ritual has been performed.

they move on to dry land and spend the rest of their lives in holes in the ground.

How do you tell a frog from a toad?

A lot of people confess to having a feeling of distaste towards toads, and it is true that toads are often uglier than frogs. Toads are compact, and have a drier, warty skin. Their faces are flatter than frogs' and their legs are shorter. They spend most of their lives on dry land, and move about more ponderously than frogs, either by walking or by making small hops. Toads like to find themselves a shelter under a stone or some leaves, and only come out when the temperature and the weather suit them. Frogs are much more active, agile and lively animals than toads. They can swim well, and can also jump great distances.

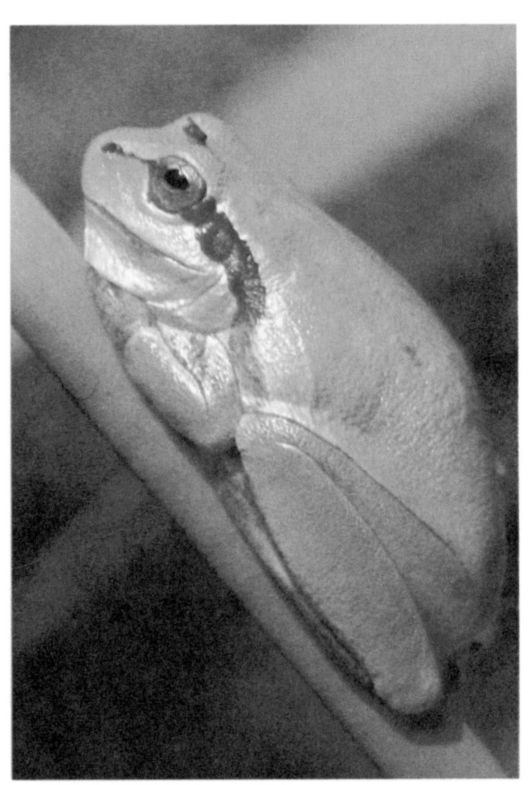

Do frogs live in trees?

Frogs have adapted themselves to all kinds of living conditions. There are some 500 species of tree-dwelling frogs, which have fingers equipped with adhesive suckers. In Malaysia there is even a variety of tree-frog called a 'flying frog', which is specially adapted for a gliding kind of flight. Its feet are almost entirely webbed, and when it jumps from a great height it spreads them out, which helps it to glide. It really drops from the top of trees rather than flying properly. This enables it to catch insects which it couldn't catch by leaping from the ground. It can also escape from snakes in this manner.

Top: **The common frog is quite common in our part of the world. It is distinguished from the edible frog by the dark patches beside its eyes. It comes in all shades of brown.**
Above: **The natterjack toad *(Bufo calamita)* lives in sandy soil and coastal regions.**
Left: **Tree-frogs are most common in tropical regions. Most of them feed on insects living in tree-bark or under leaves. They have sucker-like discs on their toes which enable them to climb up smooth surfaces.**

Fish

Fish have played an important part in the process of evolution; for it was from fish that the first land animals arose. They are the most numerous inhabitants of water, and are found in fresh, salt and brackish conditions.

Above: **The common pirana (*Serrasalmus nattereri*). It has a terrible reputation, which it richly deserves. This little member of the salmon family, shaped like a carp about 10cm long, is one of the most fearsome flesh-eaters in the world.**

Below: **The *Melanotaenia nigrans* is about 7cm long. You can see it in an aquarium.**

Do fishes have skeletons?

This is an important question, because one of the ways that biologists divide animals is into vertebrates and invertebrates, according to whether or not they have a vertebral column, or spine. The spine is part of the skeleton. The spine is a hard column made up of movable bones which supports the back. The ribs, skull and limb bones are also part of the skeleton. The cavity containing the body organs – such as the heart and lungs – is protected by the rib cage bones. Run your hand down the middle of a friend's back, or your own; the bumps you can feel are the vertebrae, and the whole lot make up the vertebral column.

Now imagine a nice grilled herring. The bones in a line down the centre are the vertebral column. So fish must be classified as vertebrates.

How do fish swim?

You may have thought that fish swim with their fins, but although most fishes make movements with their fins, fishes swim by making S-shaped movements with the rear half of their body and the tail.

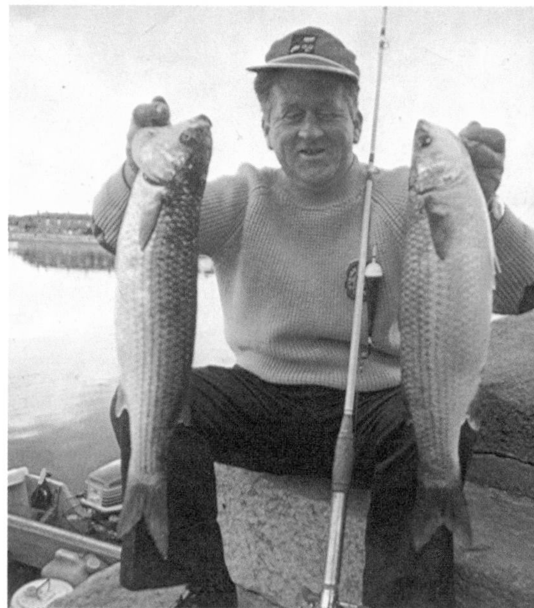

Fishing isn't always a vital necessity. Lots of people fish just as a sport or hobby.

Of course, it takes muscles to make these swimming movements. These are the white flesh of the fish, running down both sides of the body. They are the part you eat.

You can't eat the very end of the tail, which is called the caudal fin. This consists of a membrane, or fine skin, on a framework of bony spokes, and it enables the fish to make very wide swishing movements to increase its speed when swimming. The fish is thus able to propel itself forward by making a series of side to side movements with its tail.

Before examining the fins, let us have a look at the body. It has an interesting shape, really like a rain-drop, with the round, flat head at the front and the tail end narrowing to a point. You can see this from the front as well as from the sides and top and bottom. Zoologists have proved that this is the shape best suited to movement in water. In other words, a fish, being streamlined, meets with less resistance from the water so that it can swim very fast. The same thing goes for racing cars, ships, aeroplanes and everything else that's designed to move with speed or with little resistance.

Although fish wouldn't get very far without some means of moving themselves forward, they also need steering and balancing organs. These come in the form of fins. There are two kinds of fins, paired and single, all made up of a fine skin supported by slender, bony rods called fin-rays. These are sometimes so sharp that an inexperienced fisherman, who may not be careful how he handles a fish, can hurt himself on the dorsal fin.

The paired fins include the pectoral fins, which are near the gills, and the pelvic fins, usually about half-way down the belly. These act as brakes. If the fish wants to stop, it simply turns its paired fins against the water. These paired fins – in particular the pectoral fins – also enable the fish to swim vertically – upwards or downwards – by placing them at a slightly oblique angle.

Another important swimming organ in some fish is the swim-bladder, a sort of gas bag in the fish's body, usually connected to the throat. This can be filled up with gas to make the fish lighter. Thus, when the bladder is empty, with almost no gas in it, the fish is relatively heavy and has a tendency to sink. To climb up again it has to blow up the swim-bladder.

The main function of single fins is to help the fish move in a straight line. They serve the same purpose as the keel of a boat, which is to prevent it from rolling over sideways. The fish has two fixed fins, the dorsal fin on its back and the anal fin on its underside. The caudal fin, or tail fin, is one of the single fins.

How do fishes breathe?

You have already read in this book about gills. You can visualize them as a book full of pages covered with tiny blood vessels. The oxygen in the water (there's more in cold

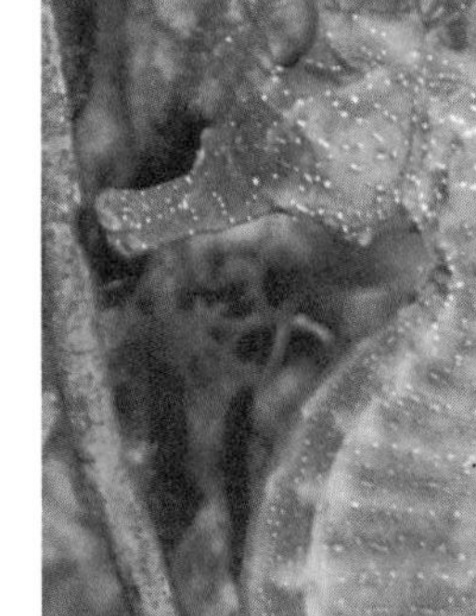

Above: The sea-horse, with its horse-shaped head, is a real fish although it doesn't look like one. It swims upright, using only its dorsal fin. It has a very tiny mouth which it can't open, so it has to suck in its food. The sea-horse also looks after its babies in a rather unusual way: the female lays her eggs in a fold in the male's stomach, and the young fish are carried about in this pouch until they can look after themselves.

Left: The cardinal tetra, originally thought to be a sub-group of the famous neon tetra, is one of the most beautiful aquarium fishes. The red colouring of its underside continues up under its throat, differentiating it from the subtropical neon tetra. Its back is a magnificent brilliant blue which can turn bright green in reaction to shock or a change of temperature. In a subtropical aquarium these fish group themselves in schools at a temperature of 23° to 25°C.

Below left: The African cichlid *(Haplochromis enchilus)* carries its fertilized eggs in its mouth. When they hatch out the mother fish keeps the babies round her and feeds them on food she has chewed up beforehand.

Below right: Our rivers used to be full of these beautiful fish, salmon, but nowadays their numbers have been reduced by pollution. Adult salmon spend most of their lives in the sea, but they always lay their eggs in fresh water. They are famous for the spectacular leaps they make when swimming upstream.

Above: **The *Glyphidontops hemicyaneus* is a small fish, about 7cm long. A shoal of these tiny fishes is capable of chasing off a large octopus.**

water than in warm) passes through these fine membranes into the blood, while carbon dioxide is filtered out and goes back into the water. This continuous process of taking in oxygen and getting rid of carbon dioxide is maintained by the movements the fish makes as it opens and closes its mouth in the water. If the fish leaves the water the 'pages' cling to each other so that the gills become like a closed book. A fish is specially designed to breathe the oxygen dissolved in water. A fish can't survive unless it stays in water; if it is taken out, it dies. When a fisherman takes a fish out of the water to remove the hook, he must return it to the water quickly so it can continue breathing.

Why do fish never bump into each other?

As well as the swim-bladder, which is an important organ for keeping the fish buoyant, fishes also possess an organ which can detect vibrations in the water – this is called the lateral line. You can often see this line in the form of a thin, sometimes coloured stripe, along the sides of a fish. The latteral line consists of a long tube going from the head to the tail of the fish, and contains a whole series of smaller tubes which are in contact with the water around the fish. It looks rather like a comb. When the fish swims along, the water round it moves. The waves it makes are picked up as vibrations by the nerves in the lateral line. This enables the fish to sense if there is anything in its way.
Fish can detect movements and probably shapes; they can discern sound vibrations, are sensitive to touch and are aware of the taste and smell of anything immersed or dissolved in the water.
The sense of balance is extremely important, too. This sense is situated in the semicircular canals of the ear. In the internal ear there are also some chalky formations called otoliths which tell the fish whether it is the correct way up or not.

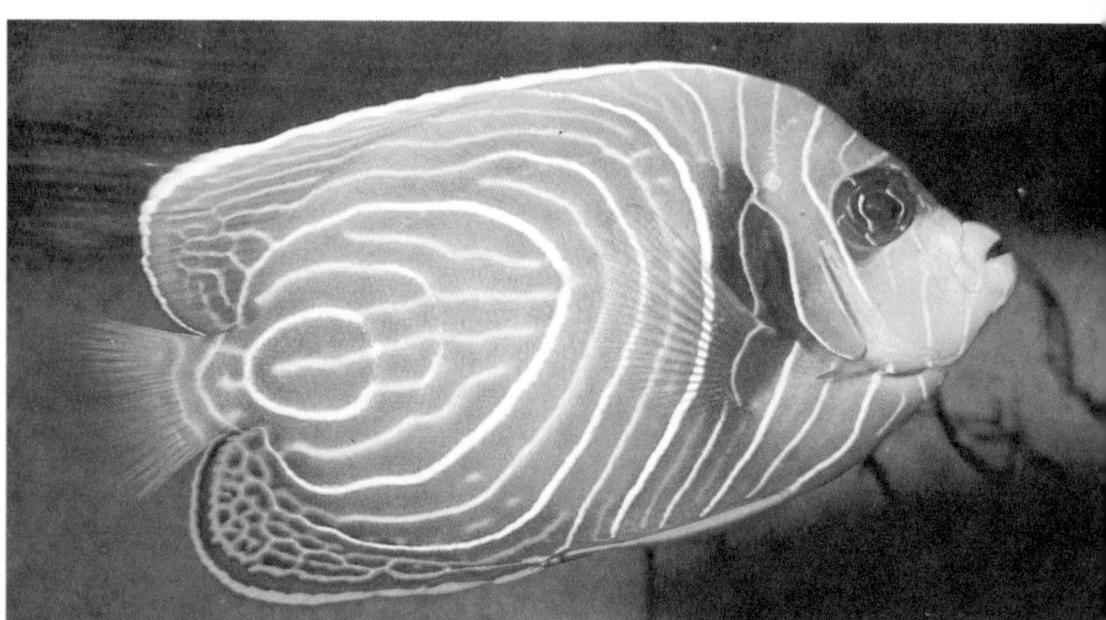

Right: **A young *Pomacanthus imperator.* It is difficult to describe its appearance, as the babies look quite different from the adults. If they didn't, the adults would chase them away or eat them.**
Below: **The two-coloured surgeon fish owes its name to the scalpel-shaped spine a centimetre long at the base of its tail. The fish can use it as a weapon; when it lashes its tail it can cause some nasty injuries.**

What is a flatfish?

To begin with, there are some genuine flatfish, and others which just *look* like flatfish. For example, plaice, turbot, soles and dabs, are proper flatfish.

Rays look like flatfish, but together with sharks they belong to a different group of fishes, that of the cartilaginous fishes. Cartilaginous fishes have a simpler body system than the type of fish called bony fish – which includes flatfish, as well as fish such as herrings. Cartilaginous fish also have different shaped bodies and tails; the upper part of the tail is usually larger than the lower part.

Rays are flattened from top to bottom. Real flatfish (which as we have seen are bony fish) are far more complex than that. When they are small they look like other fish. But they grow up flattened from side to side, so that one side becomes the under side, and the fins that appear to go around them are in fact their dorsal, pelvic and anal fins. The lower eye also moves round to the top side. Their mouths have also grown to one side. With their peculiar shape they are well suited to live buried in the sand on the seabed, however.

Above: *The platax* ***(Platax orbicularis)****.* **When they are frightened, these fishes slowly sink to the bottom like dead leaves.**

What do we use fish for?

First of all, fish are very good to eat, whether boiled, baked, grilled or fried. They contain many of the proteins we need, and which are only otherwise found in meat and vegetables.

Then you can go fishing, either by yourself, or with an experienced angler who knows about fishing methods and how to maintain the natural balance of water life.

An easier way of watching the various habits of fish would be to get your own collection together in an aquarium. It's also a good way of observing the relationship that exists between fishes and other water-animals and plants. Plenty of books will tell you how to do this.

Below left: **The jack-in-the-box lives in the sandy depths, where it burrows holes at least 35cm deep.** ***Below right:*** **The white-tailed surgeon fish is a beautiful fish which can live in aquariums filled with warm sea-water. The spines on their tails can do a lot of damage to other fish. They eat a lot of algae, and in aquariums they are often fed on spinach.**

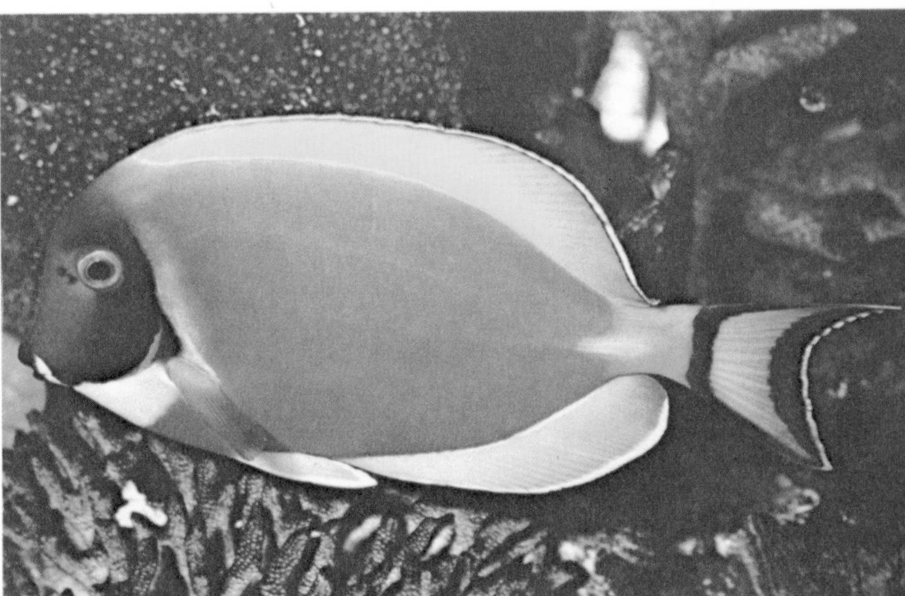

Above: The eggs of the stick insect shown on the right. Although the males and females mate, the females are able to lay eggs without mating. So a single stick-insect can produce a whole family. Stick insects imitate branches and twigs, and there are leaf insects that look like leaves – they are a perfect example of imitation as a means of camouflage. At rest, they can scarcely be distinguished from the branches or leaves of the plants they live and feed on.

Insects

Although insects make up by far the largest group of animals in the world, many people know practically nothing about them. Usually our knowledge of insects is limited to admiring the beauty of butterflies or scratching ourselves when we get bitten by a mosquito.

What is an insect?

There's a lot of confusion about what insects actually are. How can you tell an insect from all the other sorts of tiny creatures?

If you look at an insect, with or without a magnifying glass, you can see that its body is made up of three main parts: the head, thorax and abdomen. Creatures that do not possess this clear distinction belong to other species in the animal world. For example, animals with a clearly separate head but whose thorax and body merge into one (like many crustaceans) are not insects, even if they are very small.

Another important feature is the number of legs. All adult insects have six legs, or perhaps it would be more correct to say that most insects have three pairs of legs. These legs are attached to the thorax, never to any other part of the body, and that's one of the best ways of being sure that it's an insect. For example, a spider has eight legs – or rather, four pairs of legs, and that's one reason why it isn't an insect, but instead belongs to a separate group. A third characteristic is a bit more tricky, because there are many exceptions to the rule, but generally speaking, insects have two pairs of wings which are attached to the hard shell of the thorax.

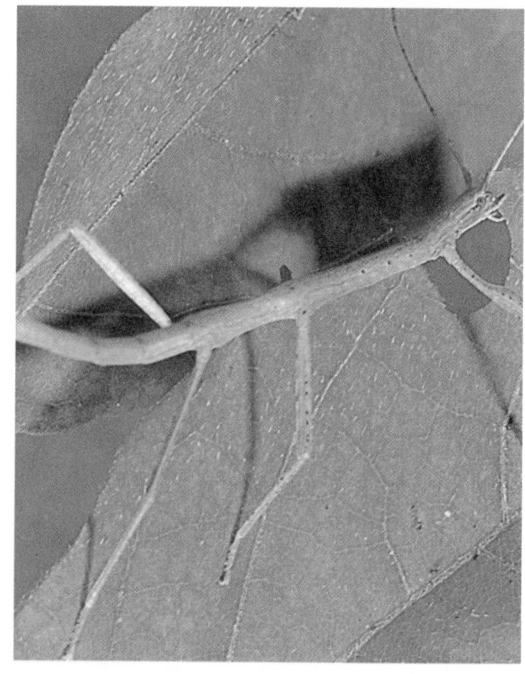

However, many insects – for example, members of the Diptera order, which includes flies and mosquitoes – only have two wings.

Opposite: Long-horned grasshoppers *(Tettigonidae)* are very attractive creatures, usually green, and distinguished by their long antennae. In European countries the most common grasshopper is the great green grasshopper *(Tettigonia viridissima)*; its loud chirping can usually be heard throughout August and September. This noise is called stridulation; long-horned grasshoppers produce it by rubbing their front wings together, while short-horned grasshoppers rub their hind legs against their wings. Grasshoppers are immediately recognizable by their back legs, which are very long in proportion to the rest of the body, and enable them to leap very high. To jump, they contract their legs and straighten them out again quickly.

Other types of insect either never have wings or only have them during a certain phase of their life. Coleoptera (beetles) do have four wings, but the front pair is hardened into wing cases, called elytra. Underneath these is another pair of wings which are folded up when not in use for flying. Have a look at a ladybird or some other small beetle when not in flight, and you will see the elytra.
Many insects, in their larvae stage, look completely different from the adults. Think of the caterpillar, which is a young butterfly. The butterfly is an insect, for you can see clearly that it has a head, a thorax and an abdomen, six legs and four wings.

Do insects have skeletons?

If by the word 'skeleton' we mean a structure consisting of a series of bones surrounded by muscles, organs and skin, then it is true to say that the insect does not have one, and is therefore an invertebrate. However, it does have a very strong, rigid structure to which its muscles and tissues are attached, and which protects its delicate inner organs. So insects have a kind of hard skeleton on the outside, which is called an exoskeleton. It is called an exoskeleton because 'exo' means outside; hence it is an 'outside skeleton'.
Let us take a look at a relation of the insect class, the shrimp. When it's boiled for eating you can remove its shell, and inside you find the soft muscles and organs. What you have removed is its exoskeleton, for all the arthropods (which includes insects, spiders, crabs, shrimps, etc.) have them.
The exoskeleton is very important, first of all as a defence against natural threats, like predators. Clearly this shell can't protect the

Above: **The field cricket *(Gryllus campestris)* is distinguished by its fairly short antennae and wings which don't go beyond the rear part of the body – the abdomen. Like house crickets, field crickets are famous for their loud chirping.**
Below: **This insect is a member of the cicada family *(Cicadidae).* Male cicadas have a special drum-like organ, called a tymbal, covered with two membranes placed in the lower part of the body. This complicated mechanism produces such a loud stridulation that crickets have the reputation of being the noisiest insect of all.**

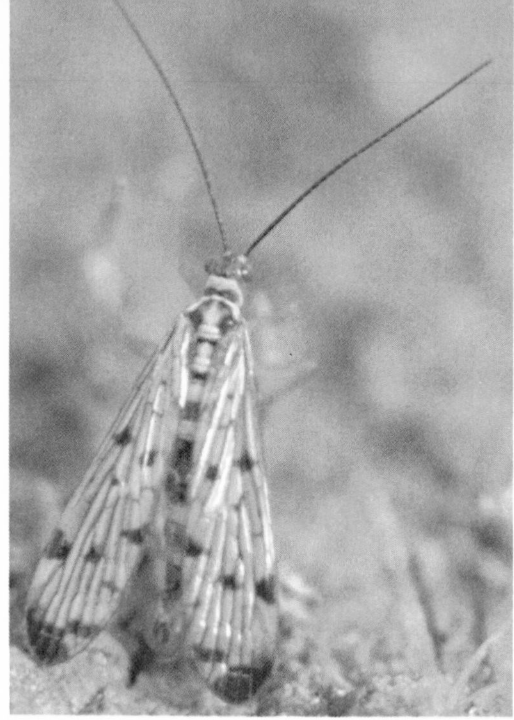

insect against everything; birds and moles, for example, aren't at all put off by it. They simply crunch it up to eat the insect within. To defend itself against enemies like these, insects have to use other methods, like the ability to bite or sting, sometimes using poison. We are familiar with this among mosquitoes, wasps, ants and others. The exoskeleton has another means of protection in the form of colouring, which can be used either as a form of concealment or to scare others away. This is used, for instance, by many butterflies. Predators are startled when a peacock butterfly suddenly opens out its wings, and this gives the butterfly time to escape. The exoskeleton has a wax layer to avoid the body losing water in land-dwelling insects. And finally, there are also some insects which have such a horrific appearance that they fool their enemies into thinking they are very dangerous, so that they are often left alone. Similarly, other insects may have an unpleasant smell or taste, so predators avoid them.

How do insects fly?

Insects use their hard exoskeleton for flying. The flight of birds and the flight of insects may have a similar end-result, but the mechanisms involved are completely different. (Resemblances like this are called analagous, and are often found in nature.) Birds and bats fly by means of wings operated by muscles attached between the breastbone and the 'arms'. In insects, however, there are movable joints between the wings and the thorax; the wings are not rigidly fixed to the thorax, but are in fact outgrowths from its hard wall provided with blood vessels (which you can clearly see in the wings of flies and butterflies). An insect uses the muscles attached inside the exoskeleton to alter its shape and pull the wings up and down. Thus, when the horizontal muscles which run between the top and bottom of the thorax contract the thorax becomes longer, taking on an oval shape, and the wings are forced down; when the muscles attached between the back and front of the exoskeleton contract, the thorax becomes flatter and wider and the wings are pulled up again. These movements all happen very quickly, and enable the insect's wings to beat quickly.

Why do insects lay so many eggs?

If you are interested in nature, you might have looked under a leaf and seen an enormous number of insect eggs laid there. The reason there are so many is

Left: There are five different species of scorpion fly _(Panorpa communis)_ in our part of the world. They are quite small insects which take their name from the pincers at the end of the male's abdomen.
Below: The little housefly _(Fannia canicularis)_ is an important member of the diptera family, which have two wings.
The large photo at the bottom shows a dung-beetle. The characteristics of the coleoptera are clearly visible here – the front wings are hardened into elytra.

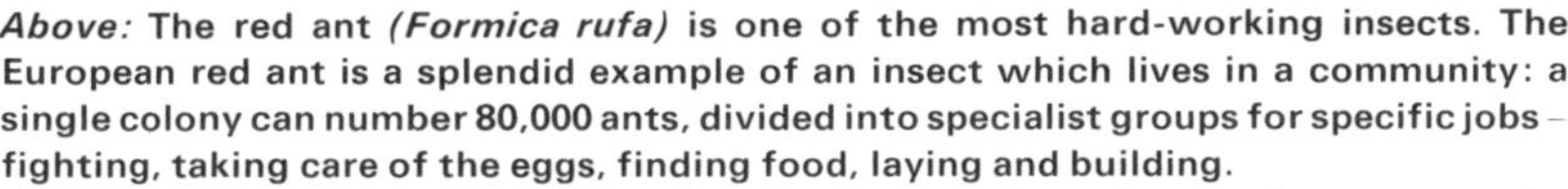

Above: The red ant *(Formica rufa)* is one of the most hard-working insects. The European red ant is a splendid example of an insect which lives in a community: a single colony can number 80,000 ants, divided into specialist groups for specific jobs – fighting, taking care of the eggs, finding food, laying and building.
Above right: The brimstone butterfly *(Gonepteryx rhamni)* owes its name to the yellow colouring of the male. Butterflies are good examples of metamorphosis, with their eggs hatching out as caterpillars.
Opposite: The eggs of the peacock butterfly *(Vanessa io)* in the process of hatching out. The caterpillars will in turn become chrysalids, from which the fully-grown butterfly finally emerges.

because the enemies of insects – chiefly other insects – eat enormous quantities of them. Generally the eggs are quite well protected against frost and drought, although a great many more hatch out after a mild winter than after a hard one. Even many larvae and caterpillars – which are the newly hatched young – get eaten up before they can grow into adults. So, for there to be enough adult insects, there have to be a lot of eggs.

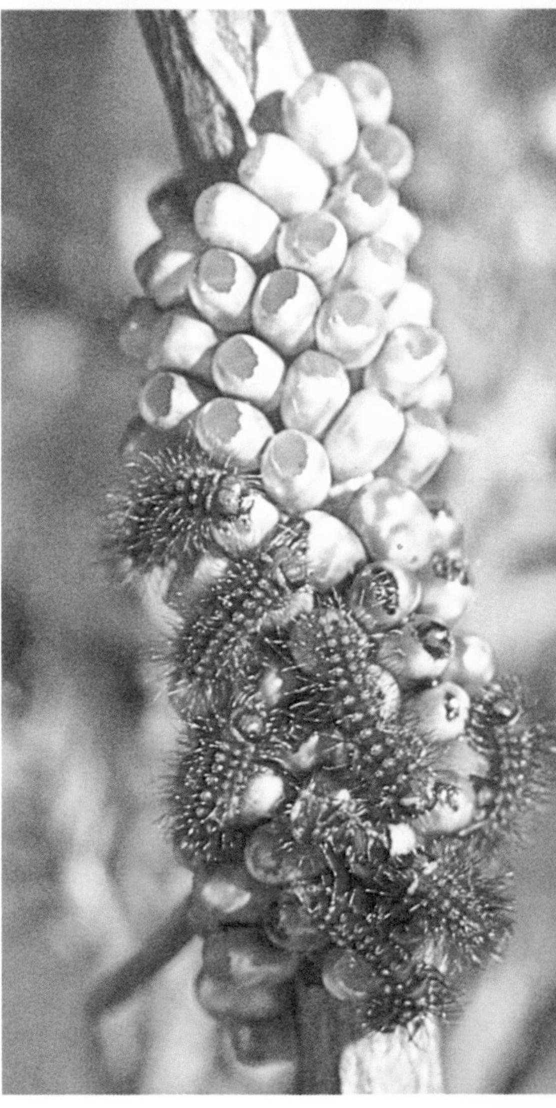

Why shouldn't we use anti-insect sprays?

Insects form the largest group in the whole animal kingdom, and are an important link in the balance of nature. Very often they carry pollen to plants, and they provide a large source of food for other creatures, such as birds, fishes, amphibians, reptiles, and insect-eating mammals.
When we use poisonous chemicals to kill harmful insects, the poison also enters the bodies of these insectivores – as biologists call these insect-eating animals. Moreover, the insectivores are eaten in their turn by predators – which is sometimes man himself. So when we use these sprays we are not only destroying the insect life, but also all the animals in this food chain, at the same time reducing the supply of fertilizer that feeds the plant kingdom.
Sometimes these insect-killing chemicals can cause damage to the egg shells of birds which eat the insects or makes them produce sterile young.

Lower Animals

The great majority of the animal kingdom – nearly 95 per cent – consists of 'lower animals'. Some zoologists include all the invertebrates as lower animals, others only call the most primitive invertebrates 'lowly'.

Above: **The *Porcellio scaber* can be found under any stone and in any damp place.**
Opposite: **The starfish belongs to the order of Forcipulata. You can clearly see its legs, head and body. Its body is not in fact the same all over; at one place it has a kind of scale called the madreporite, which lets water in through a system of vessels, enabling the suckers on its legs to function.**
Below: **The garden spider *(Araneus diadematus)* is very common everywhere. Despite its eight clearly constructed legs, it is considered a lower animal.**

Why are some animals called lower'?

When we talk of lower animals, we don't mean they are low down on the ground. What we mean is that they are primitive in body form and function. On the scale of evolution, with the unicellular animals on the bottom rung and man at the top with other highly specialized animals, lower animals come low down the scale. They were probably the earliest forms of life, and the history of their evolution goes back for thousands of millions of years.

The origin and development of life on earth – which is what evolution is – probably began in the warm oceans with a unicellular plant similar to the *phytoplankton* of today, many varieties of which still live in the sea and in fresh water. Phytoplankton, like other green plants, is able to manufacture the food it needs out of the minerals present in seawater, using the energy from sunlight. These microscopic plants have also made animal life possible on land, for they provided food for the first sea animals, which in turn evolved into land-dwelling forms. The earliest forms of animal life must have been very similar to some of the tiny zooplankton creatures which exist today.

Are there many lower animals?

There are a great many species of lower animals (if we mean all invertebrates) and a great number of individual animals within each species. For instance, there are nearly a million known species of insects alone! We shall look at the major groups of invertebrates now, starting with the most advanced and finishing with the most lowly.The most advanced is the Cephalochordata, the best known species of which is the amphioxus. These animals are a link between the invertebrates and the vertebrates, and they have a spinal cord, an organ going down the back which supports them, like the bones of the vertebral column in vertebrates.

There is no vertebral column in echinoderms, whose name – which means prickle-skinned' – comes from the fact that some members of the species have tiny spines made of lime or silicon. These include starfish, sea-cucumbers, sea-urchins, sand dollars and brittle stars. All echinoderms are marine animals.

By far the largest group of animals is that of the arthropods. These animals have limbs divided into several parts. The different sections of the legs, antennae and mouth parts can be clearly seen. Insects, crabs, lobsters, prawns, scorpions, ticks and spiders are all arthropods; so are water-fleas and shrimps. Arthropods can occur in almost all environments – on land, in the sea and in fresh water.

Arthropods probably originally developed from segmented worms, whose bodies can usually be seen to be divided into subdivisions, or segments. Have a look at an earthworm, which is a very well known member of this group. Its body is entirely made up of separate rings. Other segmented worms include leeches and peacock worms.

Above: **The garden snail *(Cepaea hortensis)* is a fine example of a mollusc. Its shell is often attractively striped. The different shades of colour may act as a camouflage against blackbirds, among others. The markings tend to vary according to the snail's habitat.**

Another very large class (containing many thousands of species) is that of the molluscs, which you probably know best as slugs and snails. Shell-bearing molluscs are in turn divided into *univalves* (or gastropods), like snails; and *bivales* like cockles and mussels. Octopuses and cuttlefish also belong to the mollusc group. The 'cuttlebone', which you can find on beaches and which is hung up in bird cages, is regarded by biologists as its shell, although it's actually inside the cuttlefish.

Molluscs and segmented worms have evolved from all kinds of roundworms and flatworms, even more simply formed, and from tiny animals which live in colonies.

Corals and jellyfish belong to the large group of coelenterates and are sometimes considered as links between the higher, more advanced animals and the lowliest forms of all, the sponges and the unicellular protozoans.

Unicellular animals and plants provide a huge source of food, especially in the colder seas, and thus make it possible for other forms of life to exist.

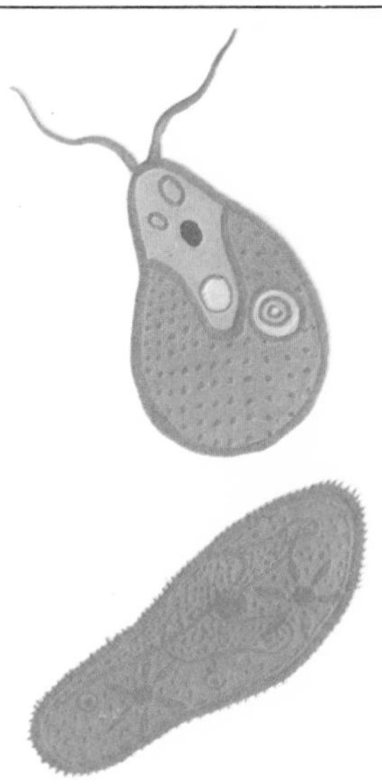

Where unicellular creatures are concerned, it's sometimes hard to tell if we are dealing with a plant or an animal. This tiny chamydomanas belongs on the 'plant side' of the animal kingdom. It is an animal which can make its own food, just like a plant. The same goes for the volvox, a tiny animal which lives in colonies, and some other related colonial animals. In this drawing you can also see a paramecium *(Paramecium caudatum)*, a unicellular animal measuring about 0.3mm.

Below: **If you're not an expert, its very difficult to put a label on creatures like the sea-anemone, sea-cucumber or dahlia-anemone *(Tealia felina)* shown here. They look like plants, but they are true animals belonging to the coelenterate group, and which catch their prey with poisonous tentacles.**

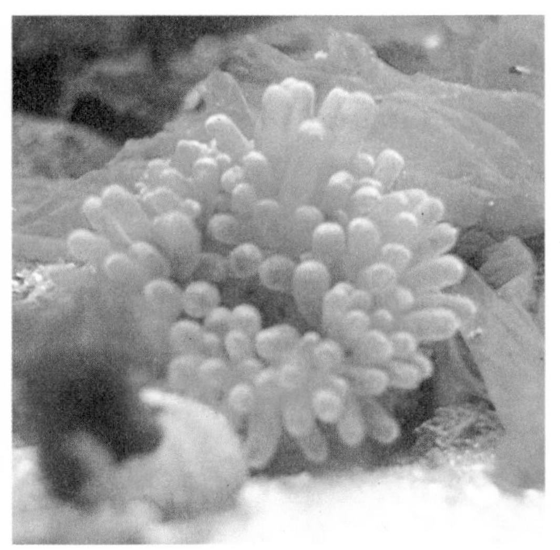

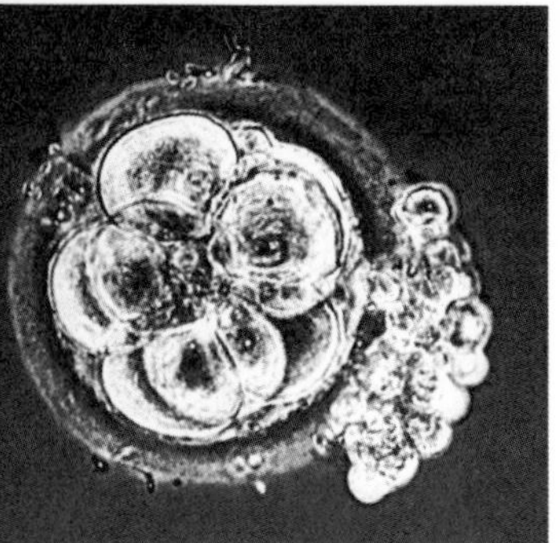

Man

The Human Body

Of all forms of life on earth. Man has reached the most advanced stage of evolution. His brain gives him the ability to think and to adapt his surroundings to suit his own needs.

Above: **Once the human egg, or ovum, has been fertilized in the fallopian tube, it quickly begins to develop. It takes nine months for it to reach full maturity, and during this time it goes through a vast number of important changes.**

Below left: **An embryo a few weeks old inside the womb or uterus. The limbs are already starting to form and you can see the umbilical cord.**
Below right: **The embryo has reached the foetus stage. It looks much more like a little human being. However, it doesn't look anything like a fully-grown baby yet – the head is much too big in relation to the body.**

What distinguishes Man from other vertebrates?

As far as his general make-up is concerned, Man belongs in the category of vertebrates, just like horses and cows. Newly born babies are fed in exactly the same way as any other mammal.

It is obvious, however, that Man is very different from other animals because of his more highly developed brain. This enables him to think before he acts, to tell right from wrong, to have a memory and to use his will-power; it has also allowed him to explore the worlds of thought and imagination. Moreover he has been able to use his capacity for thinking to trace his own history and that of animals and the environment. The lessons he has learned from history help him to plan for the future.

What is the skeleton for, and what is it made of?

The skeleton is the framework of the human body. It is made up of hundreds of bones, made of salts containing calcium, which support the body. Most of the muscles which enable us to move are attached to our bones. They also serve to protect some of our vital organs. The place where two bones meet is called a joint.

Looking at the skeleton from the head down, we start with the skull, which is made up of a series of bony plates joined to each other by sutures. The brain case, or cranium, protects the cerebrum (fore brain), the cerebellum (mid-brain) and the medulla (hind brain). The lower jaw is linked to the cranium by joints, and like the upper jaw it contains teeth – canines, incisors, premolars

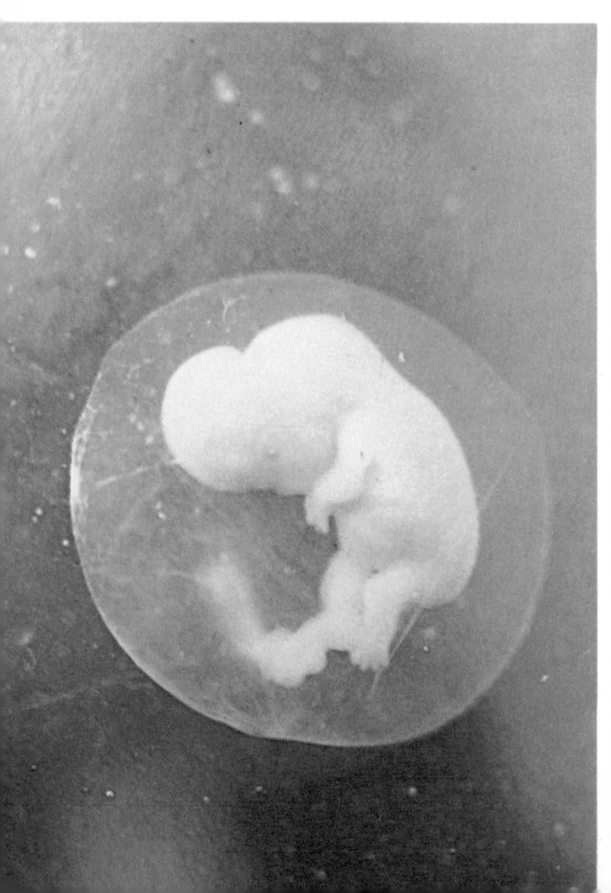

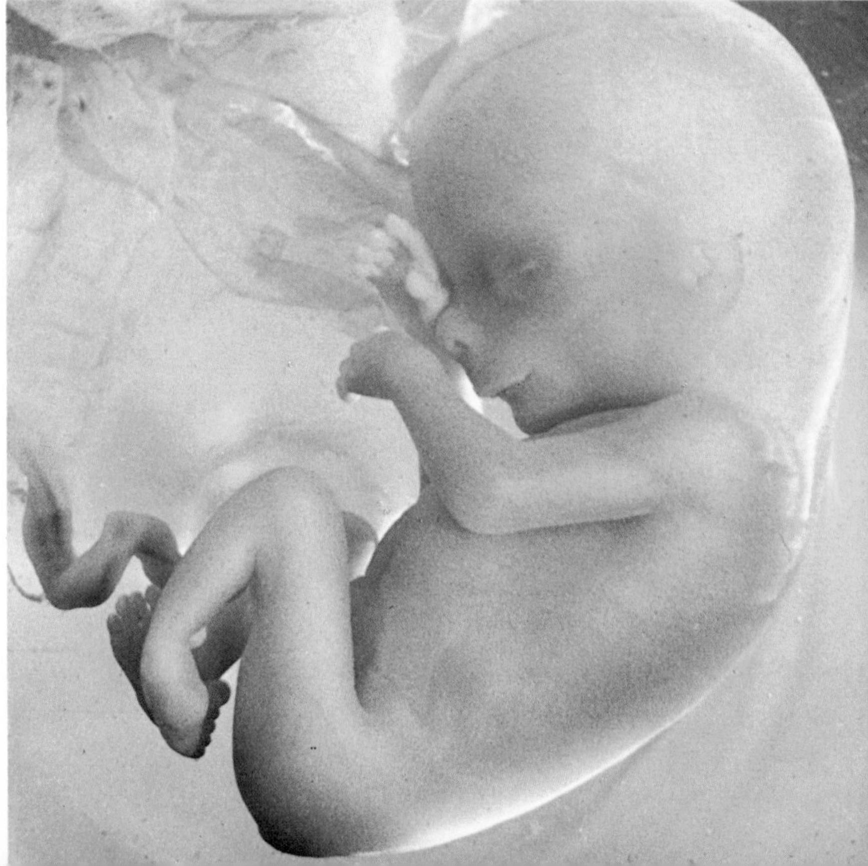

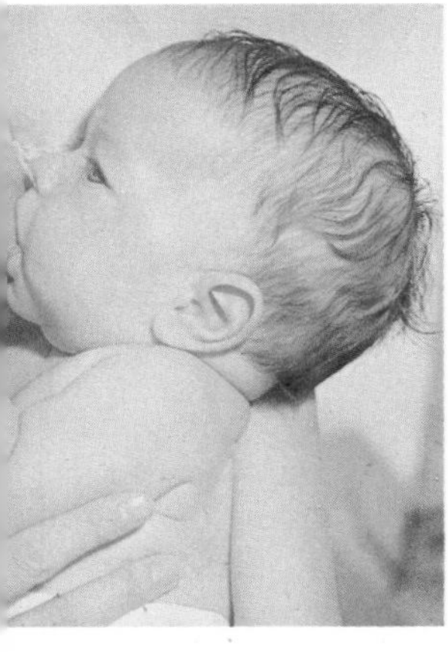

A baby suckling at the breast. For some time after its birth the human baby drinks its mother's milk. These days, however, many mothers use bottles instead, with a teat on the end.

Above: Louis Pasteur, the French doctor who invented pasteurization, the purification of foodstuffs. Milk, for example, is brought to a temperature of 100°C for a few moments, which destroys all the bacteria.
Right: Sleep and dreams. Children and adults dream while they're asleep. Humans spend about a third of their lives sleeping. During sleep, a number of our organs go on functioning – our heart, lungs, etc. – while most of our other muscles and part of our brain are at rest.

and molars. The occiput, or back part of the skull, rests on top of the spine or vertebral column, the central axis which is the chief support of the human body.
Going down the spine we come to the sacrum and the pelvis. These two parts of the skeleton support the vertebral column and also contain two sockets into which the hip joints fit. The leg is made up of the following bones: the femur, the tibia and the fibula. Then come the foot bones: tarsals, metatarsals and phalanges (toe-bones). The arm bones consist of the humerus, the ulna and the radius, to which the hand is attached.
The thorax, or chest cavity, is made up of twelve ribs on each side and the breastbone, or sternum; and the arms are connected to the body at the shoulders by the clavicle or collar-bone, and the scapulae or shoulder-blades.

Where do we find cartilage?

Most of our bones are in fact made up of cartilaginous matter which has hardened, or ossified. Not all cartilage turns to bone, however, and we find cartilage as such in some parts of the body, like the bridge of the nose, and the ears. And it is cartilage that covers our joints and lines the joint sockets. It also links the vertebrae (small bones forming a jointed rod) to one another and keeps the ribs attached to the breastbone.
Each vertebra has a hole in it. The spinal cord passes through these holes and in this way it is protected by the vertebrae.

What are muscles for, and how do they work?

Our muscles enable us to move. Movements are performed either voluntarily, when we decide to move, or they can occur involuntarily. So there are two types of muscle: the red muscles, which are also called voluntary or striped (but excluding the heart, which is also red and striped but is not a voluntary muscle), and the unstriped or involuntary muscles, which are pale in colour. Involuntary muscles are controlled by the section of the nervous system known as the autonomic nervous system. The red muscles are made up of filaments and under a microscope they do look striped. They react quickly to the direct command of the will. The unstriped muscles work slowly, and we have no voluntary control over them; they are totally governed by the autonomic nervous system. They hardly ever get tired. This type of muscle is found in the intestines and throughout the digestive system as a whole. Thanks to these, necessary body functions are automatically carried out without any conscious effort.

Apart from this distinction, muscles are also differentiated according to their shape and their attachment to the body. There are, of course, the muscles of the skeleton which are attached to the bones, and circular muscles, including those going round the mouth, and the muscles of the eye, the anus, the bladder and the wall of the oesophagus inside the throat. Other muscles control the opening and closing of the orifices in the body.
Finally, muscles are attached to bones by tendons. These have a rather rubbery consistency, though they are not really elastic; they are, however, very tough.

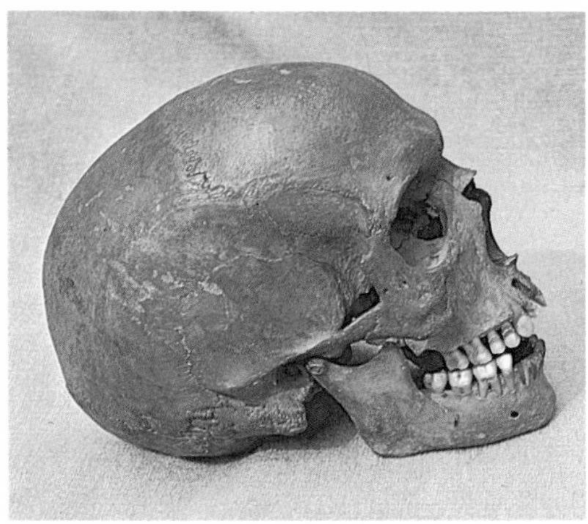

The skull of *homo sapiens* ('wise' or 'rational' man). Even today it is extremely difficult to be certain about the origins of mankind. What we can tell, however, by close examination of the skeletons and skulls of human beings, is that man has been living on earth for a very long time.

What is our heart for? Why do we have veins and arteries?

The heart is a dark red, striped muscle, which does not usually get tired. It acts as a pump, sending blood to the veins and arteries and taking it back in again as it comes round the body. The circulatory system is a one-way system. It is an extremely important part of the mechanism which maintains life in the body. Another very important phenomenon for the survival of the organism is to be found in the lungs. There the blood is charged with oxygen and gets rid of the carbon dioxide it has accumulated during its journey through the cells of the body. Next, the left side of the heart sends the red, oxygen-enriched blood into the arteries to distribute oxygen to every cell. Oxygen is essential to enable cells to stay alive. Chemical processes, which together are called metabolism, take place inside the cells. Metabolism enables food to be converted into the components of the body: the processes involved require oxygen and produce carbon dioxide. The carbon dioxide then passes into the blood and is returned to the lungs through a whole series of blood vessels called the veins. It is then breathed out of the lungs.

Arteries have thick, muscular walls, while veins are thinner and softer. When the blood is full of oxygen it is bright red; when it contains organic wastes it becomes darker in colour. The right side of the heart pumps the blood to the lungs, where it is renewed and enriched with oxygen before returning to the circulatory system.

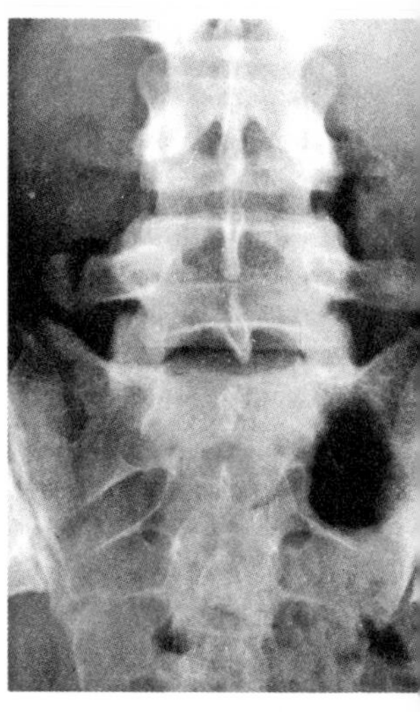

Above: An X-ray of the pelvis and sacrum, together with some lumbar vertebrae. X-rays are electro-magnetic waves invisible to the naked eye. They can easily penetrate flesh, but can't go through bones. They were discovered and put to use by the German physicist, Wilhelm Röntgen. In 1901 he was rewarded for his discovery by being given the Nobel Prize for physics.

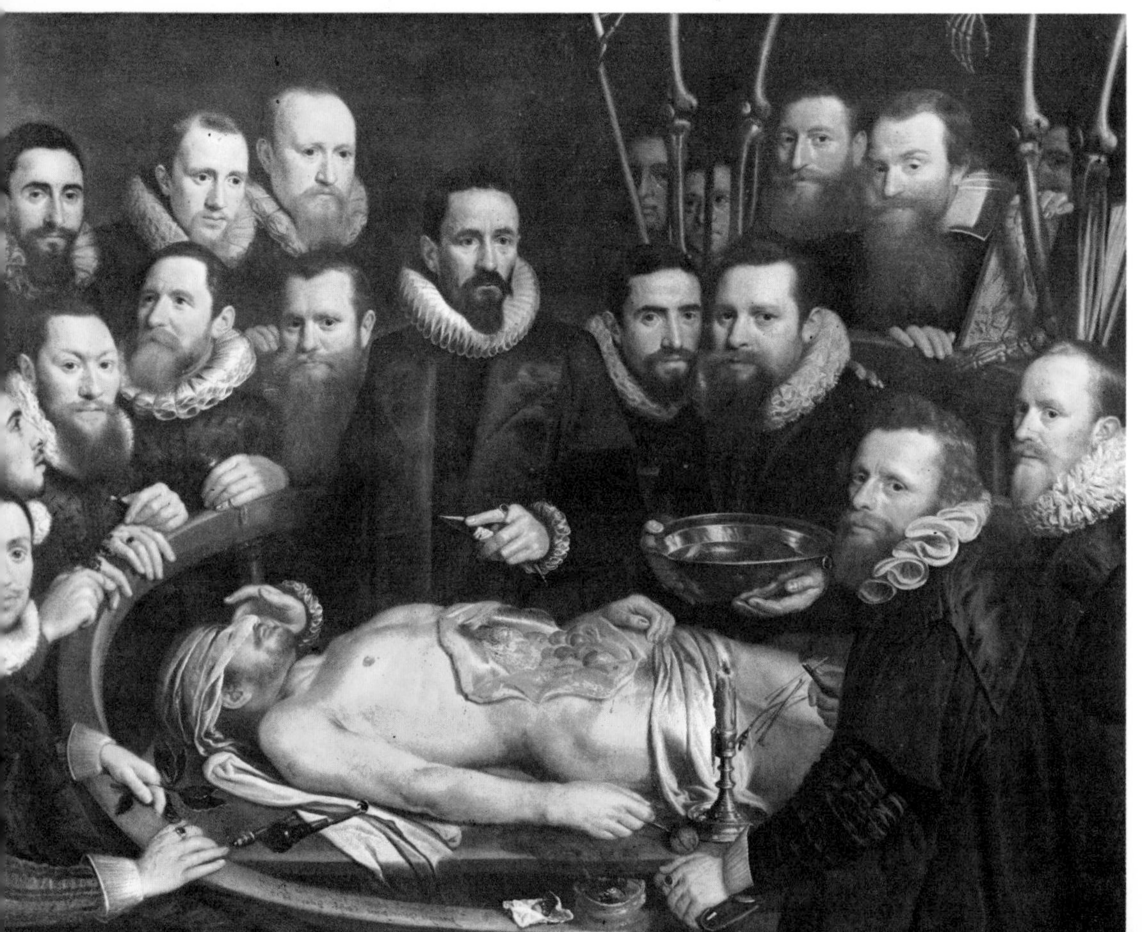

Left: The Anatomy Lesson, an oil-painting by Michiel Janszoon van Mierevelt of Delft (1567–1641). The canvas shows Dr van Meer surrounded by students. Part of the chest and stomach of the body lying down have been dissected. All medical students have to study anatomy, so that they know exactly where all the organs, muscles and so on are placed in the body. Van Mierevelt's paintings are displayed in museums in most large cities.

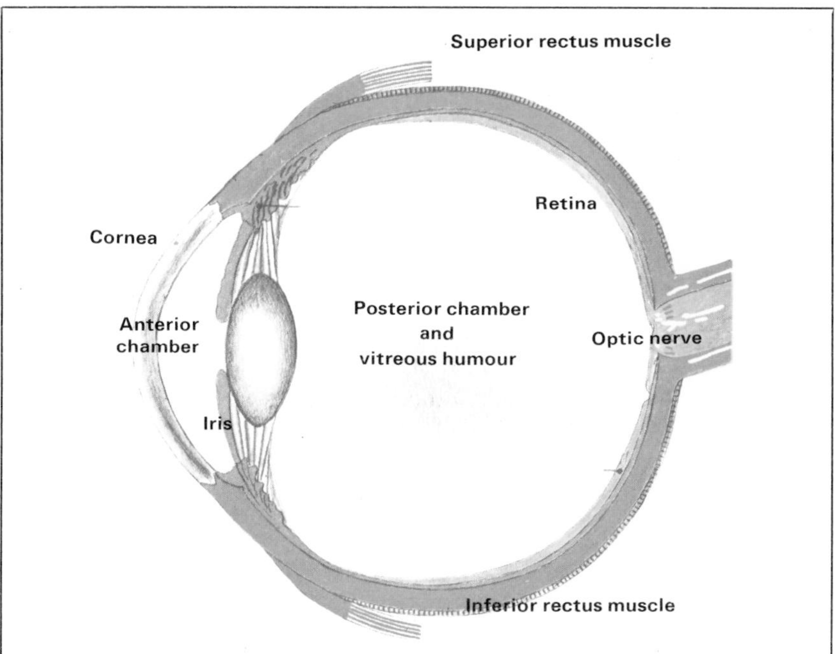

A cross-section of the eye. The eye enables us to experience objects and living things in the form of images. It is the organ of sight. The eye is equipped with a lens, just like a camera. The lens is adjusted automatically so that the brain receives as clear a picture as possible of what it is looking at – not too blurred, not too big, not too small and not too far away.

What is blood made of and what does it do?

The body of an adult man or woman contains approximately five litres of blood. Blood is made of plasma, blood platelets and red and white corpuscles, and it also carries a wide variety of nutrients (food) which the cells of the body need, together with waste products. By circulating round the body the blood delivers food and oxygen throughout the organism, and also takes away waste products – particularly carbon dioxide, which it carries to the lungs where the toxins (poisons) are exchanged for oxygen. It also conveys certain kinds of waste matter to the kidneys, where these toxins are disposed of in the urine.

Plasma is a colourless liquid which contains the blood cells. There are three types of blood cell: red and white corpuscles, which we've already mentioned, and blood platelets. Blood cells are produced in the bone marrow.

The red blood corpuscles are coloured by a substance called haemoglobin. By means of a rather complicated chemical process the haemoglobin takes in oxygen, and, in an equally complex chemical process, carbon dioxide. Thus its job is to transfer carbon dioxide to the lungs via small blood vessels called capillaries. Every molecule of haemoglobin contains an atom of iron. White corpuscles are colourless blood cells, containing no colouring matter. They look greyish-white and can change shape. There are several kinds of white corpuscle including 'polynuclear' corpuscles, which have lobed nuclei so that they seem to have more than one nucleus, and 'mononuclear' corpuscles with spherical nuclei. These two types of corpuscle can wrap themselves round disease-carrying germs and eat them up; this is called phagocytosis.

Finally, there are the blood platelets. They are not coloured, either, and are not round as you might have thought from their name. They are much smaller than the red and white corpuscles, but have an extremely important part to play in helping the blood to clot. When a scab forms on top of a wound, this is thanks to the work of the blood platelets.

Below: A little boy being vaccinated. His body will now produce special antibodies to fight germs.

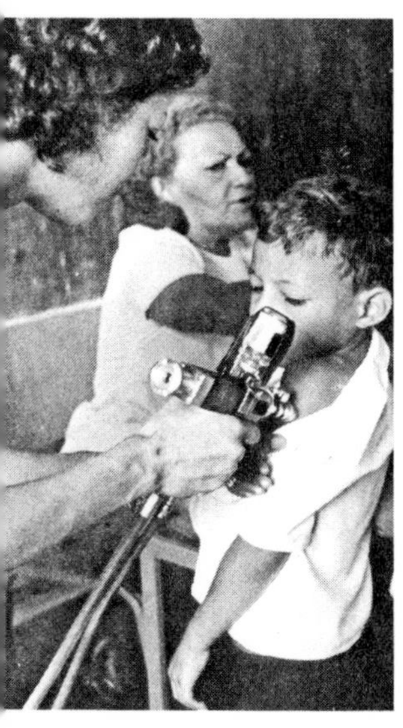

How does the body get rid of its wastes?

Two of the most important organs in our excretory system – the system that gets rid of waste products – are the kidneys. They are found in the lower half of the back.

Attached to the kidneys are two narrow tubes called ureters, which lead to the bladder. Blood is pumped by the heart into the kidneys, where it passes through millions of filters so that the blood cells and many sorts of nutrients remain in the blood, while a lot of water and many waste materials are filtered out. This waste fluid, which is called urine, passes into the ureters and down to the bladder, where it collects.

Another set of organs which get rid of waste matter are the sweat or perspiration glands in the skin. By secreting perspiration they get rid of some of the excess water from the body, together with various salts which

Over three thousand million human beings live on planet Earth. Among them are many types or races of men, distinguished from each other by the colour of their skin, habitat, language, way of life and religion.
Top left: **An Arab from the Lebanon, a small country in the Middle East.**
Bottom left: **A Greek fisherman. The history and language of ancient Greece are taught in some schools. The ancient Greek language is a 'dead' language; no-one speaks it nowadays.**
Above right: **A Lap hunter surrounded by reindeer antlers. Lapland belongs to four different countries – Norway, Sweden, Finland and the Soviet Union. In these countries the reindeer is a domestic animal.**

could be harmful in over-large quantities. When perspiration evaporates it serves its most important function of cooling the body.

The lungs are also organs which have to work efficiently to get rid of the water and the carbon dioxide produced by our bodies. Carbon dioxide is a gas which results from the metabolism inside the cells. It is taken to the lungs by the blood and the red corpuscles which circulate round the body.

Some people also regard the liver as a mainly excretory organ, since it secretes bile which is emptied into the intestines. Bile contains the waste products of haemoglobin destruction, but it also performs some useful functions for the organism. It is important in the digestion of fats because it breaks them down into tiny droplets. Finally, the solid or semi-solid waste products of the body, which consist of the remaining parts of the food that have not been digested by the organism, are called faeces. They are evacuated through the anus.

What do we eat and why?

We have to eat to keep our cells alive. The different categories of basic foodstuffs can be listed more or less exactly as follows:

a) *Carbohydrates:* these are sugars, starches, and cellulose which is present in the cell walls of plants.

b) *Proteins:* these are contained in meat, fish, fowl and all other organisms which have been alive at some time. These include mushrooms, shellfish (mussels, crabs, etc.), and all plants, although some plants or parts of plants, such as soya beans, contain much more than others.

c) *Fats:* these may be animal fats or vegetable oils (olive, coconut, peanut, etc.).

d) *Water:* at first this might not seem very important, but water is found in all foodstuffs and is vital for the organism. Water forms about eighty per cent of the human body.

f) *Vitamins:* these are rather remarkable substances; there are many kinds of vitamin –

too many to list here. They are not food as such, but they are indispensable to the healthy functioning of the body, and help it to fight efficiently against invasion by germs and viruses.

The oesophagus is a tube passing through the chest, equipped with white, unstriped muscles which push the food down into the stomach. This is the sole function of the oesophagus. The oesophagus, stomach and intestines form the alimentary canal or gut. The alimentary canal is concerned with the digestion (breaking down) of food into simple substances by chemical compounds called enzymes. The simple substances are absorbed through the intestines into the blood system for use by the rest of the body.

What are our sense organs?

We have many kinds of sense organs, both inside and outside the body. The most obvious ones are the organs of sight, sound, smell, taste and touch. The chief organ of taste is the tongue. It can tell the difference between salt, sweet, bitter and sour, by means of its many papillae or taste buds, cells which can distinguish tastes.

Our nose gives us information about smells by means of the olfactory (smelling) nerves. It is one of the most important sense organs because it tells us about the quality of the air we breathe, also helping our sense of taste.

For information about the organ of hearing, the ear, you should refer to the chapter on sound.

Sight (see the cross-section of the eye on page 101) is also of special importance in man's relationship with his surroundings. Thanks to the eye muscles we can move our eyes and look in the direction we want to.

Our sense of touch is governed by the nervous system. We also have sense organs enabling us to feel if something touches our skin, and to feel hot, cold and pain. Even deep inside our bodies we can feel pressure and pain.

Top row of photographs, left to right: **A young native girl from Kenya. A young girl from Taiwan carrying her younger sister on her back. Like the Eskimo in the next photograph she belongs to the Mongol type. A Makir from the Parana River area of Brazil.**

Bottom row of photographs, left to right: **Young Maori girl from New Zealand. The Maoris are part of the Mongol race, but they have certain 'white' characteristics. The Indonesian (a Javanese peasant) in the centre picture also originated from the Mongol race. His skin is brown. South America has many white people as well as those people of Red Indian and white descent. This is particularly true of Paraguay, Peru and Bolivia. This Bolivian farmer and his wife have typical Red Indian features.**

Above: Flint axes were used for the first time in our part of the world about 300,000 to 400,000 years ago. They would be chipped down from pear-shaped stones.

History

The First Human Beings

The first human beings lived about 800,000 years ago. Ancient historians sometimes called them hominids or anthropoids. After the Ice Ages mankind began to evolve more and more quickly.

Where do we get our information about the first men?

There are no written documents – that's why we talk about these times as being *pre*-historic. But the first humans left traces of themselves which tell us about their lives. We have learned a great deal from the archaeological excavations of the sites where they used to live. For example, there are the contents of tombs, which may include clothes and jewels. Even if a tomb contains nothing but bones archaeologists can establish the period when the person was buried, and sometimes even their age at death. The tools and weapons used by early men also give us a lot of information about their way of life. When archaeologists make discoveries like these they often come across some very surprising facts.

Was pre-historic man like us?

Pre-historic man knew how to think, how to use tools and how to make fire. Experts have been able to find all this out by studying ancient skulls. The one found in the

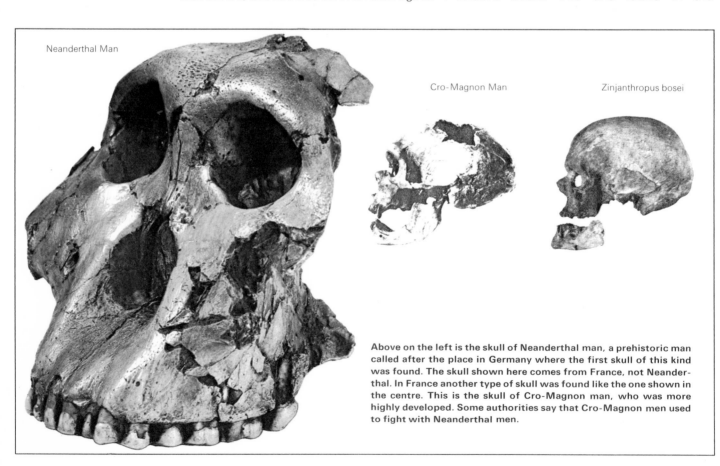

Neanderthal Man

Cro-Magnon Man

Zinjanthropus bosei

Above on the left is the skull of Neanderthal man, a prehistoric man called after the place in Germany where the first skull of this kind was found. The skull shown here comes from France, not Neanderthal. In France another type of skull was found like the one shown in the centre. This is the skull of Cro-Magnon man, who was more highly developed. Some authorities say that Cro-Magnon men used to fight with Neanderthal men.

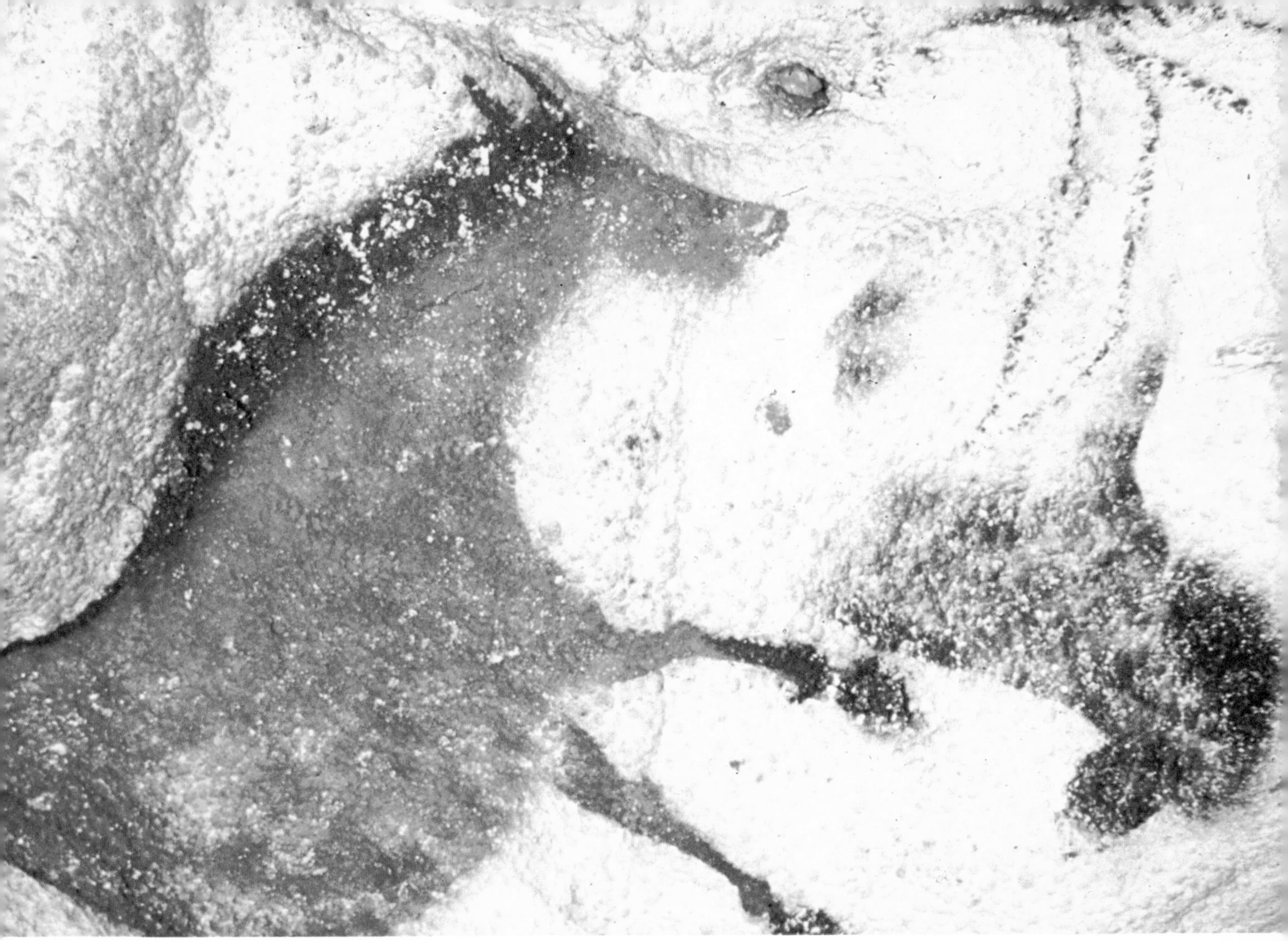

Neanderthal valley in Germany is a typical example. Skulls like this have been found in France and other regions, and from it the experts have been able to give us a description of Neanderthal man. He was squat, muscular, with a large flat skull, a receding forehead and jutting eyebrows; he had a strong jaw but no chin.

In 1868 Cro-Magnon man was discovered; he had a straight forehead and he did have a chin – he therefore looked more like us.

How did our ancestors eat?

It is assumed that the very first humans used to live on fruit and plants. Then they started to hunt. Improvements in hunting techniques and weapons enabled them to catch animals more quickly; they would roast the meat and extract the marrow from the bones.

Above: **In 1940 some boys were playing in the Lascaux region in France, when suddenly their dog disappeared. When the boys went to look for it, one of them discovered a deep hole in the ground. Some archaeologists began excavating the caves below, and found these wall-paintings; they estimated that they must have been painted some 16,000 years earlier.**

Opposite: **Lake Constance lies between Switzerland and Germany. In prehistoric times people used to live there in huts built on stilts above the water. At this period man was already advanced enough to have found a method of closing his front door – he already knew about bolts!**

Did the first men wear clothes?

They used to cover themselves with animal skins to keep out the cold. They soon realised that bear-skins were warmer than deer-hides, and began to take more trouble over preparing them. Later, they started using animal and vegetable fibres to make garments.

Ancient Egypt

The priests of ancient Egypt called their land 'the gift of the river'. Every year the banks of the river Nile are covered in alluvium, which makes the surrounding fields very fertile.

How civilized were the ancient Egyptians?

About 3400 B.C. Menes, King of Upper Egypt, invaded and conquered Lower Egypt. From then on Egypt was a single kingdom. The history of Egypt in the time of the pharaohs (Egyptian kings) included numerous gods; some, like Horus, were worshipped throughout the land. Egypt was divided into provinces; at the head of each province was a minister appointed by the pharaoh. He had to make sure that the taxes were paid and that the water which overflowed from the Nile every year was distributed evenly through the fields. The ancient Egyptians already had a calendar of 365 days a year.

What are hieroglyphs like?

Tutankhamen became pharaoh at the age of nine. Of course, the power had to be entrusted to ministers and priests. The young king only ruled for nine years; he died at the age of 18. No one knows the cause of his death, but we do know that he had a truly royal funeral. The golden mask shown here was found in his tomb in 1922.

Hieroglyphs are the symbols used in Egyptian writing. For example, the name of the first Egyptian pharaoh, *Narmer*, would be written by first drawing a fish, which stood for 'nar', and underneath it a little chisel, meaning 'mer'.

In this way the Egyptians wrote a great many words on their monuments. We are more familiar with carved hieroglyphs, but they could be painted, too.

Left: **Here you can see slaves harvesting by hand. Agriculture was very important in Egypt. Sowing was done at particular times of the year. The peasants had to wait on the edges of the fields for the arrival of the pharaoh, his priests, his servants and soldiers. The pharaoh would take some fresh mud from an irrigation canal, and the priests would chant while the rich river mud was scattered over the fields.**

Above: Thebes was situated near modern Luxor, on the east bank of the Nile. It was called the 'city of a hundred gates'. Around the site are some impressive temple ruins and also a number of royal tombs from the age of the Pharaohs.

Could people write letters with hieroglyphs?

Not everyone knew how to use these symbols. It was the task of the scribes to write letters, and they learned to write more quickly. They used a kind of paper made from papyrus, a water reed – and they also used pens made out of reeds. With this equipment they were able to write more quickly and they found a way of simplifying complicated hieroglyphs and linking up the symbols. But before they could be regarded as experts in this new form of writing, they had to practise a great deal. The simplified kind of writing was called hieratic writing.

What are pyramids?

They are the tombs of pharaohs. Around 2600 B.C. King Cheops chose a site in the Gizeh region for his tomb. With the help of his faithful servant and minister Hemon, he drew up plans for a tomb 147 metres high! Thousands of labourers were needed to build it, and they had to be given food and drink, and the whole project needed a great deal of organization. Hundreds of stone-cutters hewed great blocks from quarries to be taken to Gizeh; the only way the blocks could be carried was by river, when the waters of the Nile were at the right level. At Gizeh the blocks were cut down to the required size. Foundations were laid out in a square, and the first stones put in place. After that the work got harder and harder as the pyramid grew higher. The heavy stones had to be hoisted up the sides. A single block could weigh 15,000 kg. Supervisors watched closely to see that the blocks were put in place correctly and to make sure that the level of the building was kept horizontal. At long last, the final stone was set in place and the pyramid was complete. It had taken twenty years to build, and over two million blocks of stone had been laid.

The tombs of pharaohs, noblemen and other important people were placed inside pyramids like this one and those built after it. The Egyptians left food, clothing, jewels and weapons in the funeral chambers, for they believed that the dead would need them for life in the after-world. The next pyramids were not as big as the Great Pyramid of Cheops, and were therefore less expensive to build.

Below: The Rosetta stone. This flat stone was discovered by an officer during Napoleon's campaigns in Egypt from 1798 to 1801. He realised that the inscriptions on it must be three versions of the same text. This stone enabled J. F. Champollion to decipher hieroglyphs. The Rosetta stone is kept in the British Museum, in London.

Above: Thebes lay in the south of Egypt; about 1900 B.C. it was the Egyptian capital. The kings reigning in those times worshipped the Theban gods, in particular one called Amun, the invisible god of the air. Very early on the name of this god became incorporated with the sun-god, Ra, and the new god, Amun-Ra became supreme. The goddess Nut offered nourishment to the Egyptians. She is often represented on the walls of richly-decorated tombs.

Where were the pyramids built?

The first funeral monument was built by King Zoser. This was a step-pyramid: its sides sloped upwards in tiers and it had a flat top. In about 1500 B.C., after the first pyramids had been built, Tuthmosis chose a valley in the Luxor region as the burial-place of the pharaohs. It was given the name of Valley of the Kings, or Valley of the Dead. Later, the sepulchres were plundered by tomb-robbers, and so after this tombs were better hidden and much harder to get at.

Babylonia and Persia

Two thousand years before Christ Babylonia was a powerful empire in Asia. It lay between two rivers, the Tigris and the Euphrates. After a long period of prosperity it was conquered by Cyrus, king of the Persians.

We know about ancient towns and cities thanks to the work of archaeologists. One of them, Robert Koldeway, began digging on a site where he hoped to find the remains of the city of Babylon. His hopes were rewarded. Today the greater part of the city has been uncovered. These excavations give us an idea of what life in Babylon was like. The picture below shows one of the magnificent city gates.

What was the capital of Babylonia?

The capital of Babylonia was called Babylon, or Babel. It was a splendid city on the bank of the Euphrates, and was the seat of government for the immense kingdom which was ruled over by great kings like Hammurabi and Nebuchadnezzar II. The huge fortified walls around it were as thick as two chariots placed end to end. The gates of the city were architectural jewels. Most of all, visitors used to admire the hanging gardens of Nebuchadnezzar's palace, which were arranged on high terraces and watered by an ingenious irrigation system. A kind of temple called a *ziggurat* also rose above the city; it was actually a tower built in tiers, at the top of which stood the temple. It seemed to reach the sky. In the city lived many artisans, including leather-workers, soapmakers, metal-forgers and glass-makers. There were doctors, too, who knew a great many remedies and even performed operations. And there were astronomers who drew up a calendar and even mapped the movements of the stars. Religion played an important part in the life of these people.

What was the Babylonian captivity?

In the land of Canaan the Israelites had completely forgotten over the centuries that they were supposed to follow the laws of Moses. Prophets denounced their way of life and predicted a dark future for them. Most of the Istraelites wouldn't listen to the prophets, and one day it was too late. The Babylonians invaded the Land of Canaan. In 597 B.C. King Nebuchadnezzar seized the city of Jerusalem and took many of its inhabitants back into exile in Babylon. A few years later, in 586 B.C., the Jews who had stayed in Canaan revolted. The Babylonians returned: this time Jerusalem was completely destroyed and hundreds of Jews were imprisoned in Babylon. It slowly dawned on the Israelites that their prophets had been right.

Opposite: **The Ishtar gate at Babylon. The Babylonians often carved animals on the monuments they erected in their capital beside the Euphrates.**

Left: A scene from daily life, carved on Darius's tomb.
Below: One of the expeditions led by Darius. One of the last campaigns he conducted was his war against the Greeks.

Why did the Persians call King Cyrus 'Father'?

Cyrus, King of the Persians, was a brave warrior who often led his troops into battle, but he wasn't a cruel man. On the contrary, he showed kindness to his conquered enemies and was famous everywhere for his generosity. When he captured the city of Babylon he was welcomed by all the inhabitants. Cyrus immediately saw to it that the Jews were returned to their own country. This earned him the friendship of many nations. Jews, Greeks, Babylonians and others were allowed to keep their own way of life and their religion; they were even allowed to keep their leaders. Millions of people looked on Cyrus with respect. He was so good to his own people that they gave him the nickname of 'Father'. Cyrus died in battle in 530 B.C.

Why was Darius called 'King of Kings'?

By means of numerous conquests and alliances Cyrus's successor, Darius, considerably enlarged his empire. In the north it stretched from the Danube in Bulgaria across Turkey to the mountains of Asia Minor, and in the south from Egypt and the Mediterranean coast as far as the banks of the Indus river in India. The empire was divided into twenty provinces, and Darius entrusted their administration to *satraps*, Persian nobles who governed in his name. The different parts of this vast empire were linked to each other by a network of roads along which travelled numbers of trading caravans. Darius was nicknamed 'the merchant' because he took an active part in trade.

When Alexander the Great became king, he decided to set out to conquer the world. Thus it came about that Troy, Syria, Phoenicia and Egypt all fell under Greek domination. Alexander then crossed the plains of Persia and Turkestan and, after defeating the Persians, reached India. He died at the age of only thirty-two, but he had been responsible for many cultural exchanges. The peoples he conquered were not reduced to slavery but came under the influence of Greek civilization.

Below: Cuneiform writing first appeared in Mesopotamia about 2500 B.C. Cuneiform characters were engraved on clay tablets. They were made up of straight lines and triangles. Experts have succeeded in deciphering all the combinations of these signs and unravelling their meaning.

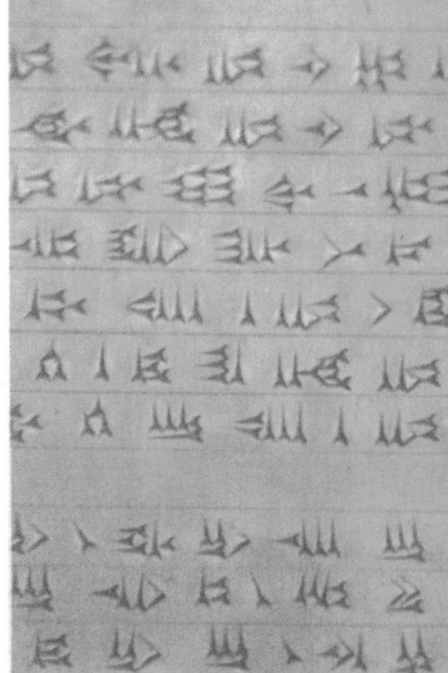

Greek Civilization

About 400 B.C. some nomadic tribes left Russia and headed south. When they got as far as the Mediterranean they settled there, despite the heat and the rugged conditions of the region.

Above: A large number of ancient Greek vases have been preserved. They were often beautifully decorated. On this vase you can see a picture of a relay race.

What was Greek civilization?

The people who settled in Greece borrowed elements from the civilizations of Egypt, Phoenicia, Mesopotamia and India. Greek civilization emerged from the blending of all these cultures.

Who was Homer?

A poet called Homer lived in Greece around the ninth and eighth centuries before Christ. Homer is famous as the author of two great epics, the *Iliad* and the *Odyssey*. The *Iliad* tells the story of the capture of Troy, a city in Asia Minor. The *Odyssey* relates the adventures of Ulysses, who wandered through the world after the Trojan war.

When the Greeks couldn't agree among themselves, their gods often intervened in their affairs. They took on human form and, like humans, could succumb to feelings of jealousy or vanity. Some of these divinities even stirred up quarrels.

Below: The Acropolis of Athens. 'Acropolis' means citadel or fortification. Later it became a religious centre. The temple of the Parthenon, dedicated to the goddess Athena, is clearly outlined against the sky.
Right: In architecture a caryatid is a support. Here the caryatids are shaped like women.

Why do people say that the Greeks were civilized?

The ancient Greeks had an enormous thirst for knowledge.

Thales of Miletus studied the movements of the stars and could predict eclipses of the sun. He was a mathematician, physician, astronomer, geographer and philosopher.

Phythagoras was the father of mathematics. His chief discoveries were the multiplication tables, the decimal system, and the theorem concerning the square on the hypotenuse – Phythagoras's theorem.

Democritus established that everything is made up of a quantity of tiny particles called 'atoms'.

In the fifth century B.C. there were already philologists living in Greece – scholars who studied languages. Architects and sculptors often used to work together, a very fruitful collaboration whose results can still be seen in the splendid temples and buildings of the age.

The oracle of Apollo at Delphi: an oracle tells the wishes of the gods through a priestess in their service. Its message is often ambiguous.

Far left: The ruins of a temple dedicated to Athena, goddess of war and also of prosperity and peace. The architecture is characterized by Doric columns, which have no base or pediment and have a very simple capital at the top.
Above left: The oracle of Apollo at Delphi. Apollo was the Greek god of beauty and goodness. He was the leader of the nine muses, who protected the arts. The place where he was most highly venerated was Delphi, where his oracle was kept.
The oracle of Apollo at Delphi: an oracle tells the wishes of the gods through a priestess in their service. Its message is often ambigous.
Below left: Corinth was a large and important town in antiquity. In former times there was a splendid temple there dedicated to Apollo; today all that is left of it are a few Corinthian columns. These are different from Doric columns (see page 140).

Greek citizens were obliged to keep the laws. It was in Greece that the principle of democracy was born, under which all citizens enjoyed equal rights.
Aeschylus, Sophocles and Euripides wrote plays which are still performed today. The historian Herodotus wrote an account of his travels to Egypt which is very valuable to us. Thucydides and Demosthenes turned public speaking into an art. It was Socrates who pronounced the famous maxim: 'Know thyself'. His pupil, Plato, sought to know the true, the beautiful and the good. Socrates invented the Socratic method of argument, by questions and answers.

How did Greek civilization spread?

Many Greeks left their country and travelled to places in the Mediterranean area, like Sicily, southern Italy and Asia Minor. They also settled in Marseilles, in France. From there they travelled even further afield: Pytheas, for example, adventured as far as Scandinavia.
Alexander the Great spread Greek civilization even more widely. He was the son of Philip, King of Macedonia. When Alexander succeeded his father he was 20 years old. He had been the pupil of Aristotle, and was remarkable for his courage and intelligence. He travelled with his armies through Asia Minor and Palestine, and went on to India, a country which until then was known to the Greeks only by name. He marched through the Punjab and established Greek colonies there. Alexander often absorbed the soldiers of armies that he defeated into his own army, and so he was travelling with men of many nations.
Under Alexander the size of the world known to the Greeks was quadrupled and the two great cultures of Greece and Persia were linked in one Greek-speaking nation.

Below: Alexander the Great lived from 356 to 323 B.C. He beat the Persian satraps and King Darius III had to acknowledge defeat. Alexander's many conquests led to the massive expansion of Greek civilization throughout the world.

Above: The legend tells us that Romulus and Remus were suckled by a she-wolf. When they reached manhood, they decided to found a city. They were working hard together when Remus, who was jealous of his brother, mockingly jumped over the furrow which marked the boundaries of the city. Romulus killed him in a fit of fury.

The Roman Empire

The influence of Rome is still present in our civilization today – our language and our alphabet have their origins in the culture of ancient Rome, and European law is based on Roman law.

When was Rome founded?

According to ancient accounts, Rome was founded in 753 B.C. This date has to be regarded as approximate because, of course, cities take more than a year to build. It was built on top of Mount Palatine near the River Tiber. On this hill was a small village consisting of huts; its inhabitants lived by agriculture and rearing stock. Strangers who came too close regarded them as excellent fighters, and they had a deep-rooted sense of discipline. This village was probably one of several which one day joined up to form a town. The Roman legend tells us that twin boys, Romulus and Remus, who descended from the royal family that ruled Alba, were thrown into the Tiber by their uncle. They didn't drown, however – they were carried by the waters of the river to the foot of the Palatine hill. There a she-wolf who had just given birth to cubs approached the two babies and suckled them. Romulus was the one chosen by the gods to be the founder of Rome. But Remus, who was jealous, scornfully jumped over the future boundary of the city, and Romulus killed him. That was how Romulus became the first king of Rome.

Who governed Rome?

According to the ancient legends, Rome had seven kings: Romulus, Numa Pompilius, Tullus Hostilius, Ancus Martius, Lucius Tarquinius Priscus, Servius Tullius and Lucius Tarquinus Superbus.

In 509 B.C. there was a revolt, and the Romans dethroned the king, Lucius Tarquinius Superbus (Tarquin the Superb) who had been a harsh ruler. Royalty was replaced by the Republic, with two Consuls at its head. These were elected for a year at a time.

Above: Cicero was a highly intelligent Roman. He was a great orator, and was also a writer, and he played an important role in politics. He lived from 106 to 43 B.C. He was a great defender of the republican regime. His writings are still read today.

Right: A painting which has been very carefully detached from the wall it was painted on. For nineteen centuries it lay buried under a layer of lava two and a half metres thick. This fresco decorated the villa of a rich Roman at Pompeii. Similar discoveries bear witness to the comfortable life led by this villa-owner. Unfortunately, not everyone was able to enjoy the riches of Italy in this way.

Above: **Cato was a Roman statesman who persistently demanded the destruction of Carthage in North Africa. For many years the Romans were engaged in the Punic Wars against Carthage. Cato also criticized people who indulged in corruption and excessive luxury. He and his wife led a simple life.**

Later other magistrates, under the authority of the Consuls, were likewise elected annually, two by two. These were the *praetors*, who were responsible for matters of administration and justice; the *quaestors*, in charge of finance; and the *aediles*, who were the guardians of public affairs.

During the period of the Republic, however, Rome went through a number of difficulties. Clashes broke out between the *patricians*, the rich and powerful citizens, and the *plebeians*, members of the working classes. The patricians were much more powerful and had more influence over the government since the two Consuls were chosen from among them. As Rome also had to cope with numerous wars, unity among its people was essential. Around 400 B.C. the country was invaded by the Gauls. They destroyed the city of Rome and fled with enormous booty.

Julius Caesar re-established order after a civil war in 80 B.C. The first emperor was Augustus, and other emperors followed him. The Roman empire, however, became very corrupt, and gradually her power diminished. The last emperor was overthrown in 476 A.D.

Why is Pompeii important?

In 79 A.D. the city of Pompeii was buried by an eruption from Vesuvius. It was completely covered by a layer of volcanic debris several metres thick. A number of thorough excavations have enabled us to recreate an accurate picture of life in Roman times. Under the thick lava all kinds of objects have been found, including both everyday articles and rarer objects. There were cushions in the rooms, and low tables (which were very useful for the Romans, who ate their meals lying down), mosaic pavements, wall-paintings, sculptures and fountains in the gardens surrounding the villas.

The excavations have brought to light a remarkably well-preserved city. They confirm that the rich certainly lived a very pleasant life, but they also show us that poverty, too, existed in Pompeii.

Right: **Roman villas in Britain must have looked quite like this. The Romans sent their troops to the far reaches of Europe, even to conquer Britain. They settled almost everywhere, particularly in Belgium, France and Britain. Most of the inhabitants of these conquered regions adopted the conquerors' way of life. It was not very long before they started living in houses which were very luxurious for the times, with the living quarters and the stables cleverly separated. These well-off people even had a kind of under-floor central heating. The Roman word 'villa' is still used in European countries today.**

The Middle Ages

The Middle Ages are a very important period in our history. They began with the fall of the last Roman Emperor and ended about the time when Christopher Columbus discovered America.

Above: Part of the Bayeux tapestry, showing William the Conqueror.

Who governed Europe after the Romans left?

Around 400 A.D. a number of tribes began to overrun Europe from east to west. The much-weakened Roman Empire was hard put to resist all these invasions, and not much was left of Roman civilization. Roman establishments and Roman roads were destroyed, and disorder reigned.
In 481 A.D. Clovis, King of the Francs, set off to conquer the neighbouring regions. He ruled his kingdom well, but his successors were weak characters who were less effective. They handed over the work of administration to governors, and it was only to be expected that one day one of these governors would seize power – as did Charles Martel (*The Hammer*). His son, Pepin, was crowned king in 752 A.D. Pepin's son, Charlemagne, turned out to be a great leader. His reign launched a new era in history and civilization.

How did the Norsemen or Vikings leave Scandinavia?

The Norseman were skilled boat-builders. Their longships were impressive and superbly made, with a narrow stern and a high prow finished off with a dragon's head. They had between 15 and 20 pairs of oars. The warriors could hang their multi-coloured shields on the side of the boat. The square sail was reinforced with canvas strips in a different colour. When they died, high-ranking Vikings would be burned with their boats.

Charlemagne helped the Pope to convert pagans to Christianity. He often went to war, partly to enlarge his kingdom, but also to protect it. And he was not only a military leader, he was a wise and just ruler as well. He helped the poor by making the nobles and the clergy pay large taxes. He was also responsible for starting schools, which were attached to the monasteries.
At that time there was no real capital city. Charlemagne used to travel through his empire, which was divided into counties governed by counts. He appointed emissaries to make sure the counts were fulfilling their task properly. Charlemagne died in 814 A.D., leaving a huge empire behind him. This was then divided into three, and straight away discord reigned once more in Europe.

Who were the Norsemen?

The Norsemen, or Vikings, were a tough, hardy race from Scandinavia. They left their own country in their Viking ships which were equipped with single sails enabling them to sail long distances. The reason they left home was that agricultural land was becoming more and more scarce in the Nordic countries. So the young peasants left their homeland to go and settle elsewhere – an unwelcome business for the people whose countries they conquered. Only two hundred years after the death of Charlemagne, they succeeded in invading and destroying his huge empire. They settled in Ireland, took control of part of England, lived in Normandy and France and even occupied Russia and Iceland. They discovered Greenland and evidence suggests that they also lived for a time in America. Some of them went to settle in Sicily in the Mediterranean.

Above: **Charlemagne was born in 742 A.D. He succeeded his father Pepin as king of the Francs at the age of 26. He defeated the Saxons, the Bavarians, the Avars and the Lombards. But he was not solely a warrior; he saw to it that his country was governed well. He encouraged learning, and schools were attached to the monasteries. The children of both rich and poor were able to attend them to learn reading, arithmetic and music. Charlemagne also helped to spread Christianity. In 800 A.D. the Pope crowned him Emperor because he had done so much to help the Church. At his death his vast empire was divided into three parts: the kingdoms of Charles, Lothair and Louis, the names of his three grandsons, who ruled over them. This partition took place in 843 A.D. and was ratified by the Treaty of Verdun.**

Above: **A medieval manuscript. The first letters on a page were heavily decorated, often with designs relating to the subject matter. As the pictures were very small they are often referred to as miniatures; the manuscripts are also called 'illuminated' manuscripts. Later on the pages became less heavily decorated and the writing less close, but the pictures were still referred to as miniatures.**
Right: **Pius II was the Pope who was head of the Christian Church from 1485. In 1459 he summoned an army to take part in a crusade to prevent the Turks from advancing further into Europe.**
Below: **Charles the Bold, Duke of Burgundy, ruled over France and the Netherlands from 1467 to 1477. He would have liked to re-establish the kingdom of Central France, but did not succeed in this aim.**

When the Vikings found some land they wanted to occupy, they set about it in a brutal way. They would subdue the local people, kill them off or chase them away, so that they could take possession of the whole territory. Thus they travelled the world, sowing terror and despair among the people they conquered.

What were the Crusades?

In the Middle Ages thousands of people used to travel from Europe on pilgrimages to the Holy Land – Palestine, where Jesus Christ had lived and the Christian religion was born. There they visited holy places such as Jerusalem, Nazareth and Bethlehem. In 1077, however, a disturbing event occurred: Jerusalem fell into the hands of the Turks. From then on, terrible tales were told of how the Turks were persecuting Christians, and these stories began to reach western Europe. The situation became so bad that in 1095 the Pope asked the European princes to intervene. In 1096 an army of knights undertook an expedition from western Europe to the Holy Land. But not all the crusaders were inspired by the same motives; some of the nobles in charge wanted to extend their possessions as far as the East, or at least to bring back a lot of booty. The serfs and peasants under them were hoping to earn their freedom.

There were eight Crusades in all, some of which never achieved their aims, and the holy cities did not remain in the crusaders' hands. One advantage of the Crusades, however, was that they introduced Europeans to new ways of life. From this period onwards trade between East and West opened up on a large scale. Little by little the nobles lost their power; the freed serfs began to settle in small villages, and towns began to grow.

What was the Order of the Golden Fleece?

It was an order of knighthood instituted by Charles the Bold's father, Philip the Good, when he was Duke of Burgundy, in 1429. The insignia of the Order consisted of a golden chain on which hung a boar.s head. It was a mark of knighthood. It was later taken up again by the Spanish and Austrian sovereigns.

What was life like in these towns?

Every town was surrounded by large walls, and very often encircled by a moat. People would have to cross drawbridges and go through huge gates to get in to them. Near the main gate there would be a gibbet, with

the corpse of a criminal hanging from it as a warning.

The roads were narrow and winding, and also very crowded. Merchants and craftsmen busily plied their trade, while children, beggars, students, peasants and housewives came and went, with dogs and pigs constantly running underfoot looking for scraps of food. So the ground would be littered with rubbish. Generally the houses were only one or two storeys high. In the centre of the town would stand a large church, the town hall and the guildhall. Guilds were associations of merchants and craftsmen. The streets were unlit, so the town was often not a very safe place.

The Renaissance

The word 'Renaissance' means 're-birth'. It is the name given to an intellectual movement which had an enormous influence on the arts and sciences, and on people's way of life, in the sixteenth century.

Above: **Queen Elizabeth I reigned from 1533 to 1603. During this time England became a great maritime power. Elizabeth could rightly be called 'queen of music and the arts', for during her reign the arts and sciences flourished. The great playwright William Shakespeare was an Elizabethan.**

What is meant by 're-birth'?

During the Middle Ages people attached almost no importance to the past. In Greece and Rome the ancient ruins were covered in weeds. In the libraries of castles and monasteries you could still find manuscripts on science and art, but they were covered in a layer of dust. When the towns began to grow people became less dependent on their feudal lords – they were no longer subordinates. Scholars were able to investigate all kinds of subjects, and once again they turned their attention to the past. Once more the old manuscripts were read. Some scholars went to Rome and even to Greece, to study the sources of our civilization. It was as if the ancient glories of Greece and Rome were being re-born in Europe.
This new phase in people's thinking and attitudes didn't start up everywhere at the same time. The Renaissance spread slowly across Europe from 1350 onwards.
Francesco Petrarch lived in Italy, where he had been born in 1304. At a very early age he showed he was an intelligent child. At school he was dissatisfied with teachers who were boring and with books which were even more boring. Realising that he had wasted seven precious years of his life in this way, he set out to discover the world for himself. During his travels he learned a great deal about the Greeks and the Romans. He travelled from town to town, looking for old manuscripts wherever he went.
Right up to his death in 1374 he took a constant interest in new subjects, not necessarily connected with book-learning. To many people's surprise he was quite capable of climbing a mountain just to enjoy the scenery: this was simply a manifestation of the new way of thinking and of looking at the world. Petrarch was the first humanist. The word *humanist* refers to someone for whom philosophy begins with the study of mankind.

Below: **Pieter Bruegel the elder, painter of peasant life, had a similar style to that of an earlier painter, Hieronymus Bosch. But the influence of the Renaissance can be clearly seen in Bruegel's paintings, particularly in the clothes worn by these Flemish peasants.**

Where was the influence of the Renaissance first felt?

First of all, in Florence. The rich merchants who governed the town wanted to show the rest of Italy that a town run by ordinary people could be as beautiful, even perhaps as glorious, as a city ruled over by nobles. The Florentines were successful in their aim, thanks to the help of the Medicis, an immensely rich banking family. They turned Florence into a leading town in the sphere of the arts and sciences.
Some of the other, older Italian towns refused to accept Florence's supremacy. Milan, Pavia, Ferrara and Venice built splendid cathedrals, libraries and palaces. Rome, where the pope had the best architects, painters and sculptors at his disposal, became a magnificent city. The new artists were not in the least like the unknown craftsmen of the Middle Ages, whose contribution to works of art and architecture had been anonymous. These artists were known by name; they were welcomed as guests and honoured in their home towns. Sometimes so much was demanded of them

that they had to get members of their families to help carry out all their orders. Among the great, internationally-famous painters were Leonardo da Vinci, Michelangelo and Raphael. Sometimes the Italian painters would accept invitations to work at the courts of foreign kings.

How did the Renaissance spread across Europe?

The King of France, Francis I, was a great admirer of all things that were Italian. He not only collected works of art from Italy; he also invited Italian artists to come and work for him in France. He commissioned leading Italian sculptors and painters, including Benvenuto, Cellini, and Leonardo da Vinci to design and decorate his palaces and organize royal entertainments. He founded the Collège de France where the progressive spirit of teaching contrasted with the tradition and conservatism of the Sorbonne. His love of Italian things was so great that he would rather have liked to conquer the whole of Italy!

So it was that a great peaceable army came out of Italy, crossing the Alps to spread all over Europe. First of all came merchants with their rolls of silk and wool; then the artists and scholars. The paintings and books they brought with them contained new ideas about humanity, and they encouraged others to begin their own investigations. Some countries sent scholars to Italy to work and study there. Others, like France, sent their armies. Even so, Leonardo da Vinci accepted Francis I's offer to join his service for seven thousand gold pieces and a château of his own in France.

The Italian merchants and bankers did good business with the Low Countries, Flanders and Germany. With the profits they built splendid palaces in the towns of Italy. In the cathedrals of northern Europe Italian artists discovered a wealth of works of art and a level of learning that was the equal of their own. So an exchange of ideas took place, resulting in a merging of the artistic skills of various countries.

For example, the Italians learned the technique of oil painting, while the German, Albrecht Dürer, learned in Italy how to draw a perfectly-proportioned figure. Erasmus, a Dutchman who travelled widely, was given the title of 'Prince of Humanism'. In Spain the most famous painter of the time was El Greco, and Cervantes was writing his *Don Quixote.* In England Queen Elizabeth met the Florentine Duke Orsini, with whom she could converse in his own tongue, Italian. A striking example of the Renaissance spirit was Sir Philip Sidney, who could wield a pen as well as a sword. And finally, Shakespeare borrowed the subjects of many of his plays from Italian romances.

Above left: By the sixteenth century the original function of a castle – to serve as a fortress – had died out. This splendid French château was built at Chenonceaux in the Renaissance style.
Above right: The church of San Giorgio Maggiore in Venice. Venice retained status of city-state from the seventh to the eighth century. Around 1500 it was the richest and most powerful city in Italy.
Below: Lorenzo de Medici was the founder of a rich banking family, and from 1469 onwards he was in practice the true ruler of the town of Florence.

The Reformation and the Age of Discovery

The works of the ancient philosophers were being studied once more. The passion for truth and knowledge led at the same time to the Reformation and the great voyages of discovery.

Above: Philip II of Spain was fortunate to keep his Catholic influence in the south of the Low Countries when the Eighty Years War came to an end in 1648. *Left, from top to bottom:* Martin Luther lived from 1483 to 1546. He and Calvin were the central figures of the Reformation. He first studied law, and then entered the Augustinian order as a monk. Disapproving of a number of abuses in the Church, he wrote ninety-five theses on a paper which he nailed on the church door of Wittenberg castle in 1517.

Erasmus was a famous humanist who came from the north of the Low Countries. He was a very wise man who preached that tolerance should be practised as far as possible. He kept himself apart from the religious conflict that raged violently during his lifetime in many parts of Europe. His best-known book is *In Praise of Folly*. In it he criticized the wicked ways of society and the Church.

Thomas More was a friend of Erasmus. He held a high position in the English government. He was executed by Henry VIII for objecting to the founding of the Church of England with the king at its head.

Who wanted to introduce reforms in the Church?

At the end of the fourteenth century a priest named John Wycliffe lived in England. He was a wise man, who disapproved of the bad ways the Catholic Church had got into. For example, he objected to the existence of two popes competing for authority. In Prague in Czechoslovakia, Jan Huss, who had read his books and approved of what they said, began to propagate Wycliffe's ideas. But he paid with his life for doing this.

In Europe more and more people began to demand religious reforms. The Church of Rome itself took some action, and tried to ensure that there was a greater number of honest priests who worked hard and lived good lives. But many people felt that the Church had not done enough. When Martin Luther visited Rome in 1510 he saw a number of scandalous things going on there. He was appalled at the way the priests lived. On his return to Germany he worked at the University of Wittenberg, and there he became convinced that the most important element in man's relations with God was faith. This led him to break with the Church and Rome. Many people agreed with him and turned away from the doctrines imposed by Rome.

Zwingli was a reformer who lived in the town of Zurich in Switzerland. He was a gentle man, who tried to understand other people's points of view. He was not just concerned with saving the soul for the next life; he also did all that he could to help people with the every-day problems of this life.

Another important reformer was John Calvin. He had read Luther's books while a student in Paris. At the age of twenty-one he had an experience which he felt sure was a call from God. From that moment on he devoted himself completely to the new religion, and because of this he had to leave Paris after a time. He settled in Switzerland and there wrote a book on how the Church should be re-organized.

What was the Counter-Reformation?

In the heart of the Catholic Church monks as well as powerful cardinals began to discuss how they could bring about a revival to improve matters. So began a kind of 'cleaning-up' process. The Church gave up a lot of its bad behaviour and wicked ways.

The Spaniard Ignatius de Loyola founded the Jesuit Order, whose task was to defend the Catholic faith. In the meantime, the King of Spain had given ecclesiastical judges the right to inflict punishment on anyone who didn't respect the laws of the Church.

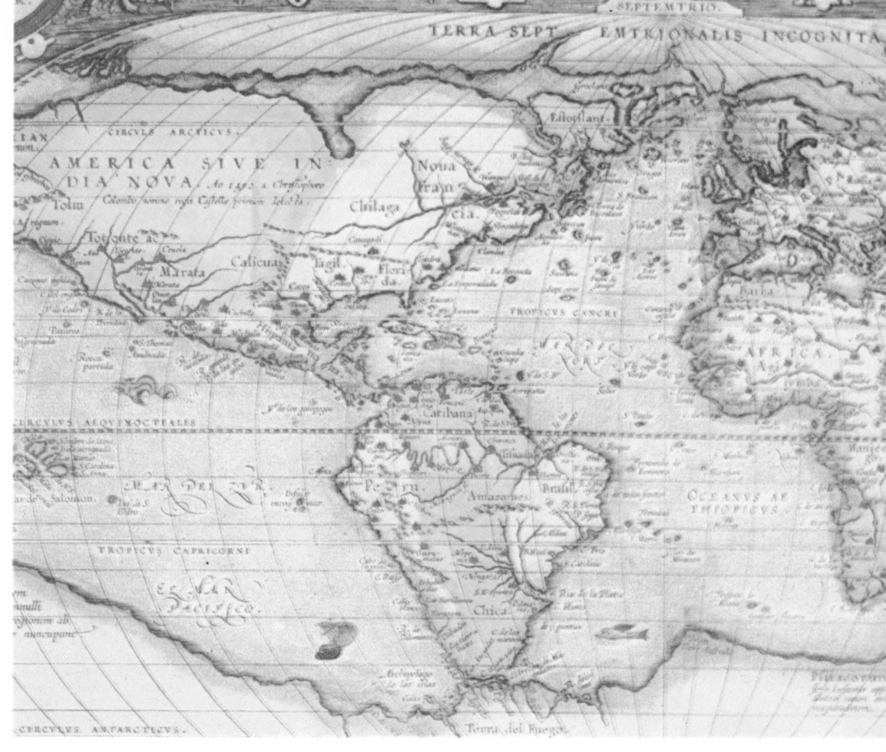

How was Columbus's voyage different from earlier ones?

The Portuguese prince, Henry the Navigator, wanted to find a sea route to the East so that he could take part in the spice trade. He set up a school of navigation at his court, and encouraged ship-building. In order to try out his ships and their crews he ordered them to sail as far as possible towards the west. That was how the Azores were discovered. This was followed by several expeditions along the coasts of Africa. In 1497 Vasco da Gama set sail eastwards towards Asia. The voyage was a success. After that Portugal sent soldiers to far distant countries to set up fortified trading posts.

Columbus headed west, hoping to reach India by that route; he thought it must be possible, since the world was round. He had no idea that on his voyage he would come up against a whole new continent – America. With money from Spain he equipped the *Santa María*, the *Niña* and the *Pinta*. In all, his fleet was manned by over eighty hands. The anchor was weighed on 3rd August 1492. After a difficult voyage, Columbus reached dry land on 12th October. Thinking he had arrived in India, he called the people he found there 'Indians', and the land became known as the West Indies. He made three further voyages to the New World.

Many others followed him, including Amerigo Vespucci, after whom the new continent was named. Magellan embarked on a voyage which was supposed to take him all round the world, but he died on the journey. Sebastian del Cano took command, and although only the *Victoria* and a few of the sailors who had originally set out on the fleet of five ships actually returned, the first voyage round the world was achieved. At last no one could doubt that the world was round.

More than two centuries later, in 1768, Captain Cook led an expedition to the Pacific Ocean. He had been given the task of visiting as many islands as possible and putting them on the map. After this he undertook two more voyages, with the object of finding a north-west passage to America. These missions failed, but he came back with a wealth of new information.

Above: **More and more voyages of exploration set out from western Europe, and information about hitherto unknown regions accumulated. Maps were drawn with increasing accuracy. The map shown here was drawn up by a Flemish cartographer, Abraham Ortelius. After drawing this map he had it printed. Such maps were a great help to other explorers. As exploration progressed they were corrected and updated, and new discoveries were included on them.**

Far left: **Vasco da Gama discovered the sea-route to India. He was a great navigator, but also a cruel man.**
Left: **Christopher Columbus was born about 1450 at Genoa, and died in 1506. He undertook four voyages to the New World.**
Right: **Captain James Cook was another great sailor. During his three voyages he covered about 300,000km in sailing vessels. He had a great knowledge of geography and was an excellent mathematician and astonomer.**

Above: Blaise Pascal lived in France from 1623 to 1662. He started by studying mathematics, science and philosophy at an early age, and he could rightly be described as a child prodigy. At the age of 19 he invented a calculating machine. After his death his *Pensées* *('Thoughts')* were published, in which he defended the belief that man's true happiness is to be found in God, and that God is the ultimate aim of the body, mind and heart.

Right: Louis XIV became king at the age of five. He wisely surrounded himself with capable ministers such as Louvois and Colbert. He wanted to make France a great and powerful nation. His reign, which lasted from 1643 to 1715, was above all characterized by magnificence and splendour. The other European countries had to unite to set a limit on French dominance. During Louis XIV's reign new ideas became increasingly widespread among scientists and philosophers.

The Age of Enlightenment

The Age of Enlightenment is the name given to a period dominated by the rationalist philosophy, which held that truth should be sought by reason and reason alone. During the eighteenth century rationalism influenced not only philosophers but heads of state as well.

What is meant by the word Rationalism?

Rationalism is the name of a doctrine which was popular between 1700 and 1800. Rationalism held that if man used his reason properly he could understand everything that took place an earth.

The man who started all this was an Englishman, Sir Francis Bacon. He put forward a new way of thinking which consisted of putting facts together and looking for the general principles to be found hidden amongst them. At first this method of study was applied only to science, but the new ideas also began to filter into the world of philosophy. Among the new philosophers was the Frenchman, René Descartes, who was also a great mathematician.

Thomas Hobbes was an English philosopher who also studied mathematics. In his books he set out to show that since men are basically selfish they need an all-powerful government or sovereign to keep society in order. In the Low Countries Benedict Spinoza was developing his own theories. The Englishman John Locke kept very close to every-day reality; he wrote several essays on economics, politics and education. Like Sir Isaac Newton, the great physicist who investigated the laws of nature, Locke tried to discover laws that would enable men to improve themselves and society. The thinking of Newton and Locke was taken up in other countries, and applied to all kinds of fields. Thus the eighteenth century acquired its title of Age of Enlightenment.

What were the main features of the Age of Enlightenment?

The main characteristic of this period was a belief in the power of human reason. In the Middle Ages a similar trust had been placed in nature and in a society which was the expression of God's will. During and after the Renaissance, such beliefs had been set in doubt. Scientific research had shown that there were laws to be found in nature.

The old ways of thinking were given up, and in great cities like London and Paris politicians and learned men met to discuss the latest ideas. More and more people wanted to know what was going on, and the journals and periodicals were read with close attention.

An outstanding writer of the day was Daniel Defoe, one of whose books was *Robinson Crusoe.* In his writing he was able at the same time to entertain his readers and to instruct them.

The approach to science at the universities underwent changes, as did ideas on the education of children. The pioneer of modern education was Pestalozzi. People were trying to change society, to 'humanize' it.

Far left: Tsar Peter the Great lived from 1672 to 1725. He was ruling the great Russian Empire at the age of ten. He gave himself the task of modernizing Russia; with this aim in mind he visited the countries of western Europe and even worked in Dutch and English shipyards.
Left: Frederick William II of Prussia lived from 1744 to 1797. He was a great admirer of Voltaire and invited him to come and live at his court. But Voltaire quarrelled with his host about how the new ideas should be put into practice, and took his leave.
Below: George Washington lived from 1732 to 1799. In 1774 he was put at the head of the American troops who were fighting for independence from Britain, who wanted America to remain a colony. On 4 July 1776 American Independence was declared, and in 1789 George Washington became the first American president. He held this position until 1797, during which time he was re-elected once. Once the United States had been instituted the new ideas on government were put widely into practice. This was owing to the influence of John Locke, whose ideas had been spread by people who had settled in the New World over the years. The Declaration of Independence of 1776 proclaimed truths which were applicable to everyone, anywhere in the world, and most of the people agreed with it. One of the truths contained in the Declaration was that all men are equal. It also declared that everyone has a right to life, liberty and the pursuit of happiness. The task of the government was also set out in great detail. The Americans knew what they were fighting for: independence, the expression of natural rights possessed by everyone, and a government under which all men would be free and treated as equals.

Who were the enlightened despots?

Enlightened despots were rulers who had absolute power but who were nonetheless concerned for the welfare of their subjects. Among the enlightened despots of the eighteenth century was Peter the Great, Tsar of Russia. The government of his large country lay in his hands alone; however he improved the conditions of life in Russia by putting into practice the ideas and methods he had learned during his travels in western Europe. Later the Empress Catherine the Great introduced more reforms in Russia.
Joseph II, Emperor of Austria, was another ruler who would allow his subjects no say in the government but nonetheless did all he could for them. But the greatest enlightened despot of all was Frederick the Great of Prussia. He regarded himself as the servant of his nation.
These rulers were full of goodwill, but there was one thing they forgot—that one day their power would come to an end. All the improvements they made depended on the benevolence of a single person, the head of state.

What was the *Encyclopédie*?

The *Encyclopédie* was a work in twenty-one volumes published in France between 1751 and 1772, and edited by Denis Diderot. The idea behind it was to publish a series of books which would contain all the ideas and all the knowledge acquired by man, in the light of current philosophy. The work was dedicted to Francis Bacon, founder of the new doctrine. The French government disapproved of the contents of the *Encyclopédie*, and tried, though in vain, to suppress it.
The most famous contributor was Voltaire, a writer whose criticisms spared no-one. He spent a considerable part of his life outside France, and was a frequent visitor at the courts of England and Russia. He was a great defender of liberty and human rights. Despite all this, however, ordinary people were not very aware of the 'enlightened age'.

The French Revolution and the Nineteenth Century

There was a great revolution in France in 1789. It finally came to an end when Napoleon seized power in 1799. The French Revolution heralded the reforms of the nineteenth century.

What changes did the Revolution bring about in France?

First of all, people tried to put the new ideas into practice – for example, the belief that all people should be equal. The divisions of society into nobility, clergy and bourgeoisie were abolished; from now on, everyone was simply to be a French citizen. The King didn't rule in accordance with the new ways of thinking – so, royalty was done away with, and the kingdom of France became a republic. The motto of the French revolution was 'Liberty, Equality, Fraternity'. It was written into the Declaration of the Rights of Man.

After the Revolution, France remained in a state of disturbance. On 21 January 1793 the King, Louis XVI, was guillotined for 'conspiring against the liberty of the subject, and criminal action against the safety of the State'. The form of government changed another four times before the country finally became a republic.

Right: **Napoleon Bonaparte was born in 1769 in Corsica and died in exile on the island of Saint Helena in 1821. He began his career as an army officer, and rapidly rose in rank as a result of his many victories. He overthrew the 'Directory' which was governing France at the time, and seized power. He conducted a great many wars before he was finally exiled.**

Below: **The Bastille in Paris was a fortress which was used as a prison. The people regarded it as a symbol of the hated authority of the king. On 13 July 1789 they took it by force, killed the guards and set free the prisoners. After that, they razed it to the ground.**

What happened after Napoleon seized power in 1799?

First, he set the internal affairs of the country in order; this helped him to remain popular with the people. Then he cast an eye on countries abroad, and threw Europe into a series of bloody wars. He crowned himself Emperor, and won many battles. But finally he was beaten at Waterloo by the British and the Prussians. He was sent into exile, and delegates from the conquering nations met together at Vienna. There they decided the fate of Europe with little regard for the wishes of the ordinary people. The decisions taken at the Congress of Vienna thus became a new source of divisiveness and oppression.

What happened in other countries after the French Revolution?

The ordinary people who were being oppressed by the Emperor of Austria, the Sultan of Turkey and the Tsar of Russia wanted to gain their liberty too. The events

Above: From 18 September 1814 to 9 June 1815, after the fall of Napoleon, delegates from the European governments met at the Congress of Vienna. There they decided the fate of millions of people, without any real regard for what these people wanted.

in France and the earlier declaration of independence by the British colonists in America. gave them new hope and courage. The French Revolution was followed by a series of revolts in the name of liberty. In other countries people became aware of the concept of nationality, and Italy and Germany took steps towards becoming united countries. In South America the inhabitants of the Spanish and Portuguese colonies revolted against the mother countries.

What was the Victorian era?

The period during the nineteenth century when Queen Victoria ruled Britain is called the Victorian era. Queen Victoria came to the throne in 1837 at the age of nineteen. During her reign England enjoyed an age of prosperity and well-being; it seemed as though the Queen and her people were specially protected by God – which also meant that everyone should lead a virtuous life and work hard. There were all kinds of rules and regulations about what people could and could not do.

The Queen encouraged these attitudes believing that they would safeguard Britain from moral decadence. But not all foreigners thought like this; many considered it a hypocritical way of life. However at the Great Exhibition in 1851 the British exhibits were the most outstanding, and there were many new inventions and discoveries in Britain during the Victorian era.

Victoria was married in 1840 to her German cousin, Albert; they had nine children who were given a very strict and straightlaced education. During Victoria's reign legislation was introduced to stop women and children working in the mines. The working day in factories was limited to a maximum of ten hours, and the number of people having a right to vote was increased (though it wasn't till 1928 that every person over twenty-one was given the vote).

During the Victorian era Britain's power also grew outside Europe. Disraeli, a Prime Minister, proclaimed the Queen Empress of India. After the opening of the Suez Canal Egypt was almost entirely under British control. The age which bore Victoria's name came to an end with her death on 22 January 1901.

Above: Queen Victoria reigned over England from 1837 to 1901. For many British people she was a symbol of the nation's glory. Her children and grandchildren were connected by marriage to nearly all the ruling families in Europe.
Right: An English street during the Victorian era.

Modern Times

The first half of the twentieth century was largely overshadowed by the two world wars. Millions of men lost their lives, and the decision to explode the Atom Bomb was a serious one, whose effects are still with us today.

Above: **Lenin's real name was Vladimir Ulyanov. He lived from 1870 to 1924. He had to leave his country because he wanted to bring about changes. With the help of some Germans he returned to the U.S.S.R., which was involved in the First World War and was in a very bad state. He led the October Revolution in 1917, set up the government of the Soviet Union, and concluded peace with Germany.**

Why did the First World War break out?

In the twentieth century it became increasingly clear that there was a great deal of tension between the various European countries. One nation would find it intolerable if another nation's trade and industry were flourishing; some countries felt humiliated by those who had won wars against them in the past. The politicians and military leaders before 1914 nearly all held to the belief that when agreement could not be reached the only thing to do was to go to war.

Slowly but surely two camps began to form. On one side were Germany, Austria and Italy; on the other, Britain, France and Russia. Both groups signed pacts, promising support for the other members should war break out.

The incident that triggered off the war was the assassination of the Archduke Francis Ferdinand of Austria and his wife, at Sarajevo, in Serbia. The Austrian government immediately declared war upon Serbia. Germany offered to help Austria, and Serbia asked Russia for assistance. Russia immediately consulted France. When they had made sure that France would remain their ally, the Russian generals lined up their troops along the Austrian and German borders. The Germans demanded their withdrawal. When they refused, Germany declared war on Russia on 1 August 1914, and on France on 3 August. Germany immediately invaded Belgium, and England, too, declared war, on 4 August 1914. Thus a whole network of alliances had thrown entire nations into a war which they didn't want at all.

What was the course of the First World War?

In August 1914 few people thought that the war would last longer than a few weeks or months. The military leaders believed that modern weapons would bring the conflict to a speedy end. In Germany plans had been prepared well beforehand to fight Russia in the East and France in the West. First, the German army had to defeat France; then they were to turn against Russia. It was a well known fact that the Russian army was very slow in mobilizing; Germany would have plenty of time to move its troops from west to east.

But the war didn't go as Germany had planned. The French were not instantly wiped out, and the German troops became bogged down in northern France, where the horrible war of the trenches took place. During the next four years, millions of victims fell in the most terrible war ever experienced by humanity.

Then the U.S.A. entered the war in 1917 because of violent attacks against the central powers by German submarines, and the threat that all ships found in certain areas around Britain and France would be sunk without warning. This brought about a

Below: **The Emperor William II ruled over Germany from 1888 to 1918, but he had no aptitude for government. In 1918, when the German army refused to take his orders, he fled to Holland. He is shown here among a group of officers during a visit by the Archduke Francis Ferdinand of Austria. The Archduke was assassinated in 1914 on a visit to Sarajevo. There was a violent reaction to this event, culminating in the outbreak of the First World War.**

turning-point in the conflict. The war came to an end in 1918. England and even more so France, heavily ravaged by the war, owed huge debts to America. Among the defeated nations the situation was even worse. Europe was in a state of total disorder.

Right: **Aeroplanes were used for the first time during the First World War, in small-scale aerial battles. Here we see an encounter between French and German planes.**

Below: **Thomas Woodrow Wilson was president of the U.S.A. from 1913 to 1921. It was he who declared war on Germany in 1917. In January 1918 he issued his Fourteen Points, which were intended to guarantee lasting peace after the end of the war with Germany.**

What was happening in Russia?

In 1914 the great Russian army was confronted by a well-equipped, well-trained German army. The Russians had poor weapons and were not prepared for warfare. During the next few years the Germans were able to make the conquest of vast territories. In 1917, following revolts in the army and in St Petersburg, the Russian Tsar abdicated. The new government decided to continue the war, but it became increasingly clear that the country had had enough. The Russian people were ready to follow anyone who would promise them peace and better living conditions. This was when Lenin appeared on the scene, at the head of a party called the Bolsheviks. In November 1917 the Bolshevik party seized power and in March 1918 peace was signed with Germany. Under the terms of the peace treaty Russia lost a great deal of territory; the Bolsheviks were not happy about this, but Russia was too weakened to go on fighting.

What happened in Germany after the First World War?

After the fall of its empire, Germany became a republic. The people's representatives met at Weimar. In 1919 disturbances arose because of disagreements between the political parties, who were accusing each other of murder and assassination. They even blamed each other for the military defeat. The government had been obliged to sign the Treaty of Versailles in 1918, which annoyed many people, since the treaty stated that Germany and its allies were responsible for starting the war. The feelings of hatred that had existed before the war were not dead. The Emperor had fled – but his generals remained. The judiciary, the police, civil servants and school teachers all clung to the attitudes that had prevailed at the time of the empire. German pride had been deeply wounded because the victorious nations had granted Poland a large piece of German territory. From then on it is not surprising that a number of political parties appeared, extolling the past glories of the German state.

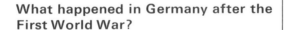

Opposite: **The First World War was a total war. The civil population of Europe was as involved in it as the army and the navy. Civilians often suffered from food shortages. The occupying powers, who were in control of the distribution of supplies, often had nothing to give their own army. When this happened they would plunder the harvest and kill the cattle. The ordinary people in areas where fighting was going on had to look after themselves as best they could in these conditions of hunger, destruction and chaos.**

Above: **Adolf Hitler was born in 1889. He was Austrian by birth. In 1921 he became leader of the National Socialist German Workers' Party, the N.S.D.A.P. In 1924, while in prison after a failed attempt to seize power, he wrote *Mein Kampf*, in which he set out his party's political programme. He gained a large following with his thunderous speeches, and became head of state in 1934. He ruled as a dictator, which means that there was no limits to his power. So Germany became a one-party state – the Nazi party, directed by Hitler himself. Human rights were brutally violated.**

In 1932 one of these parties, the N.S.D.A.P., obtained 37 per cent of the votes. Its leader was Adolf Hitler, who immediately insisted on being made head of the government. He was supported by the commercial world, which saw him as the man who could re-establish peace inside Germany. Once Hitler was in power he proclaimed a number of emergency laws. He took all the power into his own hands. The Jews were persecuted, the political parties were dissolved, the arts came under Hitler's control, and children had to be brought up along lines dictated by him.

What brought about a second world war?

From the start, Hitler wanted to ignore the Treaty of Versailles. Slowly, Germany re-armed. The countries who had fought against her did nothing to prevent it, for during all the time he was preparing for war, Hitler was talking of peace – and everyone believed him. He even began to have the feeling that the other nations would do nothing when he took back the Rhineland, which Germany had lost under the Treaty of Versailles.

In March 1936 the German army suddenly marched on the Rhineland. And, as Hitler had expected, Britain did nothing; neither did France. Everyone was afraid of war. In October 1936 Hitler made an alliance with Mussolini, in Italy, which was given the name of the 'Rome–Berlin Axis', after the capital cities of the two countries concerned. Later, Japan joined them too. A month after this, Hitler announced that the German people needed more *lebensraum* (living space). He wanted to conquer Austria. Some of the Austrians wanted to join with Germany, and Hitler encouraged them. So, on 14 March 1938, with nothing to stop them, the German troops marched into Austria, which Hitler had declared to be a part of Germany. Once again, none of the other countries dared to intervene.

Next Hitler turned his attention to the Sudetenland and Czechoslovakia. There partisans were trying hard to rouse the people against the Czech government. Hitler let them get on with it. He was able to deceive Britain and France, and Czechoslovakia was slowly swallowed up by the German state. Despite all this, Hitler was a little afraid of the Russians, even although their military power was diminished following the First World War and the Revolution. He set out to create a rapprochement with them, and on 19 August 1939 the amazing news broke that Germany and Russia had signed an agreement not to attack each other. Hitler felt free to carry on.

Next, it was the turn of Poland. On 1 September 1939 Germany attacked Poland,

Opposite: **The German army was well trained; it was highly disciplined and well organized. With its large number of lorries, tanks, armoured cars and other vehicles it was able to attack with speed. This gave rise to a new technique of warfare, the *Blitzkrieg*, or 'lightning war'.**

at the cost of many innocent lives. This time, two days later, England and France declared war on Germany. The Second World War had begun. It had taken a long time to decide to put an end to the aggression of Hitler and his allies.

What was the course of the Second World War?

Below: **Winston Churchill became Prime Minister of Great Britain on 10 May 1940. Roosevelt, Stalin and Churchill made up the 'big three' of the allies. Churchill was a great leader, thanks to whom Britain held fast in the combat against Nazi Germany.**

As soon as Germany had invaded the western frontier of Poland, the Russians attacked its eastern frontier. Russia and Germany shared the booty.

Then, in April 1940, Germany invaded Denmark and Norway, and very shortly these countries were occupied by German troops. On 10 May 1940 the German war machine swung round once more. The Netherlands, Belgium and Luxembourg were defeated and the German army moved onwards towards France.

Near Dunkirk in northern France 340,000 British troops were stranded, threatened by the German army; the only way to save them was to evacuate them to Britain and all kinds of emergency vessels were used. The evacuation took place between 29 May and 3 June.

Meanwhile, Winston Churchill had succeeded Chamberlain as Prime Minister of Britain. On 5 June Germany launched the major attack which Churchill had predicted. France capitulated. Now Hitler could concentrate on Britain. Thus began the Battle of Britain, a battle in the skies which went on for eighty-four days and was finally won by the pilots of the Royal Air Force.

Below: **Dwight D. Eisenhower was the American general who successfully commanded the disembarkation of the Allies into Europe. After his return to the U.S.A. he became a popular politician and was twice elected president.**

The German fleet was in trouble, too. In North Africa the Italians were losing ground, and the Germans had to go to their aid. The same thing happened in Greece. Hitler did not want to stop, however, and he attacked Russia. Now Britain and Russia were allies. And finally the U.S.A. entered the war, too, after a surprise attack by the Japanese on Pearl Habor. The new allies decided to defeat Germany first; then they would deal with Japan.

First, in 1942 and 1943, the Germans were pushed out of North Africa. In February 1943 the German army was also defeated at Stalingrad in the Soviet Union. Then the allies invaded Italy, and removed Mussolini from power.

D-Day

D-Day was the code-name for 6 June 1944, the day set for the allied armies to land in Normandy. This was the last phase of the Second World War. For months soldiers and equipment arrived in the British Isles. Everything was carried out as secretly as possible. The army which was to take part in the landings was commanded by General Eisenhower. He had 10,000 aeroplanes at his disposal and 4,000 ships, which together were to transport over a quarter of a million soldiers across the Channel. This gigantic army was made up of men from all the countries at war with Germany.

Finally, on 6 June 1944, the great Normandy landings took place. Under the command of General Eisenhower troops of many nations fought the German army. One after the other Hitler's allies deserted him. After one last great offensive the German army was pushed back into Germany. On 7 May 1945 Germany surrendered.

The war officially came to an end on 2 September 1945, after the terrible Atom Bomb had been dropped on the Japanese cities of Hiroshima and Nagasaki. Many years later people were still dying from the effects of those atomic explosions. The war was still claiming thousands of victims long after it had come to an end and peace had been restored in most countries.

The Present Day

After the Second World War Europe recuperated with remarkable speed. Throughout western Europe this recovery was followed by a period of prosperity. But after the war Russia was the predominant military power in Europe, and rivalry between Russia and the U.S.A. soon became apparent.

What was the 'Cold War'?

The Cold War was the name given to the state of hostility between western Europe and the U.S.A. on the one hand and the Communist countries on the other. It arose mainly out of the disagreements between East and West which had started during the Second World War.

The two sides used many means of opposing each other without resorting to the direct use of arms. However, the Cold War led a number of countries to embark on programmes of re-armament. The western nations made an effort to get closer to each other through the North Atlantic Treaty Organization. The East European Communist countries reacted to this by signing the Warsaw Pact.

How did the Cold War come to an end?

First of all, a certain rapprochement took place between the American President Eisenhower and the new Russian leader, Krushchev. Then the Cold War reached a crisis. In 1959 Fidel Castro had seized power in Cuba, and during the next few years Cuba's ties with the Soviet Union had become increasingly strong. The U.S.A. was not happy about this. In 1962 it became known that Russia was installing missile

Above top: **Charles de Gaulle lived from 1890 to 1970. He was not only an experienced general, he was also a great politician. During the Second World War he led the French resistance against Germany, and until 1946 he was provisional head of the French government. From 1959 to 1969 he was President of the French Republic.**
Above: **Mao Tse-tung led the Chinese communists from the twenties until his death. Over the years the Chinese Communist Party became increasingly independent, and frictions began to arise between China and the Soviet Union.**
Below right: **After the Second World War the Vietnam War continued until the seventies. It came to an end in 1976.**
Below left: **A meeting of the Security Council. This is a department of the United Nations Organization. Its task is to promote peace all over the world. It has fifteen members.**

bases in Cuba, and the Americans saw this as an immediate threat to their own country. All over the world, tension was rising. Would there be another war? Would atomic weapons be used?
In the U.S.A., John F. Kennedy had become president. Like the Russian leader, Krushchev, he had a great sense of responsibility. He and Krushchev reached an agreement, and the Soviet Union withdrew the weapons that had represented such a threat to America. Everyone was able to breathe again.

What were the main features of the Sixties?

The Cold War was followed by a period of détente. Kennedy and Krushchev met for talks. In 1963 an important treaty was signed between the U.S.A. and the Soviet Union, putting an end to military experiments with atomic explosions. This pact reinforced the spirit of mutual trust which was steadily building up.
In the Sixties, too, many African and Asian colonies declared their independence, and they now have a voice at the United Nations, the great organization of nations which has its headquarters in New York. The events in Cuba had repercussions in the South American countries, where many people became aware of the wretched conditions they were forced to live in.
Among the wealthier nations a form of aid to under-developed countries was started up. The Vietnam War made people all over the world realise that the difficulties lay not only between East and West, but also between North and South. In the Middle East antagonism between the Arabs and the Israelis also led to war.
There was a rift between the Soviet Union and China. It first became apparent in 1958 when Russia refused to make atomic weapons available to China. By the end of 1964 China had exploded her own atomic bomb. During this time, too, man was also setting out to conquer space. In 1961 the Russian Yuri Gagarin was the first man in space; after this the U.S.A. and the Soviet Union both made enormous strides in space exploration. And in 1969 American astronauts were the first men to set foot on the moon.

What has been happening during the Seventies?

People had been becoming increasingly aware that in many 'Third World' countries conditions will never get better so long as the west continues to live in luxury and ignore their plight. During the Seventies scientists have been looking for improved ways of dividing the world's resources among its inhabitants.
American involvement in the Vietnam War has finally come to an end, and with the decrease in hostilities the Vietnamese must now turn their energies to improving their living conditions and their economy. But much of the bitterness still lingers, and a lasting solution has yet to appear.
Hostility is still going on between the Israelis and the Palestinians. The Palestinians are disputing with the Israelis the right to own territory in Israel. There are continuous bloody encounters between them and their neighbouring country, the Lebanon, is involved in these. President Sadat of Egypt paid a visit to his colleague Begin in Israel. Begin in turn went to Egypt at Christmas, 1977. Both countries hope for a solution to the Middle-Eastern conflict, for they consider that there has been enough bloodshed.

Above: The Israeli army is well-equipped and its morale is high. In the past it has proved its effectiveness at keeping out invaders.
Below: A wrecked Egyptian lorry. Although they enjoyed a period of success, the Egyptians had to admit defeat during their last military conflict with Israel.

Culture

Music

Music is one of the many forms of art by which man expresses himself. The word encompasses singing in the bath just as much as beating a drum or playing the organ.

Opposite: A tom-tom. A tom-tom is a percussion instrument like a drum, which is well known all over the East. It is often played with extraordinary skill.
Below left: Detail from *The Coronation of the Virgin* by Fra Angelico. You can see an angel carrying a brass instrument which was played in Fra Angelico's day. The figure in the centre is plucking the strings of a lute. In the bottom right-hand corner you can see part of another lute viewed from the side. When it was held in the position shown here. The lute was played with a bow.

What is music?

Music is formed by a series of sounds. As each sound is made it travels through the air in the form of sound-waves. These waves are received by our auditory organ, the ear. The music is then transmitted to the brain as a collection of resonant impulses. To make music, the best sounds are clear notes which vibrate well.
However, not everyone appreciates the same kinds of sound, with the result that music can be very varied indeed. Different kinds of instruments are used to produce different sounds. These vary throughout the world. Each country has its own distinct style of music. In addition, people's tastes change over the years. And finally, man is always inventing new kinds of musical instruments.

What causes differences in pitch?

High notes are produced by a large number of vibrations per second; similarly, we hear low notes when there are very few vibrations per second. Between the highest and lowest number of vibrations lies a whole range of notes which we, as human beings, can hear. But it also happens that some notes are too high for our ears to hear, and the same thing applies to extremely low notes. Sometimes animals can hear notes which we cannot; for example, a dog can

How many different kinds of music are there?

Music can be classified in various ways. There is instrumental music, in which instruments only are used. Chamber music is written to be played by a small number of musicians. A symphony has to be executed by a symphonic orchestra consisting of at least 80 musicians. There are also scores written for one particular instrument; we call these concertos – violin, piano, flute or organ concertos for example. Folk music is the music of the people whose popularity lasts over a fairly long period of time. Hymns are songs of the people, and so are national anthems, the songs chosen by nations to symbolize the ties between people living in the same country. Pop music is a light kind of music in the tradition of rock and roll and the music of Elvis Presley, the Beatles and the Rolling Stones. Lastly, we should note that western music is very different from eastern music, for instance the kind played in India.

Left: **Joseph Haydn, an Austrian composer who lived from 1732 to 1809. Being a nice-natured man, he wrote music that is graceful and well-balanced, and often humorous. He composed symphonies, chamber music and piano pieces. His oratories, *The Creation* and *The Seasons* are still very impressive.**
Centre: **Wolfgang Amadeus Mozart, another Austrian composer. He was the musical genius of the nighteenth century. At the age of six he was giving piano recitals, and he began composing at the age of seven. He turned the piano concerto into a popular form of music. In 1781 this famous composer died, in poverty and deserted by everyone.**
Right: **Ludwig van Beethoven, a German composer of Flemish origin. He was born in Bonn in 1770, and died in 1827. He is regarded as one of the greatest composers, and his music is still played a great deal today.**

pick up the high note produced by a dog whistle.

When a piano is properly tuned, each string produces exactly the right number of vibrations, and these are arranged so that each note will give a different sound.

How is music made?

Anyone who wants to play a musical instrument must first have lessons in how to produce the sounds he wants to hear. Then he must choose what he wants to play – whether he wishes to interpret a composition of his own, or follow a musical score indicating the right notes to play. A score is written music; it is covered with symbols which have a particular meaning for the musician. They have been written down by someone else, the creator who originally thought of the music – in other words, the composer.

What different kinds of instrument are there?

It is possible to divide musical instruments into three categories – string instruments, wind instruments, and percussion instruments. String instruments – the violin, for example – can be played with the help of a bow which is drawn across the strings. Strings can also be plucked; the sounds produced in this way have quite a different resonance – think of the guitar, banjo, mandoline or double-bass. Stringed instruments also include key-board instruments.

Wind instruments are divided into woodwinds and brass. Among the woodwinds we find the oboe, the bassoon and the clarinet. The trumpet and tuba belong to the brass section. In general we can say that wind instruments produce a more piercing sound than stringed instruments.

In the percussion section, everyone is familiar with the drum, but there are others, too. There are kettle-drums, which are shaped a bit like saucepans and are tuned very precisely. Then come the triangle, the cymbals, one or more gongs, the bass drum, the tambourine, the castanets and the rattle. We may find many of these instruments together in a large orchestra, whereas a small group may use only a few instruments to produce a different musical effect.

Edward Kennedy Ellington was the full name of the man known to jazz history as 'Duke' Ellington. He was one of the greatest composers of jazz music. The 'Duke' was also an excellent pianist and one of the top band leaders. Many great jazz musicians have played under him. Duke Ellington was born in 1889 and became famous from 1924 onwards. This giant of the jazz world died in 1974.

What is jazz?

Jazz was born out of the popular music of North American black people. The first compositions date from the end of the nineteenth and beginning of the twentieth century. Jazz was extremely popular between 1920 and 1940, thanks to the invention of the gramophone. Percussion and wind instruments play a major part in it, and jazz musicians are often left free to improvise on a basic theme.

Painting

This form of art includes painting on wood, fabric and paper; other modes are painting on walls (murals and frescoes) and painting on glass.

Did painting already exist in ancient times?

The ancient Egyptians painted the walls of their temples and decorated their tombs with scenes of every-day life. They used colours such as blue, green, rust-red, yellow, black and white, and their human figures were always drawn in profile.

Frescoes have also been found on walls in Mesopotamia. The Etruscans, who ruled in Italy before the Romans, left tomb-paintings behind them. Finally, the Romans themselves had richly decorated houses, with walls covered in frescoes; the over-all effect was often rather untidy by our standards. We also have canvasses dating from the first two centuries after Jesus Christ, representing the faces of the dead immortalized in wax.

What do we know about painting in the Middle Ages?

Monks reproduced books by copying them out by hand. The first letters of each chapter would be decorated (or illuminated) with great care and detail. They depicted the scenes from the New Testament or the Book of Psalms which were the subject of the main text. At first this was only practised in England and Ireland; then, during the reign of Charlemagne and his successors, the art of illumination spread among monks all over Europe.

At this period the inside walls of churches were decorated with frescoes – which are painted on to a wall while the plaster is still wet. Later, when the architectural style changed, churches were also given stained glass windows, and the art of decorating with glass was born.

What was the first picture painted by man?

The pictures found in prehistoric caves show that man's interest in those days was very much centred on animals. Moreover, according to the experts, prehistoric men painted their lifelike pictures of animals because they believed that this would give them power over them. The need for this feeling of superiority over animals was naturally very important, since prehistoric men were under constant threat of attack by wild beasts. They also needed to feel stronger when they went out hunting. Our ancestors used both brushes and their fingers to create these animal paintings on their cave walls. They used colours such as red-brown, yellow and black.

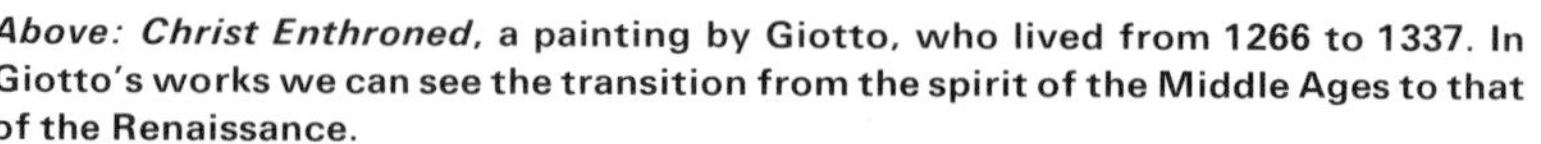

Above: *Christ Enthroned*, a painting by Giotto, who lived from 1266 to 1337. In Giotto's works we can see the transition from the spirit of the Middle Ages to that of the Renaissance.
Left: Hans Holbein was a skilled painter and draftsman who lived from 1497 to 1543. He was a painter at the court of Henry VIII, and also sculpted several lifelike busts of the king.
Below: Study of the heads of old men, by Leonardo da Vinci, one of the greatest artists of all times.

Sir Anthony van Dyck was a Flemish painter who lived from 1559 to 1641. He was best known for his portraits. Here he is shown in one of his own paintings. He had a particular liking for subjects taken from the Bible. Van Dyck worked for a long time at the English court. After Rubens, he was the most important painter of the seventeenth century.

How was painting 're-born' during the Renaissance?

After the Middle Ages, people began to look back to the 'classical' age of the Romans, and to try to imitate them, particularly in their art, and so the age was known as a 'rebirth'.

During the Renaissance the rules of perspective were discovered, and artists learned how to represent three-dimensional objects on a flat surface. In Florence these rules were worked out mathematically, but in Flanders they were deduced from the constant and painstaking observation of reality.

At first paintings only portrayed religious subjects. However, there is a *Virgin and Child* painted in 1452 by Filippo Lippi which already contains the seeds of secular art.

Then it became the fashion among the rich to have their own portraits painted. Orders came in so thick and fast that painters were hard put to carry them out. Raphael painted the portrait of the Pope in Rome; Titian painted the Emperor Charles V. Holbein, a German, painted King Henry VIII of England with a meticulous care for accuracy.

In Renaissance paintings artists abandoned the principle that the scene portrayed must be seen through a window.

At this time Italian painters were already highly thought of, particularly Giotto. But Flemish painting became extremely important, too. Jan van Eyck was the first of a whole line of great painters, the best known of whom are Rogier van der Weyden, Hugo van der Goes and Hans Memlic. Then there was Hieronymus Bosch, who had a completely individual style of his own.

What are the characteristics of the Baroque period (about 1550 to 1700)?

The Council of Trent summoned by the Pope to condemn the Reformation and define Church doctrine was over, but its effects continued to reverberate in the world of art. Artists had a new attitude towards religious subjects and portrayed them in a new way. The painter focussed on what seemed most important to him, and drew attention to it with a new use of light, vivid and slanting. Many European painters of the seventeenth century adopted this technique. One of the

Above: A self-portrait by Rembrandt van Ryn, who lived from 1606 to 1669. His life's work consists of 350 paintings, 300 engravings and 1600 drawings. One of his favourite subjects was mankind.
Opposite: Studies of a negro's head, signed by Peter Paul Rubens, a Flemish contemporary of Rembrandt. In 1610, Rubens founded a great studio.

Opposite: Paul Gauguin was a French painter who lived from 1848 to 1903. In his early days as an artist he belonged to the group of painters calling themselves *Impressionists*. He was the first person to put Europeans in touch with artistic styles from other parts of the world. One of his favourite places was Tahiti, in the Pacific, where he painted this picture of young Tahitian girls.

Below: Joannes Vermeer of Delft lived from 1632 to 1675. He is chiefly famous for his pictures of people in their homes. These paintings are not very large, but their impact comes from his extraordinary use of colour. Here we show a detail from a painting called *The Lacemaker*.

most famous was Rembrandt van Ryn, who is famous for his skilful use of light and shade.

Baroque art is also characterized by a new way of applying paint to the canvas. Light colours are contrasted with darker ones to make the subject stand out in relief. Seen close to, these works give the impression of having been rather carelessly done, and the effect is better when they are looked at from a distance.

Like other painters of his period, Frans Hals of Harlem painted some wonderful portraits. Favourite themes of the Baroque period include landscapes and interiors; Rembrandt, Vermeer and Jan Steen were masters of these themes.

What is a fake?

A fake is a form of artistic fraud. It is sold to the buyer as the original work of a great master, with the object of making a lot of money.

Who was van Meegeren?

Hans van Meegeren was a Dutch painter who died in 1847. He was a great artist, but unknown. He made his name in history by forging the works of Vermeer; he signed a number of his own paintings with the name of the famous painter, who had recently been discovered. Only later were they found out to be fakes.

Other famous painters of the period were Velazquez in Spain and Sir Peter Paul Rubens of Antwerp. In France, Nicolas Poussin was highly successful; his meticulous, severe style is diametrically opposed to that of Rubens.

What are the distinctive features of the rococo style in painting?

The Rococo style tends to be lighter, and more escapist than the Baroque.

Rococo art was best represented in France. The great master of this style was Watteau. His paintings are notable for their lightness and gracefulness. His favourite subjects were love, pomp, luxury and magnificence.

What happened to painting before and after the French Revolution?

In 1760 painters in Germany were trying to imitate Raphael. In France, Greuze chose to paint scenes of everyday life, showing the virtues of the bourgeoisie. David, also French, took his subjects from Greek mythology; his style was sobre and severe.

Opposite: This picture, painted in 1942 by Picasso, is called ***Still Life with Skull of an Ox***. Pablo Picasso was a Spanish painter, born in 1881. At an early age he left his country to live in France. On his death in 1973 the French state inherited part of his enormous output.

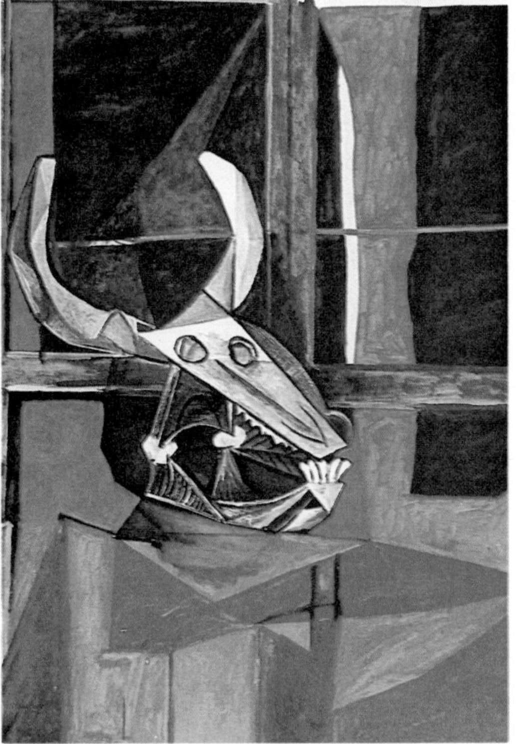

Below: Self-portrait by the Dutch painter Vincent van Gogh, who lived from 1853 to 1890. In France he came into contact with the Impressionists and began using very deep colours contrasted with very light ones. He depicted nature in his own personal way. He thus became the precursor of Expressionism.
Right: ***Woman by a Window*** by Marc Chagall, a Russian painter who worked mainly in Paris. In his work the boundaries between dream and reality are blurred. His style strongly influenced the artistic movement called Surrealism.

In England, William Blake was inspired by the works of Michelangelo. After this, English painters, including Turner, took a new interest in landscape. Following the Romantic movement one of the first painters to set up his easel out of doors was Constable. He was closely followed by the French painters, around 1830, principally Rousseau, Corot and Millet. Landscape painting was also taken up in Germany.

What invention influenced painting, and what were the results of this?

After photography had been invented by Niepce it became popular as a novelty among painters in the 1840s. Courbet, Manet, Degas, Cézanne and Breitner all used photographs as a starting point for their paintings.
Some artists reacted against it, however, by laying greater stress on contrasts of shapes and colours. The Cubists went to the extreme of trying to represent on a flat surface an object seen from several angles at once.
Meanwhile the Impressionists, with Monet at the forefront, had been experimenting with techniques based principally on colour and light. Other Impressionist painters were Manet, Renoir, and – again – Degas.
Seurat invented Pointillism and Gauguin simplified forms, filling his canvases with flat shapes in warm colours.
In the work of Vincent Van Gogh, one of the 'Post Impressionists', colour and shape are subordinated to interior rhythm; his paintings still look very modern today.

Why is 1912 an important date for contemporary painting?

That was the year when Duchamp painted a picture in which he expressed 'movement'. This innovation was followed by a number of artistic movements with names ending in '-ism'. Among the great artists of the period were Picasso, Kandinsky, Modigliani, Pollock and Appel, all of whom were painters of 'movement'.
With Pop Art there has been a return to every-day reality; the most important Pop artists are Oldenburg and Warhol, who are also well-known in other fields of the arts.

Sculpture

Sculpture is an art form which consists of chiselling, carving, moulding or otherwise working on particular materials. The result is a three-dimensional object or likeness.

Above: Athena Lemnia, a Roman copy of a work by the Greek sculptor Phidias. **Below:** Part of a stone carving representing scenes from the travels of Darius. This Mesopotamian work of art was discovered on the site of ancient Persepolis.

Was sculpture practised in ancient times?

Men were painting and carving images – often of the animals they hunted – long before they could even write.

The Egyptians carved wooden statues in the image of their pharaohs, and placed them in their funeral chambers. Many of them have been preserved. Great stone statues have also been found – some of them 4 metres high. Sometimes these depicted animals.

In the region lying between the Tigris and the Euphrates the statue of a king has been found dating from about 2,400 B.C., together with stone effigies of warriors and gods from a later period.

The Greeks laid great importance on the human body. They placed statues around their temples in honour of the gods. Often a warrior-hero or a great athlete would be immortalized in sculpture showing the athlete in motion, as in the sculpture of the discus thrower by Myron. Temple friezes were also decorated with bas-reliefs depicting famous people. One of the greatest Greek sculptors was Phidias; others were Praxiteles, Scopas and Lysippus. After Phidias a more decorative style developed. With the conquests of Alexander the Great the artistic ideas of the Greeks were disseminated through a number of countries.

The Romans had a great admiration for the Greek sculptors, and used to copy them. When they conquered Greece in the second century after Christ, they carried off a large number of sculptures. And anything they couldn't take to Rome, they copied on the spot!

It is due to the Romans' boundless admiration for Greek art that over the centuries the inhabitants of Europe were able to become acquainted with ancient Greek and Roman sculptures.

Where do we find medieval sculpture?

Sculpture did exist during the Middle Ages, but it was entirely in the service of religion, so that it is mainly to be found in churches and monasteries. At first it was not allowed to be classed as a monumental art, and was limited to craftwork, but after the twelfth century it began to appear on tombstones and in church portals.

The covers of the books transcribed by the monks were often decorated in relief; sometimes these decorations would be carved in ivory.

Opposite: Gothic sculpture on the exterior of Rheims cathedral. The figures shown are all seen from the front, two by two. In sculptures of people the posture is often accentuated by the folds of the garments. In Gothic cathedrals sculpture was not limited to doorways. The whole façade, the buttresses and even the arches were decorated with sculpture, too.

Around 1015 the church of Hildesheim in Germany was endowed with bronze doors carved with scenes from the Bible. Carved decorations began to appear on wooden doors, too. Relief work, in stone, wood or metal, depicting biblical scenes, was very popular.

In Italy famous sculptors included Nicola Pisano, Giovanni Pisano, Andrea Pisano, Luca della Robbia, Giotto and Arnolfo Cambio.

In Germany only a few sculptures were to be found in churches. In France, on the other hand, a Romanesque style of sculpture came into being, related to the architectural style of the churches being built at the time. Bas-reliefs appeared on the pediments and capitals of pillars.

With the arrival of the Gothic style, Gothic churches sprang up almost everywhere in Europe. A change took place in the art of sculpture, too, and it became more delicate. Statues were placed on plinths and a great deal of attention was paid to the details of their clothes, particularly the folds. Their facial expressions became more lively, reflecting the sculptors' desire to give their work a more human touch. Inside the churches, tall pillars and elegant stained glass windows took over from sculpture, which eventually faded out.

What happened to sculpture after the Middle Ages?

Sculptors continued to contribute their skills to the adornment of churches and monasteries, but they also began to receive orders for statues which had no connection with religion.

In 1453 Donatello sculpted an equestrian statue of the Italian military leader Gattemaleta; it was very similar to the ancient statue of the Roman Emperor Marcus Aurelius, which was still preserved at that date. Thus there was a renewed interest in classical antiquity in the world of sculpture. Donatello's statue captured the feeling of movement of the horse, and was very realistic. Many sculptors tried to follow him and then work became increasingly decorative and ornamental.

This new style of art was part of the Renaissance – which means 're-birth' or 'renewal'. Many artists began producing work that reflected the new style. The most famous of them was Michelangelo.

How did sculpture develop during the twentieth century?

Two of the great names of twentieth-century sculpture are Ossip Zadkine and Naum Gabo, both Russian by birth. We should also mention the delicate, almost transparent sculpture of the Swiss sculptor Giacometti, which forms a direct contrast with the monumental works of the British Henry Moore. Moore is famous for his reclining figures. He has a great instinct for shape and texture, and although he uses abstract techniques, his work is never completely abstract.

In North America Calder is producing extremely lightweight works called mobiles; these are made up of a number of separate parts, and when they are hung up the different sections are constantly in motion, creating a composition that looks different from moment to moment.

Top: **Michelangelo's *Pieta*. *Pieta* is an Italian word denoting the Virgin Mary weeping over the body of her Son, which lies in her lap. Michelangelo was an Italian artist of the Renaissance period.**
Above: Children bathing. **The impression of lightheartedness is enhanced by the fact that the sculptor, Stio Blomberg, has succeeded in lifting the group away from the ground, which it only touches at one or two carefully chosen points.**

Literature

Literature is a form of art which is expressed by the written or spoken word. The artist who chooses this medium tries to communicate his impressions to others by the choice of the right words.

Below: Sophocles lived in the fifth century B.C. He wrote tragedies which were often performed in ancient Greece. A hundred and twenty-three of his plays have been preserved.

What forms does literature take?

It is possible to classify literature in several ways. Firstly, there are popular stories – folk and fairy tales, which come from the ordinary people, and include for example the tales of the brothers Grimm. Then there is the more cultivated literary form, in which a particular author expresses his own thoughts and feelings.

But we can also make the following classification: the narrative, or epic, lyric poetry (in which the writer communicates his feelings), and drama. In this last literary form, a writer's ideas are generally interpreted by a theatrical performance. Myths, fairy-tales and legends are stories in which the imagination plays a great part; these three forms belong to the narrative genres, which also includes the epic. Epics are long narratives, usually relating the story of an important event or the life-story of a hero. *The Song of Roland* is a poem in this category. Milton's poem, 'Paradise Lost', is a very good example of an epic work.

Ballads are stories told in verse. Fables and parables are stories which teach a lesson. Short stories and novels are literary forms which can keep us enthralled for whole evenings at a time. These are written in prose.

The biographies and autobiographies of famous people concentrate on past events in the life of the person concerned which the writer considers to be important.

Lyric poetry can include songs, and elegies, and also satirical verse, in which the poet expresses his disapproval of a situation or person, as in the poetry of Alexander Pope, for example.

Writers have a third way of expressing themselves – play-writing.

The Greek theatre developed out of the religious ceremonies performed in honour of the god Dionysos. It was started up in about 535 B.C. by the person who conducted these ceremonies. The theatre flourished in ancient Greece thanks to playwrights like Aeschylus, Sophocles, Euripides and Aristophanes. These plays were usually tragic.

In the Roman theatre the emphasis was more on comedy, while in Europe drama centred for a long time around religion. Religious themes were not dropped until very late on.

These days sad plays, usually ending in the death or downfall of someone, are called tragedies and funny plays which have happy endings are called comedies or farces. The theatre can also be divided into modern and classical. And if a theatrical work is performed to music, it is called an opera, an operetta or a musical comedy, depending upon the style of the work.

Below: In ancient Greece the town of Epidaurus lay in the Argolis region. Its theatre was the pride of the local people. It has been preserved over the centuries and many plays are still acted there. Although it is very big, the actors can be heard by the whole audience. The architect of this remarkable building was Polycletes.

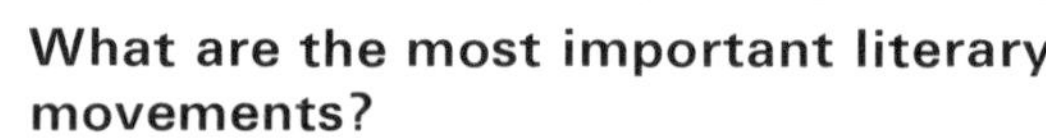

What are the most important literary movements?

In the Middle Ages the main literary forms were epic or narrative poems, lyrics and religious poems. One of the most famous early poets is Chaucer, often referred to as the 'Father of English poetry', the author of *The Canterbury Tales*.

During the sixteenth century the Elizabethan love lyric, based on the Italian Petrarchan sonnet, became popular. Wyatt,

Above right: **Dante was a great Italian poet of the Renaissance. This painting shows his meeting with Beatrice, his beloved. Dante dedicated some remarkable verses to her.**
Top left: **Goethe was a German writer and poet. He was one of the great figures of the Romantic movement.**
Above left: **Shaw was a highly talented playwright and critic. He was awarded the Nobel Prize for Literature in 1925.**
Below: **The Russian writer Dostoievsky, who lived from 1821 to 1881, was one of the giants of world literature.**
Below right: **Detail of a sculpture by Rodin of Balzac, one of the greatest novelists of all time.**

Surrey and Sidney wrote many sonnets.
Early drama took the form of *tableaux* or miracle plays. These depicted scenes from the Bible.
Drama was very popular with the Elizabethans, and the greatest dramatist of all was William Shakespeare, whose plays are still performed and enjoyed today. Other dramatists of the period include Marlowe, who wrote *Dr Faustus*, and Ben Jonson.
At the beginning of the seventeenth century a new style of poetry began to emerge. It was known as metaphysical poetry because of the unusual concepts and images employed by poets like Donne and Herbert to express their emotions.
Plays were banned during Oliver Cromwell's time, and it was not until Charles II came to the throne in 1660 that they could again be performed in public. Called Restoration plays, these were often light-hearted comedies, contrasting with the darkness of the Putiran era. Playwrights include Sheridan and Wycherley.
The novel began to emerge as a literary form towards the end of the seventeenth century with John Bunyan's *Pilgrim's Progress*, Defoe's *Robinson Crusoe*, and later Swift, Richardson and Fielding.
The eighteenth century, the 'Age of Reason', included famous satirists like Pope and Swift.
This was followed in the early nineteenth century by the romantic movement in poetry, led by William Wordsworth, 'the poet of the lakes', Coleridge, Shelley, Keats and Byron.
The nineteenth century saw the emergence of the great novelists, including Charles Dickens, George Eliot, Jane Austen, the Bronte sisters and Walter Scott.
Plays had suffered a decline since the Restoration, but at the end of the century Wilde and Shaw were writing plays. Shaw's most famous works include *Pygmalion* and *St Joan*.
In our own age playwrights include T. S. Eliot, Beckett, Pinter, John Osborne, Alan Ayckbourne. Poets include Eliot, Yeats, Auden and Gerald Manley Hopkins. Some of today's novelists are Hardy, Conrad, Orwell, Huxley, H. G. Wells, Woolf, Henry James, Joyce, D. H. Lawrence and Graham Greene.

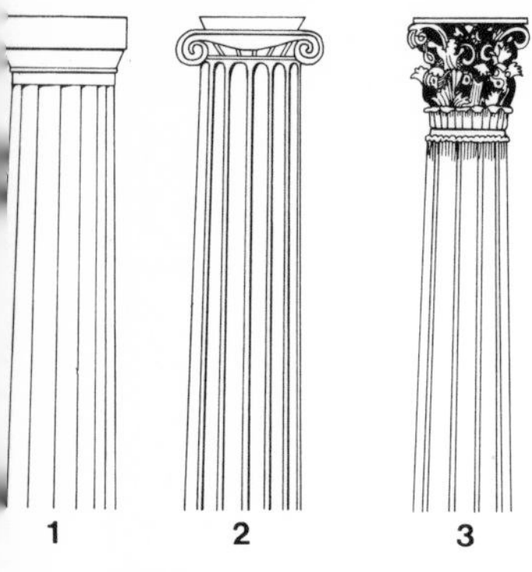

Above: The three orders of Greek column. (1) The Doric column is the oldest; it was in use in the fifth century B.C. From 450 B.C. it was replaced by (2) the Ionic column; there is a scroll on each side of the capital between the column and the angular superstructure. (3) Finally, from 350 B.C. the Corinthian column made its appearance. It is more tapered than the two earlier ones and is topped with a heavily decorated capital.

Above right: Masons at work. This illustration dates from the thirteenth century. At the time pulleys were already in use, and the builder had a mortar-trough. With the help of simple tools like a plumb-line he was able to check whether the work was being carried out according to plan. The artisans who worked on buildings such as cathedrals used to travel from town to town.

Architecture

Building styles and shapes and exterior decorations change over the course of time, and depend on the architect.

What do we know about the architecture of ancient times?

Between 1300 and 1800 B.C. the Egyptians built their pyramids, which were stone tombs for their pharaohs. They were built out of huge blocks of stone placed on top of each other in a series of squares which narrowed as they grew nearer the top. These stone blocks were hauled up the sides using human strength alone. There are also some remains of Egyptian temples of the same period, and from the few ruins that are left we have a very good idea of the architectural abilities of the Egyptians.

In Asia – the region between the Tigris and Euphrates rivers – buildings were chiefly made of clay, which could be moulded into bricks and baked in the sun. Only one instance of natural stone has been discovered, used in some foundations. After some time the clay bricks would crumble, so that all the

buildings of this period have vanished into dust.

The early Greeks, around 900 B.C., built temples out of wood with clay walls. Several hundred years later they began to build temples in stone, though the roofs were still wooden, tiled over. The Greek temple was built in a rectangle, surrounded by pillars. These were made of round blocks of stone placed on top of each other and interlocking. The friezes and triangular tympan were decorated.

The Greeks were already familiar with

Opposite: The ruins of an imposing Greek temple on the Acroplis of Athens. Originally the word 'acropolis' meant 'fortress'. Later, the Athens acropolis became a centre of worship. The Parthenon is a temple dedicated to the goddess Athena. It was supported by Doric columns, the remains of which can still be seen on the rocky hill overlooking Athens. Phidias, the famous Greek sculptor, carved a great many statues and friezes for this collection of temples.

When the Roman Empire of the west broke up, the Roman Empire of the east remained a great power. The buildings of this period reflect both western and eastern influences combined. The Emperor Justinian ruled over this great empire from 527 to 665 A.D. Around 530 A.D. he witnessed the building of the monastery of St Catherine on what was almost an island in the Sinai desert, between the Red Sea and the Gulf of Aqaba.

In the Middle Ages, people tried to make their towns more secure by building thick walls around them. Carcassonne in France is a typical example of these fortified medieval towns. The walls and fortifications were restored in the nineteenth century under the direction of Viollet-le-Duc.

What form did freemasonry take in the past?

Freemasonry is a movement that exists in several countries. Its aim is to promote the welfare of all mankind. Its organization is based on the medieval guilds of stonemasons and builders. Masons keep their organizations and ceremonies secret; in the past there was even more secrecy about them than there is now. The members of a group – called a lodge – are generally divided into three degrees, as in the old days – apprentice, fellow of the craft, and master mason. Their symbols are the tolls that used to be used in cathedral building. Often only initiates know the secret method of handling them.

blocks and tackle, and used them frequently. They were also very skilful at decorating the interior of their homes.
The Romans copied the Greeks in many ways, but they introduced a new architectural feature of their own, the arch constructed of wedge-shaped stones, examples of which they had come across in the East. They were also among the first to use concrete and bricks for building their baths and temples. They developed a very powerful form of mortar, faced with brick on marble, and this advance enabled them to build huge roofs. This changed the style and function of their buildings, and we find a large number of theatres, ampitheatres, domed temples, public baths and aqueducts.
For fortresses and aqueducts they would bake bricks on the building site; if they wanted to use brick to support a lot of weight they had to make very precise calculations. The Colosseum, which is four storeys high, the Arch of Titus and the Pantheon still bear witness to the skill of Roman architects.

Are there any remains of antique architecture in Europe?

As long as people had no permanent dwelling place, there could be no question of architecture. Then, when whole tribes began to accept the Christian religion, small churches began to spring up. Remnants of Frankish architecture can be found, dating from the Merovingian period. In addition, there are some churches and monasteries which were built in Charlemagne's reign. Most of the remains of this period can be found at Aix-la-Chapelle in Germany and at Autun and Auxerre in France. The style of most of these buildings was copied from the Romans.

In the twelfth century, French architects discovered a technique for building churches entirely out of stone. They gave the vaulted ceilings and arches a more pointed shape. However, they didn't as yet attempt to make very wide openings in the thick walls which supported the heavy roofs, and the churches remained dark inside.

This was the birth of the Romanesque, or Norman, style, characterized by heavy, square buildings, lit by only a few windows and held up by thick walls with no buttresses. There are some good examples in Burgundy (Vézelay, Paray-le-Monial), Poitou (Poitiers), and in the south of France (Arles, Moissac), and in Durham, Ely and Peterborough cathedrals in England.

From the thirteenth century onwards a great number of high-vaulted churches and cathedrals began to appear around Paris. They were supported by stone arches and butresses round the outside. In most cases the façade was flanked by two towers, framing the triangular gables of the centre nave, which contained a magnificent rose-window. The main doorways would be richly decorated with sculptures.

The same techniques were used for building castles and houses. This is particularly noticeable on the exterior walls, for inside, the different storeys were divided up into square rooms without ribbed vaulting. Among the great monuments of this period we should mention Chartres cathedral, Notre-Dame of Paris, Notre-Dame of Reims, and the cathedral of St Denis. In

Opposite: During the Renaissance period castles were no longer used as fortresses, for no fortifications could withstand the onslaught of the cannons now used in warfare. Castles were replaced by beautiful palaces and châteaux. The château of Chenonceaux in France was built in the Renaissance style and has all of the characteristics of the period. One of its unusual features is the wing built over the river Cher.

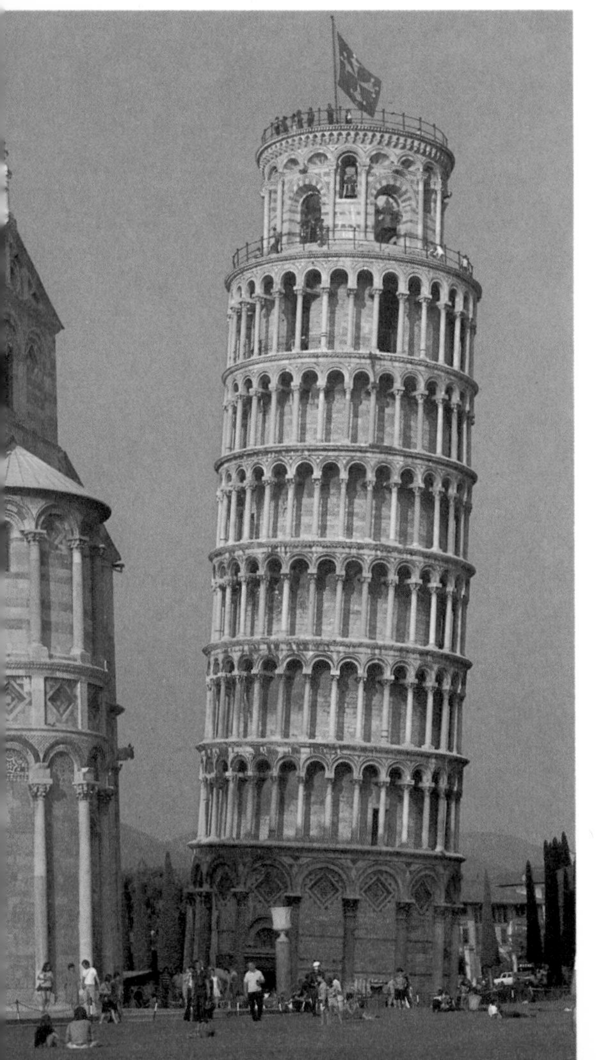

Left: Romanesque architecture in Italy is typified by façades decorated with galleries and pillars. One of the customs of the period was to build a separate bell-tower at the side of the church. An example of this can be found in the cathedral of Pisa, which was completed in 1090. After it was built, the bell-tower began to lean to one side, and it still leans today. When building the foundations, the architect had not taken the type of soil into account, and they began to sink in the marshy ground.

Right: Fischer van Erlach was an Austrian architect who lived from 1656 to 1723. The Baroque style can be clearly seen in his work. He designed the Palace of Schönbrunn, which was built for the Empress Maria Theresa. Between 1744 and 1749 a number of major alterations were carried out on this building.

Top: The Taj Mahal, a tomb at Agra in India. It was built in the seventeenth century by Shah Jehan, for his wife.
Above: A very different building – the royal palace at Bangkok, capital of Thailand.
Right: Brasilia, the new capital of Brazil, was designed by the famous architect Oscar Niemeyer. The photograph shows the tower of the underground cathedral. For the architect, this tower is 'a crown of thorns, which lacerates as it draws tighter'. Niemeyer was the first man in history to be given the opportunity of designing an entire city without worrying about cost. Brasilia was thus created as a whole in just a few years.

Britain an example of this type of architecture, known as Gothic, can be found at Gloucester cathedral.

Were the new Renaissance ideas also reflected in architecture?

The architectural style of the Renaissance was a return to the strict lines of Greek buildings. Here, too, the classical style was in favour. In church and house building the aim was simplicity, shapes being restricted to the straight line and the circle.

What is the Baroque style?

Whereas the lines of the Renaissance had been strict and classical, the sixteenth and seventeenth centuries gave birth to a much more grandiose and florid style. This appeared first in Italy, in the churches and palaces built at this time.

The German states and Spain were strongly influenced by this new movement. But in France, the Baroque style was in competition with the rise of Classicism, which was characterized by fidelity to the Greek and Roman architectural styles. The principal examples of Baroque are to be found in the interior of large buildings like the château of Amboise, Azay-le-Rideau, Blois, Chambord and Chenonceaux. It did not appear in architecture until later, with the château of Fontainebleau, the Louvre, etc.

In the eighteenth century there was a complete return to the past. Little by little during the nineteenth century concrete began to be used as a building material.

What are the characteristics of modern architecture?

The principles on which modern architecture is based are efficiency and simplicity. Materials used are steel, glass and concrete. Units are pre-cast in concrete in special workshops and transported ready-made to the building site.

The most famous architects of our own times are the Dutchman Rietveld, the American Wright, the Swiss Le Corbusier and the Brazilian Niemeyer – the creator of Brasilia, the new capital of Brazil.

The art of the cinema

Workers leaving a factory was the subject of the first film to be shown in public in the nineteenth century; it was made by the Frenchman, Auguste Lumière. Enormous developments have taken place since.

Above: Louis Lumière lived from 1864 to 1948. He and his brother Auguste, a chemist, were the pioneers of cinematography.

What do you need to make a film?

A series of images has to be recorded on a continuous strip of film. For this photographic equipment is needed, including cameras for taking the pictures and materials for developing the film. Then a machine is needed to project the reel of film.

At the cinema we don't just look at pictures, we also hear the actors' dialogue, and the sounds that accompany the action. This is possible because alongside the reel of film is a strip with the sound recorded on it. The projector has a special system built into it for projecting sound films; this includes a sound-head which amplifies the sounds recorded on the sound-track, and reproduces them through loudspeakers, for the audience.

How was the cinema born?

The first important event in the history of the cinema was the discovery made by two Frenchmen, Niepce and Daguerre, in 1824 and 1839 respectively, of a way of printing images on film. Not long afterwards another Frenchman, Marey, announced that he had invented the 'photographic rifle'; this invention made it possible to take twelve pictures per second, with the help of a revolving chamber.

In the nineteenth century a Belgian scientist called Plateau invented a children's toy which was an important step in the development of cinematography. In fact, he called his invention a children's cinematograph. After this it appeared in various forms under names such as the *Zoetrope* and the *Praxinoscope*. Eventually a *Praxinoscope* was produced which could project a simple moving picture of the kind which today would be called an animated cartoon.

Who made the first film?

Auguste Lumière built the first camera

Below: Charlie Chaplin was born in 1889 and died in 1977. He was active in several areas of the film business, but is above all famous as an actor of tragi-comic roles.

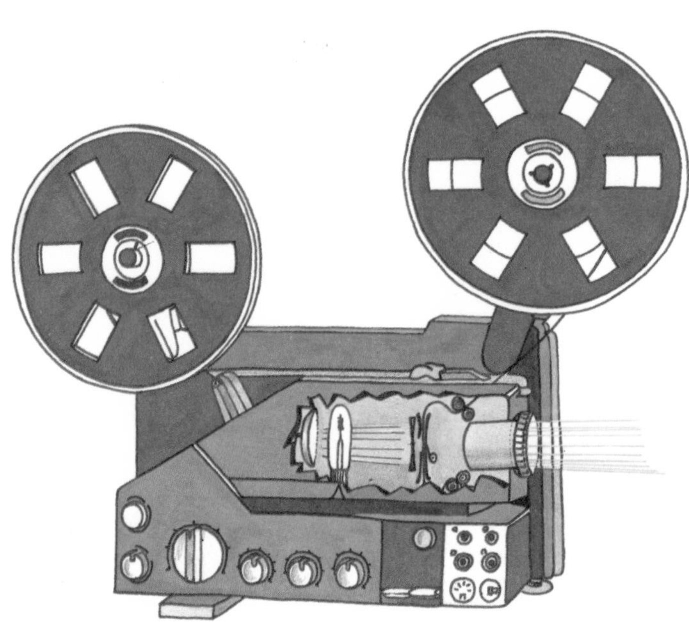

A film projector projects a certain number of images on to a screen. Each image represents a progressive stage of a movement. Our brain retains the pictures for an instant longer than the eye records them, so that what we see is a continuous action.

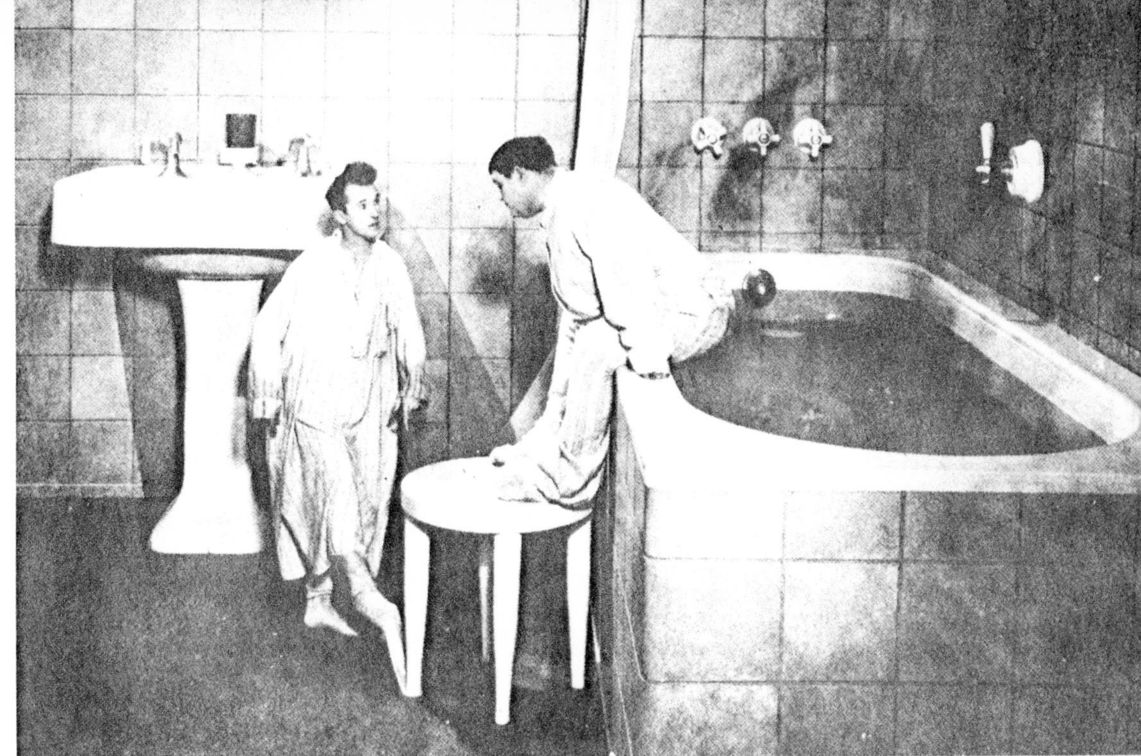

which could record a large number of images per second on a strip of film which could then be developed. Among his first films was one of workers coming out of their factory on their way home.

Lumière announced his discovery in February 1895, and on 22 March it was shown in public for the first time. It was a phenomenal success.

After this, several people began making films in various parts of the world. These early films appear very jerky to us. Although there were some good productions, the modern cinema only really began in 1927, when it became possible to reproduce both sound and pictures at the same time. Until then, the actors' dialogue had had to be conveyed in the form of captions projected between the scenes. Very often the story would be told in the cinema by a person who accompanied the action by playing on the piano. These were known as 'silent' movies, and the new films called 'talkies'. Colour was not used until the 1930s, and then in only few a few films.

What does a reel of cinema film look like?

To take a picture with a moving camera, we use a reel of film, taking care that it doesn't get exposed to the light. When we start filming the camera records a certain number of images per second on to the film. When these are projected, our eyes see them as a continuous moving picture. On the developed film the pictures are almost too small to make out, and they have to be projected on to a screen to be seen properly. Both camera and projector include a mechanism for making the film go round. There are small holes along the edges of the film to ensure that it goes round at a regular speed. The film shown here has holes down one side only, but some types of film have holes along both sides. Amateur film-makers chiefly use 16mm film, but film is also available 70mm wide.

Does it take a lot of people to make a film?

Yes, the production of a film demands the participation of a great number of people. There are the writers who write the scripts and the actors who perform them, people who design and look after the costumes, workmen who build the sets, make-up artistes who get the actors ready, the director and his assistants who are in charge of the actors' performances, and there are cameramen, and sound and lighting technicians. Once the film has been taken it has to be developed by laboratory staff. Then the sound has to be synchronized with the picture. Once this is done, the film goes to another laboratory where copies are made, so that the same film can be shown in several cinemas at once all over the world. People are needed to distribute the copies. And lastly, there are the cinema staff and the projectionists who help us to enjoy the film when it is shown in our cinema.

Dancing

Dancing is the art of moving the body in rhythm. People have always danced, all over the world. Nevertheless, there are enormous differences between the dances of different nations.

Above: Photograph of a performance by the Ballet of Copenhagen, capital of Denmark.
Below: The Zulus are a black race from southern Africa, belonging to the group called Bantus. They live mainly by agriculture, cattle-herding and hunting. They have a very rich heritage. Over the centuries they have developed a wealth of folklore and tradition, including their national dances.

How is dancing classified?

It is possible to make several kinds of classification. There is solo dancing and dancing in a group, depending on how many people are taking part. Groups of dancers may form patterns such as lines or circles, and of course there are many other possible variations.

We can also divide dancing into classical and modern dance.

Some kinds of dance are traditional to different nations. These are called folk-dances, and often they are very old. They are performed in groups and are part of the people's cultural heritage. In some countries there are dances performed only by men and others only by women.

Another kind of dance is created to accompany particular pieces of music; this is called ballet.

There are also various forms of modern dance, performed mainly to modern light music, which are taught in specialized schools.

Finally, there is social dancing. At a formal ball the couples have to follow strict rules, moving in a set pattern to each piece of music; for example in a waltz or fox trot. In discotheques they can move about more freely to the rhythm of the latest hits.

Where are folk dances performed?

Folk dances are performed by people the world over. In Holland, for example, there are still clog-dances, performed by people wearing clogs. They vary from one region to another. In Eastern Europe, Latin America and some African countries, national folk-dance companies have been formed.

With the assistance of the authorities these groups organize public performances of their national dances. They don't always limit themselves to dancing in their own countries; they often travel to other parts of the world to perform their traditional dances. Often, folk dances are performed for the benefit of tourists, and held on certain days to uphold ancient traditions, like the Furry Dances in Cornwall.

What is ballet?

The word ballet denotes dancing as an art-form. Ballets may tell a story, or they may consist of a series of individual dances. They are performed by a company of male and female dancers. Before ballet dancers can perform on the stage they have to go through a very rigid training of exercises, which they start learning in childhood. One of the most famous ballet companies of all is Russia's Bolshoi ballet, which travels all over the world.

The Royal Ballet is a very famous ballet

school. But after leaving a ballet school, dancers have to go on practising for the rest of their careers.

The person who creates dances is called a choreographer. He may design a ballet by inventing a series of steps and movements to go with a piece of music he particularly likes – though this is not always the case. Then the work has to be rehearsed, which may take quite a long time. When it is performed in public the ballet is usually accompanied by an orchestra. Sometimes recorded music is used, but a performance with an orchestra is of course much more effective.

Maurice Béjart is the professional name of M. Berger, a dancer and choreographer born in Marseilles on 1 January 1927. He formed his own dance company in 1952 and called it the *Ballets de l'Etoile*. He goes in for a modern dance style as well as classical, and also uses jazz and movements taken from Oriental dancing. His best known ballets are *Haut Voltage*, *Signes*, *Symphonie pour un Homme Seul*, *Roméo et Juliette*, and *Sacre du Printemps*.

Currently, the Ballets du Vingtième Siècle are looking for new forms of expression in the realm of dance.

In Britain, famous choreographers include Sir Frederick Ashton, whose ballets include Cinderella, Sylvia, and Ondine, Dame Ninette de Valois, founder of the Royal Ballet, and Martha Graham, who was instrumental in founding The London School of Contemporary Dance.

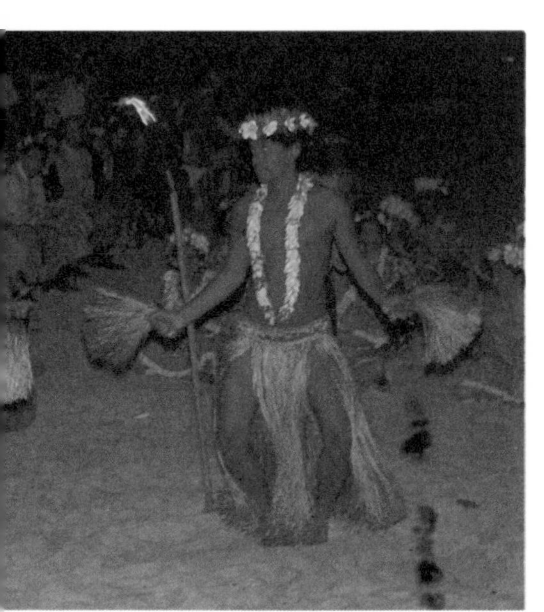

Above: The 'corps de ballet' practising. The corps de ballet is the overall name given to the dancers in a ballet company. During rehearsals the dancers wear light, comfortable clothing which allows them freedom of movement.
Below, left: The Tamara dance. This dance is performed in Tahiti, a large Pacific island which is a French colony.
Below: A typical Tyrolean dance. The women's skirts whirl around to the rhythm of the music, while the men, in leather shorts, clap their hands to beat time.

Is dancing still an art?

Art has always been a means by which feelings are expressed. But to achieve this in dance, the dancer must possess certain talents. Whether the dance they perform is an art or not must depend on how gifted they are. Very often people who dance aren't thinking about art at all – people go to discos, for example, simply to enjoy themselves.

One particular kind of dancing as a form of recreation is formation dancing, in which a group of dancers go through a series of steps and movements to a changing rhythm. Formation dancing is very popular at the moment in the West, and in northern Europe. International competitions are organized every year to choose the best dancers.

Anyone who takes part in a modern dance group, performing to jazz or soul music, is also getting an excellent form of physical exercise.

When dancing is just a pleasant way of spending one's spare time, it can't really be considered as an art form. It's quite another matter when a dance is created by a choreographer and performed by professionals. Then it can reach a level at which it can justly be described as an art.

How human beings live

Man's particular characteristics are his upright stance, the difference between the functions of his hands and feet, the larger size of his brain, his ability to speak and his highly developed intelligence.

Above: **Indonesian woman carrying a burden on her head. When a man carries something on his head he wears a headband as well.**
Right: **As groups of people become more advanced, the children no longer stay at home to learn all they need to know about life from their parents.**
Below: **This young woman's canine teeth have been filed down. This custom still continues in parts of Indonesia.**

What is meant by a primitive way of life?

The word 'primitive' is often used in a critical fashion; some people automatically take it to mean something of little value, with a lot wrong with it. Looked at from this point of view, people leading a primitive life might be thought to be living in very poor conditions. This is not so.

Races, tribes or other groups of people are referred to as 'primitive' when only their basic needs can be met. Very often the desire for change doesn't arise, simply because at their present stage there is no possibility of any further development.

Primitive people are usually people living in the wild. They are content with what nature has to offer them. They are mainly to be found living as nomadic tribes in virgin forests or on islands. Their lives remain primitive because even if they wanted to make contact with other people in the rest of the world, the natural barriers in their way are too big to cross as they live in very inaccessible parts of the world. Thus their traditions are kept up without being affected by outside influences.

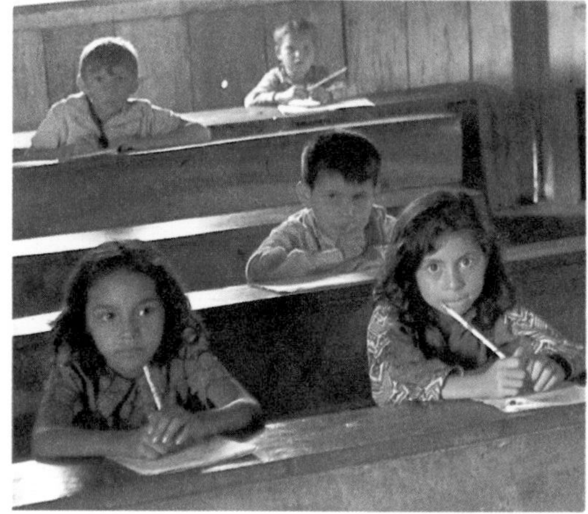

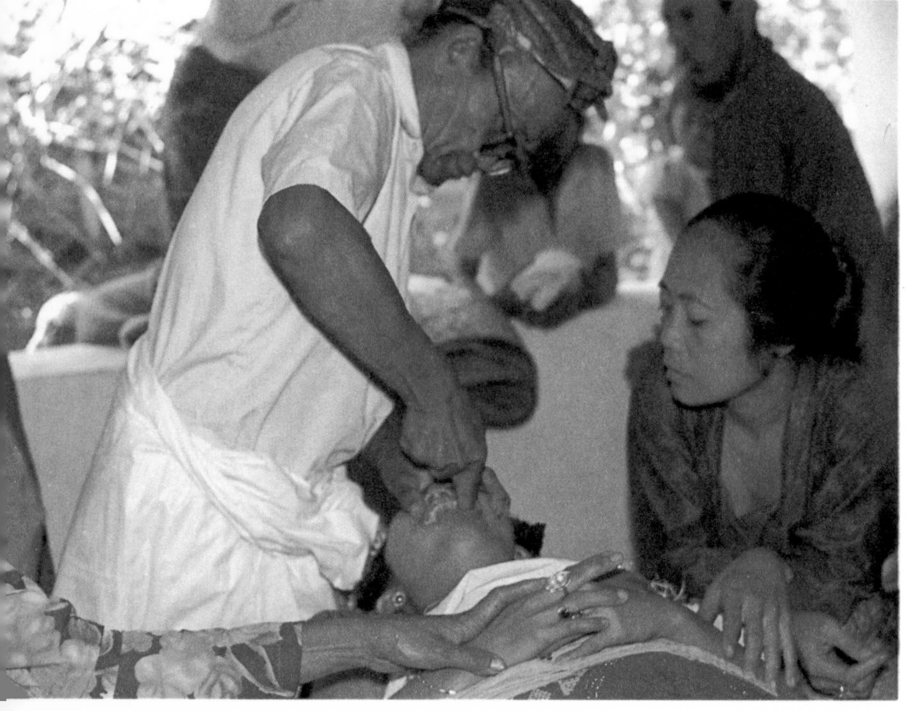

In some cases nature itself forces people to live in a primitive way. This is the case with the Eskimos, for example, who inhabit the polar regions. There are few natural resources, and so they live in houses made from blocks of snow, and eat mainly fish and whalemeat.

Primitive people are satisfied to lead their daily lives in exactly the same way as their parents and grandparents. They live just as their ancestors did.

However, now that more and more means of communications are being made between different kinds of people, the number of primitive people is growing smaller.

What do people wear?

The most simple form of clothing was originally the animal skin, which was worn primarily to protect the body. Another very simple form of dress is the loincloth, a primitive garment made of fabric or leaves which is worn round the waist to serve as a skirt or trousers.

Opposite: People who live off the land need to know how to prepare the crops they grow so that these can be used as food. So among farming tribes you will always find a millstone, a mortar and a pestle. The use of these involves a considerable amount of physical effort, at certain times of the year. This hard work is left almost exclusively to the women. This applies equally to the rice farmers of Indonesia and the African cassava growers.
Right: At the bottom of the page you can see Kenyan women busy with this work.

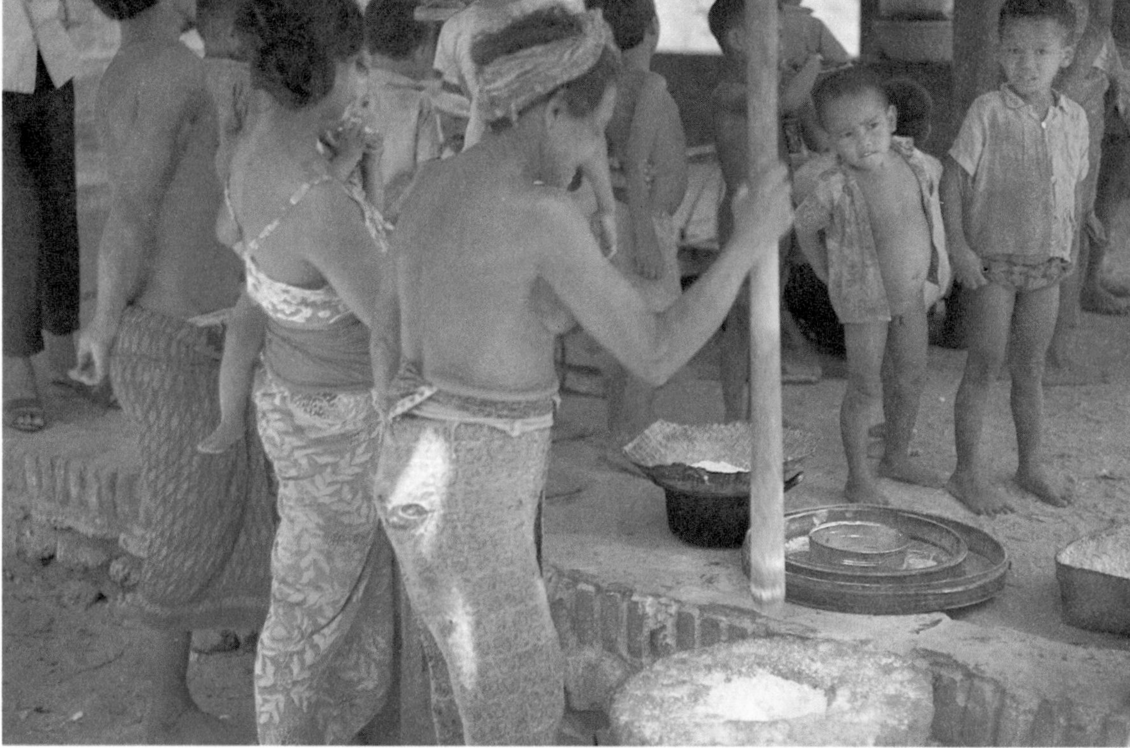

Another simply-made garment is the poncho, a large square of vicuna wool with a hole in the centre for the head to go through. Some Indian tribes join the front and back of the poncho together by sewing them under the arms.

Eskimos make garments for themselves based on the same principle as the poncho. After sewing two skins together at the shoulders and under the arms, they then attach two long sleeves and a hood. This garment is made of fur, which keeps them well protected against the cold. They also wear shirts, with or without sleeves.

In Europe we wear coats and overcoats to protect us against cold or wet weather.

The Japanese kimono is a kind of coat. It consists of a long tunic with sleeves, which crosses over at the front and is held together by a wide belt.

A jacket is a short coat which has become an habitual item of western dress for both men and women.

Most European men wear trousers. Women – who traditionally have worn skirts or dresses – are now tending more often to wear trousers because they are comfortable and practical. For young people the most popular type of trousers in recent years has been jeans, often described as young people's 'uniform'.

The feet are protected by shoes. These are usually made from leather, or other animal skins but nowadays synthetic, man-made materials are being used increasingly.

How do people get married in primitive societies?

Marriages take place very simply. Primitive people regard marriage as such a normal state that they don't need to make a big fuss about it. When a man and a woman take all their belongings and go to live in the same hut or house, the couple is considered to be married. This is what happens in Polynesia today.

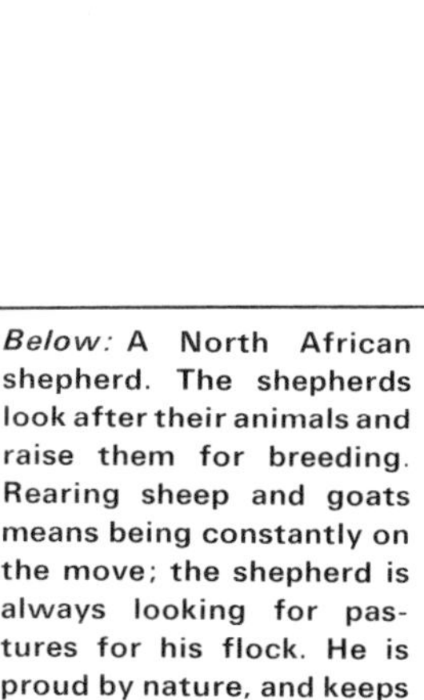

Below: A North African shepherd. The shepherds look after their animals and raise them for breeding. Rearing sheep and goats means being constantly on the move; the shepherd is always looking for pastures for his flock. He is proud by nature, and keeps himself apart from the other farming folk.

How do people make themselves look more attractive?

Everyone has a certain amount of vanity in them. When people want to beautify themselves they find all kinds of ways of decorating their bodies.

The members of the Dayak tribe of Borneo live almost naked. When a young man performs a dance for his future wife, he dresses up in rich materials and adorns himself with feathers.

In other regions there are other circumstances when people use clothes to make themselves look special. People who hold a leading position in a society stand out from the crowd by wearing specific clothes or decorations suited to their function. For example, everyone knows about the crowns and ermine robes worn by royalty. Elsewhere there are other forms of dress and decoration that indicate that the wearer holds a position of great power. The kings of the Hawaiian islands, for example, used to wear a cape of yellow and red feathers, and a helmet-shaped head-dress in the same colours.

Many forms of decoration have a religious significance and are worn to protect the wearer; among these are amulets and medallions.

In some parts of the world, people even used to change the appearance of certain parts of the body. In a region of Zaire the members of one tribe used to keep their babies' heads strapped flat between two wooden boards, which gave them unnaturally elongated skulls. In Burma women's necks used to be elongated. The Dayaks enlarged the lobes of their ears by wearing wooden discs in them, and in Africa some people still use wooden discs to make their lower lips bigger. The Chinese used to bind the feet of their little girls so that they would stay small. In Africa and Indonesia people used to have their teeth filed to a point. Tattooing is not confined to western Europe; it has been practised for a very long time all over the world, from Japan to England.

Anyone who wants to improve their appearance pays attention to their hair. This applies equally to European ladies and to women and girls in West Africa. There are many methods of dressing hair, and fashions vary from country to country. Hair can be plaited, curled, cut short or piled in a bun.

Top: **A Masai woman with her child. The Masais are a tribe living in Kenya, rearing cattle and sheep and living as nomads. Because of a shortage of good pasture lands, however, they are now having to settle down on permanent sites and restrict the size of their herds.**
Above: **A group of folk dancers from the Black Forest.**

Right: **The Quetchu Indians live around Lake Titicaca. This is the highest lake in the world, lying at an altitude of 3,850m above sea level in the Andes, on the borders of Bolivia and Peru. The Indians have been living there for centuries. They make small canoes out of reeds very like the papyrus reeds used by the ancient Egyptians. This gave Thor Heyerdahl the idea which inspired his 'Ra' voyage. He set out to prove that there was a connection between the civilizations of Egypt and America, by crossing the Atlantic from Egypt to America, via Morocco.**

Some people cover themselves in paint for certain occasions. The Australian aborigines and some Africans do this. Red Indians make use of different colours for particular purposes, using one colour when they dance and a different one when they are going out to fight.

Nearly everywhere in the world people make necklaces and jewellery out of teeth, shells or precious metals. Precious stones have always been used as a form of bodily decoration. Wearing clothes can also be said to be a way of making oneself more attractive.

How have people made homes for themselves?

All over the world since man first came into being, people have sought places where they could shelter from the wind and cold. Very often this would include gathering round a fire to keep warm. Prehistoric men used to live in caves, and the Vedda people of Sri Lanka still do. If there were no caves people had to build their own shelters. The simplest solution was the windbreak, consisting of some short branches stuck in the ground and hung about with leaves or animal skins. Windbreaks like this provided shelter for groups of nomads, and Indians would use them when they travelled across the prairies of North America.

Above right: **The burning of a dead body is called cremation. It is a very common practice in the west. In Far Eastern countries, cremation has a religious significance; it is supposed to help the soul to free itself from the body.**
Below right: **A burial on the Indonesian island of Celebes. An image of the dead person is placed in a gallery in front of the cave where the tomb is kept.**

Then people extended this simple system into a circle, and at a later stage put a roof over it. Now it was beginning to look like a proper dwelling. Dome-roofed huts like this are still used among the Pygmies. A tent made of skins is very common among the tribes of central Asia; it is called a *yourt*. The Eskimos' igloo, a hut built out of snow, is also round-shaped, and has a very low door. The round hut was followed by the conical hut, consisting of long branches leaning against each other at the top to form a cone; the sides would then be filled in with leaves, twigs, clay or tree-bark. The Laps of Northern Europe still live in conical huts like this. Another kind of dwelling place is the round hut with walls of straw, clay and twigs with a cone-shaped roof on top. This kind of hut is still very common in Africa.

Later on still, huts began to be built in a square, and this shape became very common all over the world. The Polynesian's hut on his Pacific island is built in a square, just like our own houses or flats. Only the building materials are different.

With stone, people can make buildings that are solid, long-lasting and strong. The Pueblo Indians built stone houses. Some were even built on top of one another, like a primitive form of our own blocks of flats.

According to the prevailing conditions, homes have been built in trees, on stilts or on high ground, the building materials used depending mainly on the local climate.

A lot of problems were solved for people

Below: **Buildings have been made out of stone for many centuries now. Stone enables people to build solid, long-lasting homes to shelter them from the climate. Once square buildings began to be made, individual styles developed in various parts of the world, with roofs in thatch, slate or tiles. This photo shows a typical farm in the Campine region.**

Different kinds of buildings and houses vary in size and design. These differences are manifested in various ways according to the building methods used at different stages of man's development. Buildings also vary according to their function. A building in which lessons are given will look different from a hospital. The differences will be even more evident inside.
Below: **Manhattan is an island on the Hudson river, and is a part of New York City. It is the business centre of this city of millionaires. Many large companies like to have their offices there. That's why, for decades now, space has been saved by building upwards, in the form of skyscrapers. One of the most impressive buildings there is the World Trade Center.**
Right above: **A charming Swiss village built on a mountain slope. The houses are solidly constructed so as not to be damaged by avalanches.**
Right below: **Some of the Peruvian Indian tribes living along the banks of Lake Titicaca build light straw huts on floating rafts.**

when they began to join together and live close to each other in groups. This was particularly necessary in the case of primitive people who had few means of protecting themselves, both from other tribes, and wild animals. Groups of people began to settle down together in village communities; later on, the first towns appeared. Migrant or nomadic tribes set up their tents in camps; their villages would be the places where they gathered together. They would travel from place to place in search of food, or fresh water, and grazing ground for their animals. They would move on again when they had exhausted the supplies.

What is man's most basic need?

Man's most basic need of all is food. He eats vegetable produce, meat and fish. Primitive people find their food supplies in nature. Leaves, fruits, roots, slugs, insects and reptiles are all edible.

In Pygmy tribes the women look after the basic food supplies, and the men add variety to the menu by going out to hunt big game. Anything in nature that can be eaten has been eaten by man. In the old days some men were cannibals; they ate human flesh. In our own part of the world, advertising has a strong influence on what we eat.

Some people can't always eat what they'd like to because of religious sanctions; an example of this is the sacred cow of India.

Different groups of people choose what will go into their daily menus; they acquire habitual tastes and come to enjoy or dislike certain dishes.

The uses to which some foods are put can also vary. The Kirghiz of Asia eat a great deal of butter, but there are some black African tribes who prefer to smear it over their skin.

Gradually mankind learned to harvest the crops and use them for food. Rice is a basic foodstuff for the major part of humanity. In North and Central America, as in Central Africa, maize was for a long time regarded as an essential food. These days it is used as a basis for many every-day foodstuffs. The potato plant comes from America. In the Pacific Islands, sweet potatoes, bananas, breadfruit and coconuts are the usual ingredients of meals.

Wheat and other cereal crops were taken from Europe to other parts of the world, where people learned to cultivate them.

Maize is an important cereal crop. It used to be particularly important in North, South and Central America. The Indians living in the south-western regions of the U.S.A. used to hold religious ceremonies to encourage their crops to grow. Sometimes these would last for a whole day. During these rites, they would pray to Mother Nature to send rain or a favourable wind. At present maize is also used as cattle-fodder. Popcorn is a way of cooking maize which is very popular in America; you can buy it here, too.

Above: Priests in Katmandu, capital of Nepal in Asia. Priests are an every-day sight in the city, which is famous for its many magnificent Buddhist and Hindu temples and palaces. A few years ago numbers of young westerners were drawn to the East. They found all kinds of ways of getting to Katmandu so that they could achieve greater understanding and wisdom through meditation.

How do people eat?

It isn't necessary to boil, bake or fry everything we eat. Fruits are eaten raw, for instance, and so are some roots and other parts of plants. Crustaceans, too, worms and small fish can be eaten raw. Both the Polynesians and the Eskimos eat raw fish.
To cook food, people need not only fire, but cooking equipment as well. That's why many primitive peoples grill or roast their meat, rather than boiling it, for example, because they lack the material to make a container which could be used for boiling.
In the Pacific, the local people dig a hole in the ground and line its sides with stones. Then they light a fire in it and cover it over. When the stones are red hot, they put sucking pigs inside, wrapped up in leaves. Two hours later the meat is perfectly cooked and smells delicious. Despite the introduction of cooking utensils, this primitive cooking method is still very widespread.
There are other ways of cooking food, too, without using pots and pans. Think of a chicken on a spit. One American Indian tribe used to use wooden buckets, water and red-hot stones.
To carry food to their mouths, the first thing people used was their fingers. Primitive people often eat from the same pot, sometimes using a knife or fork. Nature has also provided man with some useful 'plates' and 'cups' in the form of bark, coconut shells and banana leaves.
In the western world we use knives, forks, spoons and plates, which come in different shapes and sizes. Originally, only one set of cutlery would be needed, but nowadays, we use different kinds of knives and forks for each dish. In China, chopsticks are used to eat with. The Chinese eat a lot of rice, for which these are very suitable, and food in the traditional Chinese dishes is often cut into very small pieces before being cooked. It is therefore easier to chew.
The food we eat today is very different from the food our ancestors would have eaten. It is only this century that tinned, frozen and packeted food has become widely available, but we would find it hard to imagine life without these 'convenience foods'.
Nowadays, we can make soup from a tin within minutes, select a joint of meat from a deep freeze, have vegetables all the year round from packets and exotic fruits from many countries from tins, and even our desserts can be ready made for us and stored in a deep freeze. Our bread can be bought ready sliced and cakes and puddings can be quickly and easily made from powder mixes, and finally, if even this seems too complicated, we can even buy food ready cooked, and merely re-heat it.

Why do men fight one another?

When fighting arose among primitive peoples it was often because strangers invaded a tribal territory for no good reason while the menfolk were out hunting. Or a tribe would go into battle out of a firm conviction that its members alone were actually humans. Killing the members of another tribe could even be considered a praiseworthy thing to do. This is the case, for example, with certain tribes of New Guinea. Battles are dangerous, but what is important is the glory that can be won during them. War happens when organized groups of men fight each other with weapons. In warfare, military leaders are placed at the head of armies, and conduct the course of the battles. Some races are more warlike by nature than others. This is the case with the Bedouin, for example, who are always looking for new grazing lands for their herds. Some people still fight with clubs.

How did trade originate?

The simplest form of trading is exchange or barter, when one object is handed over in order to obtain another. Among even the most primitive peoples the mutual exchange of animals, objects or natural produce used to take place everywhere. Thus the African pygmies exchange the game they've killed while hunting with other Africans for good weapons.

In an area where several different kinds of crop were produced, a farmer with a good supply of one crop might still need something produced by another farmer. This is how, little by little, markets began to grow where these exchanges could take place. Discussions about the value of the goods exchanged could sometimes last a very long time.

It was only at a later stage that the value of articles began to be expressed in terms of money. Sometimes rare objects, which had no value in themselves, were used as currency. These could be exchanged for useful items, such as food, or weapons and implements. The Indians of north-east America used to use a particular kind of shell which could only be found among rocks deep under water. It was its rarity that made it valuable. Much later, people began using precious metals, bills of exchange and bank-notes.

These days, banks and other financial organizations are essential to the growth of a country's economy. Each country has its own currency and monetary system. Organizations like this not only facilitate financial operations, they also lend capital both to individuals and to industry. From the financial point of view international relations have also improved a great deal. At the present moment Eurocheques make it possible for people to spend their holidays in different parts of Europe without having to take different currency with them.

***Right:* Thai boxing, a very tough sport practised in Thailand.**
***Below:* Member of the Chani tribe of Irian Jaya, formerly Dutch New Guinea.**

How do we tell who's who?

At birth, parents choose a first name for their child. In some countries the child takes its father's surname, and in some the names of both father and mother.

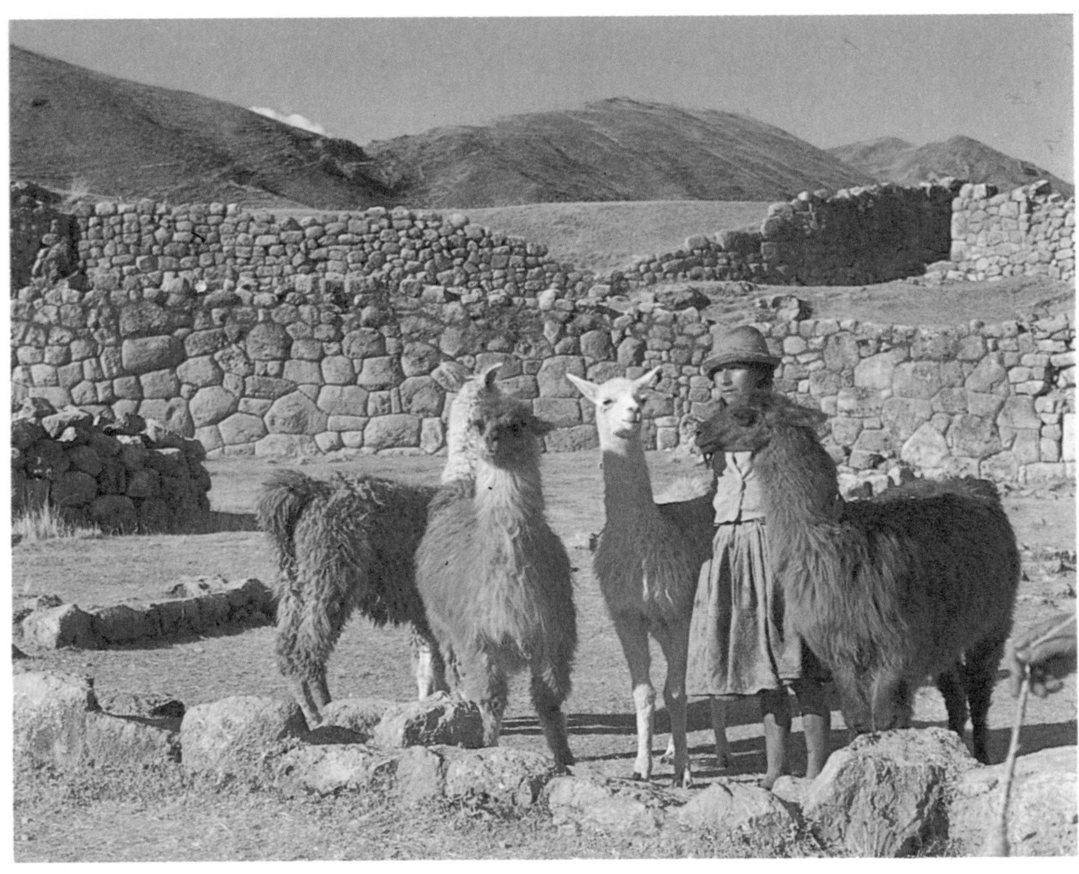

Opposite: Man can carry his own loads, but he can also use animals to carry them for him. In South America llamas are the perfect beasts of burden. In fact, they can only carry light loads, but there are enough of them available to serve the needs of the Indian population. As well as being pack-animals, llamas are a good source of wool. They can also be killed for meat. Altogether it would seem that the llama – which is a distant relation of the camel, and a familiar sight in the Andes mountains of South America – is indispensable to the Indian mountain people.

Below: Nepal is an independent kingdom in the Himalayas. It is inhabited by people who are accustomed to the harsh climate and snowcapped peaks of the Himalayas. It's there that the highest mountain in the world can be found: Mount Everest, which is 8,882m high. The summit of Everest was reached for the first time by an expedition led by Sir Edmund Hillary. Nepalese mountaineers called Sherpas took part in this difficult ascent.

In Britain parents must have their babies registered with the local Registrar of Births. In this way people's names are entered in the records of the state, and they can be kept track of.

What are the main stages during a person's life-time?

At birth, the infant is helpless. Its needs have to be completely taken care of by its parents, or it is handed over to another person to be looked after. This happens in most Jewish kibbutzim, for example, where there is one person who is responsible for the care of the children of the whole community.

In former times little girls had to watch their mothers going about their work, for later they would have to fulfil all these household tasks themselves. It was unthinkable for a woman to take up any occupation other than housework and the care of her husband and children. A boy had to follow in his father's footsteps and practise the same profession as him. Today it is very unusual to come across customs like this. In the western world, with a very few exceptions, every young person is free to choose his or her own career.

Becoming an adult is celebrated differently in different parts of the world. Among many people a ceremony is held to mark a young person's coming of age. Among others, boys may have to go through trials of physical strength, and cannot be considered as men until they have come through these tests. In the Catholic church the ceremony of confirmation marks the child's entry into adulthood.

In the west, once young men and women have come of age they are free to marry whoever they wish. In some parts of the world marriage takes place while the boy and girl are still very young; in this case they are chosen for each other by their parents.

During their life together a man and a woman may have children, who in time grow up and get married, and set up a home. In some countries they do not move away and the family units become very large.

Every human being is mortal, and most people believe to some extent in a life after death. The form this will take is interpreted differently according to different religious beliefs.

Sports and games

When their daily work is done, people need to relax, both mentally and physically. Games and sports are the ideal way to get the relaxation we all need.

Above: **Now that working hours are shorter, people have more and more spare time, and how to fill their leisure hours is becoming an ever-increasing problem. One way in which people can relax is to go to a leisure centre, where they can spend their time very pleasantly. The leisure centre shown above is at Brasschaat in Belgium.**
Below: **Lots of people find life on the water a good way of relaxing. Every year more and more people are taking up water sports, and the seas and lakes are becoming increasingly crowded. There are many expert yachtsmen around, and international yachtsmen are in evidence too.**

What kind of sports did man first practise?

The first sports practised by man were designed to strengthen the body. Because of this, there are very few places in the world where some type of wrestling, for example, has never been popular. After a while, various rules are developed. During a wrestling bout even the very primitive men of Tierra del Fuego, at the southern tip of South America, had to keep to certain rules.
Races of different kinds were also very popular. The Hopi Indians, for example, were fast runners. And some races were held on horseback, with the object of covering a certain distance in the shortest possible time. Today horse-racing still continues to attract a lot of interest.
The North American Indians played a lot of ball games. In other parts of the world, a long time ago, people would play games with an object resembling a ball. These ball-games were the precursors of today's team-games, like basket ball and football.
It was only natural that people living in tropical islands surrounded by water and enjoying a hot climate should take up water sports. And these are still practised today by the people who live in the Pacific islands lying in the triangle formed by the Hawaiian Islands, New Zealand and Easter Island. They often organize swimming and rowing competitions. Surfing also originates from this part of the world. For centuries now, surfers have been riding the waves towards the beaches, skilfully balanced on wooden boards, and the sport has spread to other countries.
Another Polynesian sport was javelin throwing, which used to be practised in other parts of the world, too. This early form of sport was especially popular with the Bantus. It is a useful preparation for both hunting and fighting.
In Asia and Africa people used to practise sports demanding physical skills which approached the art of acrobatics; these required both suppleness and physical strength.

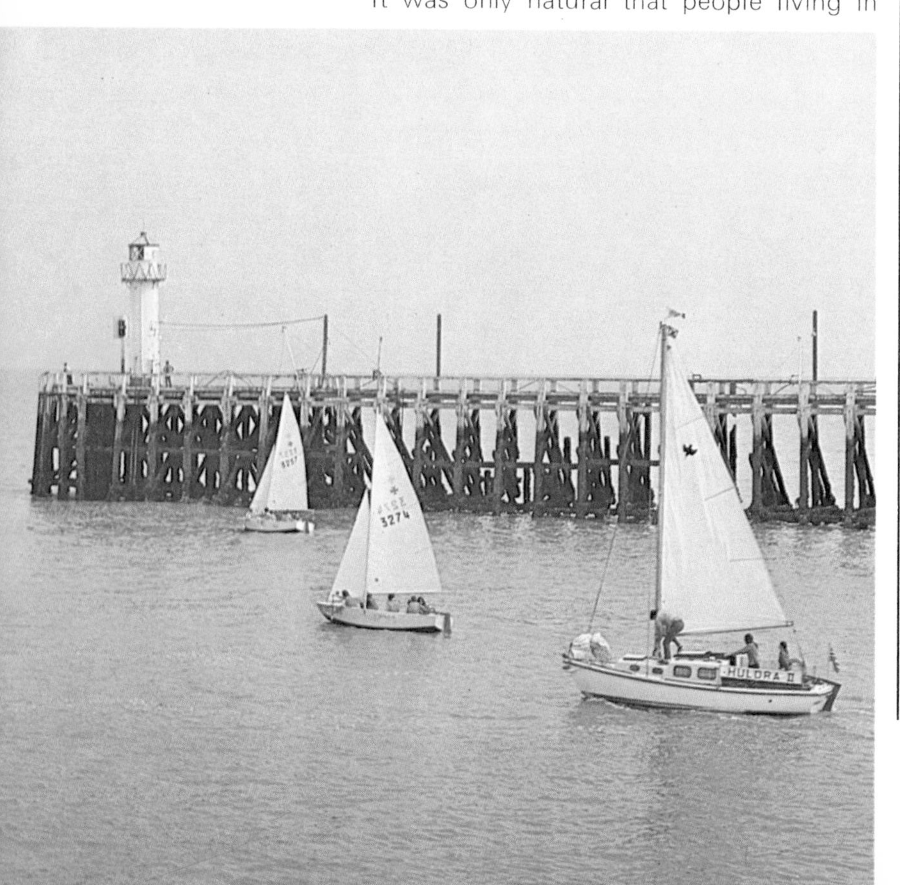

What games did children once play?

In the old days, as now, children used to spend a lot of time playing. Very often it would be their fathers' job to provide toys for them. Red Indian fathers, for example, used to make attractive dolls for their little girls. The Maori children in New Zealand used to play with dolls which had arms and legs that could be moved with strings. The little boys also had model fortresses and liked to play war games. In many countries the spinning top was a popular children's toy. Today, all over the world, there are regulations drawn up by specialists governing the manufacture and safety of toys and games.

What games did grownups once play?

In Polynesia, stilt-walking used to be a very

popular pastime. Elsewhere, people played with skipping ropes and could perform quite complicated steps with them.
The primitive peoples of Africa and America used to enjoy board-games in which luck played a large part – games of chance, in fact. They would use small sticks, stones, or animal-bones.
However far back we look into history, we can always find people playing games. So it seems that the inhabitants of the earth find play a basic necessity, as a means of relaxation, exercise and preparation for their daily activities.

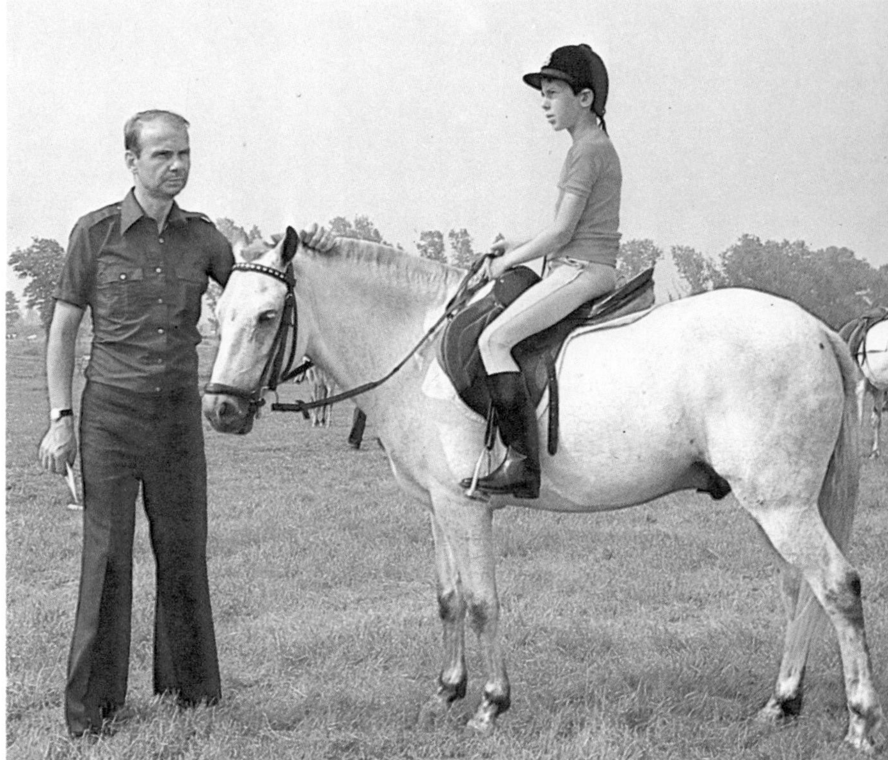

What do sports consist of in our part of the world?

In the Middle Ages tournaments and hunting were regarded as sports reserved for princes and noblemen. In England the sport of hunting was almost a fine art. In the first place, the participants were far less interested in the quarry than in the sheer pleasure of testing their strength. It was a case of man pitting his wits, skill and endurance against the animal world.
Later, all this changed. People had to work hard to earn their daily bread, and sports were regarded as a change of activity, an opportunity to relax at the end of a long day's work. People who took up sports aimed to achieve high performances. Rowing, boxing, wrestling, riding and various forms of athletics were first practised in England. Very soon sports were being practised all over western Europe.
During the two last centuries people began to realise that exercise was good for them. It helped the body to stay supple and strong; it ensured sound health and also, it was said, kept the temper sweet. The French philosopher Rousseau and the German educationalist Muths were strong advocates of physical education. Friedrich Jahn, a German – also called 'Vater Jahn' – recommended young people to take up gymnastics; he had a political aim in mind – to strengthen the unity of the German people.
In England sports developed with greater freedom. Games were played in schools, and it became the custom for matches to be played between different schools. Cricket, rugby and football developed as popular team games, and have had a great effect upon the way we spend our leisure time.

Above: **Horse-riding is no longer a sport reserved exclusively for the rich. These days there are plenty of pony clubs and riding schools everywhere, where children can learn to ride.**
Below: **Tennis is a game played by two or four people. Whether played as singles or doubles, it consists of using a racquet to send the ball from one side of the net to the other.**

How have sports and games reached their present stage?

In England rules were established for all branches of sport. They were soon adopted by other countries, with a few changes. The man who introduced football to the Netherlands – where its popularity cannot be disputed – was Pim Mulier; he took the first football back from England in 1883. Around 1850 the first professional sportsmen made their appearance on sports grounds, in the form of runners – both sprinters and long-distance runners, the distances being set by British standards. They went in for very intensive training. When they won, there

were big cash prizes for them to take home. In 1864 a race took place for the first time between the undergraduates of Oxford and Cambridge Universities. In 1867 the first race was held on a proper cindered track. From then on, athletics of all kinds began to enjoy a great rise in popularity, particularly in the U.S.A. Black American runners came to the fore, and broke many of the records. Nowadays there are many athletic competitions, on all levels, from school sports days to contests between nations.

What are the Olympic Games?

A very long time ago in ancient Greece, between 776 B.C. and 393 A.D., a series of sporting contests were held every four years at the town of Olympia. They were organized in honour of the Greeks' supreme god, Zeus. The Greeks believed that Zeus had provided them with music and games so that they could fight courageously and live freely.

The place where these games took place was of course sacred. At first the celebrations lasted for three days; later they took five days. They were a purely masculine event. Women were not allowed to take part in the contests, and were not even welcome as spectators. Olympic winners would be crowned with a wreath of olive leaves. Very often the town which had sent a winning champion to the games would build a statue in his honour.

A special feature of the Olympic Games was that while they were taking place a truce was held in the internecine struggles between the different tribes and towns of Greece. In 340 B.C. professional sportsmen took part in the games for the first time, but the historians of the day considered them lacking in the proper sporting spirit. After that, the games deteriorated. In 393 A.D. they were abolished by the Emperor Theodosius, who decided that they were being conducted unfairly.

Many centuries later, in 1894, a French baron, Pierre de Coubertin, founded an organization with the purpose of bringing new life to sporting events. In 1896 the new-style Olympic Games were held for the first time at Athens. Coubertin's idea was that the games should not be entered into solely with the aim of winning; he wanted them to be a kind of celebration in honour of physical culture and the sporting spirit. In 1896 only twelve countries competed, and there were only two hundred and eighty five competitors – nowadays there are over ten thousand entrants from nearly every country in the world.

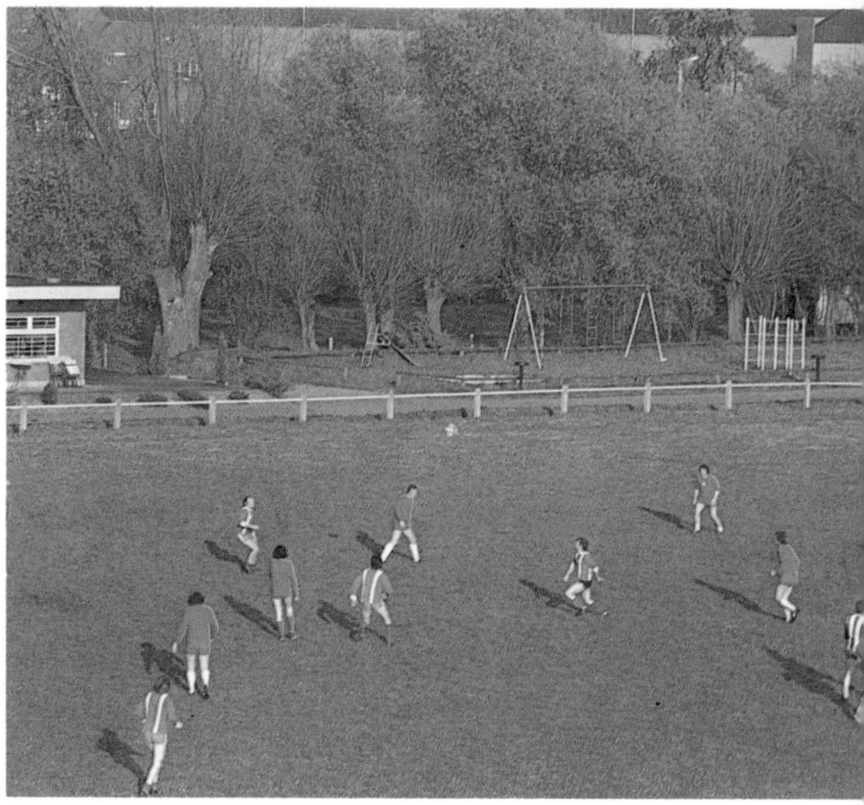

Above: **Football is a popular interational sport. Matches are held both nationally and internationally.**
Below: **Skiing is the art of sliding on snow on wooden or metal skis which are bent upwards at the tip. The sport is growing more and more popular, and the number of skiers is greatly increasing.**

Are the Olympic Games still held every four years?

Yes, that still happens today. The four-yearly games are only cancelled under extreme circumstances – as in 1916, for example, the year when the First World War was at its height. Similarly, the games of 1940 and 1944 could not be held, for during those years the nations of the world were once again engaged in combat; the Second World War had broken out.

The games are held in a different city each time, and these cities are chosen many years in advance. Huge stadiums and sports complexes, catering for every sport, are specially built.

Why are some sports not popular all over the world?

There are several reasons. In the first place, there is the nature of the land and the climate of the country. People can't go in for mountain-climbing in the Pacific Islands, and in Egypt there's very little interest in skiing. Another difficulty which may arise is the question of money. Anyone who wants to take up polo, for instance, must be rich enough to own the requisite number of horses. The character of the local people also plays a part in their choice of sports. In the U.S.A. rodeos are regarded as first-class sporting events, while in the Netherlands no-one seems to be interested in them. And there are some sports which are traditional to certain countries, like wrestling in Japan

Above right: **Golf originally came from Scotland. The object of the game is to send a small ball from the starting point to the final hole by hitting it as few times as possible. A golf course comprises 18 holes, and players have to get their own ball into each one before going on to the next. This is a game played both by amateurs and professionals.**

What are the Olympic sports?

There are a variety of Olympic events, for women as well as men. Both men and women take part in swimming, athletics and fencing. The men go in for boxing and wrestling. Judo is also regarded as an Olympic sport, and so are weight-lifting and gymnastics. Then there are canoe races for both men and women. There are a few contests, like cycle-racing and shooting, which are held outside the Olympic programme. Equestrian events are always very exciting to watch. For team games like football, handball, basket ball, volley ball and hockey, each country tries to pick its best teams to send to the games. Competitions and matches in all the games and sports mentioned above are held in the summer.

Winter sports form a sub-section of the Olympic Games. They include skiing, ice-skating, ski-jumping, the bobsleigh and toboggan. The only team game in the winter sports is ice hockey. The first separate Winter Games was held in 1924, in the French Alps. The Winter Games have to be held at a different venue from the rest of the events, to ensure suitable snow conditions.

Does bullfighting come under the heading of sport? In Spain, for instance, the bull is always killed at the end of the fight – though in some countries the bull may not be killed. In our own country most people strongly disapprove of customs that seem barbaric. However, in Spain and South America people feel quite differently about bullfights, and in these countries they are a form of national entertainment.

What is the longest distance run by the Olympic runners?

The longest race is the Marathon, in which participants have to run 42.2 kilometres as fast as possible. This distance has not been chosen arbitrarily; there is a whole story behind it.

In the year 490 B.C. the Persians invaded Greece. The Greek historian Herodotus tells us that an Olympic champion called Dimedon was present at the Battle of Marathon, where the Greeks defeated the Persians. Dimedon was sent to carry the news back to the city of Athens as quickly as possible. He raced back to Athens and announced the good news. Then, completely exhausted, he fell to the ground and died.

Another historian, Lucianus, tells us that the message-bearer had a different name; according to him the first Marathon runner was called Philipides. There is yet another version of the story, related by a third historian – Plutarch.

Now people are beginning to doubt whether the first Marathon race, with its fatal outcome, ever happened at all. We don't even know exactly where the battle between the Greeks and the Persians took place. However the tradition is kept and the race continues to be held, attracting many spectators.

When the first modern Olympic Games were held in 1896, the programme included the first official Marathon Race, which was actually run between Marathon and Athens. The first champion over this distance was a Greek peasant, Louis Spyros. One of the greatest Marathon runners was the Ethiopian Alebe Bikila, who ran the race in 1964 in 2 hours, 12 minutes and 11.2 seconds.

Transport and communication

Left: A modern racing car looks very different from the first motor cars. It is largely due to the experiments carried out on racing cars that motor cars have the form which we are familiar with today. Note the low, aerodynamically-shaped bodywork and the extra-wide tyres. The engine is so large that there is only room for one man.

Motor cars

Below: The main features shown in this diagram are to provide comfort and safety both for the driver and for passengers.

In the past our ancestors travelled on foot or by horse. This took a long time and could be very tiring. Today, travelling is very much easier, thanks to the motor car.

How were motor cars invented?

The American word for a car is an automobile – which means a vehicle which moves by itself. Men had been trying to invent a vehicle of this kind since ancient times. The first carts were pushed or pulled by men, who had to use all their strength and weight to get them along. Later, this job was taken over by draught animals such as horses, oxen, elephants or donkeys. Later still, people tried to make a vehicle which was driven by the force of the wind.
Then the Frenchman Joseph Cugnot produced a steam-driven vehicle, the earliest forerunner of the car, and the principle of steam power was further developed by the Englishman James Watt. But it was not until the invention of the internal combustion engine that progress in this direction could really be made. Nowadays, motor cars have engines with several cylinders. The explosions which take place inside these cylinders enable motor cars to travel at high speeds. But the story is not yet over. People are always looking for new ways to power vehicles and have already experimented successfully with electric cars. Gas turbine engines have also been tried, though these so far have not been suitable for passenger vehicles.

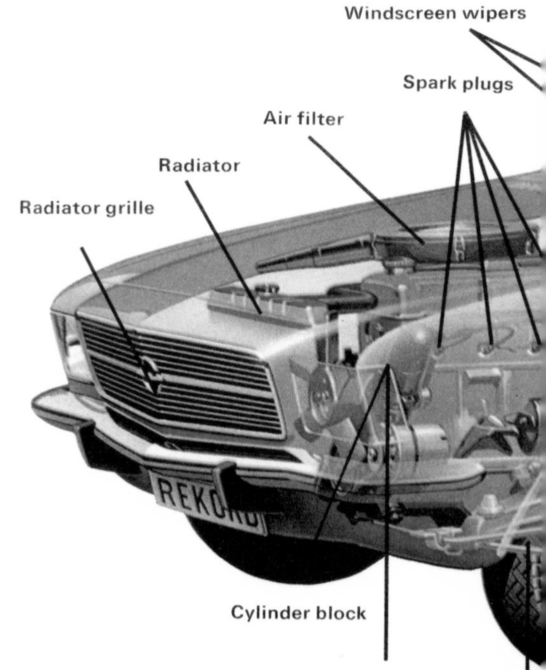

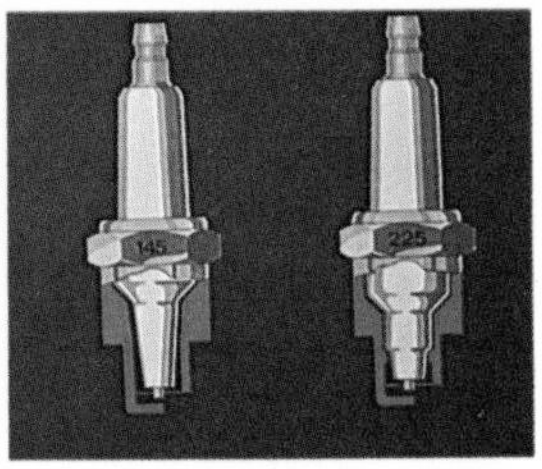

Above: Spark plugs have electrodes which produce sparks, enabling the gases contained in the cylinder to explode.
Below: The battery provides the current which is needed for starting the vehicle. It also provides power for lighting etc., even when the car is stationary.

What makes a good car?

The creators of the car started from two fundamental principles – a motor car must be fast and it must be reliable. Once these conditions had been satisfied, attention could be paid to factors such as comfort and safety.
Today there are certain safety requirements which any car must conform to in order to be able to travel on public roads.
The car's engine should make as little noise as possible. The noise level must be kept below certain legal limits, and this is why silencers are fitted. The pollution from the car's exhaust system must be kept as low as possible. For this reason the quantity of lead in petrol is reduced as far as possible. In some places you can buy lead-free petrol. The car should have a cooling system to reduce the risk of overheating to a minimum, and the electrical system must be perfect. The tyres are also very important, for once a car skids it is practically impossible to control. For the car to be easy to drive it needs a good suspension system which keeps the tyres in contact with the road even on a bad surface. This contact is essential for effective braking. Brakes must be powerful enough to enable a large car to stop in the shortest possible time.
A car must have brakes at the front and back and also be equipped with a handbrake. There must be powerful headlamps for driving at night to enable the driver to see and, equally important, to be seen in the darkness. They must be adjusted to give a good view without dazzling oncoming drivers.
A horn and windscreen wipers and washers also play a part in making the car safe for the driver and for other road users.
To give protection in case the car should be involved in an accident seat belts must be fitted. Laminated glass, which will crack but not shatter, may be fitted. The bodywork should be able to absorb the impact while keeping the passenger compartment intact.

When were cars first built?

When steam engines were first used to drive the pumps in the English mines in the

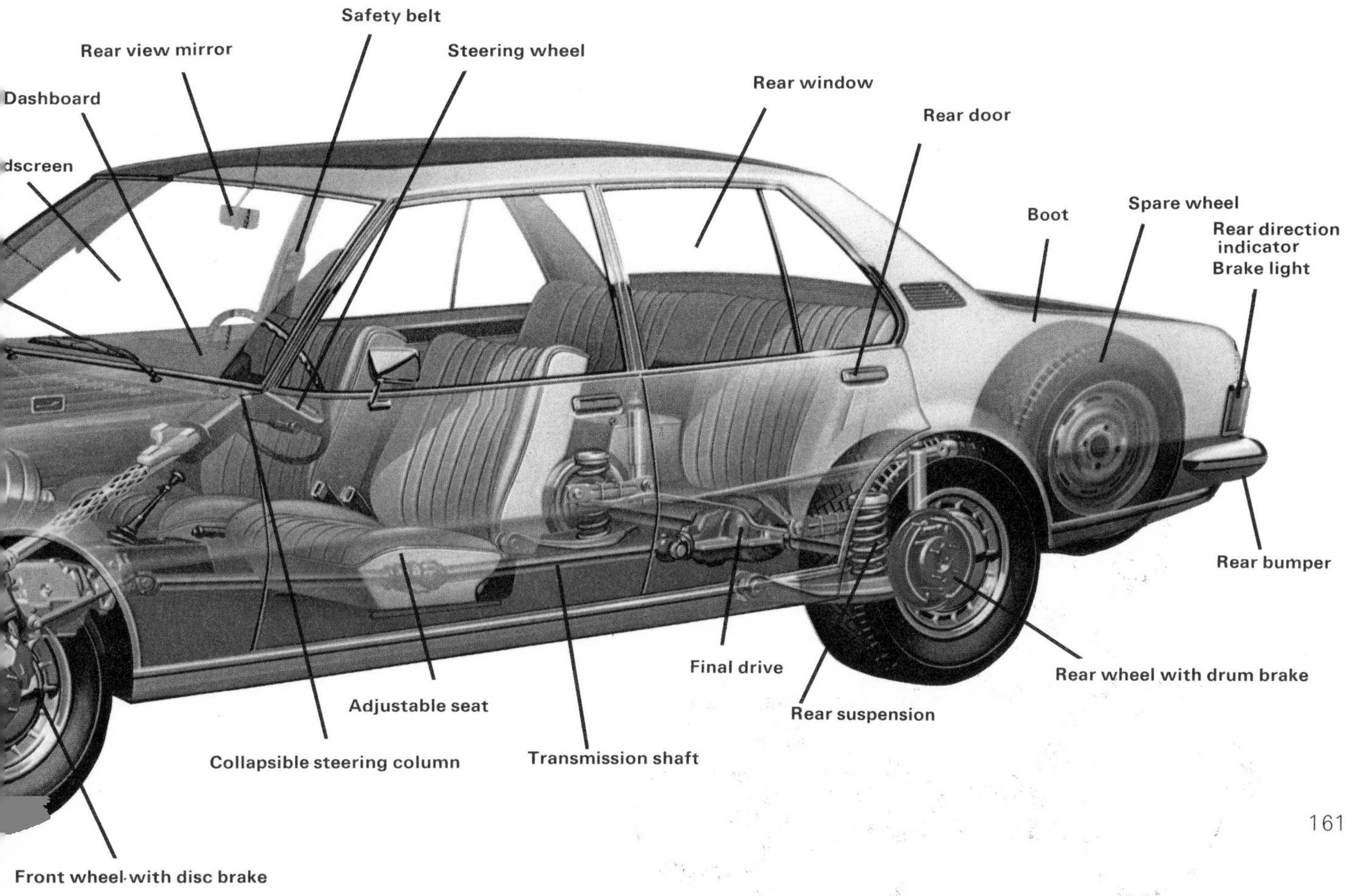

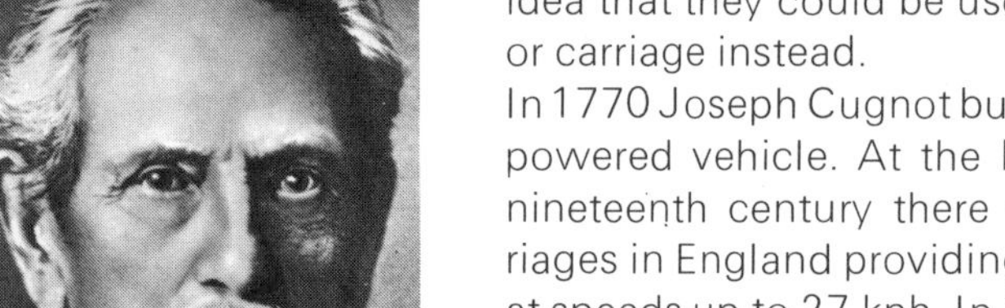

Above: **Karl Benz built one of the first practical and usable cars in 1885. It had three wheels and an engine of about 2-3 hp.**
Below: **After working in a factory in Cologne, Gottlieb Daimler went into business on his own. In 1885 he built the first motorcycle. The engine had only one cylinder and developed ½ h.p.**

eighteenth century, people quickly had the idea that they could be used to move a cart or carriage instead.

In 1770 Joseph Cugnot built the first steam-powered vehicle. At the beginning of the nineteenth century there were steam carriages in England providing regular services at speeds up to 27 kph. In 1860 the Belgian Etienne Lenoir invented a car powered by gas, and in 1864 the Austrian Siegfried Marcus used an engine running on petrol vapour. He solved the problem of electrical ignition in the cylinders and invented the first spark plugs. When the German Nikolaus Otto invented the four-stroke engine in 1876, thus providing the first smooth running power unit, the motor car was ready to be sold to the public. The first men to sell motor cars were the Germans Gottlieb Daimler and Karl Benz.

Great progress was being made in France, too. The Count de Dion and Emil Levassor improved both the petrol engine and the external shape of the motor car. The original coach shape used hitherto was abandoned and the engine was placed at the front. It now had a gearbox and transmission to the rear wheels.

It was in the United States, however, that the first steps were taken towards providing a 'car for every man'. In 1900, mass production and conveyor-belt methods of manufacture first appeared. By 1912 the Ford factories were already producing 20,000 cars a year, or about 70 cars each working day.

How were the new cars tested?

Once the motor car had arrived there was stiff competition among the automobile manufacturers. They all tried to win the public's favour by making cars which were faster and more manoeuvrable, offering more performance and greater safety. At first they had difficulty in combining the two. In the cars used for motor racing, safety was often sacrificed to speed, but sometimes speed itself had to be sacrificed for the sake of reliability. Many inventions and technical developments were tried out on racing cars, and the results of these experiments were applied in manufacturing ordinary cars for sale to the general public.

Today, racing is not so important for the evolution of the motor car. Motor-races are still given a lot of publicity, but they have become a traditional event, a kind of festival which is held every year. The competitions known as rallies, which test the endurance of the car (and the driver) have done much to improve the robustness of present-day cars. Nowadays the length of a car's life is considered more important than its speed, especially in the case of cars made for the general public.

How has the motor car changed our society?

As everyone wanted to have his own car in order to move around more freely, the motor industry grew rapidly. Enormous factories were built in which thousands of workers could earn their living. And as cars became more and more refined, more specialized workers were needed. All kinds of specialists were trained. Each one worked on a particular section of the car and was thoroughly familiar with it, but knew nothing about the other sections. Conveyor-belt production methods and standard measurements were introduced, so that large numbers of identical cars could be quickly produced.

Each worker made one very small part of the

Left: **1898 Benz Comfortable, built by Karl Benz.**

How an internal combustion engine works. The petrol pump feeds a small quantity of petrol into the engine. This is mixed with air and vaporized into a gas; the mixture is then fed into the cylinder, where it explodes. The force of the explosion pushes the piston downwards and turns the crankshaft. As there are several cylinders functioning one after the other, the engine turns smoothly. The fan cools the engine, while the distributor ensures that each spark plug produces a spark at the right time for the explosion to take place.

car, which then passed to the next worker, who fitted another part. This method resulted in faster production, but meant that expertise and a pride in the finished product disappeared from the factories. The workers rapidly became exhausted and depressed by the monotony of what they were doing, and because they could no longer see a clear relationship between their own tasks and the end product there was no incentive to produce a better piece of work than the next man. Ideally, a balance needs to be found between the advantages and disadvantages of this type of work.

Below: View of a motor car factory in the 1920s (the Minerva factory at Mortsel in Belgium). Both the workers' clothing and the building and machines look outdated. Production methods were uneconomical, and not many cars could be produced each day. All of these factors would help to explain why the factory was unable to keep up with its competitors.

The fact remains that the motor industry has become an important source of income for many countries, and any changes could result in adverse effects on their economy. In addition to the car factories themselves there are innumberable branches of industry which live off motor cars. We need think only of the paint, glass and tyre manufacturers. Petrol and oil distributors also play their part in the car industry. Then there are the garages, coachbuilders and so on. The motor car has indeed changed our society.

The modern road system is designed for cars. Roads have been widened and improved, and the road network has become larger, with more intersections. The large numbers of cars on the road has brought changes in the highway code and traffic regulations; new bridges and tunnels have been built. But in the final analysis, it is man himseff who has changed the most. Once he could travel quickly and easily he began to move around more and more. Nowadays, practically everyone can go abroad. Anyone who has travelled once wants to go again, and to go further. Travelling enables us to meet people from other countries and other cultures.

But the car has also brought disadvantages. The roads have become more danerous, and not a day passes without our hearing or reading about some terrible accident. Every year several thousand people are killed, and many more injured, and it is children who are put most at risk by the motor car. All things considered, the motor car can be said to occupy a very important place in our society. Some people even seem to worship it. Everything has to give way to the motor car, and buying and running one costs a great deal of money. Nevertheless, people still keep buying cars, and will no doubt go on doing so as long as they are able to, as there is no doubt that a car is a very great asset in our society. Many large companies now supply cars to their executives, who often have to travel to different parts of the country for important meetings.

Trains

For a number of years before the appearance of aircraft and motor cars, it was the trains of the national and international railways which took the place of horse-drawn carriages in taking travellers to see distant places and to visit the people who lived there.

Above: **George Stephenson (1781–1848), an English mining engineer, who invented the first steam locomotive; it was used to draw heavy wagons full of coal.**
Top right: **A silver mine in Alsace in the seventeenth century. In the background can be seen the wagons running on wooden rails which were already being used to carry the silver ore. These were pushed along by the workers themselves.**
Bottom right: **Stephenson's *Rocket*, one of the first steam locomotives. Note the tall chimney and the cylinder and piston at the side.**
Below: **A 'modern' steam locomotive – obviously a much more complicated machine than the *Rocket*.**

Who really invented the train?

In fact, no-one did. The train was the result of a whole series of developments carried out over a number of years. Little carts running on wooden rails were already being used in mines in the sixteenth and seventeenth centuries. Later, iron rails were introduced. The wheels had a raised flange to prevent the carts from coming off the rails, and at first they were pulled through the galleries by men or horses. At the beginning of the nineteenth century George Stephenson invented the steam locomotive and the first railways appeared in several countries. The first electric train journey was made at the Berlin Exhibition of 1879. The diesel-electric train made its appearance in Europe around 1935. This type of train did not need overhead wiring or a pick-up rail. It is only since the Second World War that overhead wiring has become the standard system in Europe. A vast system of signals and points was installed to ensure the safe passage of traffic on the rail network. Where trains crossed ordinary roads, level crossings were installed, most of which now have automatically operated safety barriers with flashing lights. Trains now travel at speeds well over 100 k.p.h.

What use is a train?

A train is chiefly useful for carrying people. For more than a century millions of people have been using trains to get to their place of work or go on holiday safely and quickly. The train was the main means of transport before the coming of the motor car, and even today there are many people who prefer to take the train and leave their car at home, so that they can arrive relaxed and rested at their destination. Because they can carry relatively large quantities at a time, trains are also widely used for transporting goods. The train's main disadvantage is that it is confined to its rails, and there are many places it cannot serve. This problem is still a pressing one today. It is particularly inconvenient for industry, which relies on the rapid distribution and delivery of its products and raw materials.

Is there a future for trains?

Obviously, trains will have to struggle hard to meet the competition offered by road and air travel. To remain competitive they will have to improve considerably, and great emphasis must be laid on qualities such as speed, reliability and comfort. The speed of rail travel can be increased if electric trains are introduced on more routes. Where there is no overhead wiring, diesel-electric trains must be used; these are trains in which the electric current to drive the train is produced by a diesel engine. Rails must also be modified to take higher speeds. Trains running on a single rail have already been tried out, most notably in Japan and Germany. These monorails, as they are called, reach higher speeds than normal trains.
Speed is obviously an important factor in carrying passengers, but it is probably even more important in carrying goods, when these have to be delivered quickly to distant destinations. Travel by train must also be comfortable enough to attract large numbers of passengers. Fares must be cheap, and passenger train interiors must be clean and comfortable and the service must be regular and reliable. Although it is often quicker, and less tiring, to travel between large towns on the train, one problem is that the more remote places are often not near a railway station.

Top: **An electric locomotive of the type currently used for goods trains. The arm which picks up electricity from the overhead wires can be clearly seen.**
Centre: **A diesel-electric locomotive. This time there is no arm to pick up the current. Instead the current is produced by a diesel engine. It is still an electric locomotive, but one with its own generator.**
Bottom: **A Japanese 'monorail', which runs on a single rail. These trains reach very high speeds, and are used chiefly for long distances.**

Ships

Since time immemorial men have built craft for voyages of discovery, for transporting goods over long distances or for conquering new territory across water. Today ships are chiefly used for carrying heavy, unmanageable cargoes such as oil.

Above: When ships are damaged below the water-line or their hulls need to be examined for maintenance, they are put into dry dock, out of the water. This makes working on them very much easier. Most large ports have dry docks.
Below: A vessel of ancient Egypt. It moves gracefully through the water, driven by oars and a sail. It has no rudder – the two slaves at the stern guide it with an oar.
Right: Model of a 'ship of the line, fourth grade, called Caesar and dating from 1807'. Note the large number of sails, which enables the ship to travel at high speed. The double row of cannons provided a formidable armament.

What kind of ships were used in ancient times?

The first ships in which man ventured on the sea were very simply constructed of wood or bundles of papyrus. Some small boats were even made of tanned leather. These vessels had only the wind or oars to move them along and the men who put out to sea in them must have been very courageous. Ships were first used for commerce and voyages of exploration. Later they were useful for war, and many exciting stories are told of the naval battles fought in those far-off times. Some ships were specially designed for transporting large numbers of soldiers. Since they used oars, they were no longer dependent on the wind, and even made regular crossings of the Mediterranean. These galleys were rowed by slaves chained to the oarsman's benches; many of them were lost in shipwrecks.

Though these boats did have faults, they brought many countries commercial prosperity. In those days, and indeed today, the most powerful countries were those which had a substantial fleet. This was the case with Spain, Portugal, the Netherlands and England.

What influence did the voyages of exploration have on ship-building?

When men had understood that the earth was a globe and that they could sail right round it, they began to construct larger and stronger ships so as to be able to make longer voyages. Large, solidly-built sailing ships left the ports of Europe to trade in unknown lands. Warships went with them to protect them from pirates. The first expedition that was to sail right round the world set off in 1519.

After the sailing ships came steamships, which were less dependent on the winds and tides. They were faster and could carry larger loads; wood was gradually replaced by iron and steel in their construction.

As engines became more powerful, the size of the vessels had to change. Diesel engines

Top right: **A modern port. There are spacious, well-equipped berths for the ships, and the large cranes on the quay provide rapid unloading. Some cargo ships are specially fitted to carry containers.**
Bottom right: **The Hovercraft, a fast and modern means of passenger transport over short distances. This vessel rides on a cushion of air and is driven forward by propellers. There is a regular hovercraft link between France and England.**

Below: **A cargo ship with cabins for passengers. Its large carrying capacity means that transport costs are kept low, but it does not go very fast. Passengers who have the time can go on cruises in boats like this. Note the radar and radio aerials, both vital aids to safety.**

replaced steam, making ships faster and more reliable. In large ships today the skills of the sailor have, to some extent, been replaced by the skills of the technician.

What is the future of sea transport?

In order to compete with aircraft, ships need to develop very rapidly. New means of propulsion are now being used, and some ships work by atomic power. Giant oil tankers can carry enormous quantities at a time, keeping transport costs very low.
In passenger transport, ships have already lost the battle against aircraft. The great ocean liners are outdated, but hydrofoils and hovercraft provide high-speed passenger transport over short distances.
In cargo transport, a ship's larger capacity makes up for its lack of speed. Better port facilities ensure a fast and regular flow of cargo traffic.

Aircraft

Man has always envied the ability of birds to fly, and has often tried to imitate them. According to ancient Greek legend it was in attempting to fly that Icarus met his death.

Above: **Louis Blériot was the pioneer of aerial navigation in France. He lived from 1872 to 1936. He was the first man to cross the Channel by air, in 1909.**
Right: **A Piper Comanche – an ideal business aircraft. Planes like this are used more and more frequently for business trips. Many large towns have landing strips for these machines.**
Below: **A Boeing 747. This enormous 'Jumbo' jet can carry hundreds of passengers at a time. Only larger airports can accommodate such aircraft.**

Has man often tried to fly?

The air which surrounds the earth like an envelope is not dense enough to carry a man, so he must use other means to fly. The first air voyages were made in balloons filled with hot air. Later these balloons were filled with very light gas. Both types of balloon are still used today. After balloons, people experimented with gliders, which were launched from hilltops. Airships were also popular, and today they are used for advertising. The early airships used hydrogen, which could be very dangerous, but modern airships use the much safer gas, helium.
A great step forward was made when aircraft were fitted with internal combustion engines – still a recent discovery at the time. These could combine lightness with power. With an internal combustion engine, an aircraft could take off from the ground. Later the jet engine was invented, and higher speeds were possible. But with the introduction of rockets, travel above the surface of the earth underwent a real change. As these rockets flew above the atmosphere where the air could no longer support them, wings became unnecessary.

How did aircraft develop so rapidly?

Flying aeroplanes was initially regarded as a pastime for daredevils. But as their potential was understood aeroplanes soon came to be seen as a serious subject worthy of a great deal of thought and scientific study. Petrol engines were improved, and people learned the basic rules of aerodynamics. They realised, too, that when they used aircraft, rivers, mountains and seas were less of an obstacle than with traditional methods of transport.
During the First World War the aeroplane proved an efficient means of observing and attacking the enemy, and the race began to build faster, more reliable machines. After the war these efforts continued because industry had already been set up to develop aircraft. Flights were made over the oceans to far-off countries. The post, cargo and passengers could be carried at high speed. Then came the Second World War which was largely won thanks to the aeroplane. After the war, large jet aircraft appeared which could travel faster than the speed of sound. The aeroplane is not just an amusement for the foolhardy – everyone makes use of it.

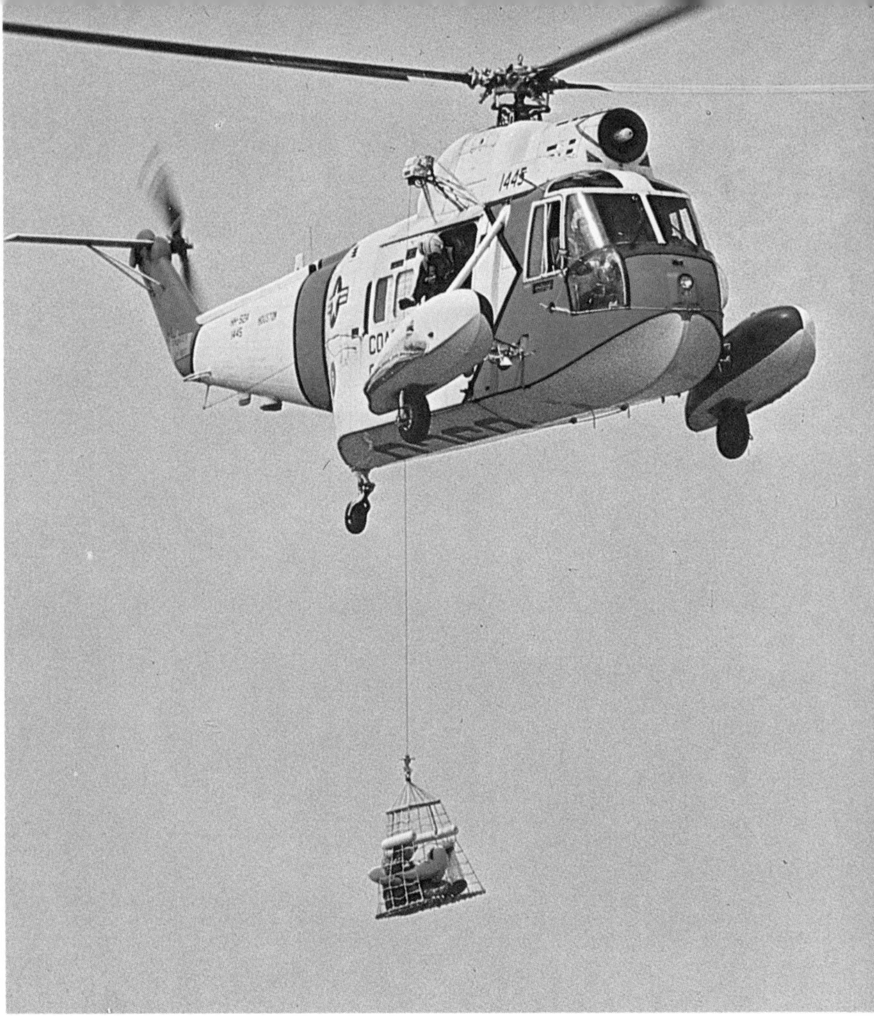

What sort of aircraft are there and what are they used for?

The shape and fittings of an aircraft are often determined by the use it is intended for. Obviously, military aircraft will not be the same as airliners. Military aircraft have to carry bombs and rockets without attracting too much attention. Civil airliners on the other hand have to carry their passengers in comfort and safety. Famous aircraft manufacturers include Douglas, Fokker, Convair, Lockheed, Tupolev and Dassault. The helicopter is a special type of aircraft. It has no wings, and rises from the ground and flies by means of rotors. The great advantage of the helicopter is that it needs very little space for take-off and landing.
The smallest aircraft are used for pleasure and business travel. Gliders are still in fashion too, and even balloons haven't been forgotten.

Has air travel changed our society?

Aviation has brought an overwhelming change in many areas. The speed with which aircraft move from one place to another has influenced services on the ground. As aircraft became larger and heavier, longer runways were needed, and airports had to be able to receive more passengers, provide food for them, handle their baggage and arrange parking and transport facilities. As the number of planes grew, traffic regulations had to be changed. Developments in electronics have helped to increase safety; now aircraft can land in bad weather by instruments alone. Thanks to the aeroplane, people can travel round the world more easily and do so more often.

Top left: **The control tower of an airport; it is from here that air traffic is controlled.**
Bottom left: **View of a large airport in Japan.**
Right: **A helicopter in action. As it can hover, i.e. stand still in the air, it can be used anywhere.**

Does a helicopter have wings?

At first sight one would say not, but this is an illusion. The big rotor at the top of the machine works in two ways. First of all it lifts the helicopter into the air, then it can be tilted slightly to move the machine in any direction. The great advantage of the helicopter is its ability to go up and down vertically. It needs very little space to land in, and can do so on the top of a building, on the deck of a ship, or on a platform in a forest clearing or any kind of open ground.

Interplanetary travel

Some time before the aeroplane was invented, the French writer Jules Verne wrote a book about a trip to the moon. People reading these adventures at the time thought his ideas impossible.

Above: **Yuri Gagarin (1934–1968), an officer in the Soviet Air Force. He was the first man to travel into space. On 12 April 1961 he completed an elliptical orbit round the earth.**
Below: **A rocket lifts off from Cape Canaveral in the United States. It was from here that the Apollo space craft took off for the Moon.**

How do rockets and jet engines work?

Early aircraft were propelled by an internal combustion engine driving a propeller. The propeller draws the air from in front of it and drives it backwards with a great deal of force, thus pushing the aircraft forwards. This motion gives the wings the 'lift' which carries the plane off the ground. During the Second World War and the period which followed, people experimented with rockets and jet propulsion. In jet engines fuel is combined with air and expelled from the engine to drive the aircraft along. It was soon found that very high speeds could be reached with this type of propulsion. The sound barrier was broken. Rockets combine two fuels and also use exhaust gases for propulsion, and the speeds which they have reached have opened up new possibilities for the future. Now only small aircraft are designed with propellers.

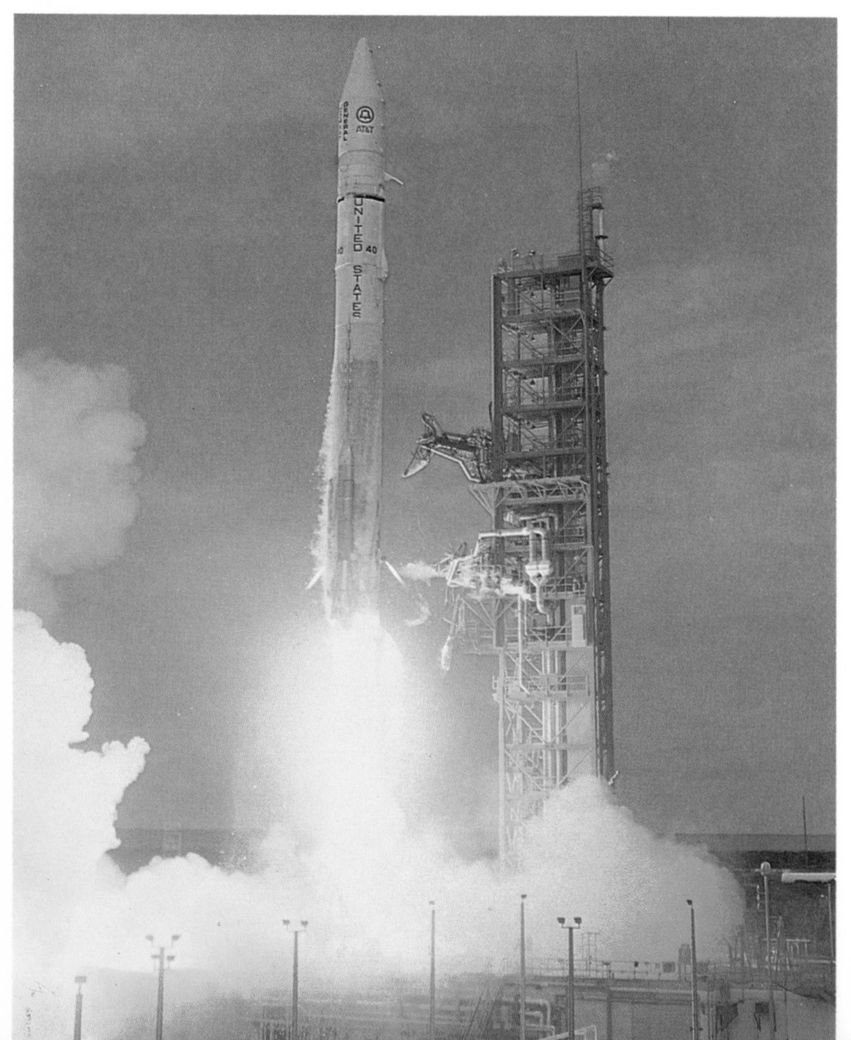

How did interplanetary travel begin?

In fact space travel began on 4 October 1957, the date on which the Soviet Union launched the first satellite, called *Sputnik*. This satellite circled the earth more than 1,400 times, carrying scientific instruments but no crew. Its workings were transmitted back to earth by radio. Once this first step had been taken both the Soviet Union and the United States began sending more satellites into orbit. A satellite must be at least 100 km away from the earth to be able to go into orbit. By giving it a precise speed, its exact course can be calculated.

On 12 April 1961, the Soviet Union sent the first man into space. It was an important step forward. The astronaut's name was Yuri Gagarin; he circled the earth in just under one and a half hours and landed again safely. The first American astronaut, Alan Shepard, was sent into space on 5 May 1961.

All these space journeys, both manned and unmanned, were intended to increase man's knowledge of space, and particularly of the radiations in our universe and the thickness of the atmosphere which surrounds us. Satellites were sent into orbit round the earth to facilitate communications with other parts of the world. Tests were also carried out in preparation for journeys to the moon and the other planets.

Earlybird, the first purely commercial communications satellite, was put into orbit on 16 April 1965. It allowed live satellite television pictures to be sent across the Atlantic for the first time. *Earlybird* was followed by other satellites, which today form a network for the whole world.

What were the results of this 'space race'?

On 11 and 12 August 1962, the Soviet Union sent two men at once round the earth. On 16 June 1963 Valentina Tereshkova became the first woman astronaut. On 12 October 1964 three men (Vladimir Komarov, Boris Yegorov and Konstantin Feoktistov) were launched into space simultaneously. The United States worked hard to catch up. On 23 March 1965 the first American space flight by two men was made by Virgil Grissom and John W. Young in *Gemini III*. Meanwhile, more unmanned ships were sent out to assemble data on long space voyages. The first target was the Moon. On 3 February 1966 the Soviet Union made a successful landing on it with *Luna IX*. This was followed some months later by the American *Surveyor I* (2 June 1966). However, not everything went according to plan; accidents happened both in Russia and the US, considerably slowing down the programmes. On 28 January 1967 fire broke out in the *Apollo* space capsule during tests on the ground, and Virgil Grissom, Edgar H. White and Roger Chaffee lost their lives. In the USSR, Vladimir Komarov was killed in an unsuccessful landing on 24 April 1967.

Accidents could, and did, happen while the spacecraft were away from earth. During the *Apollo XIII* mission to the Moon there was an explosion in an oxygen tank, and major electrical problems were caused. By living in the Lunar Excursion Model for the rest of the trip and returning to the command module only to re-enter the Earth's atmosphere they survived, and returned safely home.

Nevertheless there were other, important successes. The American astronauts Frank Borman, James A. Lovell and William Anders made the first flight in lunar orbit with *Apollo VIII* from 21 to 27 December 1968. Finally on 21 July 1969 the first landing of a man on the Moon took place – that of the Lunar Module from Apollo XI. The first man to set foot on lunar soil was Neil Armstrong. His companion Edwin Aldrin followed him a few moments later. Meanwhile Michael Collins was orbiting the Moon in the cabin of *Apollo XI* itself. *Apollo XII* with Charles Conrad and Alan L. Bean on board also landed on the Moon to carry out scientific research. *Apollo XIII* had to turn back, as we have already seen, but *Apollo XIV* reached the moon with the astronauts Alan Shepard, Stuart Roosa and Edgar D. Mitchell.

The Soviet Union preferred to send unmanned rockets. In September 1970 *Luna XVI* landed on the Moon to gather samples of rock and then returned to earth with its load. On 17 November 1970 the Russians landed a small vehicle (*Lunokhod I*) on the Moon, one which could be controlled from the earth. *Lunokhod I* carried out measurements which were radioed back to earth.

Above: Inside a space craft. Note the small size of the capsule in relation to the rocket itself. The astronauts' accommodation is further limited by the large number of navigation instruments. The couches take up a lot of space but are essential to cushion the astronauts against the forces generated by the launching.
Left: Model of a lunar module. As there is no air on the Moon, a streamlined shape is not needed. The legs have disc-shaped feet to prevent the module from sinking into the lunar surface. Rocket motors let it down gently and enable it to take off. The lunar module has to contain all the equipment of the space craft itself.

What was learned from these trips to the Moon?

The return of the spaceships from the Moon was always awaited impatiently on earth. But what did the samples of rock gathered on the Moon tell us? Scientists have already concluded that the Moon and the Earth are each as old as the other. Lunar rock is not very different in composition from that of the Earth, and it also appears that there were volcanic eruptions on the Moon. No minerals or crystallized water have ever been found, however, which seems to prove that there was never any water on the Moon.

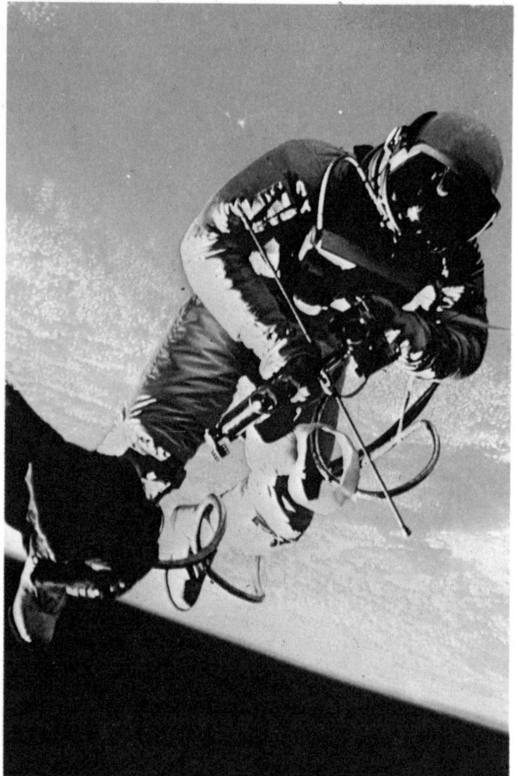

Above: **An astronaut leaves his space craft to examine or repair the outside. As the Earth's gravity is very weak at this altitude, the astronaut does not fall towards it.**
Below: **An Apollo space craft on the way to the Moon. There is not much left of the giant rocket which left the Kennedy Space Centre. The three lower stages have burned out and been jettisoned, and only the space capsule with its rocket engine attached remains.**

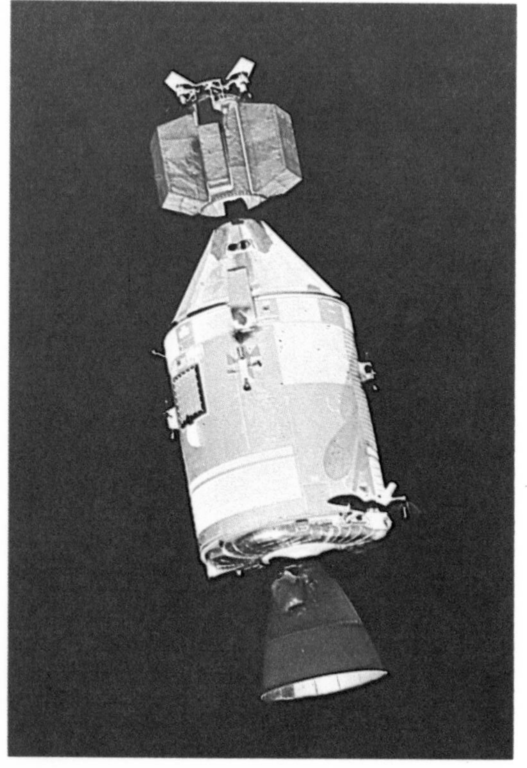

What is the basic difference between the Earth and the Moon?

The Moon is a satellite of the Earth, which orbits round our Earth at an average distance of 384,400 km. The moon is the smaller of the two. Its diameter is 3,500 km, while that of the Earth is 12,700 km. As a result the Moon is lighter than the Earth, and this has a number of important consequences. Its gravitational pull, for example, is only one-sixth of that of the Earth.

The Earth has a thick atmospheric layer which is totally absent from the Moon. On the Moon there is a vacuum. Shadows are crisp and jet black, because there is no air to reflect the sunlight. The sky is a deep black, too; the 'blue' sky which is familiar to us on earth is merely a consequence of the atmosphere. There are no clouds, and no weather to speak of. There is no sound, and all communication among astronauts on the Moon has to take place by radio. One unpleasant consequence of the lack of atmosphere is the extreme variations in temperature. On the Earth these are absorbed by the atmosphere, but this is not possible on the Moon. At midday the temperature reaches 100°C, but at night it can fall to 150°C below zero. As gravity is less on the Moon, a man only weighs one-sixth of his normal weight on Earth. For the same reason, a rocket needs less acceleration to take off from the Moon. Thus the take-off of the lunar module to rejoin the *Apollo* spacecraft orbiting the Moon was much easier than its original departure from the Earth.

The lunar surface is not flat; there are many mountains and craters, the latter probably caused by the impact of meteorites. On Earth these meteorites would burn up in the atmosphere and be seen only as 'shooting stars'. Because the Moon has no atmosphere they crash heavily – even in the low gravity – and cause enormous craters. The mountains of the Moon are higher than those on Earth. There are no signs of present or past life, which is only to be expected in view of the lack of atmosphere. In fact, the Moon is hardly the ideal place to go for a holiday.

Was the journey to the Moon the end of the story, or is it a point of departure for other voyages of exploration in space?

The teams of scientists who sent a man to the Moon and brought him back to Earth safely no doubt thought that that was the end of their task. Their object had been achieved. In fact reaching the Moon was just one tiny step in the exploration of space. But it was an important one. If we had not taken the first step, we should not be where we are today. The trips to the Moon taught us a lot about space travel. Problems such as taking off from the Earth and re-entering the atmosphere had to be resolved. The experience gained in this field will be invaluable on longer journeys. The Moon expeditions also taught us a lot about the effects of space travel on the human body. Also, a whole range of measuring and analyzing devices were developed and used.

One thing is certain – man will continue to explore further into the

Universe. A spacecraft has already reached the next target, Mars, a planet which has always been a source of fascination for man. Photographs have been taken and sent back to the earth, but their analysis has proved disappointing. The surface greatly resembles that of the Moon, and the atmosphere is even thinner than had been thought at first. There may possibly be water in the form of ice, but so far no sign of life has been found. No one knows when a manned landing will be possible.
One line of space exploration on which the U.S.S.R. has been concentrating is sending men into space for very long periods in orbit, to see how they react physically and mentally.

What will happen in the future?

Man has reached the Moon, unmanned space craft have been sent to Mars and other planets to take photographs and deposit measuring instruments. Nevertheless, all this is only a beginning. From the beginning the idea has been to build inhabited space stations orbiting the Earth. The possibilities opened up by such stations seem limitless, and they will certainly be an invaluable source of scientific information. Studies have also been done on the possibility of collecting solar energy and transmitting it back to Earth. Because we are threatened with a shortage of energy, scientists are doing everything they can to carry out these projects as quickly as possible. Technically, such a scheme is probably possible, but there are other problems of an entirely different kind. If they are to be carried out, these plans will need international research and co-operation, and so far this has not been achieved. They will entail a vast amount of work at government level, and it is to be hoped that the great powers such as the United States and the Soviet Union might decide to collaborate on this research.
Perhaps these projects will help to eliminate global conflicts by engaging the major powers in something which is of common interest to all of them. The plans for the great space stations have been in existence for a long time, and we also have the rockets to put them in orbit. The rest is just a question of time.
So far, all craft sent into space have been used only once, and large parts have been jettisoned in space. To overcome this waste the Americans have developed the Space Shuttle, which takes off like a spacecraft — rising vertically on rocket motors — to put a payload into orbit. When the mission is completed the craft will glide back to Earth, like a conventional aircraft, with its engines shut down. It will land on a runway about 6,000 m long. Present tests are being done on a salt lake so that additional landing space is available if necessary.
Another major problem is how we can one day travel to other solar systems. The distances involved are so enormous that even at the speed of light a lifetime would not be long enough to reach them. In the meantime, we have enough problems to resolve on the shorter journeys. New developments in aviation still make headlines in the newspapers, but there are many facts about space which the public never hears of. There are several thousand satellites orbiting the earth. In addition to communications and weather satellites there are a whole range of military satellites circling round us like spies. If they enable the great powers to maintain a balance, we can only be thankful for them. Thus space technology makes its own contribution to peace in the world.

Above: An astronaut on the Moon. His space-suit keeps him at a constant temperature and supplies him with oxygen.
Below: The return to earth is a complex operation. As soon as the capsule re-enters the atmosphere, parachutes open to slow it down.

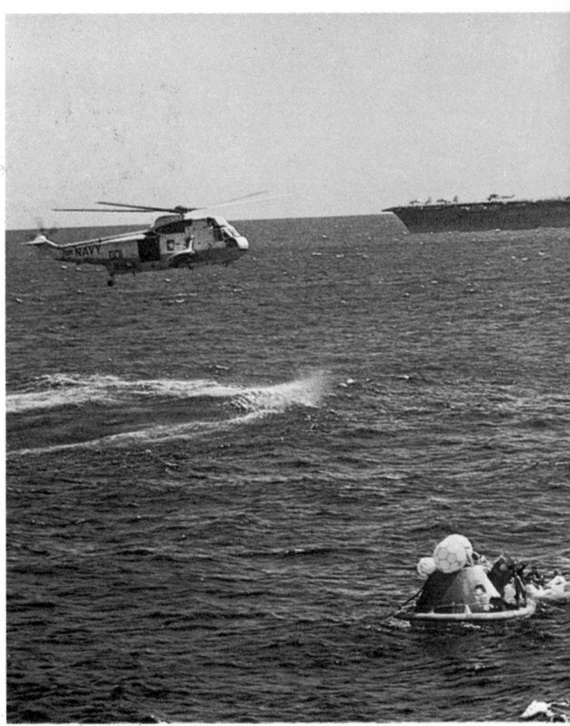

Radio and television

Today, everyone knows what radio is. We only have to press a button to fill the living room with music. But we don't always remember that there is a lot more to radio than that.

Above: Guglielmo Marconi (1874–1937). Italian by birth, he received no support for his experiments in his native country. He carried out the first radio communication with France in 1899, from England.

How did it all begin?

The existence of radio waves had already been demonstrated in 1886, by a German physicist, Heinrich Hertz, who discovered that they behaved in much the same way as light waves.

In 1896, Guglielmo Marconi, an Italian electrical engineer, left Italy for England to work on his great passion – the transmission of signals without wires. In 1898 he established a radio link between France and England, and in 1901 between England and America. In 1909 Marconi received the Nobel Prize for Physics in recognition of his achievements. At first the signals transmitted by radio took the form of faint whistling sounds which could be used to send messages by means of the Morse Code. Later, when the microphone was invented, great improvements were made. Radio could be used to transmit and receive the spoken word and even music.

But radio had many further possibilities which were not yet exhausted. Television, radar, stereophonic music, remote control, were all developed in record time. These improvements were all very important for man. The first vibrations which Marconi sent along his waves were to lead to more innovations than he could have ever imagined. Research is still going on, and science and technology are still developing radio and electronics.

What changes did radio bring?

Developments in wireless communication inspired an increasing desire for knowledge about electricity and its applications. The study of electronics became more and more popular and continues to be so today; it has developed a long way beyond simple wireless-telegraphy. There have been innumerable new inventions and improvements, and all humanity has benefited from them.

The radio has become an important piece of domestic apparatus. It has been followed by television, the tape-recorder, the record-player, pocket calculators, baby alarms, digital watches, etc. All these electronic

Right: Modern stereo systems are to be found in many households. Their main components are a record-player or tape-recorder with an amplifier and a pair of loudspeakers. These are often very expensive, but records can lose a lot of their quality if the loudspeakers do not faithfully reproduce their sounds. For stereo music two are needed, placed at least a metre apart. Good loudspeakers can transmit sounds ranging between 50 and 20,000 cycles per second. When buying a system it is advisable to ask if the amplifier can produce these frequencies.

devices have become part of everyday life in our society, and new investigations and inventions are always being carried out to find ways to make life easier. In some modern supermarkets the assistant needs only to pass a labelled item through her electronic check-out. This registers the cost, adds up the items and also keeps a check on the amount of stock that will then have to be re-ordered.

What does radio mean for man?

Radio has come to occupy a special place in our life. Radio news bulletins and weather reports keep us informed of what is going on. Through them we have a better knowledge both of our own country and of the rest of the world. Radio is the fastest means of communication we have. We can hear a speech which the President of the United States makes to his people the moment he pronounces it. We were able to follow the experiences of the first men on the Moon as they took place. A catastrophe happening in some far-off region is immediately communicated to the rest of the world, enabling aid to be quickly organized.
Radio also provides us with a great deal of amusement and recreation, broadcasting instructive and cultural programmes. We can all hear the best orchestras and artists in our own homes, and follow an infinite variety of events. For all this to happen, large studios and giant transmitters are needed. To people who know very little about electronics, they look like enormous laboratories. But a lot of work needs to be done to improve the quality of the transmissions and keep them at a high level. Highly qualified technicians and famous artists work together to produce high quality programmes. It needs a lot more work than one might imagine to make a recording or a direct broadcast. There are hundreds of people waiting to go to work at the press of a button; all of them make their living from radio.
A radio is often a housebound person's link with what's happening in the world. It keeps people in touch with current events and political and economic moves, and it also keeps them abreast of developments in the areas of science, music, theatre and fashion. Unlike watching television, which takes

Left: **A vast amount of complex equipment is needed to ensure high quality recordings on record or tape. A studio must be completely soundproofed to shut out extraneous noises, and even with the most perfect equipment it is still very difficult to make perfect recordings. To record music in stereo several microphones are needed. Specialized technicians monitor the result to make sure that it is of high quality.**

one's whole attention, listening to the radio can be combined with many other activities.

How does radio serve mankind?

The part which radio has played in the past, and still plays in expeditions of exploration, clearly proves how useful it is for groups of people isolated from the rest of the world. It can provide essential information about supplies running out, the state of health of members of the expedition, etc. Weather bulletins and family news reach the farthest corners of the earth instantaneously. Often it happens that whole areas are suddenly isolated as the result of some catastrophe such as an earthquake or floods. In moments like these help is needed quickly, and again radio provides the solution. Some people are so enthusiastic about radio that they have made contacting people in other countries with simple transmitters and receivers their hobby. For these radio 'hams' radio is a source of relaxation and helps to promote international friendship.

Was television something new?

Television is still a relatively recent development, at least for the public, for it did not appear in people's homes until the 1950s. But for the experts, television as a means of transmitting pictures by radio has existed for

Above: **A radio transmitter and receiver at the South Pole. Radio is very important for linking people in far-flung regions with their homeland, and every expedition has its own radio operator, who is responsible for maintaining communications. The photo shows one of these operators transmitting the results of research. He receives the answers to questions, family messages and meteorological bulletins.**

Above: John Logie Baird (1888–1946), a Scottish pioneer of television. In 1926 he gave the first television demonstrations in the world. In 1928 he was already demonstrating colour television.
Bottom left: The aerial is an important part of a radio or television station. The length of the antenna and the height of the aerial mast are critical for its proper functioning.
Bottom right: A television camera in action. The operator's earphones and microphone keep him in constant contact with the director, who watches the pictures on a monitor screen.

a great deal longer. The first television transmissions were made in England in 1926 by the Scotsman John Logie Baird.

But while technical knowledge had advanced this far, its practical realization still presented too many problems. The Second World War held up progress because people had other things than television to think about. It was only after the war that it made great strides. This progress was partly due to the war itself, which greatly developed people's knowledge of electronics. In the period which followed, this knowledge was applied to television, and radio itself was improved. Television soon appeared in the home and came to occupy an important place there. Large studios full of electronic equipment were built to record and broadcast programmes and more and more sophisticated outside broadcast techniques were developed. Television transmitters need aerials several hundred feet high if they are to cover the widest possible area, and even so relay stations and communications satellites are needed for television to reach the whole world.

Closed circuit television was also developed, and is used in such places as hospital operating theatres, to show observers an operation, or banks, as an additional security precaution.

Has television influenced our society?

A large number of people are concerned with television every day – technicians, cameramen, programmers and of course artists. Thus television plays an important role in our society. This role is sometimes positive, but it can also at times be unhealthy, if the material shown on television has an adverse effect on the viewer. Through television we receive images from all parts of the world and our knowledge of mankind is extended.

But not all of television's effects are beneficial. Audiences in cinemas and theatres have greatly declined. There have been changes in the home too. Whereas people once spent the evenings working or studying, many now spend a large part of the evening watching television programmes.

What is radio's connection with space?

Man's last great voyages of exploration have taken him beyond the earth. The early space flights, the lunar expeditions and the sending of spaceships to distant planets could never have taken place without radio.

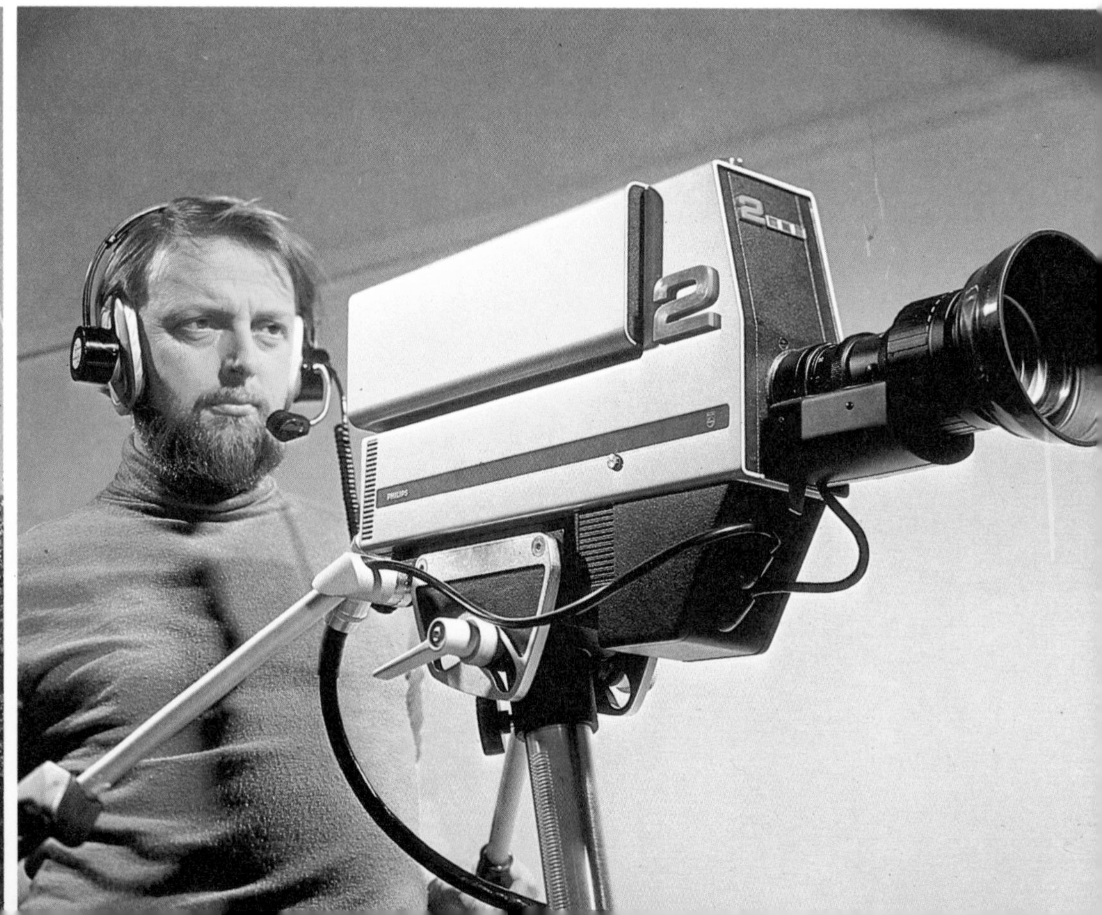

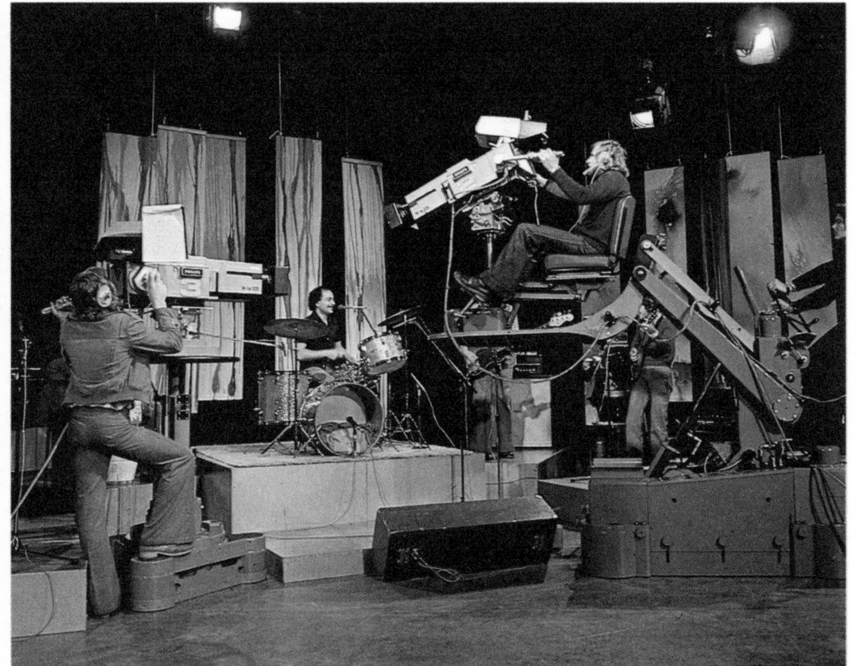

Above: **View of a television studio during a recording. The part of the studio which we see here is very small compared with the space taken up by the equipment needed for the cameras, microphones and lighting. When several different cameras are working at the same time, it is the director who decides which of the images will be transmitted. The cameras can be turned in any direction and moved up and down. Very strong lighting is needed for transmission in colour. The lamps used give out a great deal of heat as well as light. Producing a television programme is a very hot business!**

The space capsules in which man travels the cosmos are really complex laboratories containing more equipment than men. Unmanned vessels, too, are used to explore space and the planets. It is radio which makes communication between the space capsule and Earth possible. The receivers respond to the faintest of signals transmitted over a distance of hundreds of thousands of miles. We can still remember the television camera which was landed on the Moon and controlled from Earth. Radio was important in the early space flights, which were unmanned, because it kept scientists on the ground in touch with what was happening in the spacecraft. It was important in later flights because it was the astronauts' only means of communication with their base.

As the waves emitted by radio and television transmitters do not follow the curvatures of the earth, their aerials need to be very high. The higher they are, the better the reception. That is why artificial satellites have been placed in orbit round the earth. Radio signals are transmitted to the satellites, and sent back to earth over a wide area. This is how we receive images transmitted from America. But to do this requires special aerials which are too large and too expensive for ordinary television stations. Perhaps one day this system too will be improved, for technological progress never stops. Who would have thought a hundred years ago that a man would one day walk on the moon?

What are the other uses of radio?

Finally we must look at the ways in which radio and television help navigation by air and sea. Every ship and airliner today is in constant contact by radio with one of the many seaports or airports. Radio is able to supply instant help and information when necessary. Atmospheric changes can produce unexpected dangers such as fog or storms in the path of an aircraft or ship. These changes in weather are detected by satellites and transmitted to ground stations, which relay them to the ships and aircraft. Maps and photographs of the weather situation are transmitted with all the necessary data to the captain, who is responsible for the safety of his passengers or load.

At ports and airports, radar and television ensure safety even in bad weather. The thickest rain-clouds and fog are no obstacle for radar; whatever the conditions, its images will still show the obstacles in the path of a ship or aircraft.

A car radio is a much-welcomed piece of equipment. Its music can help to keep the driver awake on long journeys, and its traffic bulletins can provide him with useful information.

Community radio, or local radio, has become more popular in recent years. Its aim is to bring the people of one area together by bringing them local news and events, giving weather and traffic reports for that particular area, and often giving local people the chance to broadcast their views on issues that affect their community.

Right: **A radio telescope makes an excellent device for receiving and transmitting signals from and to satellites. Aerials like this must be able to turn in any direction to follow the satellite's course. They can receive signals from a wide range of angles and are, as it were, the 'eyes and the ears' of the earth.**

The telephone

It is difficult to imagine an office or a modern building without telephones. Only when we find ourselves without a telephone do we realize how useful it is.

Above: Alexander Graham Bell (1847–1922) was an American physicist of Scottish origins. He is considered the inventor of the telephone.
Right: Demonstrating a telegraph apparatus in America.
Below: A model of the first telephone. Obviously, it was not very easy to use in practice.
Bottom: An old fashioned telephone. The handle was used to call the exchange.

How does the telephone work?

The Scottish-born American Alexander Graham Bell is generally accepted as the inventor of the telephone. He had discovered that the sound waves created by the human voice could be used to make a small metallic plate vibrate. Under this plate were carbon granules which clustered together or separated in sympathy with the vibrations, thereby altering their resistance to electrical current. Thus when a current was passed through the plate, the vibrations caused by the sound waves altered its intensity. These variations in current were conveyed to another plate in the receiver by means of electro-magnets, causing it to vibrate in the same pattern as the voice. In this way, the spoken word could be sent along a wire. Naturally the telephone has been considerably improved since then, and it can now communicate over much longer distances.

What is the difference between the telephone and the telegraph?

The telegraph only transmitted the simplest of signals – a whistle or a buzz. The microphone had not yet been invented, and so a code was needed to transform letters into a combination of dots and dashes. This was the Morse Code. It was a good and effective system in itself, but its disadvantages compared with the telephone are obvious. Both the sender and the person who received the message had to know morse well, and the speed at which messages could be sent was much slower than by telephone. This is one of the main reasons why the telephone can be considered an improvement over the telegraph. Also, the telephone can transmit music as well as the spoken word. Speech – and music – transmitted by telephone are distorted however. This is because only part of the sound is received by the listener. But enough sound gets through for the listener to understand the message, and for him to recognize the speech patterns so that he knows who is talking to him.
Nevertheless, the telegraph continued in use for a long time. When wireless communication was first invented, the techniques of the telegraph, including morse, were adapted for its use. Naturally a great deal of progress has been made since then,

but such was the importance of the telegraph that it still has its uses today.

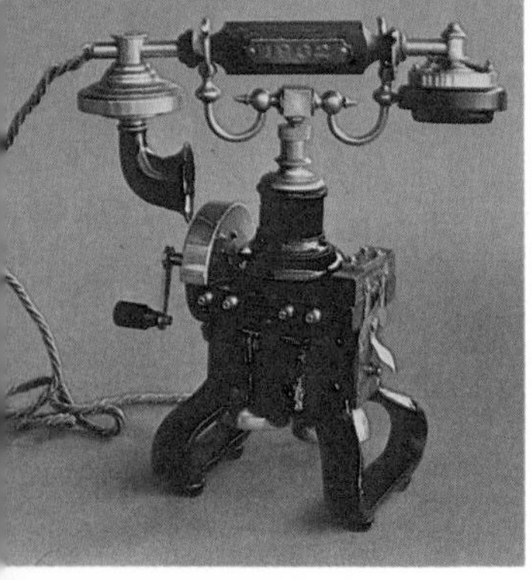

How has the telephone changed since its invention?

At first, people had to go to the post office to use the telephone. When a person wanted to make a call he had to give the number to an operator, who made the connection. Later, telephones were fitted with dials, so that anyone could call the number he wanted. The connection was made automatically at the exchange. The system developed rapidly, and many national telephone networks are now almost completely automatic. Most of the European countries and other places such as Canada and the United States can be called automatically. It is therefore very easy to run up a very expensive bill in a very short time! Communications with other countries are no longer by cable but by radio transmitters linking the different exchanges. Thanks to these new developments, anyone can telephone from one continent to another.

Can we expect changes or improvements in the telephone system in the near future?

Telephones will undoubtedly be improved in the future. The dial will be replaced by push-buttons. This will not be a very important change, but will enable the number to be chosen more quickly. Although push-button sets are already available telephone exchanges must be adapted to them. A greater step forward will be the use of the telephone together with television, so that the caller and the person to whom he is talking can see each other.
Technically, this type of communication is still possible, but from a practical point of view it still poses a lot of problems, not least financial ones. It will make telephoning more expensive, but it can be done. Telephone lines are also used for other purposes besides personal and business conversations. They are used for telex communications, which can also be made by wireless. Press agencies use this method a great deal for collecting news. Even photographs can be transmitted along the telephone lines.
All these different systems enable mankind to learn quickly and accurately what is going on on the other side of the world. The social and commercial interchanges which are essential to the peoples of the world are well served by this complex system of communications, whether in the form of radio, the telephone, telex or television. It depends on the circumstances which means of communication is used, but one thing is certain—people have now come to depend so much on receiving information quickly and easily that there will always be a demand for better and more efficient communication systems.

Above: **A modern telephone exchange. There is no room for the operator – none is needed. Thanks to modern electronics, this compact piece of equipment enables people to communicate with the whole world.**

Left: **The telephone as a means of communication. It is very important to be able to communicate with others both in business and in everyday life. News from all over the world can be transmitted in record time. The telephone also has many other services to offer. To know the exact time, we need only dial a number. The telephone can supply weather information or the latest stock market prices.**

Science and technology

Argriculture and forestry

Agriculture is the deliberate use of nature to produce food and other products such as wood, wool or flowers. It can be divided into horticulture, animal husbandry and forestry.

Above: **The Netherlands are famous throughout the world for their tulip fields. Tulips are not native plants of Holland, however; they were first cultivated in Turkey, where they grow wild. The first tulip appeared in the Netherlands in the sixteenth century. At the time, growing tulips was a rich man's pastime, and astronomical prices were paid for a single bulb.**
Below: **Romanian farmers taking a moment's rest in the fields.**

How did agriculture develop?

In prehistoric times, men lived by hunting, fishing and food-gathering. They fed on the edible plants and fruits which they found in the forests. They did not live in one place but roamed the country in search of food. When men settled in one place they began to till the earth around them and cultivate edible plants. At first they only grew things for their own use, to complement the products of hunting and fishing. Later the work was divided; some people went hunting or fishing, while others specialized in growing plants to feed the whole community. When it was discovered that some wild animals could be tamed, animal husbandry began. Little by little, the places where people lived grew, together with the population.

Later, agriculture was practised on a larger scale. Simple tools such as hoes and ploughs were made. At first these tools were made of stone and wood, but later metal was used. This primitive type of mechanization enabled larger areas of land to be cultivated, so that bigger crops could be produced. Over the centuries methods of cultivation improved constantly. A whole series of agricultural machines were invented which made work in the fields quicker and easier. The use of chemical fertilizers increased the harvests, and insecticides reduced the number of pests attacking the crops. Nowadays, many larger farms tend to specialize in one main crop, for example, wheat, which will be grown on a large scale, and then sold, and possibly exported. Large ranches specialize in rearing cattle or sheep. Smaller farms still continue to grow a variety of crops and keep several kinds of animals.

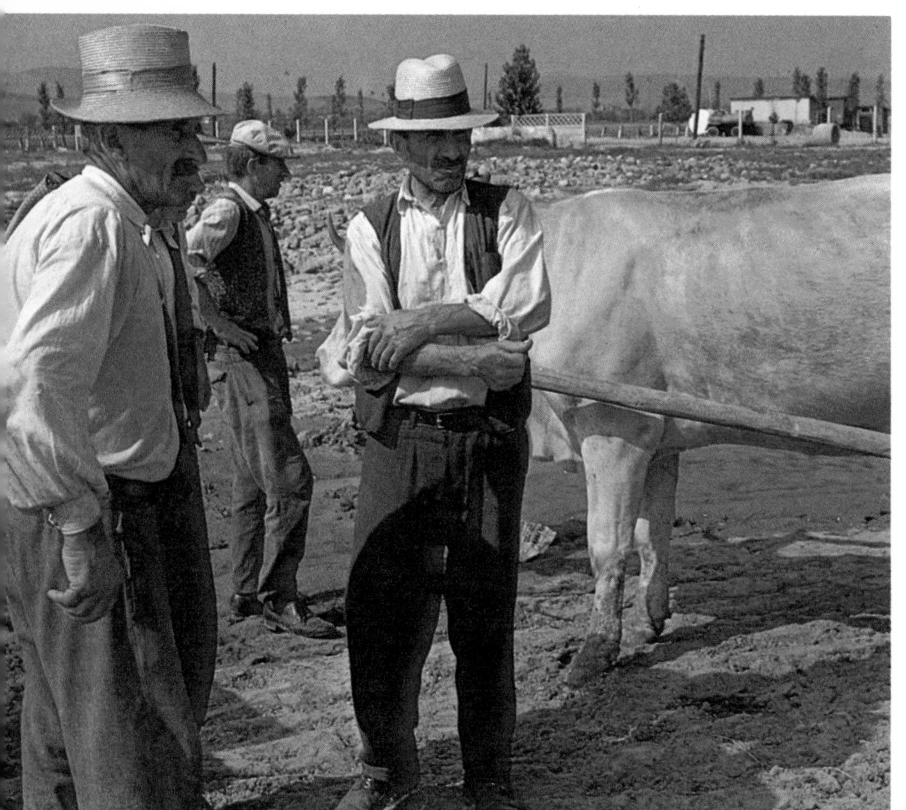

Why is fertilizer needed?

Plants contain chlorophyll, and this enables them to make their own sugar with the sun's rays, so that they have their own food supply. But at the same time there are certain elements in the soil which are essential for good crops. The plant absorbs them as it absorbs water, by its roots. The essential elements are nitrogen, phosphorus, potassium and magnesium. Small quantities of copper, manganese, zinc and iron are also needed. At harvest time these elements are removed from the soil at the same time as the plant, and so the ground has to be fed with fertilizer to prevent it becoming unproductive. Formerly, horse manure was the chief fertilizer used. It is still used widely, but additional chemical fertilizer is also needed to produce good harvests.

In spite of the great advantages of chemical fertilizers, manure is still essential for agriculture, since it contains organic elements which improve the quality of the soil. If the same crop is grown year after year, the soil will eventually become exhausted, so that, as well as spreading fertilizer, it is sometimes necessary to rotate crops, allowing each field a year in which to lie fallow.

Which domestic animals are used in agriculture?

Among the chief domestic animals used in agriculture are cattle. Cattle are probably descended from the primitive ox which was still to be found in our regions in the seventeenth century. Bovines (and other grass-eating animals) have molars covered in ridges of enamel which enable them to chew the grass which they feed on very finely. They are ruminants. Their digestive tract is very long, so that it can cope with a diet of vegetable matter. The stomach itself consists of four compartments. Grass which has not been chewed accumulates in the rumen, or first stomach, then passes into the honeycomb, or second stomach, before rising into the mouth to be chewed. Then it passes through the third stomach into the fourth, or rennet, stomach, where it is digested. In summer the cows are sent out to graze in the pastures. A pasture of one hectare produces enough grass to feed two or three cows for a year. Cattle produce chiefly milk, cheese, butter, meat and leather. The best known varieties are the British Highland Hereford and Aberdeen Angus and the French Charolais, all raised for their meat, and dairy breeds such as the Friesian, Holstein, Jersey and Guernsey.

The pig has been used as a domestic animal for more than 8000 years. Men started by domesticating wild pigs captured in the forest. Then around 1800, farmers began crossing European pigs with Chinese varieties to produce new breeds. The best known of these is the white Yorkshire pig, which has a small head and pointed ears. The Berkshire pig was produced in the same way and is dark, also with pointed ears. The so-called Landrace varieties are native European breeds, all white with long, floppy ears. In modern piggeries some pigs are reared for breeding while others are fattened for slaughter.

Above: **A farm. In former times each district had its own characteristic type of farm, but now the buildings are tending to become more uniform.**
Left: **Sunflowers are cultivated for their seeds, which have a very high oil content.**
Below: **Haystacks are becomingly increasingly rare. We seldom see grass drying in the fields today; instead it is dried under cover by means of hot air.**

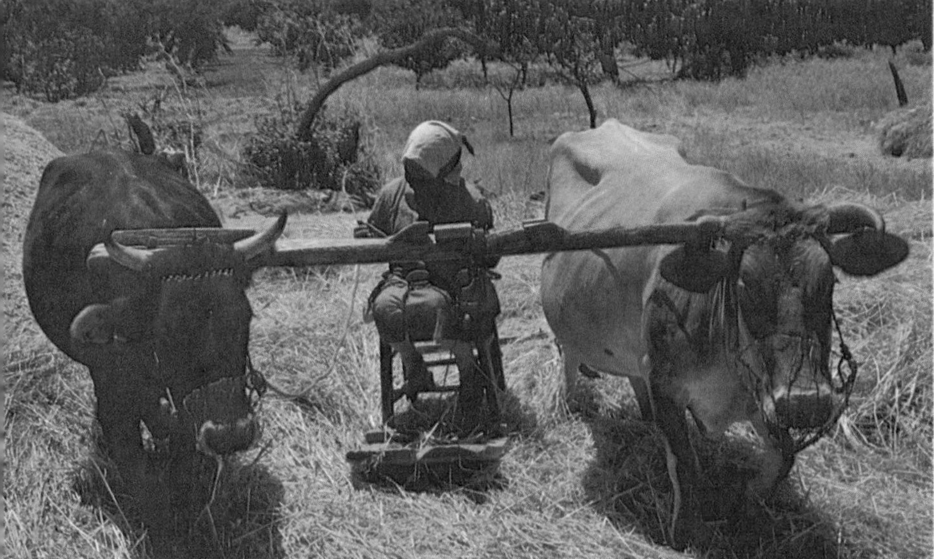

Top right: **Shepherds in Spain.**
Top left: **Agriculture is still very primitive in developing countries like Nepal. There is little mechanization, because it is too expensive, and farmers ploughing with oxen are an everyday sight.**
Bottom left: **A Greek woman using a pair of oxen for ploughing.**
Bottom right: **Our modern agricultural units are usually highly mechanized. The photograph shows a combine harvester. This machine can do the work of dozens of men in a short space of time. It both harvests the grain and threshes it in a continuous operation.**

Sheep are raised for their wool and their meat. Formerly, ovines (sheep) were of far greater economic importance than they are today, as the produced good fertilizer. Since the introduction of chemical fertilizer, their numbers have declined considerably. The best known wool-producing breed is the Merino, while in Britain, breeds such as the Cheviot and the Scottish Blackface, the Bluefaced and Border Leicesters and the Suffolk and Dorset are raised for wool and meat production.
Goats are found chiefly in the developing countries, where they take the place of cattle. They give similar products at a lower cost.
Poultry farming is chiefly concerned with chickens. Chicken farms are becoming more and more specialized. Some are solely hatcheries, concerned with breeding, others are engaged in egg production and some in fattening chickens for the table.
Horses are no longer very important in modern agriculture, since tractors can do their work more quickly.

What are forests used for?

In countries such as Brazil and Indonesia, wood from the forests is in great demand and forms an important part of the economy. These tropical woods are used in Western countries for building and for the furniture industry. The wood in European forests is less precious and serves largely for the manufacture of chipboard, paper and cellulose, or as fire-wood.
On the other hand, the recreational use of forests in Europe is much greater, as a result of the growth of the population and the increase in leisure activities. City-dwellers who live in the 'concrete jungle' and breathe in the polluted city atmosphere day after day have a particularly strong need to take a

Right: **The trunks of conifers usually contain resin. Some types of resin are used for making turpentine.**
Bottom right: **The rubber tree *(Hevea Brasiliensis)* is a native of South America. Today there are large rubber plantations in south-east Asia and Africa. The tree is cultivated for its sap, known as latex. To collect the latex, horizontal cuts are made in the trunk and the liquid flows into containers fixed beneath the cut. The latex is turned into rubber in factories.**
Below: **Canada is one of the world's great wood producers. Rivers are used to transport the trunks, which float on the water.**

walk in the country from time to time.
Another important function of forests is their protective role. First of all the trees protect the soil against erosion, anchoring it in place with their roots and restraining the force of the water which runs down slopes and hillsides after heavy rain. Often trees are specially planted in areas where there has been much erosion. They also protect man and the animals by providing them with oxygen and they purify the air by collecting dust particles. Finally, the forest provides a refuge for all kinds of wild plants and animals which are threatened with extinction by human activities such as the building of houses, roads etc.

What are the main activities of forestry?

Although forests are used for recreational activities more than anything else, wood production nevertheless remains an important factor. Forestry is making sure the woodland is well kept and grows properly. The forester cannot cut down trees as he pleases, he needs to think which trees are ready for cutting and which will need to be replanted. A section of forest which has been cleared should be replanted in the autumn with young trees from a nursery. The plantation is usually enclosed by a wire fence to protect it from deer and other animals, who might break down or eat the young trees. For the first few years, all the forester needs to do is to remove the weeds which tend to grow around the young shoots. These would kill the tree by taking all the nourishment from the soil. Later, the tree needs to be surrounded in such a way that light reaches it only from the top while it is growing. This helps it to grow straight upwards and reduces the number of side branches. It also avoids the formation of knots in the wood. From time to time the plantation is thinned out, and any diseased wood or trees with irregular growth, such as a double or crooked crown, are removed. Trees which are hindering the growth of others are also cut down. If the thinning has been carried out properly, the trees will reach their standard height with a minimum

number of side branches in fifty years. Later the plantation may be thinned further so that the best trees can have enough space to develop properly. After ninety to a hundred years, the trees are cut down with a power saw. The tops, side branches and bark are removed, and the wood is then sold to a sawmill, paper mill or other concern which uses wood as a raw material.

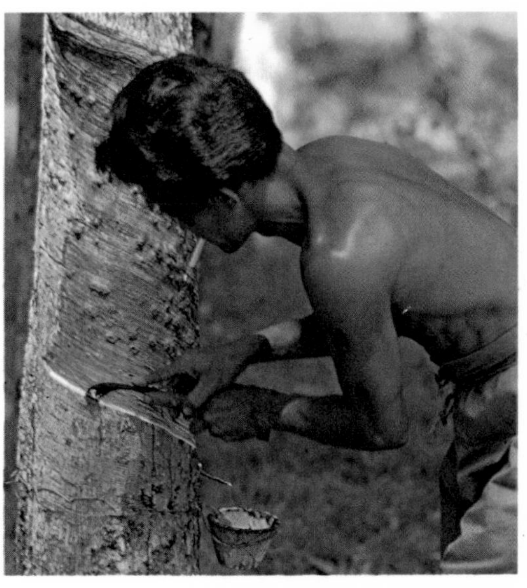

Textiles

A textile is any material which contains fibres suitable for making cloth. The word textile is derived from the latin textilis *meaning woven or plaited.*

Above: Sheep farming is an important activity in New Zealand, which is one of the world's main wool producers. The wool is transported in its raw form to countries all over the world, where it is spun and then used by the textile industry.
Right: Shearing the wool from the sheep is done quickly and easily with electric clippers.

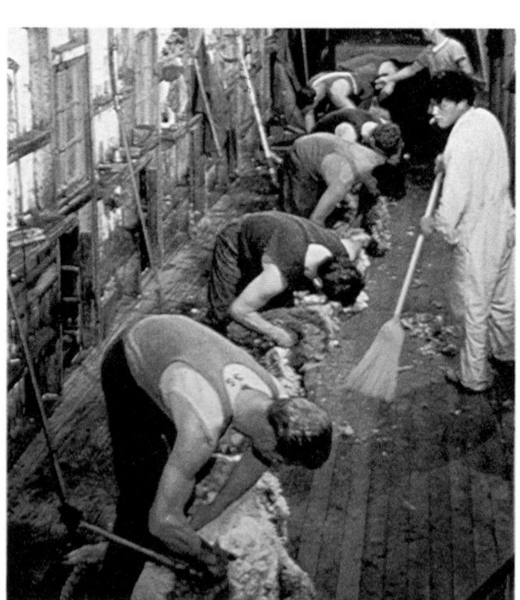

What are the most primitive forms of textile production?

Long ago the natives of Africa and South America beat and crushed bark and used the fibres to make textiles. In South America blankets were produced by this method. The same technique is still used to produce textile fibres in the Pacific islands around the Equator. The men choose a suitable tree, which must be neither too young nor too old, and remove the bark by soaping it away with seashells. The women then soak the bark in water, leaving it for several days. The strips of soaked bark are then placed side by side on a broad wooden plank, and crushed with a block of wood. In this way large sheets of material resembling cloth are made. Another form of textile production consists of beating and pressing wool or animal hair which has been treated with grease so that it will form a felt-like textile. This method is found particularly among shepherds who keep long-haired flocks, such as the nomad tribes of Asia. The felt is made by the women outside their tents, while the men have the task of keeping the flocks.

Below: This detail from a picture by Roger van der Weyden illustrates how for many countries the people of Flanders produced elegant garments from the textiles available to them.

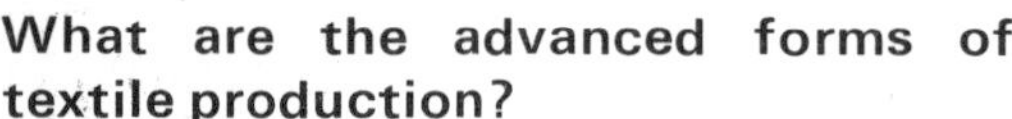

What are the advanced forms of textile production?

The advanced forms of textile production are spinning and weaving. Spinning is the production of long threads of fibrous material such as wool, silk and cotton. Either animal hair or vegetable fibres can be used. Cotton and flax are the most widely used plant fibres, although hemp, jute and sisal are used, and coconut fibre is used for matting. Wool, silk, cashmere and angora are animal fibres. Special tools such as the shuttle and spindle were not used by very primitive peoples, but in America, in the regions where cotton grew, the Indians had been using a sort of shuttle for a very long time. In Europe a rather more complicated device, the spinning wheel, was used. Thus spinning was known all over the world. Weaving requiries a more advanced technique. A society needed to have reached a certain level of development in order to be able to use a loom and make a simple piece of fabric. The art of weaving was totally unknown in the Pacific Islands, in some parts of Africa and among the Indians. In Asia, however, the loom had long been in use. Later, people began to decorate the fabrics they produced. A form of decoration invented in Indonesia is *batik*. This technique involves drawing patterns on cotton cloth and covering them with wax. The parts not covered with wax are then dyed. The operation is repeated several times with different colours. The method of weaving used by the Incas is still found among the Quechua and Aymara Indians of Peru. These examples show that people in different regions of the earth discovered long ago that fabrics could be artistically coloured.

Are all textiles woven?

No. Clothing can also be knitted. In this case wool or thread is used, and is knitted or braided with long needles. Nowadays there are even knitting machines.
Spun fibres can also be used to make lace on a bobbin. Belgian lace made in this way is world-famous.
Thread can also be worked with a crochet hook This is a long needle with a hooked end which is used to pass the thread through the loops in the crochet-work.

What is happening in the textile industry today?

For centuries, Flanders was one of the most important centres for the textile industry. The Flemish people cultivated flax, which yields a high quality vegetable fibre. These fibres were used for weaving cloth, and Flemish cloth was renowned throughout the world. France also had an important textile centre – the region around Lyons specialized in weaving silk, produced by the silk worm which lives on mulberry bushes, while in England the cotton mills of Lancashire produced cloth from Indian cotton which was then sent all over the world. The European textile industries suffered a decline with the introduction of man-made fibres, and also as a result of fierce competition from the developing countries. Countries where industry is still relatively new and salaries are still low can produce textiles at much more competitive prices. Some areas which formerly imported European textiles at high prices are now able to export the same products to Europe. Some European textile manufacturers have even gone so far as to set up factories in the developing countries, taking advantage of the cheap labour to produce their fabrics at low cost. But all this has done is to increase unemployment in the textile industry at home.
The introduction of man-made and synthetic fibres is relatively recent. Nowadays nearly every shop contains many articles made from fibres such as rayon or nylon. Rayon is made by processing natural substances to form a new fibre. Nylon is synthetic, which means that is made from chemicals.

Weaving is a method of passing threads across one another at right angles. The threads run in two directions – the warp and the weft. All looms work on this principle.

Above: **A Scottish weaver producing a piece of plaid cloth.**
Bottom left: **The art of weaving has been known in Asia for centuries.**
Bottom right: **This Thai girl is weaving in the same way as her ancestors did several thousand years ago.**

Metallurgy

Metallurgy began a very long time ago in Europe and on the continent of Asia.

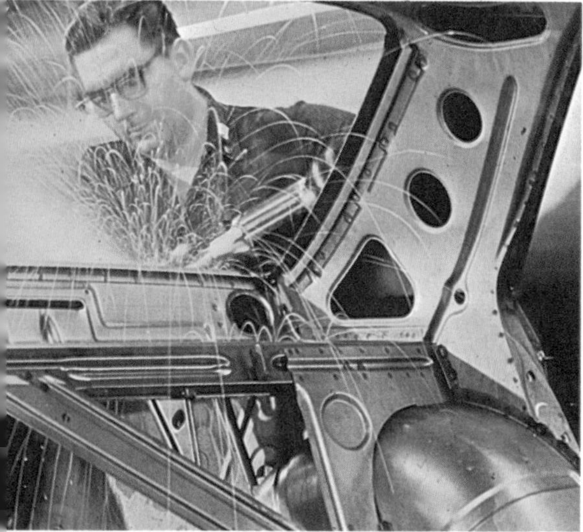

Above: **The different parts of a metal structure are welded together, using a blow-torch which works at a very high temperature. In welding, the edges of two pieces of metal are brought into contact and melted together. For this process a mixture of oxygen and acetylene is used. The blow-torch is fed by two rubber pipes carrying the two types of gas, which are mixed together and come out of a small hole, where they are lit. The mixture can be regulated to produce the critical temperature at which the two pieces of metal will melt together.**

What effect did the absence of metal have on a region's development?

In the regions where metal was unknown the primitive peoples remained in the Stone Age. This was the case, for example, with the inhabitants of a large number of islands in the Pacific Ocean. But we know from the history of the European and Asiatic peoples that their way of life progressed in great leaps and this evolution was very largely a consequence of the use of copper, bronze and iron. We also find that the introduction of metal objects among peoples who had not known them before produced an overwhelming change in their way of life. There were extensive changes in the way of life of the Pacific islanders when they started importing iron implements. Another example of social change caused by metal objects is the introduction of the gun among the Indians, who lived chiefly by hunting. The gun changed the Indian's way of hunting, and his way of life. Tribes became richer and more powerful and were able to trade with guns.

Where was copper first used?

Copper was known in Europe at an early date and used in the making of bronze during the Bronze Age, but some of the Indian tribes of America knew how to work it before its discovery by the Europeans. The Yellowknives, who lived in Canada, for example, used it for making axes and knives, and it was from this that they got their name.

Below: **A village forge. The blacksmith is working pieces of metal which are brought to red heat in the fire with the help of the bellows. When the iron is red hot the blacksmith takes it out of the flames with a pair of tongs and places it on the anvil. As the metal is then soft, it can be worked with a hammer to give it the required shape.**

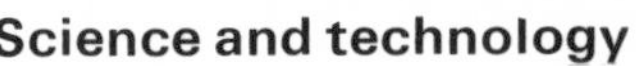

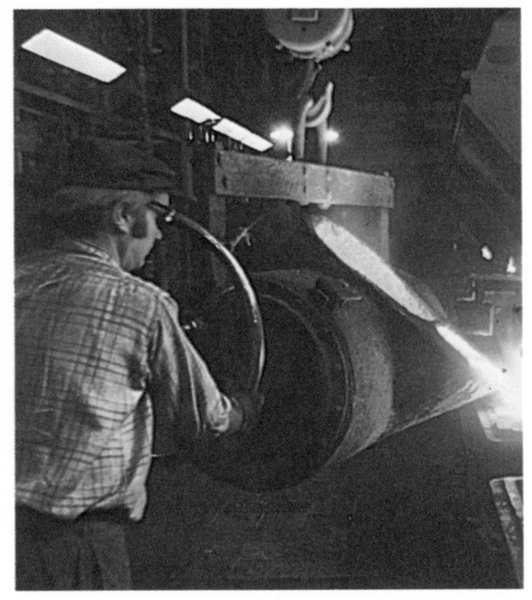

Left: **Iron is a blueish-grey metal which is extracted from iron ore. Steel is iron mixed with a small quantity of carbon (about four per cent). The process takes place in tall furnaces where the metal is heated until it turns liquid. Other substances as well as carbon may be added to the molten metal, giving it certain properties. Vanadium, for example, produces a very hard metal, while chromium makes it resistant to rust.**

They used to prospect for copper in the mountains along the river Coppermine. The Yellowknives were highly respected by the other tribes, until the Europeans came and sowed discord among the Indians.

In Peru and Mexico the use of copper had been known for centuries. It was also worked in Africa and Asia. One disadvantage of this metal was that it was relatively soft. Stone objects were more resilient.

What is bronze?

Bronze is an alloy, made from a mixture of copper and tin.

It had been known in Europe for many centuries, but in Central and South America its use was less widespread. It was also used for a number of centuries in Benin in West Africa. Works of art in bronze have been preserved from this period. Some scholars claim that it was the inhabitants of Benin who taught Western Europeans the use of bronze.

Where was iron used?

Iron was first used in the East, and, during the period of the great popular migrations, the use of iron spread throughout Europe. Soon the black Africans also began to use the metal, making strangely shaped but highly effective spears. Once Man learnt how to smelt iron ore he could make many tools.

Working in iron requires a certain level of technological development, for it involves the use of furnaces, anvils and hammers. Bellows are needed to stoke the fire and increase the heat it gives out. With their great ingenuity and imagination the black Africans invented many different types of bellows, all of which were very effective. Today the blacksmith still occupies an important place in the life of an African village. His role is comparable to that of the village blacksmith in European villages several decades ago.

Were precious metals always considered very valuable?

In Europe, gold and silver have long been considered precious metals and commanded high prices. The same was true of Asia, too. The American Indians worked these metals and valued them highly, but after the continent's discovery by Christopher Columbus and the damage done by the European invaders, working in gold and silver practically disappeared from that part of the world. Only one tribe, the Navahos of Arizona, continued this ancestral art.

Gold and silver were unsuitable for the manufacture of tools and so the more primitive peoples had little use for them. More advanced civilizations, however, knew that they were a very valuable foreign currency. Thus the Indians who lived in the Rocky Mountains of Western America thought nothing of the gold to be found in abundance in their river beds. They could not understand the gold fever which gripped the whites, and more than one Indian lost his life as a result. In California the Indian population was practically exterminated and the authorities made no attempt to intervene. Hordes of white adventurers invaded the country in search of gold, killing anyone they found in their path, during the 'gold rushes'.

Below: **Bells have been in use for many centuries. As they are made of metal they vibrate when struck by the clapper inside, producing a ringing sound. The same effect can be produced by striking them on the outside with a hammer. The man in this picture is testing a bell which he has just cast. To make a bell he must first draw a design, then make a mould to the same shape. The mould is filled with molten bronze, and when this has cooled, it is broken open. The result is a brand new bell which has to be polished and fitted with a clapper.**

Paper and printing

It is only relatively recently that paper was introduced into our part of the world; and it was several centuries after this that people had the idea of printing on it.

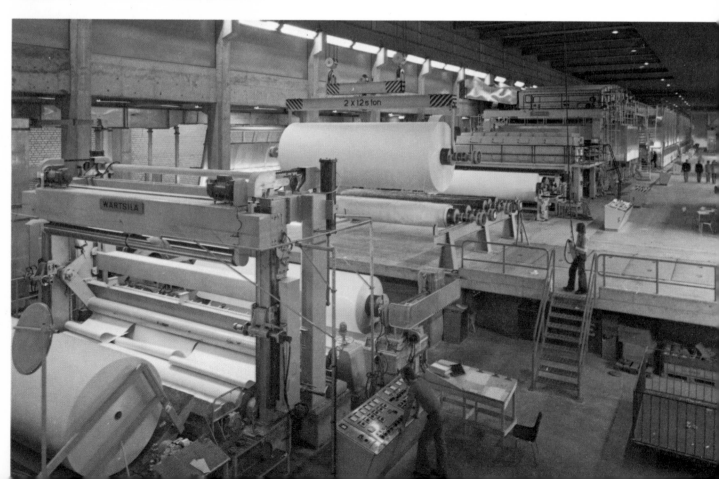

Top: **The liquid pulp used for paper making is spread in a thin layer, which is then dried.**
Centre: **The dried pulp is then pressed and glazed in a special machine.**
Bottom: **A modern paper-making machine is a large and complex piece of apparatus.**

What is paper and how is it made?

Paper is sometimes sold as sheets and sometimes sold in rolls. It is used as a packing material and is also used for writing and printing.

The Egyptians learnt to use a material made from the papyrus reed for writing on. The word 'paper' is derived from papyrus. Because papyrus does not decay, Egyptian scrolls have survived for many years. Paper was originally made from vegetable fibres which were wetted and pressed together on top of one another. It is claimed that paper was discovered by the Chinese some two thousand years ago. It made its appearance in Europe between 1000 and 1100 A.D.; before this, people had written on parchment. The vegetable fibres used for paper-making in Europe did not come directly from plants, but from linen rags. Thus the fibres were used twice over. Paper making was the first application of a technique which has become very common today and which is known as 'recycling'.

In the sixteenth century paper of excellent quality was being made from linen rags. About a hundred years later, the introduction of a new method using wood chips as a raw material enabled paper of the same quality to be made much more cheaply. Books became cheaper and newspapers were printed in greater numbers. Waste paper can now be pulped and used again.

Right: A modern offset machine. A machine like this can print in two colours at once.
This book was printed in offset. What does this mean? First of all the letters or images are formed in relief, i.e. with the details standing up from the surrounding surface. They are then printed on a sheet of smooth paper, which is photographed. The negative of the photograph is placed on a thin metal plate which is coated with albumin. A light is shone onto the plate and the albumin hardens where it is exposed under the negative. The rest of the albumin is removed, leaving a positive image on the plate. The plate is moistened, and when it is covered with ink, the latter only sticks to the plate where the layer of albumin still exists. The rest of the plate remains damp and the ink will not stick to it. The illustrations used are made up of a number of little dots which have the same function as the letters in the text. The colour illustrations are broken down into red, yellow and blue, and black is added for extra contrast. When the picture is printed, the image is built up colour by colour. After the red, yellow, blue and black have been printed, the illustration appears in its original colours.

Who invented printing?

The Chinese invented printing about a thousand years ago, using characters made of porcelain. In Europe two names are famous in connection with printing: that of Laurens Janszoon Coster of Haarlem, and that of Johannes Gutenberg of Mainz. We shall never know which one of them it was who invented printing first, but the first books appeared in the 1450s. The advent of printed books meant that knowledge was available to more people.
Originally, the characters to be printed were cut from wood and assembled to form words or phrases. They were then covered with ink and printed on damp paper. The introduction of lead characters was a great step forward. The individual letters were cast in lead and stored by the printer in a flat wooden box with numerous compartments, known as a case. In this box, every letter and sign had its own place, so that the printer could easily find the ones which he needed to make up a sentence. The letters were assembled on a composing stick and when a line had been completed it was transferred to a metal tray known as a galley, where the page was made up. Once completed the page was transferred to the press, where it was inked and printed on a sheet of damp paper.

When did this method change?

Hand printing presses were used for over 400 years, although they were very time-consuming. Steam power was first used in 1814, to print *The Times.* As machines were invented which printed faster, others were needed to compose the type faster as well. The year 1882 saw the introduction of the Linotype machine, which enabled a whole line to be composed and cast as one unit. The Monotype machine, invented in 1887, enabled single characters to be cast automatically.
Today several different methods are in use. Letterpress printing, in which lines of movable type are printed directly on to the paper, is still widely used, but offset-lithography is becoming the most common process. In this the characters are photographed on to a zinc plate and transferred to the paper via a rubber roller. Another method, which uses engraved metal plates, is photogravure.

Below: **A prehistoric drilling machine. Even in those early times, men were already thinking how they could do certain jobs more easily. This simple machine was worked by hand. A lever counterbalanced by the stones was used to exert a downward pressure.**

Machines and motors

From time immemorial, one of man's chief activities has been the invention of tool of all kinds with which to supplement his limited strength and overcome the forces o nature.

Above: **A modern hydraulically operated drilling machine works in much the same way, but here human strength is replaced by a motor. A hydraulic level provides the necessary presure.**

What in fact is a machine?

If I take a construction set and make a device full of turning wheels and shafts, can I say that I have made a machine? Not really, for by the term machine we understand a device which uses energy to perform some useful task by cutting down the amount of effort needed. This task can be of many different kinds. The machine can make our work easier, or it can speed it up. Cranes and pulleys make work easier for us by lifting heavy weights from the ground. And there are many different machines which speed work up for us.

Is the use of machinery a new phenomenon?

In his primeval state, man had no machines at his disposal. Life today is difficult to imagine without machines. We see them all around us and we use them without thinking. Everything we need during the course of a day is in some way or another the product of a machine. Perhaps you think that running water in the home is a natural phenomenon? Of course not! The tap which controls its delivery is just one of many machine products associated with running water. And then there are our clothes, our houses, our food, all of which are the product of machines. In the beginning, man used stones, wood and bones as tools. He quickly learned to shape them according to what he was going to use them for. He used stone axes and knives for hunting and cutting wood. He probably used a stick as a lever for moving large stones.
One of man's greatest inventions was the wheel. Practically all the machines which we know today are somehow made up of wheels. Wheels are needed for almost any kind of motion. Over the centuries the simple tools of primitive man have been improved and altered until they have become complex machines. Most of the machines which we know are so complicated as to be difficult to describe—an ingenious collection of wheels, shafts and levers designed to perform some useful task for man. These machines are vital to our modern society as a means of controlling the forces of nature. They are very different from those of earlier times. Modern machines have their own means of propulsion, while the first machines were operated by human strength alone. Later, animals, wind or water power were used. Today, most machines are driven by some kind of engine. Early machines usually needed someone to be present to operate them whilst they were in use, but nowadays many machines can be turned on and left to perform very complicated procedures.

What is an engine?

An engine is a very special type of machine, which transforms a quantity of energy, of a type which does not produce movement, into mechanical energy. Primitive forms of this type of machine are the sails of a ship, windmills and water-mills. The first two use the force of the wind, the third uses water as its propulsive force. Later, machines such as the steam engine, the petrol engine, the diesel engine and the electric motor were introduced.

All these machines still make use of natural forces. The force which they use is called energy. No machine could work without using some form of energy.

Where does energy come from?

We ourselves are not capable of producing enough energy for the work which these machines have to do. We have to find it elsewhere. We get it from the air, from burning coal or oil, from exploding gases, and so on. It is present everywhere in nature – in the wind, in rivers, in lightning – but we cannot always make use of it. The basic forms of energy are heat and light. Sometimes the amount of energy available and the difficulty of controlling it is quite frightening, as is the case with atomic or nuclear energy. Recently, people have begun to experiment with capturing the energy of the sun on solar panels, which are used to transform the sun's heat into electricity.

Top right: A very simple machine used in Thailand to irrigate a field with water from a nearby river. It is its simplicity which makes it so effective.
Bottom right: A cross-section of an old wooden mill, showing how it works. The millstones are fixed horizontally, so that the vertical circular movement of the sails has to be converted into a horizontal circular movement.
Below: One of man's best loved inventions – the steam train. Engines of this type could carry a large number of passengers at relatively high speeds.

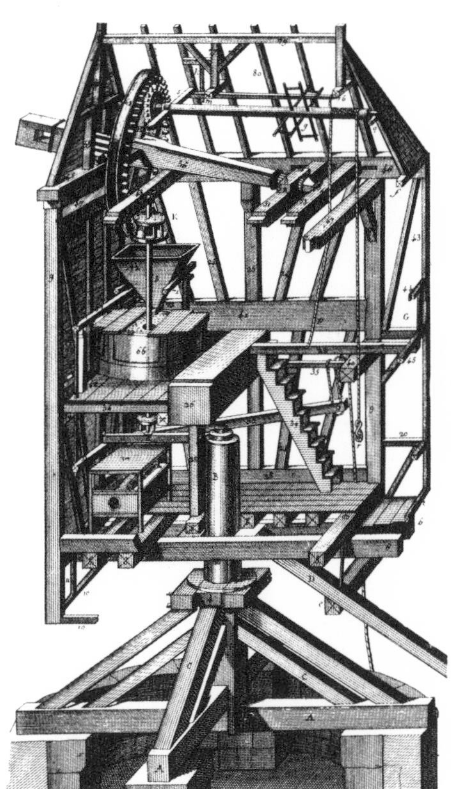

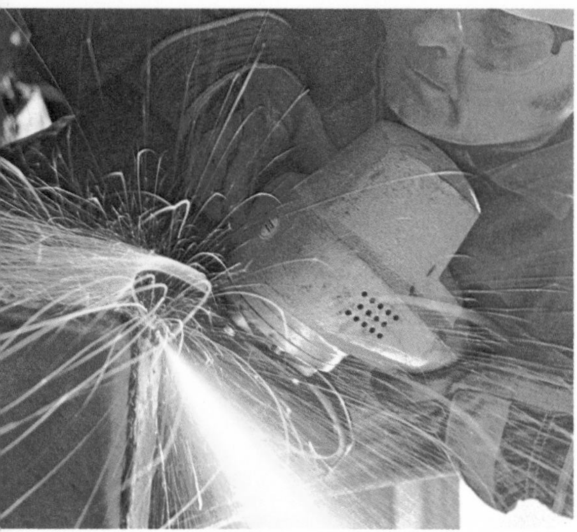

Left: **An electric machine being used to grind an iron bar. Work of this kind was long and laborious before the invention of machines. The sparks produced by the friction of the grinding wheel on the metal are clearly visible.**

Has the use of machines changed society?

The answer to this question is obviously – yes. It is precisely in order to improve and change society that man has developed tools and machines and made increasing use of them. The invention of the axe made it easier to cut down trees, and so houses could now be built from wood, and clearings could be made in the forests. The bow enabled men to shoot game at a distance simply by firing arrows. The invention of the wheel made it possible to carry in a vehicle loads which had previously been carried on the backs of men or animals. All these inventions radically changed society.

Machines provide more power to do work with, and enable it to be done faster. In former times, road surfaces were often bad because removing the rocks which were in the way was such a difficult task. Today, problems of this kind no longer exist. Any obstacle in the path of a road can be removed with cranes or mechanical shovels. If all else fails we still have dynamite. The study of physics has taught man a lot about the exploitation of natural forces and materials. This knowledge has enabled him to construct machines which are used in many different walks of life. But not all machines were created for man's welfare. Others were used as weapons of war. Guns, swords, cannon, tanks, submarines, bombs, grenades, aeroplanes and rockets – all are examples of machines used for destruction and not for human progress.

Machines have improved communications as well. We can now speak to people thousands of miles away, and hear what is happening in other countries. Remote areas can be reached and surveyed by aeroplanes.

Below: **A power drill is essential for digging up stony ground. The heavy chisel is moved up and down very quickly by means of steam, compressed air or electricity.**

Left: **A tractor at work. Tractors enable large areas of land to be ploughed by a very small number of men. Without tractors it would be impossible to cultivate the vast wheat fields in the United States, Canada and the Soviet Union.**
Bottom left: **A different kind of tractor is used in mining. Working underground is very arduous and requires a great deal of power. Remote control machines such as this are used to extract coal and ores from the earth and carry them through the mines. They make working underground very much safer.**

What is the difference between a petrol engine and a diesel engine?

The name itself indicates one difference, which is in the fuel used. One runs on petrol, the other on diesel. The latter is more economical, but the real differences lie elsewhere. A petrol engine has several cylinders, each with a spark plug in its head. A spark plug is a small device which produces sparks at regular intervals. These sparks are necessary to induce the explosion of the compressed mixture of petrol and air which drives the engine. The diesel engine also has cylinders inside which explosions take place; however these are not produced by a spark plug, for a diesel engine does not have any. Instead the vapour inside the cylinder is compressed with such force that it heats up and explodes of its own accord. Diesel engines are more robust than petrol engines.

What were the chief benefits brought by the use of machines?

The use of machines has always been of fundamental importance for society as a whole. Machines have enabled men to transform deserts and other inhospitable regions into areas suitable for people to live in. With the help of artificial irrigation, good crops can be produced almost anywhere. Roads are built across the mountains to ensure good communications. Whole areas are cleared and ploughed up for cultivation. All large-scale agricultural operations are carried out mechanically at a speed and on a scale which would have formerly been unimaginable.

Without the use of machines, operations of this kind would be impossible. But for the machines to work, iron and petroleum are needed. And to obtain the iron and petroleum, other machines are needed. Raw materials and products must both be transported quickly, and this too is the job of machines.

Machines are also used for pleasure, and for travelling. We use bicycles and cars to go to school or to work, where otherwise we would have to go on foot. We watch television and listen to the radio. Sometimes we go to the cinema. We take photographs to record pleasurable moments. None of these amusements would be possible if we did not have machines. Machines are invented for every conceivable activity – for doing sums or writing letters. People have even tried to invent a machine which was able to do everything man could. But there is one thing which such a machine could never do, and that is to think creatively, although computers are capable of complicated 'thought' processes once they have been programmed by men. Only man can really think, and it is something which he must always do if he wishes to remain master of his machines.

The measurement of time

It is difficult to imagine life without some means of measuring time. When we think of history, we do not consider time in the same way as when we hear the clock striking.

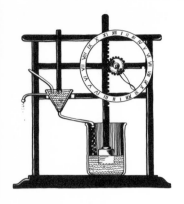

This is a water clock on which the time is indicated by a hand on a dial. The clock, which is of Egyptian origin, was connected to a reservoir from which water flowed into a receptacle through a funnel. In the container was a float attached to a toothed bar or ratchet; the teeth engaged in a cog wheel which turned the wheel of the clock.

What is time?

For centuries philosophers and other scholars have been trying to define time. A particular moment comes, goes, and never returns. It was only in the twentieth century that the great scientist Einstein found an answer to the question of what time is. For Einstein the idea of time is given to us by a clock. Many different things can serve as a clock – the earth turning on its axis, an hour glass, a watch, a heartbeat, the tides, the thickness of a layer of the earth's crust or the number of vibrations of an atom of a given substance. The kind of clock which we usually find in houses follows the laws of physics established by Newton in the seventeenth century.

How is time subdivided?

The clock strikes twelve midnight. People wish each other a happy new year and everyone sings *Auld Lang Syne*. Another year has passed, and the earth has once more travelled in a circle round the sun. The unity of time, in fact, is a natural phenomenon.

The same applies to a single day, which is the length of time it takes for the earth to make one complete revolution on its axis during its journey round the sun. The months and the seasons are also natural subdivisions of the year.

Other units of time, however, are the work of man himself. It was man who created the week of seven days, because he found it the ideal period in which to divide up activities such as business, and to introduce a period of rest or prayer. A week could just as easily have been made up of eight, or six days. He subdivided the day into hours in order to fix the moments at which he should sleep, eat or work. The hour was subdivided into minutes, and later these minutes were themselves divided into seconds. Today, hundredths and thousandths of a second are used in areas such as space travel and competitive sport, where it is necessary to be completely accurate. Races can be lost or won, and world records broken by such minute amounts of time.

How do we tell the time?

The Egyptians used to tell the time by observing the movement of the shadow cast by an obelisk. For measuring short periods they used a water clock, in which water flowed drop by drop from one container into another.

Sundials of all different kinds were used for telling the time from 4000 B.C. right up until the sixteenth century, but they were not very accurate. Very many experiments had to be carried out before an accurate system of measuring time was found. People experimented with candles, hour-glasses, falling stones and running water, and of course the position of the sun was known to be an important factor. In 1357 a water clock was built at Fez in Morocco behind a face 11 metres high. Every hour a stone fell on to a

Right: A gold watch which once belonged to Catherine I, Empress of Russia.
Below: An hour-glass used for measuring time on ships. It consists of two glass chambers linked together by a narrow passage. When the top half is full, the sand flows slowly into the bottom half.

Right: **The gear wheels of a chronometer. Chronometers are used in scientific tests, and also in sport, when they are often known as stopwatches. A chronometer is a very accurate type of watch. Its name is derived from that of Chronos, the Greek god of agriculture and the father of Zeus, and who later became the god of time. Chronos carried a scythe with which he cut down the passing years. In western Europe we know him as Old Father Time, who appears to mark the beginning of a new year.**

gong. The face contained a number of doors and at every hour also, a different door opened. Anyone who had not heard the gong could tell what time it was by looking to see which door was open.

A sundial is an old and popular device for measuring time. As the earth spins round on its axis a shadow cast by the sun gradually moves round. This movement can be mapped out and the time can be read from the clock. Like the Egyptian obelisk 'clock' it can only be used in daylight and when the sun is bright enough to cast a shadow. Part of the popularity of sundials in the past – and even today – is that very decorative models can be designed to grace any garden.

In 1900, part of a Greek calculating machine was found in the wreck of a boat which had sunk 2000 years previously. Experts recognized this piece as belonging to a forerunner of modern clock mechanisms. In an enormous Chinese water clock dating from the eleventh century a small mechanism was found which was later used as a regulator for clocks driven by gear wheels. It was a small metal shaft at the end of which hung a weight. The shaft swung to and fro, alternately holding and releasing the teeth of the drive mechanism one by one. This movement produced the familiar 'tick-tock' sound of the clock.

Later this technique was perfected in mechanical clocks. At first a system of weights was used to drive the mechanism, but later people began to make watches driven by a spring. In the seventeenth century the famous Dutch scientist Christian Huygens built the first pendulum clock. It was more accurate than existing clocks and was the first to show the seconds. Huygens then went on to invent what was almost the perfect clock regulator – the balance wheel. Huygens' two inventions were important milestones in the development of clock and watch making. Later the electronic clock was invented. Atomic clocks are the most recent invention, and caesium atomic clocks are the most accurate ever made.

Watches have undergone changes over the years too – although these portable timepieces have obviously not been in use for as long as clocks. Very accurate watches with clockwork movements have always been extremely expensive items, but since the invention of watches – and clocks – with a quartz movement accurate timepieces are available at much lower prices.

How accurate is a clock?

When several clocks had been made their accuracy could be tested by comparing them, and efforts were made to improve this accuracy. Between about 1325 and 1656, inaccuracies were reduced from 15 to 2 minutes per day. Christian Huygens used the effect of gravity on a pendulum to perfect the design of clocks, and reduced their inaccuracy to some ten seconds per day. Clocks with pendulums became fashionable from 1656. They were accurate enough to indicate minutes as well as hours. In the years which followed clock mechanisms were perfected. It was discovered that the pendulum expanded or contracted according to changes in temperature, and this had the effect of making the clock go slower or faster. The Englishman George Graham (1673–1751) succeeded in remedying this fault in 1721. His compensating clock was accurate to within one second per week In recent years the balance-wheel generally used in clocks has been replaced by the quartz crystal and as a result clocks and watches have become accurate to within some ten thousandths of a second per day. The most accurate type of clock is the caesium atomic clock, which is so precise that it would take 3000 years for it to lose a single second.

Building and construction work

Here we deal with the erection of buildings and the construction of roads and waterways.

Above: An example of the arch as it was used in architecture by the Romans. This is the Pont du Gard, an aqueduct built of bricks over the river Gard in France.
Right: A simple bridge in the Himalayas, built largely of natural materials.
Bottom left: The ruins of the pyramids, temples and palaces left by the Mayas show that they were ingenious architects.
Bottom right: The Egyptians built a large number of pyramids beside the Nile at Giza. These were enormous tombs made of blocks of natural stone. In the foreground is the famous Sphinx.

What kind of materials are used?

The first construction materials used by man were branches, wood and clay. In Arctic regions, as winter approached, the Eskimoes built igloos with blocks of snow to protect themselves from the icy cold. Buildings in the desert have thick walls made of clay and formed into blocks and baked hard. The thick walls protect the inhabitants from the heat during the day and the cold during the night. In some areas houses must have good ventilation. Sometimes, too, a house needs to be protected from attack by wild animals, and then it is built in some inaccessible place, such as a tree. As man developed and established himself in one place, his needs became more complicated. Long ago, people started making buildings of stone pillars with beams laid across them. This type of construction, known as the peristyle, existed in Egypt 3000 years ago, and it spread from there throughout the world. Later a second type of structure – the arch – was invented. Doorways were made by supporting blocks of natural stone on pillars. In regions where no stone was available, bricks were used instead. The Egyptians invented a kind of cement, which was later improved by the Romans. They constructed their buildings with a mixture of bird-lime, broken stones and powdered glass.

In the nineteenth century, cast iron and glass were widely used. Today, the chief building materials are steel, plastic and concrete. Because these materials are very strong, huge multi-storey buildings can be constructed, which means that many more offices can be contained in a relatively small area of land.

Above: A dam in Rumania. The course of a river has been altered and tne water-level has risen to produce an artificial lake. The water can be used for irrigation, but also to operate turbines which produce electricity.
Right: Twentieth century urban architecture. The building in the left foreground is the seat of the United Nations Organization in New York.
Bottom right: A modern lock system.

What developments have taken place in the twentieth century?

Man's first great architectural discovery was the peristyle; his second was the use of the arch. In the centuries after their invention, the two styles were combined and perfected. The techniques invented by the people of the Ancient World enabled men to build more and more and better and better. But in the twentieth century architecture changed completely. The use of reinforced concrete completely revolutionized building. This technique made it possible to construct floors which could support the same weight over their entire area. Thus it was no longer necessary to have many different points of support, and rooms became much larger and brighter.

The technique of surfacing roads had been known for a long time. The Romans used it to enable their army to move from place to place. The bridges they used were very simple in construction. The spectacular development of road traffic in the nineteenth and twentieth centuries brought many changes. Horse drawn carriages were replaced by cars and lorries, and many more roads became necessary. Machines were used to speed up road building and bridges were constructed mostly of concrete parts. These are capable of carrying very heavy vehicles.

New materials and working methods were also used in building dams, dykes and other earth-works. The works carried out in the Rhine Delta in the Netherlands after the great floods of 1953 are the supreme example of this type of architecture; enormous dykes were built to keep out the sea and the flooded land is gradually being reclaimed. Dutch dredgers were sent all over the world and Dutch experts in marine construction work gave other countries the benefit of their experience.

What is a lock?

A lock is used to carry a ship up or down from one water level to another. If the ship is on a higher level, the water in the lock is brought up to that level, then the lock opens and the ship enters the lock basin. The gates close again and the lock keeper lets out the water from the lock until it is at the lower level. The gates at the other end of the lock now open and the ship goes on its way. When the ship has to pass from a lower level to a higher one, the process is the same, but in reverse.

Electricity

Electricity is a form of energy which has many different applications. We use it for lighting, heating, cooking, radio, television, etc. Without electricity, life would be very different from the way it is.

Above: **André Marie Ampère (1775–1836) was a French physicist who also took an interest in mathematics, philosophy, botany and chemistry. He became especially famous for his work on electricity. The unit of intensity of electrical current, the ampere, is named after him.**
Below: **The Dane Hans Christian Ørsted (1777–1851) was a doctor who was chiefly interested in physics. He made the important discovery of the magnetic fields created by electrical currents.**
Right: **Thomas Alva Edison (1847–1931) was an American physicist who invented a whole series of electrical apparatus. His chief discoveries were the incandescent lamp, the photograph (forerunner of the gramophone) and numerous devices for photographing and projecting images. He also had a gift for improving existing inventions and making them practical for everyday use.**

What is electricity?

Electricity has existed in nature since the beginning of time, being visible in the form of lightning. The ancient Greeks discovered that when wool was rubbed against amber, the two were attracted to each other (the Greek word for amber is *elektron*). This phenomenon, which is known as static (i.e. not moving) electricity, also occurs with modern synthetic materials. It cannot however be used as a source of energy. The electricity which we make use of today is dynamic (i.e. mobile); it is in fact an electric current. In order to understand the nature of electricity, we must know something about the structure of the atom. An atom consists of a positively charged nucleus with one or more negatively charged particles – electrons – revolving around it.
The atoms which go to make up metals have a characteristic peculiarity, which is that some of the electrons are not fixed around a particular nucleus, but move freely through the metal. For this reason they are called 'free electrons'. If all these electrons can be made to move in the same direction, an electric current is produced. This can be achieved by joining the ends of a piece of metal, usually a copper wire, to a source of current, such as a battery. The strength of the current is measured in amperes, named after André Marie Ampère, a French physicist who lived from 1775 to 1836, and who did much research on this subject.

How is electricity produced?

Electricity is something which we take for granted. We have only to press a switch or put a coin in a slot for electricity to appear. But in turning on a lamp we are seeing the result of a whole series of processes which we rarely think about. Electricity comes into our houses via cables which are linked to a power station. In the power station, the electric current is produced by generators. These are gigantic dynamoes which work in very much the same way as the dynamo on a bicycle. A bicycle wheel turns the dynamo relatively slowly, but a generator needs to turn much faster than this, and so a turbine is used, the main part of which is the rotor. In mountainous regions, this rotor can be turned by the force of water descending from the mountains, but in other areas another source of energy is needed, and this is usually steam. To produce steam, we need to heat water, and this requires power, which can be produced by coal, oil, gas, or the energy emitted by the fission of a uranium atom. This last form of energy is produced in a nuclear generating station.

How is electricity transported?

Electricity is moved from one place to another through copper or aluminium cables running above or below ground. Surface cables are less expensive than underground ones, since they do not need to be insulated, although they do have the disadvantage of disfiguring the countryside. The electricity which leaves the generating station is not taken directly to the consumer, since this would result in considerable losses of energy. The current which travels along the cables produces heat, and this heat increases as the current gets stronger.

In order to reduce the loss of power through heat, the strength of the current must be reduced by raising the potential or voltage. For this reason the current first passes through a transformer which raises the potential to 275,000, sometimes 400,000 volts. It can then be led to its destination along high-tension cables running over long distances. On arrival, the voltage is reduced to some 11,000 volts in sub-stations. The current then passes along underground cables to the transformer stations which can be found in every residential district. There it is brought down to the standard voltage of 240 volts, and enters our homes as low-tension current, which can then be used for lights and domestic appliances.

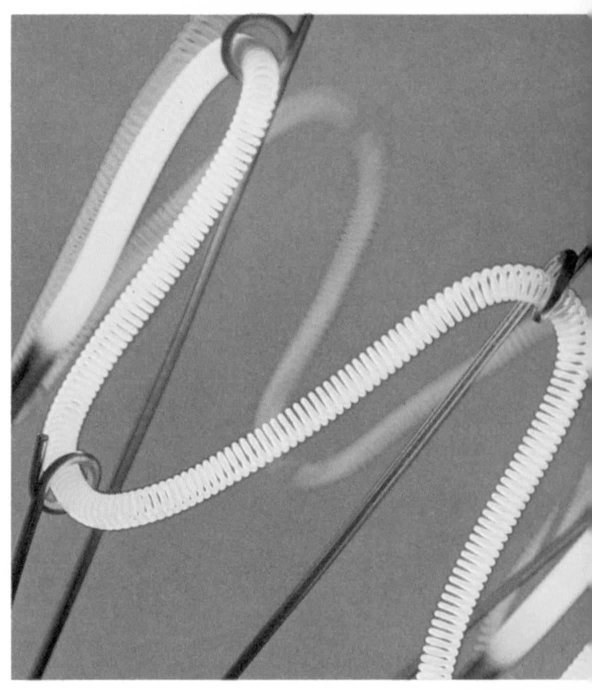

Above: This photograph shows part of a lamp filament. Filaments are made of tungsten, a metal with a very high melting point (about 3,400°C). The long, very fine wire is formed into a double spiral so that it takes up as little space as possible and can easily be introduced into the glass bulb. It is supported at several points to prevent it from collapsing under the intense heat produced.
Below: There are many different types of light bulbs, intended for a variety of different uses.

What is meant by potential?

The potential, or rather the 'potential difference', is the source of electrical current.

We can compare this to a current of water passing through a pipe. Inside the pipe, the drops of water all move in a particular direction; in an electrical cable it is the electrons which all move in the same direction. For the water to flow through the pipe, the pressure at the beginning must be higher than the pressure at the end. This difference can be produced by means of a pump. The electrons in an electrical wire are driven by the potential difference between the two ends. In order to reduce this potential difference, a sort of pump is again needed, which we can call the potential source. The wire is joined at one end to the positive pole (+) of the potential source and at the other to the negative pole (−). The current then passes from the + (high tension) to the − (low tension). The greater the difference between the two poles, the greater the amperage (i.e. the intensity of the current). The unit used to measure potential difference is the 'volt', named after the Italian physicist Alessandro Volta, who lived from 1745 to 1827.

Alessandro Volta invented the electrophorus in 1771, and then, having made a sensitive electrometer, he used it in conjunction with the electrophorus to demonstrate how electricity was produced by contact between metals. He continued his experiments after 1792 and his researches enabled him to make the first electrical classification of metals, resulting finally in the invention of the electrical battery. Batteries are used in many different machines and often have to be extremely small to fit into today's compact radios and calculators.

What is resistance?

When water is pumped through a pipe, it is held back to a greater or lesser degree by the walls of that pipe. The longer the pipe, the greater the loss of power induced by this resistance. It is easy to see that the resistance of a narrow pipe will be greater than that of a broad pipe. The material which the pipe is made of is important also. If it is smooth, it will offer less resistance than if the internal walls are rough or grooved.

In an electrical cable, the free electrons moving along it are held up every time they come into contact with the atoms which the wire is made of. The principle is the same as for the pipe. The longer the cable, the greater is the number of collisions between electrons and atoms, and hence the greater the resistance. Thin wires offer greater resistance than thick wires. Again, the material the wire is made of is important – an iron wire will offer greater resistance than a copper wire of the same thickness and length.

Some materials have a very high resistance, i.e. the current has great difficulty in passing through them. These materials are called insulators, and they include glass, plastic, porcelain and rubber. Another factor influencing resistance is temperature. When the temperature rises, the atoms move rapidly to and fro within the wire. This movement causes more collisions with the free electrons and so restricts their movement. Thus the higher the temperature the greater the resistance. There are some exceptions to this rule which we will not deal with here.

The unit of resistance is the ohm, named after the German physicist Georg Simon Ohm, who lived from 1789 to 1854.

Above: *A fairground car driven by an electric motor. Electric motors have the great advantage of being noiseless and producing no exhaust gases. On the other hand, the batteries needed for such a car to operate independently have to be frequently recharged.*
Below: *A factory producing electric light bulbs.*

How does an incandescent lamp produce light?

An incandescent lamp consists of a glass bulb containing, under a vacuum, a metal wire wound in a double spiral, which is very thin and therefore of very high resistance. When electricity is passed through this filament, the free electrons meet so much resistance that they produce heat. The wire is heated to a very high temperature and starts to burn, giving off light. Filaments can reach temperatures of more than 2000°C, and must therefore be made of a material with a very high melting point. Edison, who invented the incandescent lamp, used carbon filaments. Today they are made of tungsten, a metal which melts at around 3400°C. Tungsten also has the advantage of giving an increased resistance at a very high temperatures.

How does a fuse or circuit-breaker work?

When the current in an electrical circuit becomes too strong, there is a danger that it will cause a fire. A fuse or circuit-breaker is therefore put in as a safety measure. A fuse is made of some insulating material such as porcelain and contains a thin wire which has a very high resistance. Any electrical current coming into the house has to pass through such a device, and if the intensity of the current reaches a certain level the wire melts with the heat produced and cuts off the supply, thus preventing the electrical circuits from overheating. Fuses are classified according to the maximum current they can withstand. Thus there are fuses rated at 2 amps, 13 amps, 15 amps and 30 amps. The

Top left: A cinematic projector could not work without electricity. The light for projection is provided by a special lamp and the film is moved by an electric motor.
Bottom left: An electric tram is driven by two or more very powerful motors. The current required is provided by overhead wires. The speed of the tram depends on the amount of power fed to the motor, which the driver can regulate by means of a variable resistance. The higher the resistance, the lower the current.
Below: A traffic light is also operated by electricity.

Electricity in daily life

Electricity is one of our main sources of energy. It has become an essential part of our daily life, and is used in many different fields. Industry uses enormous quantities of electrical energy for manufacturing all kinds of products. One electrically powered machine can do the work of several men. Without electricity and its special properties, the computer, which is so vital to our society, could not have been invented. If there were no electricity in the home we would have to do without such electrical appliances as the washing machine, the dish-washer and the vacuum cleaner. Without electricity our lamps would not give out light, the radio and television would not work and the telephone would be unusable.

disadvantage of the fuse is that once it has melted either the wire or the whole fuse, according to the type, must be replaced. For this reason devices known as circuit-breakers are now being introduced, which do away with this problem. They have an automatic mechanism which cuts off the current when it becomes too high, but can be reconnected simply by pressing a button. Before replacing a fuse, or pressing the button on a circuit-breaker, the cause of the short-circuit must be traced and remedied, otherwise the fuse will blow, or the circuit-breaker drop out again. Aircraft often have complicated electrical systems which must be protected, and on many modern airliners you can see an impressive array of circuit-breakers.

Sound

Are all living organisms capable of producing and receiving sound? We do not know. Human beings we know for certain, can do both.

What is sound?

According to biologists and doctors, sound is what is perceived by the ear. Physicists are more precise; they explain that our perception of sound is the result of certain vibrations travelling through the air and reaching our eardrums. These vibrations obviously have to start somewhere, and that somewhere is what the physicists call the 'sound source'. A book falling from a table is a source of sound, so is a glass breaking on the floor. Certainly at the moment they fall, we hear a sound. Even water can be a source of sound – one thinks of rain falling against a window-pane or into a puddle. When a sound source is too far away the vibrations do not reach our ears and we hear nothing. In fact the waves produced by sounds or noises can only be transmitted through the air, water or some other specific materials. We can all remember Indians in cowboy films placing their ear to the ground in order to hear the enemy's horses approaching, and how they were able to judge which direction they were coming from with amazing accuracy. The vibration produced by the horses' hooves was transmitted through the earth.
Sound cannot travel through a vacuum, and a simple experiment often carried out in school science lessons proves this. A vacuum pump is connected to a bell jar in which has been placed an electric buzzer. As the vacuum pump removes the air from the jar the sound gets weaker and weaker. If one could create a complete vacuum inside the jar, which is practically impossible, one would hear nothing at all.

How do we perceive sound waves?

The average human being can perceive sound waves ranging from 30 to 30,000 vibrations, or cycles, per second. Our organ of hearing is actually situated in the internal ear. Curious though this may seem, the ear perceives sound less and less acutely from childhood onwards. There is nothing abnormal about this, it is simply part of the ageing process. Sound waves travel through the air at a speed of 340 metres per second; light travels very much faster, at

How an echo is produced. **Imagine it is a calm day, somewhere far from the noise of the town and with very little movement going on around you. You are standing some 150m away from a high wall and you shout a word like 'bang' towards it. You will be surprised to hear the word coming back at you one second after you have shouted it – the sound waves have bounced off the stone wall. But why the second's delay? It is very simple. We know that sound travels through air, at normal temperatures, at a speed of approximately 300m per second. The wall is 150m away from you, so the sound has to travel twice 150m (i.e. 300m) in order to reach your ears again.**

How do musical instruments produce sound?

A musical instrument produces sound waves which travel through the air and make our eardrums vibrate. The main types of musical instrument are wind instruments, stringed instruments and percussion instruments. The 'string' family includes the violin, the cello, the guitar and the mandolin.
Wind instruments are made of brass or wood. They are instruments in which sound waves are produced by blowing into a mouthpiece.
In percussion instruments, the vibration of the air is produced by striking, by hand or with sticks, a skin stretched over a wooden or metal cylinder which acts as a resonator.

300,000 km per second. This can easily be demonstrated if we watch, for example, a woodcutter felling a tree in the distance. First we see the axe strike the trunk, and it is only some moments later that we actually hear the sound of it hitting the wood.
But let us return to the organ of hearing and its relationship with the brain. Sounds are led towards the auditory canal by the external ear, which is shaped rather like a funnel, enabling it to capture the vibrations of the air more efficiently. The sound waves then strike the eardrum, which is a sensitive piece of skin or membrane. This starts to vibrate in sympathy, setting off a complex series of nervous impulses which result in the impression of hearing in a particular part of the brain. If this part of the brain is damaged for one reason or another, the person may be deaf.

What are ultra-sounds?

As we said earlier, the human ear can perceive sound waves from 30 to 30,000 vibrations per second. In recent years; scientists have tried to discover if some living beings are able to hear sounds higher than this, and they have come to the conclusion that a number of animals including walruses, dogs and bats can hear what are called ultra-sounds. These are pitched so highly that we are unable to pick them up. Since bats cannot see very well, they give out high squeaks, which will then reverberate from any solid object, so that the bat can tell where it is going.
We know that the speed of sound is 340 metres per second. This is a speed which no animal or bird could ever reach, but rockets and jet aircraft which can go faster than this have been known for a long time. 340 metres per second is the same as just 1,000 km per hour. When an aircraft reaches this speed we often hear a loud noise – the supersonic 'bang' which rattles our windows. When this happens the aircraft is said to have passed through the sound barrier.

How are sounds recorded?

In bygone days, songs, like stories, were transmitted by word of mouth. Much later a system of signs was devised which enabled music to be written down on paper and read by the musician. But the greatest revolution of all came when Thomas Edison invented the gramophone. This machine works on the following principle. The performer speaks, sings or plays an instrument in front of what we could call a 'sound funnel'. Originally this was the horn of the gramophone; now it is a microphone. A fine needle travelling over a disc or cylinder receives the vibrations caused by the sounds and engraves them in a series of small grooves. The grooves form a spiral running towards the centre of the disc, or from one end of the cylinder to the other. Once the disc, or record, has been cut, a hard matrix is made from it and this allows a series of reproductions of the record to be produced. If we then replace the gramophone needle on the disc and set it turning, it will vibrate in the same pattern as it did during the original recording. This time, however, the vibrations are fed to a loudspeaker, and the words, the music or the song which were recorded can be heard once again. A more recent discovery is the tape recorder. This device does not use a disc or a cylinder, but a tape which is covered with small metallic particles. sound is recorded on to the tape, these metallic particles are magnetized by an electronic process in a particular pattern. When the tape is passed through the machine again, it is 'read' by the recorder and the sounds are reproduced in the same pattern as that in which they were recorded.

Light and magnetic waves

Since prehistoric times, man has regarded light with reverence. Light was the Sun god, the lightning which accompanied thunder, the fire which destroyed everything in its path, and later the wood fire in his hearth.

Above: **Isaac Newton (1642–1725) is one of the most famous physicians, astronomers and mathematicians in the history of science. One of his most important discoveries was the splitting of the solar spectrum (white light) into rays of different colours. To do this he used a prism *(see below)*, through which he shone a beam of light. To his great surprise a very clear image of a rainbow appeared on the other side of the prism, made up of red, yellow, orange, green, blue, indigo and violet. Newton made numerous studies with lenses and telescopes. He was also deeply preoccupied with the phenomenon of weight.**

What is light?

Light is something which we perceive with our eyes. Scientists tell us that it is made up of electro-magnetic rays, and we will say more about this later. Biologists explain that 'everything which is registered by the eyes is light'. In the chapter on sound we learned that man possesses an auditory world and a visual world. A blind man does not have the latter, but with the help of various devices or pieces of optical apparatus, he can now lead a more or less normal existence.

What is a source of light?

The sun is the chief natural source of light. When it disappears, darkness falls.
After a great deal of painstaking investigation, scientists discovered that the earth itself does not emit light, nor does the moon. They also demonstrated that in our solar system the planets, like the earth and its satellite the moon, revolve around the sun in a perfectly regular orbit.

Isaac Newton performed a number of brilliant and amazingly simple experiments which enabled him to define the composition of solar light. What we call 'white light' is in fact made up of a wide range of different colours. By using a piece of glass called a prism, Newton was able to split light up into its different components and in this way discovered the 'solar spectrum', which consists of seven colours: red, orange, yellow, green, blue, indigo (a very dark blue) and violet. In fact we don't need a prism to see all these colours, we have only to look at a rainbow.

How can light really be defined?

This is an extremely controversial question which scientists have not yet been able to answer. However, we can carry out an experiment similar to the one which we did with sound waves. If we empty a bell jar of the air which it contains and pass a beam of light through it, we will find that, unlike the sound waves, the light waves pass through the vacuum without being diverted. Thus

Top left: A pair of binoculars. More precisely, they should be called 'prismatic binoculars', since they contain small prisms. They allow us to see distant objects with both eyes, unlike the traditional telescope, which can only be applied to one eye.
Bottom left: A microscope, of the kind often found in schools. With a microscope, we can study minute organic particles such as those found in water.
Right: Cross-section of a camera with its numerous lenses, showing how light is deflected by a mirror into the viewfinder.

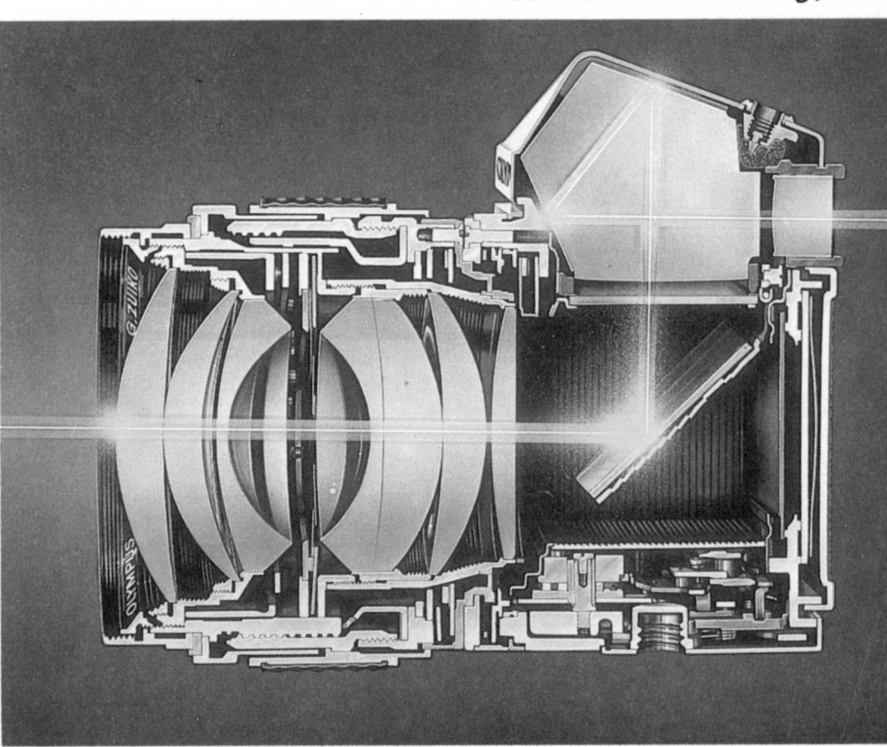

Below: Antoine van Leeuwenhoek was born in the Netherlands and died there in 1723. Far from being a scholar, Van Leeuwenhoek was an ordinary citizen who had never set foot in a university. From 1660 he was a porter at Delft town hall. It was Van Leeuwenhoek who made the first microscope, a simple device which had little in common with the sophisticated pieces of apparatus we know today. He made numerous discoveries with his primitive invention, and princes and scholars flocked to see this humble porter, whose achievements are now scarcely remembered.

we know that they can cross a vacuum. They can also pass through glass, but are wholly or partially absorbed by fog, clouds, mist, heavy rain or a great deal of snow. Solid objects such as walls or trees will not let a single light ray through. Nor can light rays turn the corner of a street. A beam of light always travels in a straight line, unless it is diverted by being reflected in a mirror.

Trees have leaves which look green because they absorb all the coloured light waves except green; a post box looks red because it absorbs all the coloured light waves except red.

Can some beings perceive ultraviolet light?

This question is important since ultraviolet rays can in some cases be harmful to human beings. However, we cannot see them with the naked eye, whereas it has been proved that bees, for example, are perfectly able to perceive them. For bees, ultraviolet rays are a kind of light. This can easily be proved by shutting the bees up in a box whose only opening is a small hole. If a red light is placed in front of the hole, nothing happens, but if a source of ultraviolet light is shone at it the bees start to move towards the hole. It would appear that red is not a visible form of light for bees, whereas ultraviolet is, since they are attracted to it. Ultraviolet rays are carried in sunlight and feed the skin with the vitamin D which they contain. Vitamin D prevents a terrible disease called rickets.

Infra-red rays cannot be perceived either by the human eye. They are so called because of their wavelength, which is greater than that of light. They are used in medicine for therapeutic purposes, because they are able to penetrate the tissues of the body. Infra-red, ultraviolet and X-rays all belong to the great family of electro-magnetic radiations. Radio waves also belong in this class; they can travel anywhere, including through a vacuum and interstellar space, at the same speed as light – 300,000 km a second.

Ultraviolet rays, which are found in minute quantities in sunlight, are harmful to the eyes, and can also be dangerous for the skin if it is exposed to them for too long. When sunbathing, it is advisable to take precautions to filter out the ultraviolet rays. Many commercial sunbathing creams have screens that will do this, but not all – so it is wise to check.

What is magnetism used for?

The phenomenon of magnetism was first put to use by man when the Chinese invented the magnetic compass. The Earth is surrounded by a magnetic field which has a north and a south pole. These magnetic poles are very close to the true geographical poles, and the needle of a compass will point towards the magnetic pole. The difference between magnetic north or south and 'true' north or south is called variation.
A piece of metal can have magnetism induced in it so that it too has a north and a south pole. The north pole of a magent will attract the south pole of another magnet, so that they stick together. This is called magnetic attraction.
If a piece of soft iron is wound round with wire and an electric current is passed through the wire the metal becomes a magnet for as long as the current flows. This is called an electro-magnet, and is very useful as it can be used to operate switches and machinery. Very large electro-magnets can be used to pick up heavy metal objects, swing them round, and put them down again.

What types of light sources do we know?

We have already said that our chief light source is the Sun. But this only gives light during part of the day. Man has sought artificial light sources since early times, and as a result of the amazing growth of technology in recent years, the number of known light sources has increased considerably.
The simplest example is a burning match. Here light is produced by a chemical process. Friction causes a spark, which ignites an inflammable material. Early fire users would try to keep the flame alight permanently because ignition was difficult. The fire could be used not only for light, but also for heat and for frightening away dangerous animals.
Our early ancestors used torches which had to be sprinkled at intervals with resin or oil to keep them alight. These torches had to be treated with great care, because they were used not only for lighting but also for heating and various other purposes. Much later, people had the idea of filling small earthenware containers with animal oil and floating a wick in it which could be set alight.
In some countries a particular type of oil was found – petroleum. This was a thick liquid which was found to give a much brighter light in the lamps of the time. Gradually, more and more elaborate lamps were devised, with adjustable wicks and shades which spread and softened the light by a process known as diffusion.
But while most houses were still using oil lamps of one kind or another, the most privileged households were already using gas for lighting.
In even richer establishments, people went on using candles, such as we still use today on festive occasions such as Christmas.

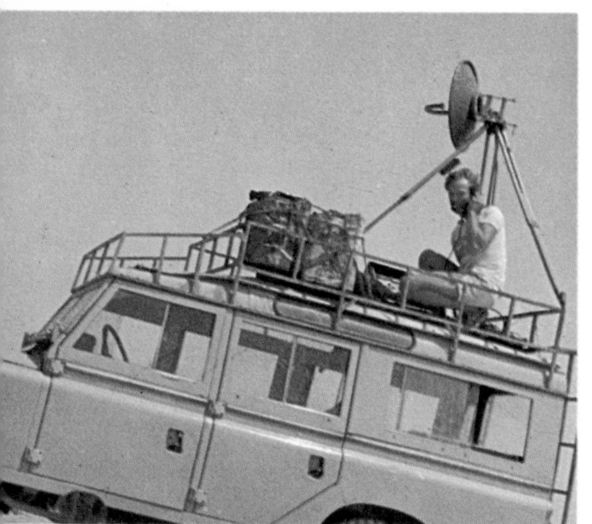

The coming of electric light

Another spectacular development in the field of lighting was Thomas Edison's invention of the electric lamp. An electric bulb is certainly more aesthetic and practical than any of the systems described so far. However, the change from gas lighting, which had meanwhile been universally adopted, to electric lighting, did not happen all at once. Today the production of electricity still depends on generators which often run on steam produced by burning coal or some other fuel. Unfortunately, sources of energy are now becoming increasingly rare. One wonders where all the fuel is going to come from which is needed to light the towns which are springing up like mushrooms, the hospitals, flats and private houses which are growing in number day by day.
Some years ago, it was thought that natural gas would provide an inexhaustible source

Left: **A mobile unit for testing radio-telephone communications in Morocco. The system uses small transmitters which need little power and can function without large aerials. Such a system obviously has enormous advantages in remote terrain or in areas occupied by enemy troops. Unfortunately, it appears that the system is easily affected by atmospheric conditions.**

Right: This photograph shows part of the radar installation used for controlling air traffic at a big airport. The word radar is an abbreviation of the words 'Radio Detection and Ranging', which means finding out the direction and distance of a solid object. The object may be an aircraft, a boat, a missile, etc. The Allied forces were already using radar at the beginning of the Second World War, which gave them a considerable advantage and increased their chances of victory. The principle of radar is simple – the apparatus emits very short radio waves, which return to their point of departure as soon as they meet a solid object. It is, in fact, the principle of the echo. The wave transmitter is always raised above ground level. Radar is now used in most ships, enabling them to find their way even in thick fog. We often see on ships a strange-looking object which turns continually. This is the radar transmitter-receiver. In the control room a beam of light on a screen shows the waves being emitted into space, and a small point of lights appears when they meet some solid body.

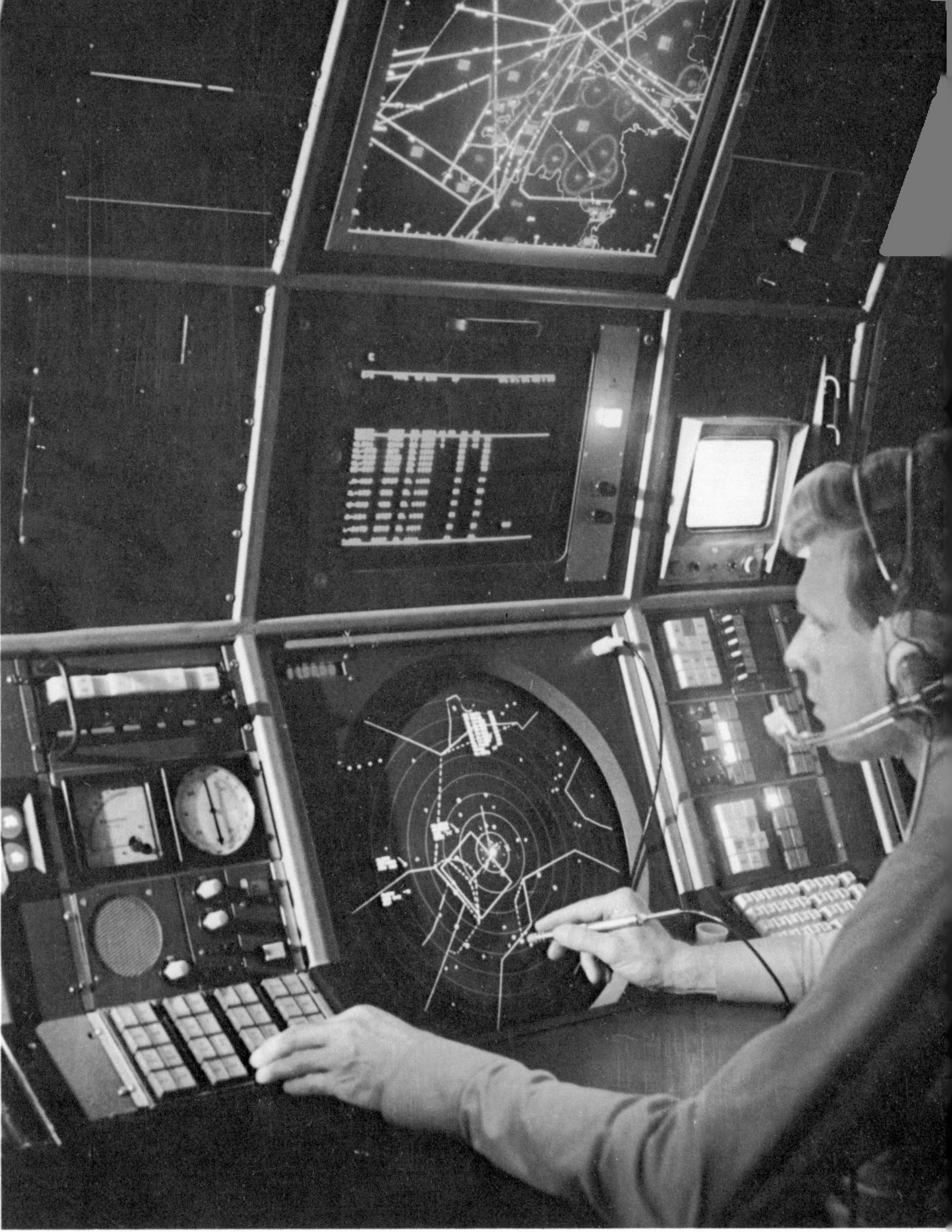

of energy to replace coal, which was becoming difficult to extract, but this no longer appears to be true.

Energy is an abstract word, but to understand something of what it means, let us try to imagine the enormous quantities of electricity which a hospital needs for lighting all the corridors, the wards and operating theatres, as well as for the innumerable machines and services which it uses. What is the answer? The possibilities of solar energy are now being investigated, and this is indeed a limitless supply, but it is even more difficult to exploit than other forms. Using the energy of the wind and the tides is another possibility.

Nuclear energy is still a possibility, and this is a thorny subject, for many people really do not know what they are talking about and are therefore afraid of it. Nevertheless its widespread use seems almost inevitable if no other way of providing electricity is found and the intricate machinery of our modern world is to be kept in motion.

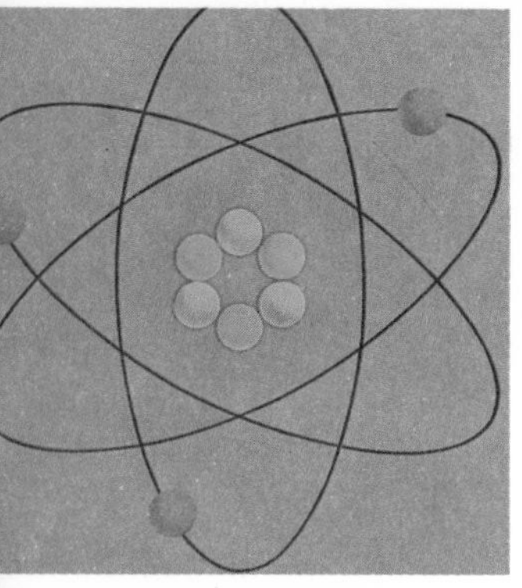

Above: A schematic representation of an atom – the smallest part of a chemical element. The word atom means 'that which cannot be divided', but after it was given this name, it was discovered that atoms themselves were made up of electrons, neutrons and protons. The last two combine to form the positive nucleus, around which revolve the negatively charged electrons.

Chemistry

In the Middle Ages, men studied alchemy. Despite the pejorative sense which has recently been given to the word, it was from alchemy that modern chemistry developed, becoming a recognized science on which much of our daily life is based.

What is studied in chemistry?

Chemistry is the study of the composition of all the materials which are found on the earth. It explains which elements go to make them up, how they are related to one another, and how their composition and properties can be changed to turn them into materials for use by industry or commercial products.

Theoretical chemists seldom concern themselves what practical use their discoveries could have, but they seldom object if other people make use of them.

What are molecules?

One of the most important discoveries made in chemistry was that all matter is made up of minute particles – originally they were thought to be the smallest – which are called molecules. Now we can define molecules as the smallest particle of any substance that retains the properties of that substance.

If one takes a jar of kitchen salt, for example, we know that it contains an infinite number of molecules of salt which are all the same size and have the same properties.

When no other molecules are mixed with them, we can talk of 'pure salt'. Over the course of time, however, it was discovered that it is impossible to obtain a substance which is totally pure.

In a number of special cases, impurities play a vital part in creating the properties for which a substance is valued. It was chiefly in analyzing chemical fertilizers that it was discovered to what extent small impurities could be important.

Once molecules were known to exist, people wondered whether chemical substances might not contain even smaller

Below: The Russian chemist Dmitri Mendeleyev. He was born in 1834, and died in 1907. His most important discovery was that of the 'periodic system' of the chemical elements, which gave rise to the so-called periodic table which is named after him. Mendeleyev's system enabled him to predict the existence of other elements before they were actually discovered.

List of the elements classified in increasing order of atomic weight

1	Hydrogen	H	29	Copper	Cu	57	Lanthanum	La	85	Astatine	At
2	Helium	He	30	Zinc	Zn	58	Cerium	Ce	86	Radon	Rn
3	Lithium	Li	31	Gallium	Ga	59	Praseodymium	Pr	87	Francium	Fr
4	Beryllium	Be	32	Germanium	Ge	60	Neodymium	Nd	88	Radium	Ra
5	Boron	B	33	Arsenic	As	61	Promethium	Pm	89	Actinium	Ac
6	Carbon	C	34	Selenium	Se	62	Samarium	Sm	90	Thorium	Th
7	Nitrogen	N	35	Bromine	Br	63	Europium	Eu	91	Protactinium	Pa
8	Oxygen	O	36	Krypton	Kr	64	Gadolinium	Gd	92	Uranium	U
9	Fluorine	F	37	Rubidium	Rb	65	Terbium	Tb	93	Neptunium	Np
10	Neon	Ne	38	Strontium	Sr	66	Dysprosium	Dy	94	Plutonium	Pu
11	Sodium	Na	39	Yttrium	Y	67	Holmium	Ho	95	Americium	Am
12	Magnesium	Mg	40	Zirconium	Zr	68	Erbium	Er	96	Curium	Cm
13	Aluminium	Al	41	Niobium	Nb	69	Thulium	Tm	97	Berkelium	Bk
14	Silicon	Si	42	Molybdenum	Mo	70	Ytterbium	Yb	98	Californium	Cf
15	Phosphorus	P	43	Technetium	Tc	71	Lutetium	Lu	99	Einsteinium	Es
16	Sulphur	S	44	Ruthenium	Ru	72	Hafnium	Hf	100	Fermium	Fm
17	Chlorine	C1	45	Rhodium	Rh	73	Tantalum	Ta	101	Mendelevium	Md
18	Argon	Ar	46	Palladium	Pd	74	Tungsten	W	102	Nobelium	No
19	Potassium	K	47	Silver	Ag	75	Rhenium	Re	103	Lawrencium	Lw
20	Calcium	Ca	48	Cadmium	Cd	76	Osmium	Os			
21	Scandium	Sc	49	Indium	In	77	Iridium	Ir			
22	Titanium	Ti	50	Tin	Sn	78	Platinum	Pt			
23	Vanadium	V	51	Antimony	Sb	79	Gold	Au			
24	Chromium	Cr	52	Tellurium	Te	80	Mercury	Hg			
25	Manganese	Mn	53	Iodine	I	81	Thallium	Tl			
26	Iron	Fe	54	Xenon	X	82	Lead	Pb			
27	Cobalt	Co	55	Caesium	Cs	83	Bismuth	Bi			
28	Nickel	Ni	56	Barium	Ba	84	Polonium	Po			

Above: Albert Einstein, born in 1897 in Ulm, Germany, went to the United States in 1934, and died there in 1955. He received the title of doctor in 1905. He is generally considered one of the most brilliant minds the world has ever known in the field of theoretical physics. He is most famous for his theory of relativity, which is still only really understood by a very small number of experts. The fact that he was Jewish prevented him from pursuing his researches in Berlin. In 1921 he was awarded the Nobel Prize for Physics.

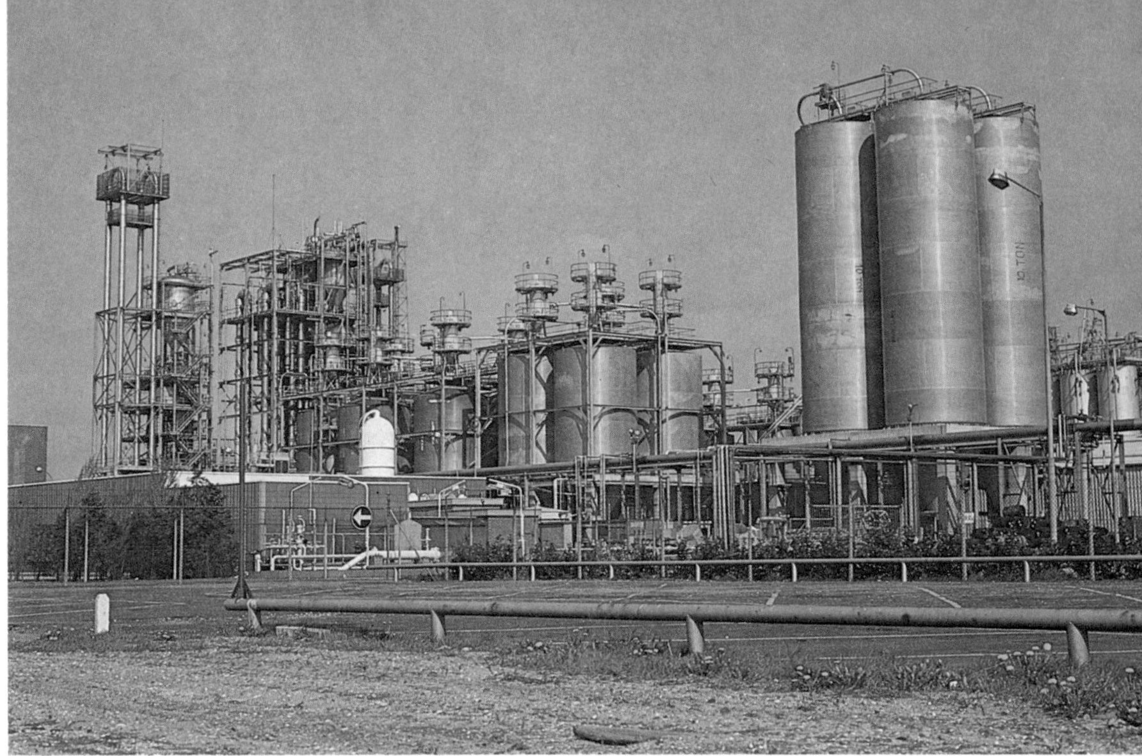

particles which made up the atoms. And this was how the theory of the atom was born.

What is the theory of the atom?

According to atomic theory, each molecule is divided into even smaller particles called atoms. (The word 'atom' comes from the Greek and means 'indivisible'.) Thus a molecule of salt contains two atoms, and a molecule of limestone contains five atoms. We shall see later that there are several kinds of atom, and that they in turn are subdivided. The subject raises a whole series of questions. How many kinds of atom are there in the universe? How are they linked together? How can they be separated? And the most important question of all – can the atom be split? We have already said that the atom

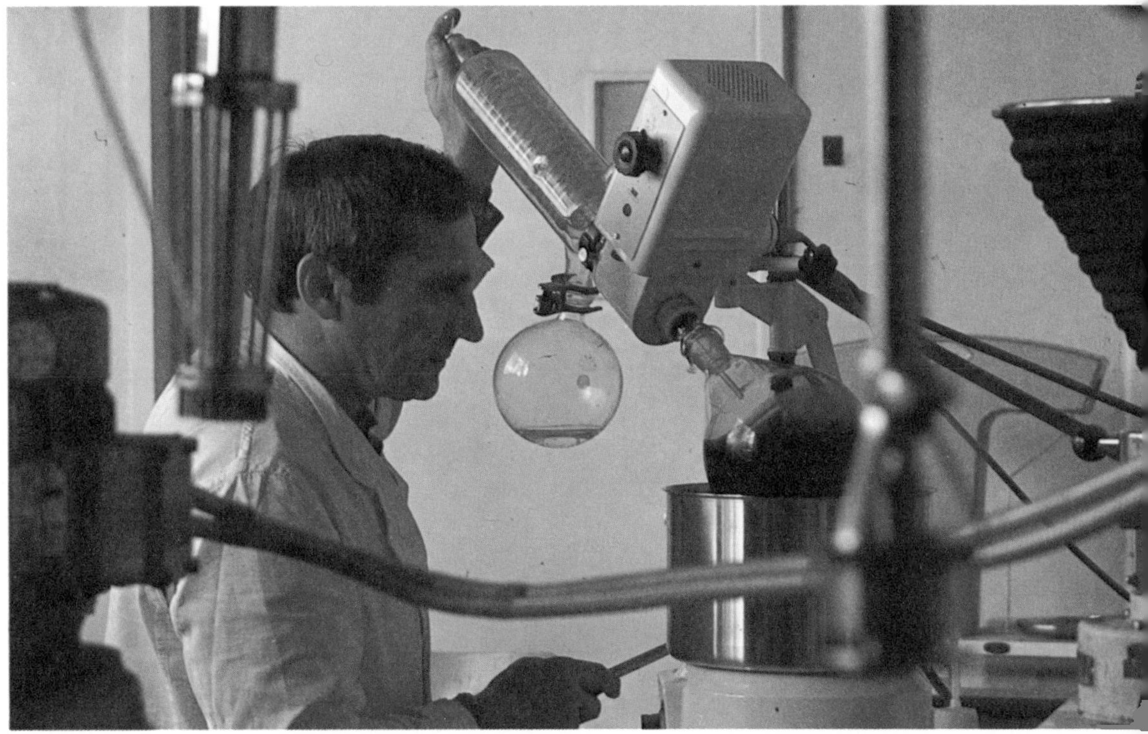

Right: Chemistry enables man to produce synthetic substances with the properties of real ones, such as rubber. Natural rubber comes from the resin of the rubber tree, which is a native of South America. In the colonial period, rubber trees were imported into the Dutch East Indies and Indonesia. Latex, which is the name for raw rubber, has a milky consistency, but can be hardened and made more consistent by a chemical process which involves heating it with sulphur. During the Second World War the fighting countries suffered an acute shortage of rubber, and after extensive research, chemists succeeded in producing artificial rubber.

can be sub-divided: once scientists discovered it was possible in theory their research had to continue. A tremendous amount of energy is needed to split an atom, and whether this energy is to be used creatively or destructively is a very important decision.

All we shall say here is that there are about a hundred kinds of atom, which form the basic elements. Some we meet every day, like those which make up water (H_2O); others are much rarer, such as gold. Others are dangerous or poisonous, such as mercury, and others again are radioactive – a problem which many people are concerned about today.

Some of these elements are found in the pure state, such as mercury, gold, silver and other metals, and also sulphur, which is not a metal. Most are found in nature linked to other elements, and this is where molecules come in. A molecule of pure salt contains only two atoms, as we have said, but most salt molecules are much more complex. There is one chemical law which never alters, however – all the molecules in a particular substance contain the same number of atoms. Thus a molecule of limestone will always consist of one calcium atom, one carbon atom and three oxygen atoms. This is not the place to explain how all these atoms are linked together. Their relationships are usually expressed by complicated formulas which serve as a reminder of their composition.

As any chemist will tell you, there are stable relationships between atoms, and unstable ones. Various chemical processes are used to make these links and to undo them. For example, strong acids acting on some substances can dissolve certain unstable links to form others. Sulphuric, hydrochloric and nitric acids are used in this way.

The atomic theory also explains some of the properties of solids, liquids and gases. In a solid each molecule has a fixed position – it cannot change its place, only vibrate slightly. In liquids the molecules can move around, so the liquid can change its shape. In gases the molecules are much further apart: most gases will fill whatever container they are put in.

The alchemists were really the forerunners of modern chemists. However strange some of their practices may seem today, their discoveries have still found an application in present-day chemistry.

Are atoms really the smallest particles?

As we have said, the word 'atom' in Greek means 'indivisible'.

However everyone knows today that this

Above: **Pierre Curie (1859–1906) married a Polish physicist, Marya Sklodowska (1867–1934) in France in 1895. The two of them carried out research of fundamental importance into radioactivity, often with extremely primitive methods. Gradually the value of the two scientists' work was recognized in France and their discoveries eventually aroused interest in other countries as well. Pierre and Marie Curie, and their colleague Antoine Becquerel, eventually received the Nobel Prize.**

Left: **Paper-making first began in China at the beginning of the modern era. Wood and other vegetable fibres were used as a raw material. The very first Chinese paper was made of silk, then hemp and the bark of the mulberry tree were used. Today, most paper is produced by the chemical treatment of wood pulp. It is to be feared that as more and more newspapers and books are produced, the demand for wood pulp will be such that trees will be felled faster than new trees can be grown.**

Right: **During and after the Second World War, numerous studies were carried out on the composition of macromolecules such as polyester. This substance can be used to make threads, fibres, discs and even films. Many clothes contain a large proportion of such synthetic fibres, which have some advantages over woollen and cotton fibres. In the photograph, a synthetic substance in the form of granules is being poured into an extruding machine. These granules will undergo a whole series of changes before appearing as the finished product.**

term is not at all appropriate, and the atom itself is made up of minute particles. It is very difficult to imagine this miniscule world and its components, but it is generally thought of as a miniature solar system, with minute 'planets' orbiting round a 'sun' which is slightly larger but still invisible to the human eye. This 'sun' is the nucleus which forms the centre of the atom. It is made up of one or more protons and several or no neutrons. Protons have a positive charge, whereas neutrons have none. Together they are called *nucleons*. A number of negatively charged particles, governed by the number of protons, revolve round the nucleus – these are the electrons.

Atoms can be combined in various different ways, and they can also be split, as is now well known.

On close observation, scientists found that particular types of atom emitted rays and particles at very high speed. Later it was found that working with these substances was highly dangerous, but it was vital to continue research on them as they promised to have important applications for medical science.

What is the difference between organic and inorganic chemistry?

Many writers make a distinction between organic and inorganic chemistry. This difference was originally explained as follows. Organic links between atoms are those in which carbon is involved, whereas inorganic links are those in which, with few exceptions, the carbon atom is not present. This difference arose from the fact that there seemed to be a difference between the molecules which make up living beings and the rest, such as water, gas, air, stone, earth etc. This distinction has become much more problematical since the creation of synthetic substances, which can themselves be considered a grouping of elements making up a living organism. Today there are thousands of organic substances to which the original difference between living and dead matter does not apply. An obvious example of such substances are the plastics, which rapidly became extremely popular, until, quite recently, people began to notice their many disadvantages. Some people even claim that the world will one day be buried under plastic waste, and they are not necessarily joking. Research must be done to teach how to break down substances as well as build them.

Photography

Newspapers, magazines and books would be very boring if they did not contain photographs. Often, such publications are bought for their photographs alone, for they form an image of our own times.

How did photography develop?

When Francis Daguerre discovered in 1839 that an image could be produced on a sensitive substance by shining a light on to it, the principle of photography became an established fact. Later the process was modified and perfected, but what happens inside today's expensive cameras is exactly the same as in the first ever produced. Today, of course, sharper lenses are used to obtain a better picture; films are of better quality and easier to handle; but the system remains the same – a sensitive substance is exposed to light to produce an image. Fragile glass plates have been replaced by unbreakable rolls of film, but these have the same sensitive coating as before. Whereas before the lens aperture had to be opened and closed by hand, this is now done by a sophisticated shutter system, and recent developments in electronics mean that this can also be done automatically. We are capable now of taking photographs in poor light and in the dark – by means of flash light. Specialist photography can also be done in the dark without flash.

Today, colour photography is within everyone's reach, and threatens to replace black and white altogether. Photography has many different and valuable uses in society.

Why are there so many different kinds of camera, and which are the best?

This is a question which people ask every day. In fact the wide variety of cameras is the result of the different preferences and requirements of their users. Technical improvements have made cameras more versatile, but they are also more complicated to use. The second part of the question is more difficult to answer. Everything depends on the person who is using the camera and what he wants to use it for. A camera which would be ideal for a professional photographer might be too complicated (and too expensive) for an amateur. A scientist would need very clear pictures in order to be able to examine the subject closely. Someone who wants to photograph landscapes, on the other hand, is not chiefly interested in precision. What he needs is a camera which is solidly built but light and easy to carry.

The size of the negative is also very important. A beginner will be most at home with a small, 35mm negative. This is ideal for black and white photography, and can also be used for colour. The photographer must also decide whether he wants prints of his work or transparencies. There are as many kinds of film as there are cameras, so many factors have to be taken into account.

Below: **A high-quality modern Japanese camera – a single lens reflex Mamiya. The image which enters the lens is conveyed to the viewfinder by a system of prisms. The advantage of this arrangement is that what one sees in the viewfinder is exactly what will appear in the photograph. The rings on the front of the lens are for altering the focus and the length of exposure. On top of the camera is a socket for a flash unit, used for taking photographs in darkness. The negative is larger than that used in small 35mm cameras, and is thus more suitable for enlargements.**

The composition of a film

A modern film is made up of several layers which are invisible to the naked eye.

1. **The emulsion, which contains the sensitive substance.**
2. **The backing, which merely supports the other layers.**
3. **The anti-halation layer, which ensures that the images are clear and precise.**

What are the uses of photography?

The main aim of photography is to transmit information about another place as quickly and accurately as possible. It can often be more powerful than words, for people react more quickly to visual stimuli. A photograph says more than any caption can, and people are more inclined to look at a picture than read a text. Photographs are international and do not need to be translated. Even the illiterate can look at a picture and understand it.

But photography has other uses besides the transmission of news. There is medical photography, for example, of which radiography (X-ray photography) is a special branch. Photography is also used in practically every different field of scientific research. Thus the journeys to the Moon would have been unthinkable without the invention of photography which gave us advance information about the surface of the Moon. Objects can be photographed with many different kinds of light—infra-red, ultraviolet and gamma rays. Astronomers have even photographed constellations which cannot be seen with the naked eye. There are thousands of satellites orbiting the earth which are continually taking photographs of our planet. Mostly they photograph clouds to provide information about the weather over a particular area.

Another important function of photography is preserving information of all different kinds. For example, famous works of art such as books, paintings or buildings are photographed so that they may be seen and appreciated by a large number of people who would otherwise be unable to study them. Photography can be an agreeable pastime, a hobby which offers an infinite variety of pleasures to the amateur, and in recent years photography has been regarded as an art form in its own right.

How did photography become popular?

Most of us have watched a pavement artist making a lightning portrait of some passer-by, and thought admiringly, 'If only I could do the same!' And we might think that photography enables us to do just that, for with a camera we can record holiday scenes or beautiful landscapes and carry their image home with us to be looked at at our leisure. On closer inspection, of course, such images are bound to be a disappointment. We realize that the photo does not convey what we expected. However accurately the scene is reproduced, it is not the same as the one we remember.

The same is true of photographic portraits. Even if they are very faithful, they do not really 'speak' to us. Nevertheless, we continue taking photographs, partly because it is so easy. We need only press a button and then give the film to a photographic studio to be developed. Even if the result is no work of art, it serves as a reminder of the scene which we have recorded. On looking at it we may remember the pleasure it gave us, and this is where the magical charm of photography lies.

The other attraction of photography for the amateur can be developing and printing his own photographs. Although this can be time-consuming, and sometimes difficult, it is a rewarding hobby.

How is a photograph produced?

Top: **Taking the picture. The intensity of the light must be measured exactly so that the correct aperture and length of exposure can be calculated. The composition of the shot is also important, and the photographer must be careful not to shoot into the sun.**

Centre: **After the film has been exposed, it is sent to the laboratory, where it is developed and enlarged automatically. Laboratory machines can develop large numbers of pictures at a time, and so costs are low. Nevertheless, some enthusiasts prefer to develop their own films.**

Bottom: **The crucial test – the pictures of our trip have arrived and can be shown to our friends. They bring back pleasant memories and remind us of amusing incidents which took place. The charm of photography lies in the fact that it enables us to relive the agreeable moments of our lives.**

The new technologies

Science and technology never stop. They are always seeking new methods and new materials which will help man to achieve greater knowledge and control over the universe, and over the survival and health of living things within it.

What are the most recent technological inventions?

There will be new inventions as long as the human brain continues to function. We seldom realize the importance of inventions at first. It is only later that they are found to have a practical application. In the case of radio, for example, a great deal of progress has been made since Marconi produced the first faint radio waves. His basic invention has been refined and improved to an extent that Marconi himself would not have imagined. Today, radio is still being developed and has many possible applications which are still to be exploited. Perhaps we shall never know the names of the scientists who today are busy perfecting existing inventions and making it possible for entirely new ones to be produced. These are the men who invented the maser, the laser and the computer – devices which have enabled science to make giant strides. The field of space technology – rockets, satellites and similar devices – has produced one invention after another in the past few years.

In present-day society there is an increasing tendency towards automation. This means that more and more machines are being built which can work effectively on their own. Automation is the result of man's wish to escape from the monotony of some kinds of work. Monotony can cause psychological problems, resulting in mistakes and inaccuracies, and present-day society cannot afford mistakes. The quality of a product must be first rate. An automatic machine can often work faster and more accurately than a man. It does not get tired and it costs less. In fact automation often seems the ideal solution, but it has many disadvantages. First of all, the machine is tending to replace man, who invented it. Opportunities for employment are becoming fewer, and the people who do work are no longer as skilled as they used to be. Today, much skilled work is undertaken by machines. For many people work is no longer the pleasure it used to be and some fear that man is losing his natural creativity. But invention will continue, even if only to solve problems created by the last invention. If automation gives people more leisure time researches will come up with new ways of filling that time.

A computer in a factory. Many offices and factories now possess a computer which can do the work of several people. The computer is given the monotonous and laborious task of recording and preserving data, thereby saving a great deal of space and time. A computer doesn't forget and it doesn't make mistakes. It can also be used for controlling the production and quality of manufactured products.

Right: A modern machine for medical diagnosis. A whole series of different rays is now available to medical science, and methods of investigating illnesses have been radically changed and improved as a result. Thus X rays can penetrate the human body and provide information on the state of its organs. They must not be used in too large quantities, however, since they can damage the bodily tissues.

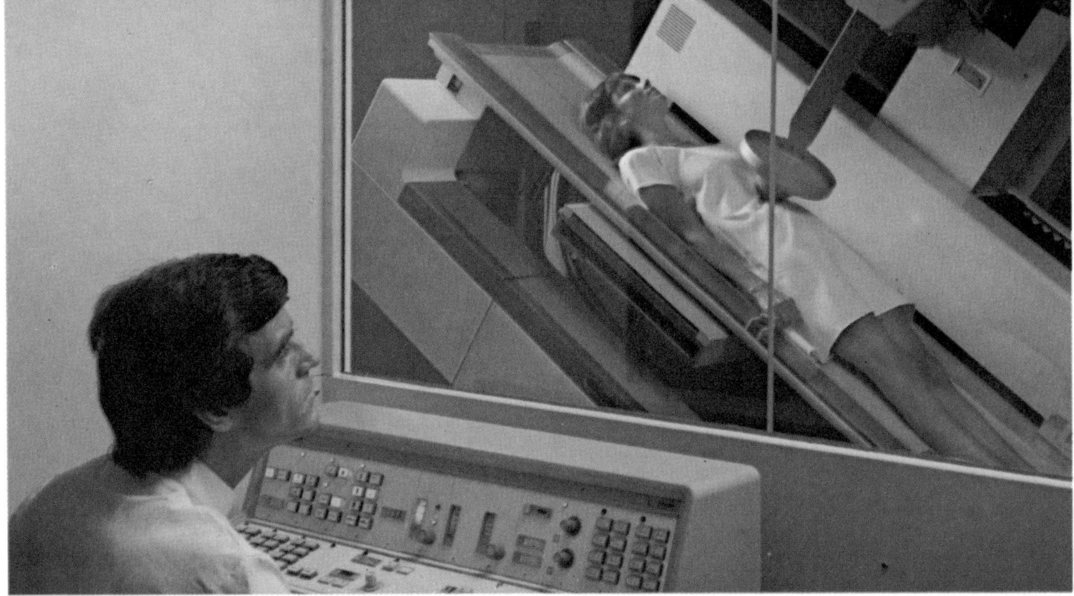

What are the chief areas in which progress is being made?

Science is no longer a single field divided into several branches. Advances made in one field are immediately applied in another, so that everyone benefits from everyone else's research. Electronics has gained much from the research carried out during the last war which resulted in the invention of radar. Originally designed as a means of detecting an enemy at a distance, radar makes use of electro-magnetic waves, which have many more applications than the simple transmission of music. Scientists researching in this field have invented the maser and the laser beam, and it is here that the greatest advances have been made. Laser beams are used in space navigation, where they serve to maintain communications and measure distances. They are also used in medicine, where they enable doctors to detect and operate on particular types of illness. X-rays are another type of wave which are used in medicine, enabling doctors to see into a person's body in order to detect ailments such as cancer. Patients are also exposed to radioactive rays as a means of combating cancer.

Another great scientific advance of recent years is the use of the catheter. A catheter is a very fine tube which can be inserted into a blood vessel in order to check its functioning. With the help of a catheter, doctors can even produce televised pictures of a patient's heart. Medical scientists will always be called upon to find new ways of treating human ailments. Although they have had great success in controlling and curing many of the old killer diseases such as smallpox and tuberculosis, there are still many diseases which debilitate and kill – such as cancer and heart illnesses. Research too, it is hoped, will eventually tell us why some children are born with physical and mental handicaps, and knowing why these things happen is the first step in preventing them.

Another important field is that of energy research. Since it seems highly likely that our present energy sources will eventually disappear, man must look for new ones. One possible source is the sun, whose rays can be used to generate electricity. Research is going on in many other fields too. Experiments are currently being carried out using the earth's heat and nuclear fission or fusion.

What is a laser beam?

In 1961 it was discovered that when certain substances were exposed to light at a particular frequency they would emit a beam of light at the same frequency, but with far greater power than could be obtained by any other method. When the materials used are glass or crystal, this light is known as laser light. As it is only of a single wavelength, laser light can be transmitted over long distances in a highly concentrated beam which has a great deal of energy. Laser beams are used for boring narrow holes in diamonds or for cutting other very hard materials, also for operating on the retina of the human eye and for making exact measurements over long distances. They can be very dangerous if they enter into contact with the human body. Laser beams have an important application in the field of telecommunications. Since they can be directed very accurately, transmission and reception are far more clear and precise than with other forms of wave.

What is holography?

Holography has been known since 1948. It is a kind of photography which creates a three-dimensional image – the hologram. Holograms have been used in scientific experiments since 1968. We all know that a certain amount of light is needed in order to produce an image on a photographic plate. As laser beams are very powerful they can be used to produce photographs with very short exposures. This means that it is possible, for example, to photograph the very short vibrations of a metal plate. If the ordinary light reflected by an object is mixed with a laser beam, an image can be produced on a photographic plate which when it is illuminated again by a laser beam after exposure will make the object appear in three dimensions. The possibilities of this new process have yet to be fully exploited, since laboratory research is very expensive. Holography is still too complicated to be used regularly on a commercial scale.

What experiments are being done at present?

Technological progress has uncovered new scientific fields whose existence was not even suspected a few years ago. It has also enabled research in existing fields to be taken further. The microscope has been greatly improved, enabling scientists to examine the minutest particles. We are all familiar with terms such as the cell, the atom, electrons and neutrons. But we have not only penetrated the microscopic world – the cosmos too has become more accessible. Today we have radio telescopes which can reach far into space and show us phenomena whose existence we would never otherwise have dreamed of.

Every day, scientific research provides us with so much data and so many figures that we need computers in order to classify and store them so that they will be available when we need them. There is so much information that it is impossible for us to know it all. Experiments are being carried out that will affect practically every sphere of our lives – health, housing, transport, work, leisure, eating and exercise, as well as all the broader and more far-reaching topics we have already discussed. In many parts of the world, scientists are working on projects which will have important consequences for all of us.

Below: **One of the latest pieces of medical apparatus – a catheter linked to a device which records the information it produces about the state of a person's blood vessels.**

What are the main problems to be solved?

Today man is faced with many vast problems, which he will have to solve with the aid of modern technology. The two main problems are those of food supply and energy.

Firstly, food. How are we to produce enough to feed a constantly growing world population? Two solutions are possible – to increase the area of cultivated land (e.g. by irrigating the deserts to make them fertile), and to increase the quality and quantity of existing produce (by combating plant disease and pests). It is more productive to grow crops on an area and use those crops as food than to use the crops as fodder for animals who will then be slaughtered to provide food. But since many people prefer to eat meat, ways of supplementing it – such as combining it with soya bean – are being investigated.

The second problem is that of energy. No matter where it comes from, whether from coal, petroleum, or animal or vegetable matter, we are consuming more energy than we produce. Soon there will not be enough to go round. Scientists have offered several solutions to the problem. One is to capture the sun's rays with solar panels. Another makes use of the earth's heat. Another is to use the force of the winds and tides. And of course there is nuclear power, which has become such a controversial subject. In fact it is not nuclear energy itself which causes so much anxiety, but rather its waste products. These can indeed be very harmful to human, animal and vegetable life, but scientists are not discouraged and are continuing their researches to find a solution to the problem. Eventually, modern technology with its vast resources will surely find one.

What have been the most spectacular inventions in recent years?

The achievements which have most captured people's imagination in recent years are of course the journeys to the Moon and the other planets. We have all seen on tele-

Right: **A lunar vehicle on the Moon. This machine was used to transport the two American astronauts and their tools and scientific apparatus on the moon's surface. During the journey to the Moon it was carried folded up in the lunar module. The lunar 'buggy' enabled the astronauts to extend their researches over a wider area. It was specially designed to travel in a complete vacuum at extreme temperatures, under low gravity and on completely unknown terrain. Each wheel is powered by a separate 36-volt electric motor. Both the front and rear wheels can be steered. The buggy enabled the astronauts to travel a distance of about 96km.**

New inventions produced by the space programme

Space navigation has given a considerable boost to technology. The problems of travelling in space are such that special laboratories had to be built in order to solve them. The success of the space programme has only been made possible by extensive technological progress which has had applications on earth as well as in space. The electronic apparatus in space craft, for example, has to take up very little room, as well as being light in weight, consuming very little current and functioning reliably for long periods. These requirements were met by the development of the transistor and the integrated circuit, two devices which have revolutionized electronics. Pocket calculators and advanced computers could never have been constructed without integrated circuits, transistors and diodes. Materials, developed for space craft, which are resistant to extremes of temperature and pressure also have their application on earth. The space programme has also brought benefits to astronomy, improving our knowledge of the planets and stars. It has aided the development of the artificial satellites which orbit the earth, providing us with meterological information, geological data, and other information such as soil fertility and the advance of plant pests and diseases. Communications satellites provide immediate links between the different parts of the world by telephone, radio and television, and spy satellites help to maintain world peace.

vision the fantastic images relayed back from the Moon and Mars. Less familiar are the space probes sent to other planets further afield. Unmanned spacecraft are even now travelling through the solar system, collecting information and sending it back to earth by radio.

Probably the most spectacular medical progress has been in the area of open heart surgery, even to the point of heart transplants. Although no other aircraft will ever have the impact of *Kitty Hawk*, the first aircraft to fly, the advent of vertical take-off and supersonic aircraft has been memorable. Tiny electronic equipment, silicone chips, the giant new oil technology – inventions and discoveries, small and large, are changing our lives daily.

The journeys by American submarines under the ice-cap to the North Pole are also less well known. We have not been able to follow their progress on television, but there can be no doubt that these expeditions were a great achievement. We can only marvel at the scientific knowledge and sophisticated technology which enabled the submarines to dive in one place, travel under the ice and surface in another place calculated in advance. Such procedures are only possible with the help of highly automated machines. Man has been interested in automatic machines since ancient times, and has long cherished the idea of a *perpetuum mobile*, a machine which could go on working indefinitely. Automation is needed in many areas of space navigation. The forces to which astronauts are subjected on take-off are such that they would be unable to manipulate the controls properly, and so many of their functions are carried out automatically. In unmanned spaceships, automatic machines replace the crew altogether, taking measurements and photographs and transmitting them back to earth. Can we expect that one day all machines, everywhere, will be similarily automated?

index

Illustrations are indicated by italic figures.

Illustration acknowledgements

Agfa-Gevaert: 209B, 211, 213; Brazilian Embassy: 143BR; Canadian Embassy: 71B, 183BL; Danish Embassy: 146T; German Embassy: 147BR, 150C; Egyptian Embassy: 26TL, 196BR; French Embassy: 65T, 117TL, 114L, 142T; Irish Embassy: 88TR, 89BR, 159T; Iranian Embassy: 39TR; Japanese Embassy: 41TL; Malaysian Embassy: 63TL; New Zealand Embassy: 58T, 184TL and TR; 197TL; Austrian Embassy: 142BR; Panamanian Embassy: 62T; Spanish Embassy: 159B; Thai Embassy: 24T; Turkish Embassy: 38T; United States Embassy: 153BL; Swedish Embassy: 101BR; Swiss Embassy: 105B; Arnhem R. and D: 16BR; 23BL; 32BL; 55T; 59LC and RC; 69T, 70T, 73C, 75TR and B, 76B, 77T, 78TL, RC and B, 80B, 81, 87T, 92, 93T, 94B, 96TL, 166T, 180T, 182BR, 193T, 197B, 205TL; Atlas Copco: 24B, 190B, 192, 193B; Bell-ITT: 178TL, CL and BL, 179, 206, 216B; Biancani: 99T; Bijnens A.: 67, 83C and B, 88B, 89T, C and BL, 90, 91, 96C; Bonhivers: 31, 69BL, 71T, 72TR, 73T and B; Bresseleers: 18TR, 33BR, 96B; Cornille F.: 141C; De Grave M.: 28T, 37B, 49TL; De Pourtales: 3C, 36TR, 39B, 41BR, 153C, 155B, 182TL, 196TR; De Vocht E.: 2L and R, 3C, 73T, 16BL, 17TL, 17RC, 20T, 22, 23B, 26LC and RC, 27R, 29B, 32BR, 33RC, 34BR, 35TR, 41BL, 43B, 45T and C, 53TL, 59T, 60B, 61B, 62B, 63TC, 63TR, 63BL and BR, 64T, 68T, 70BL, 72TL and B, 74TL, 76TL, 77BL, 78TR, 83T, 97BL, 100TR and TL, 106T and B, 107TR and B, 112, 113B, 115TL and RC, 116T, 117TR, 119BR, 120BR, 122TR, 123B, 130B, 132T and BR, 133T and CL, 134, 135T and BR, 136B, 137, 139TR and BR, 143C, 145, 148TR,149BR, 150, 151B, 154T, 156, 157, 158T, 167T, 168CR, 169TL, 176BL, 181BR, 183BR, 184B, 185BR, 190T, 191T, 194BL, 196TL, 200T, 201, 205CL, 208T, 209TR; De Wavrin: 34T, 35B, 66B, 82T, 85TR, 86, 87BL, 93B, 97T, 182TR; Dolfinarium Bruges: 66TR; Druco 61T, 167C, 177B; Imprimerie Smits: 189B; Dual: 202T, 203T; General Motors: 161, 163T, 186T, 187T; Gilis L.: 56T, 58B, 75TL, 94C; Goris F.: 66T, 140B; Gazet van Antwerpen: 27TL, 124, 125, 126, 127, 128BR, 147T, 160T, 163B; Hachette: 8; Hoyaux: 25B, 35RC, 36TL, 38BL and BR, 50BL, 102, 103, 110C and B, 111TL, TR and RC, 129, 138B, 141T, 152BR, 180B, 181T and BL, 182LC, 185BL; Lehaen: 80T; Mamiya: 205TR, 212BL; Maylin: 198; Meli-parc: 79; Musée de l'Homme: 104; Musée de Bokrijk: 186B; NASA: 171T, 172T, 173T; Musée National de Naples: 111BR; SNCB: 164C and B, 165T and C, 191BL; Philips: 174B, 176BR, 177T, 199T and BR, 200B, 203B,207, 215, 216T; Piron: 72B, 19B, 21B, 33TL, 34BL, 35TL, 36B, 37TR, 39TL, 40T and B, 42B, 44C, 45B, 46T and B, 47BL and R, 48, 49T and B, 50BR, 51, 52, 53TR and CR, 54, 107TL, 108, 109, 128BL, 136C, 143T, 147BL, 148T and B, 149T, 150B, 151T and C, 153T and C, 154B, 155T, 196BL, 197TR; Press & Pictures (P&P): 19C, 26B, 28C and B, 29T, 152CR, 158B,187B; P&P/Arnhem: 7B, 17B; P&P/Ausloos: 4, 5, 15, 30T and C, 142BL; P&T/de Ville: 162B; P&P/d'Huart: 44T and B; P&P/Durant: 99CR;P&P/Garot: 195; P&P/IL: 169TR; P&P/Japan: 169CL; P&P/Kervyn: 23C, 42T, 149BL, 185T; P&P/NASA: 168B, 170B, 171B, 172B, 173B; P&P/Tastenoy: 14TL; P&P/Thiry: 14B, 18B, 21T; P&P/Van der Vaeren: 20B, 30B, 167B; Raes: 7T, 146B; Samyn: 82C, 83B, 84T, 85T and TL, 87C; Somers P: 33TR; Tessloff: 64B; Van Autenboer T.: 3R, 18TL, 55BL and BR; Vorsselmans F: 94TL, 95; Vorsselmans L.-Verbruggen: 56B, 57T, 69B, 70BR; Voster/Koppafors: 188B, 210B, 214; Voster/PWA: 188T and C; Wuyts W: 178TR, 37TL, 43TL and TR, 183TR; Zoo d'Anvers: 66CL, 88TL.